The Worshipbook

Services and Hymns

The Worshipbook

Services and Hymns

Prepared by The Joint Committee on Worship *for* Cumberland Presbyterian Church · Presbyterian Church in the United States · The United Presbyterian Church in the United States of America

THE WESTMINSTER PRESS

Philadelphia

ACKNOWLEDGMENTS

Doubleday & Company, Inc., for quotations from *The Jerusalem Bible*. Copyright © 1966 by Darton, Longman & Todd, Ltd., and Doubleday & Company, Inc.

The Macmillan Company, for quotations from *The New Testament in Modern English*, translated by J. B. Phillips. © 1958 by J. B. Phillips.

The National Council of Churches, Division of Christian Education, for Scripture quotations from the Revised Standard Version of the Bible, copyrighted 1946 and 1952.

Oxford University Press, Inc., and Cambridge University Press, for quotations from *The New English Bible*. Copyright © the Delegates of the Oxford University Press and the Syndics of the Cambridge University Press 1961, 1970.

Oxford University Press, Inc., for litanies abridged and adapted from *The Kingdom, the Power, and the Glory*. Copyright 1933 by Oxford University Press, Inc., and Renewed 1961 by Bradford Young.

Second Printing

PUBLISHED BY THE WESTMINSTER PRESS®
PHILADELPHIA, PENNSYLVANIA

Printed in the United States of America

Preface

THE WORSHIPBOOK is in two forms. Chronologically, *The Worshipbook—Services* is first. *The Worshipbook—Services and Hymns* is second, following the first after a passage of years. All the pages of *The Worshipbook—Services* constitute the first pages of *The Worshipbook—Services and Hymns*. The second book is different from the first only in the way that the subtitles suggest. The second offers hymns. The first does not.

The Worshipbook—Services is the successor to *The Book of Common Worship* (1946). *The Worshipbook—Services and Hymns* is the successor to *The Book of Common Worship* and, for many congregations, *The Hymnal* (1933) or *The Hymnbook* (1955).

Three Churches have produced *The Worshipbook*. They are: the Cumberland Presbyterian Church, the Presbyterian Church in the United States, and The United Presbyterian Church in the United States of America. They have been served by the Joint Committee on Worship and by The Committee on Selection of Hymns, the latter reporting to the several denominations through the former. Sessions of the Joint Committee on Worship have been attended by an observer from the Reformed Church of America.

At the point in *The Worshipbook—Services and Hymns* where the hymns begin, there is a further statement about the music and hymnody in the book. This preface, therefore, contains only generalizations as to hymns, and a degree of greater detail about the services.

A principal dimension of *The Worshipbook* is its attempt to employ contemporary English in worship. The word *contemporary* needs definition. It does not mean *idiom* or *slang*, or the selection of words

5

that will call attention to their jarring strangeness, or language that reveals more the cleverness of the writer than the reality of God. It means the straightforward use of words and language in current, contemporary use in the last third of the twentieth century.

Moreover, so much of *The Worshipbook* is in the language of Scripture that the words of the new translations of the Bible have been employed. Thus, the other principal dimension of *The Worshipbook* is that it rests upon the foundation of the Holy Scriptures.

There has been no attempt to write new theology. Because the Joint Committee on Worship prepared the Directory for Worship which became part of the Constitution of The United Presbyterian Church in the United States of America, that directory has been the standard which *The Worshipbook* obeys. Nevertheless, care has been taken not to trespass against the Constitutions of the other two Churches.

The Worshipbook is a Presbyterian book. It is faithful to that tradition. *The Worshipbook* is an ecumenical book. It attempts to adopt, both in services and hymns, the best that fellow Christians in other Churches and traditions offer.

Presbyterians value freedom and variety in worship, but they emphasize equally the virtue of orderliness. It is hardly necessary to state that the book is for voluntary use. Congregations will find options offered in *The Worshipbook*. In addition, they will supply their own variations. To do so will be to please, not disappoint, those who have prepared the book. All that is claimed is that *The Worshipbook*, notably in the Service for the Lord's Day, offers one orderly and responsible way to plan for the worship of God.

There is contemporaneity in the hymns. New hymns have been written. Old hymns have been altered, where copyright and literary structure permit, so that archaic language is eliminated, and excessive introspective use of first person singular pronouns is diminished. There are folk hymns and spirituals.

The hymns have been selected, of course, in adherence to many standards. Due consideration has been given to sound theology, musical integrity, variety in the texts, variety in the tunes, and the blending of the old with the new.

There has been, however, one primary standard by which the hymns have been chosen. They have been chosen to support the services in *The Worshipbook*, particularly the Service for the Lord's

Day. If the assignment of The Committee on Selection of Hymns had been to create a general hymnal to succeed another, older hymnal, it would have offered many more hymns, with diverse and diffuse potential uses. Here, on the other hand, is a book that seeks the integrity of unity. Music is a part of worship, not apart from worship. In *The Worshipbook*, congregations should find services through which they can intelligently worship God. They should also find, in the same volume, hymns that are appropriate to those services.

The Joint Committee has been enriched in its work by the renewal of worship in other Churches. The Lord's Prayer, as it appears in the text of *The Worshipbook*, at various places, is in a version prepared by the International Consultation on English Texts. That body was composed of representatives of Roman Catholic and Protestant Churches in twenty countries, including Great Britain and the United States, where English is spoken. It is a remarkable achievement in Christian unity, blending a wide variety of both traditions and nationalities.

The same International Consultation prepared the versions of the Apostles' Creed and the Nicene Creed that *The Worshipbook* employs. For the convenience of congregations not yet ready to adopt the admittedly unfamiliar new versions of the prayer and the creeds, the Lord's Prayer, the Apostles' Creed, and the Nicene Creed are published in traditional form on the end papers of this book.

After the Second Vatican Council, the Roman Catholic Church greatly modified its Christian year, omitting many of the saints' days. In that connection, it published an entirely new lectionary, which is a list of Scripture passages, from the Old and New Testaments, for use on each Lord's Day. The members of the Joint Committee on Worship, like many other Protestants, discovered that the new Roman Catholic selections, and the manner of their organization, were remarkably in harmony with the teachings of the Reformation. The excellence of the lectionary commended itself to the committee, and with a few alterations it is offered in *The Worshipbook*.

As is known, Presbyterians are not required to follow a lectionary as they plan for worship on the Lord's Day. On the other hand, the following of a lectionary, with flexibility, helps assure a congregation that it will not, in the course of a period of years, neglect the great teachings of the Bible.

It is customary, in the preface of such a book as this, to list the members of the committee that prepared it. Inevitably, in a committee that has worked for more than a decade, there have been those who have had to leave the committee and give their attention elsewhere. They should not be held accountable for the final product of the others, but their names will nevertheless be listed.

The list does not indicate membership on one committee or the other, or membership in one church or another. It does not distinguish between laymen and ministers. It does not separate consultants from committee members. It is in alphabetical order, and the omission of further identification symbolizes the unity of the book as well as the unity of those who have served:

James Appleby, James H. Blackwood, Eugene Carson Blake, Scott Francis Brenner, Lewis A. Briner, Frank A. Brooks, Jr., Robert McAfee Brown, Wanzer H. Brunelle, David G. Buttrick, Frank H. Caldwell, Donald F. Campbell, Robert Carwithen, Dwight M. Chalmers, Rex S. Clements, Harold Davis, Theodore A. Gill, Richard W. Graves, Robert E. Grooters, Warner L. Hall, Robert H. Heinze, Thomas Holden, Edward J. Humphrey, Donald D. Kettring, Norman F. Langford, Cecil W. Lower, Joseph E. McAllaster, Dalton E. McDonald, Earl W. Morey, Jr., Marian S. Noecker, Richard M. Peek, Mary H. Plummer, John Ribble, David W. Romig, Garrett C. Roorda, Joan M. Salmon, Donald W. Stake, Jean Woodward Steele, Robert F. Stevenson, Howard S. Swan, James Rawlings Sydnor, H. William Taeusch, Hubert V. Taylor, William P. Thompson, Leonard J. Trinterud, Richard D. Wetzel, James T. Womack, Jr., H. Davis Yeuell.

Richard W. Graves died in 1969. Robert McAfee Brown was the principal writer-editor for the Directory for Worship. David G. Buttrick was the principal writer-editor for the services in *The Worshipbook*. Robert Carwithen was the editor for the musical portions of the book.

At the date of publication the chairman of the Joint Committee on Worship was Robert H. Heinze. Serving as chairmen, at successive stages of the work, were Scott Francis Brenner, Dwight M. Chalmers, Thomas Holden, and David W. Romig. The secretary was H. Davis Yeuell. He was preceded by Robert H. Heinze. John Ribble was publishing consultant.

The chairman of The Committee on Selection of Hymns was Cecil W. Lower. The secretary was Donald F. Campbell.

The Worshipbook is a new book with a new name, offered in the hope that it will serve a new age in the church. The old and well-loved title of the former book, *The Book of Common Worship*, has been sacrificed because the word *common* is no longer used as it was in times gone by. The change in title is symbolic of the attempt to help Christians, and those who may become Christians, to hear God's word, and worship him, in the language of their needs and aspirations, today.

The committees hope that *The Worshipbook* will find favor with the churches, but more, that it may be an instrument blessed by God for those who praise and serve him.

THE JOINT COMMITTEE ON WORSHIP

Memphis
Richmond
Philadelphia

Contents

Preparation for Worship

Preparation for Worship

The session will guide a congregation's preparation for worship. As people gather on the Lord's Day, they may pray, or, when there is instrumental music, give silent attention; they may wish to sing or read hymns, or to greet one another, talking together as neighbors in faith.

The following prayers may be used by members of the congregation before worship:

Eternal God: you have called us to be members of one body. Join us in Spirit with those who in all times and places have praised your name; that, having one faith, we may show the unity of your church, and bring honor to our Lord and Savior, Jesus Christ. Amen.

God our king: rule over us as we meet together, and so fill us with your Spirit, that in faith, hope, and love we may worship you, and proclaim your mighty deeds; through Jesus Christ our Lord. Amen.

Merciful God, who sent Jesus to eat and drink with sinners: lead us to your table and be present with us, weak and sinful people; that, fed by your love, we may live to praise you, remembering Jesus Christ our Savior. Amen.

Lord God: we cannot pray unless your Spirit prays in us; we cannot forgive ourselves unless your word tells mercy.

Lord God: speak your word, and send your Spirit to help us worship as we ought; for the sake of our Lord Jesus Christ. Amen.

A doxology may be sung with the choir as they make ready for worship, or one of the following prayers may be used:

God of grace: you have given us minds to know you, hearts to love you, and voices to sing your praise. Fill us with Holy

Spirit, so we may celebrate your glory, and truly worship you; through Jesus Christ our Lord. **Amen.**

Great God: you have been generous and marvelously kind. Give us such wonder, love, and gratitude that we may sing praises to you, and joyfully honor your name; through Jesus Christ our Lord. **Amen.**

Give to the Lord glory and praise!

His loving-kindness is forever.

Lift up your hearts.

We lift them to the Lord.

Praise the Lord.

The Lord's name be praised.

Amen.

And Amen.

When elders meet before worship, they may wish to say one of the following prayers:

God our Father: without your word we have nothing to say, and without your Spirit we are helpless. Give us Holy Spirit, so that we may lead your people in prayer, proclaim the good news, and gratefully praise your name; through Jesus Christ our Lord. **Amen.**

Startle us, O God, with your truth, and open our minds to your Spirit; that we may be one with your Son our Lord, and serve as his disciples; through Jesus Christ. **Amen.**

Almighty God: you have set a table before us, and called us to feast with you. Prepare us in mind and spirit to minister in your name, and to honor your Son, our Lord, Jesus Christ. **Amen.**

THE LAW OF GOD

In preparation for worship, the people may wish to think on the law of God.

The law, or the summary of the law given by our Lord Jesus, may be used in the Service for the Lord's Day immediately after the Declaration of Pardon, as a guide for the forgiven Christian who will live obedient to God.

God spoke all these words, saying, I am the Lord your God.

You shall have no other gods before me.

You shall not make for yourself a graven image, or any likeness of anything that is in heaven above, or that is in the earth beneath, or that is in the water under the earth; you shall not bow down to them or serve them.

You shall not take the name of the Lord your God in vain.

Remember the Sabbath day, to keep it holy.

Honor your father and your mother.

You shall not kill.

You shall not commit adultery.

You shall not steal.

You shall not bear false witness against your neighbor.

You shall not covet your neighbor's house; you shall not covet your neighbor's wife, or anything that is your neighbor's.

SUMMARY OF THE LAW

Our Lord Jesus said:

You shall love the Lord your God with all your heart, and with all your soul, and with all your mind. This is the great and first commandment. And a second is like it, You shall love your neighbor as yourself. On these two commandments depend all the law and the prophets.

Orders for the
Public Worship of God

OUTLINE OF THE
SERVICE FOR THE LORD'S DAY
Including the Sacrament of the Lord's Supper

THE BASIC STRUCTURE	ADDITIONS AND VARIANT FORMS
CALL TO WORSHIP	
	Versicle
HYMN OF PRAISE	
CONFESSION OF SIN	
DECLARATION OF PARDON	
RESPONSE	(Gloria, Hymn, or Psalm)
PRAYER FOR ILLUMINATION	(Or, the Collect for the Day)
OLD TESTAMENT LESSON	
	Anthem, Canticle, or Psalm
NEW TESTAMENT LESSON(S)	
SERMON	
	Ascription of Praise
	AN INVITATION
CREED	
	Hymn
	Concerns of the Church
THE PRAYERS OF THE PEOPLE	
THE PEACE	
OFFERING	
	Anthem or Special Music
	Hymn or Doxology
INVITATION TO THE LORD'S TABLE	
THE THANKSGIVING	
THE LORD'S PRAYER	
THE COMMUNION	
RESPONSE	
HYMN	
CHARGE	
BENEDICTION	

OUTLINE OF THE
SERVICE FOR THE LORD'S DAY
Including the Sacrament of Baptism

THE BASIC STRUCTURE	ADDITIONS AND VARIANT FORMS
CALL TO WORSHIP	
	Versicle
HYMN OF PRAISE	
CONFESSION OF SIN	
DECLARATION OF PARDON	
RESPONSE	(Gloria, Hymn, or Psalm)
PRAYER FOR ILLUMINATION	(Or, the Collect for the Day)
OLD TESTAMENT LESSON	
	Anthem, Canticle, or Psalm
NEW TESTAMENT LESSON(S)	
SERMON	
	Ascription of Praise
	AN INVITATION
APOSTLES' CREED	
THE SACRAMENT OF BAPTISM	
	Hymn
	Concerns of the Church
THE PRAYERS OF THE PEOPLE	
THE PEACE	
OFFERING	
	Anthem or Special Music
	Hymn or Doxology
PRAYER OF THANKSGIVING	
THE LORD'S PRAYER	
HYMN	
CHARGE	
BENEDICTION	

OUTLINE FOR THE
SERVICE FOR THE LORD'S DAY
When the Sacraments Are Omitted

THE BASIC STRUCTURE	ADDITIONS AND VARIANT FORMS
CALL TO WORSHIP	
	Versicle
HYMN OF PRAISE	
CONFESSION OF SIN	
DECLARATION OF PARDON	
RESPONSE	(Gloria, Hymn, or Psalm)
PRAYER FOR ILLUMINATION	(Or, the Collect for the Day)
OLD TESTAMENT LESSON	
	Anthem, Canticle, or Psalm
NEW TESTAMENT LESSON(S)	
SERMON	
	Ascription of Praise
	AN INVITATION
CREED	
	Hymn
	Concerns of the Church
THE PRAYERS OF THE PEOPLE	
THE PEACE	
OFFERING	
	Anthem or Special Music
	Doxology or Response
PRAYER OF THANKSGIVING	
THE LORD'S PRAYER	
HYMN	
CHARGE	
BENEDICTION	

ORDER FOR THE
PUBLIC WORSHIP OF GOD

Service for the Lord's Day

CALL TO WORSHIP

Let the people stand. The minister shall call the people to the worship of God, saying:

Let us worship God.

The minister shall say one or more of the following:

Our help is in the name of the Lord, who made heaven and earth.

God loved the world so much that he gave his only Son, so that everyone who believes in him may not be lost but may have eternal life.

Thank God, the God and Father of our Lord Jesus Christ, that in his great mercy we men have been born again into a life full of hope, through Christ's rising from the dead.

God was in Christ reconciling the world to himself—not counting their sins against them—and has commissioned us with the message of reconciliation.

The kingdom of the world has become the kingdom of our Lord and his Christ, and he will reign forever and ever.

At the name of Jesus every knee should bow and every tongue confess that Jesus Christ is Lord, to the glory of God the Father.

In the name of the Father, and of the Son, and of the Holy Spirit.

And, the following may be sung or said:

Praise the Lord.

The Lord's name be praised.

Let the people sing a psalm or a hymn of praise.

25

CONFESSION OF SIN

The minister shall say:

If we claim to be sinless, we are self-deceived and strangers to the truth. If we confess our sins, God is just, and may be trusted to forgive our sins and cleanse us from every kind of wrong.

Let us admit our sin before God:

Almighty God: in Jesus Christ you called us to be a servant people, but we do not do what you command. We are often silent when we should speak, and useless when we could be useful. We are lazy servants, timid and heartless, who turn neighbors away from your love. Have mercy on us, O God, and, though we do not deserve your care, forgive us, and free us from sin; through Jesus Christ our Lord. Amen.

Or,

The proof of God's amazing love is this: while we were sinners Christ died for us. Because we have faith in him, we dare with confidence to approach God.

Let us ask God to forgive us.   *Together*

Almighty God: you love us, but we have not loved you; you call, but we have not listened. We walk away from neighbors in need, wrapped up in our own concerns. We have gone along with evil, with prejudice, warfare, and greed. God our Father, help us to face up to ourselves, so that, as you move toward us in mercy, we may repent, turn to you, and receive forgiveness; through Jesus Christ our Lord. Amen.

The people may pray silently.

DECLARATION OF PARDON

One of the following may be said:

Hear the good news!

This statement is completely reliable and should be universally accepted: Christ Jesus entered the world to rescue sinners.

He personally bore our sins in his body on the cross, so that we might be dead to sin and be alive to all that is good.

Or,

Who is in a position to condemn? Only Christ, and Christ died for us, Christ rose for us, Christ reigns in power for us, Christ prays for us.

If a man is in Christ, he becomes a new person altogether—the past is finished and gone, everything has become fresh and new.

And,

Friends: Believe the good news of the gospel.

In Jesus Christ, we are forgiven.

Then the minister may say one of the following exhortations; or read the Summary of the Law (see page 17):

As God's own people, be merciful in action, kindly in heart, humble in mind. Be always ready to forgive as freely as the Lord has forgiven you. And, above everything else, be loving, and never forget to be thankful for what God has done for you.

Or,

Let us now obey the Lord. This is his command: to give allegiance to his Son Jesus Christ and to love one another.

Then the people may stand to sing or say the following response; or some other thanksgiving:

Give thanks to God, for he is good, his love is everlasting.

You are the Lord, giver of mercy!
You are the Christ, giver of mercy!
You are the Lord, giver of mercy!

PRAYER FOR ILLUMINATION

Before the reading of the Scripture lessons, the Collect for the Day may be used; or one of the following Prayers for Illumination, or a like prayer, may be said by the reader or by the people in unison:

Prepare our hearts, O Lord, to accept your word. Silence in us any voice but your own; that, hearing, we may also obey your will; through Jesus Christ our Lord. **Amen.**

Or,

O God, tell us what we need to hear, and show us what we ought to do to obey your Son, Jesus Christ. **Amen.**

OLD TESTAMENT LESSON

Before the Old Testament lesson, let the reader say:

The lesson is . . .
Listen for the word of God!

After the Old Testament lesson, the reader may say:

Amen.

After the lesson, there may be an anthem, a canticle, or a psalm.

NEW TESTAMENT LESSON(S)

Before the reading of the New Testament lesson, or lessons, let the reader say:

The lesson is . . .
Listen for the word of God!

After the New Testament lesson, or lessons, the reader may say:

Amen.

SERMON

When the Scripture has been read, its message shall be proclaimed in a Sermon. The Sermon may be followed by an Ascription of Praise:

Amen. Praise and glory and wisdom and thanksgiving and honor and power and strength to our God forever and ever. **Amen.**

Or,

Now to the King of all worlds, undying, invisible, the only God, be honor and glory forever and ever. **Amen.**

After the Sermon, an INVITATION may be given to any who wish to answer God's word by declaring their faith, or by renewing their obedience to Christ.

CREED

The people may stand to sing or say a Creed of the church;
or some Affirmation of Faith drawn from Scripture:

Let us say what we believe.

We believe in one God,
the Father, the Almighty,
maker of heaven and earth,
of all that is seen and unseen.

We believe in one Lord, Jesus Christ,
the only Son of God,
eternally begotten of the Father,
God from God, Light from Light,
true God from true God,
begotten, not made, one in Being with the Father.
Through him all things were made.
For us men and for our salvation
he came down from heaven:
by the power of the Holy Spirit
he was born of the Virgin Mary, and became man.
For our sake he was crucified under Pontius Pilate;
he suffered, died, and was buried.
On the third day he rose again
in fulfillment of the Scriptures;
he ascended into heaven
and is seated at the right hand of the Father.
He will come again in glory to judge the living
and the dead,
and his kingdom will have no end.

We believe in the Holy Spirit, the Lord,
the giver of life,
who proceeds from the Father and the Son.
With the Father and the Son he is worshiped
and glorified.
He has spoken through the prophets.
We believe in one holy catholic and apostolic church.
We acknowledge one baptism for the forgiveness of sins.
We look for the resurrection of the dead,
and the life of the world to come. Amen.

Or,

I believe in God, the Father almighty,
creator of heaven and earth.

I believe in Jesus Christ, his only Son, our Lord.
He was conceived by the power of the Holy Spirit
and born of the Virgin Mary.
He suffered under Pontius Pilate,
was crucified, died, and was buried.
He descended to the dead.
On the third day he rose again.
He ascended into heaven,
and is seated at the right hand of the Father.
He will come again to judge the living and the dead.

I believe in the Holy Spirit,
the holy catholic church,
the communion of saints,
the forgiveness of sins,
the resurrection of the body,
and the life everlasting. Amen.

Or,

This is the good news which we received, in which we
stand, and by which we are saved: that Christ died for our
sins according to the Scriptures, that he was buried, that
he was raised on the third day; and that he appeared to
Peter, then to the Twelve and to many faithful witnesses.

We believe he is the Christ, the Son of the living God. He
is the first and the last, the beginning and the end, he is
our Lord and our God. Amen.

A hymn may be sung.

CONCERNS OF THE CHURCH

Announcements concerning the life of the church may be
made.

THE PRAYERS OF THE PEOPLE

Prayers of Intercession may be said by a leader, or leaders, to express concerns of the church.

Or, a few or many of the following prayers may be used with the people responding, or by the people in unison.

The response, "Hear our prayer, O God," may be said instead of "Amen" after each intercession.

The following may be sung or said:

The Lord is risen.

He is risen indeed.

Then, the minister may say:

Let us pray.

Father, whose Son Jesus Christ taught us to pray: let our prayers for others be the kind you want, and not just ways of getting what we want, who already have so much in Jesus Christ, our Savior. **Amen.**

Let us pray for the world.

Silent prayer.

Lord of all the worlds that are, Savior of men: we pray for the whole creation. Order the unruly powers, deal with injustice, feed and satisfy the longing peoples, so that in freedom your children may enjoy the world you have made, and cheerfully sing your praises; through Jesus Christ our Lord. **Amen.**

Let us pray for the church.

Silent prayer.

Gracious God: you called us to be the church of Jesus Christ. Keep us one in faith and service, breaking bread together, and telling good news to the world; that men may believe you are love, and live to give you glory; through Jesus Christ our Lord. **Amen.**

Let us pray for peace.

Silent prayer.

Eternal God: send peace on earth, and put down greed, pride, and anger, which turn man against man and set nation against nation. Speed the day when wars will end and all men call you Father; through Jesus Christ our Lord. **Amen.**

Let us pray for enemies.

Silent prayer.

O God, whom we cannot love unless we love our brothers: remove hate and prejudice from us and all men, so that your children may be reconciled with those they fear, resent, or threaten; and live together in your peace; through Jesus Christ our Lord. **Amen.**

Let us pray for those who govern us.

Silent prayer.

Almighty God, ruler of men: direct those who make, administer, and judge our laws; the President of the United States and others in authority among us (especially _____); that, led by your wisdom, they may lead us in the way of righteousness; through Jesus Christ our Lord. **Amen.**

Let us pray for world leaders.

Silent prayer.

Great God our hope: give vision to those who serve the United Nations, or govern people; that, with goodwill and justice, they may take down barriers, and draw together one new world in peace; through Jesus Christ our Lord. **Amen.**

Let us pray for the work we do.

Silent prayer.

Manage us, wise God, by your Spirit, so the work we do may serve your purpose, and make this world a good home for all your children; through Jesus Christ our Lord. **Amen.**

Let us pray for the sick.

Silent prayer.

Merciful God: you bear the hurt of the world. Look with compassion on those who are sick (especially on _____); cheer them by your word, and bring health as a sign that, in your promised kingdom, there will be no more pain or crying; through Jesus Christ our Lord. **Amen.**

Let us pray for those who sorrow.

Silent prayer.

God of comfort: stand with those who sorrow (especially _____); that they may be sure that neither death nor life, nor things present nor things to come, shall separate them from your love; through Jesus Christ our Lord. **Amen.**

Let us pray for friends and families.

Silent prayer.

O God our Father: bless us and those we love, our friends and families; that, drawing close to you, we may be drawn closer to each other; through Jesus Christ our Lord. **Amen.**

God of our fathers: we praise you for all your servants who, having been faithful to you on earth, now live with you in heaven. Keep us in fellowship with them, until we meet with all your children in the joy of the kingdom; through Jesus Christ our Lord. **Amen.**

Mighty God, whose word we trust, whose Spirit prays in our prayers: sort out our requests, and further those which are helpful, and will bring about your purpose for the earth; through Jesus Christ our Lord. **Amen.**

THE PEACE

Let the minister say:

God sent the world his only Son. Since God loved us so much, we too should love one another.

Let us love one another, since love comes from God.

The peace of the Lord Jesus Christ be with you all.

The people may greet one another with a handclasp, saying: "Peace be with you."

It is fitting that the Lord's Supper be celebrated as often as each Lord's Day. If the Lord's Supper is not celebrated, let the service continue on page 38.

OFFERING

The minister shall say:

Let us bring our gifts to God.

As the offerings of the people are gathered, there may be an anthem, or other appropriate music. Then, as the offerings, which may include the bread and the wine, are brought forward, the minister shall say:

Praise God for his goodness.

A hymn or a doxology may be sung.

INVITATION TO THE LORD'S TABLE

Friends: This is the joyful feast of the people of God!

Men will come from east and west, and from north and south, and sit at table in the kingdom of God.

This is the Lord's table. Our Savior invites those who trust him to share the feast which he has prepared.

According to Luke, when our risen Lord was at table with his disciples, he took the bread, and blessed and broke it, and gave it to them. And their eyes were opened and they recognized him.

THE THANKSGIVING

The following may be sung or said:

Lift up your hearts.

We lift them to the Lord.

Give thanks to God, for he is good.

His love is everlasting.

Or,

Lift up your hearts.

We lift them up to the Lord.

Let us give thanks to the Lord our God.

It is right to give him thanks and praise.

Then, the minister may say:

Holy Lord, Father almighty, everlasting God:
[we thank you for commanding light out of darkness, for dividing the waters into sea and dry land, for creating the whole
world and calling it good. We thank you for making us in your
image to live with each other in love; for the breath of life, the
gift of speech, and freedom to choose your way. You have told
us your purpose in commandments to Moses, and called for
justice in the cry of the prophets. Through long generations, you
have been fair and kind to all your children.]*

Great and wonderful are your works, Lord God almighty. Your
ways are just and true. With men of faith from all times and
places, we lift our hearts in joyful praise, for you alone are holy:

The following may be sung or said:

Holy, holy, holy,
God of power and majesty,
heaven and earth are full of your glory,
O God most high!

Or,

Holy, holy, holy Lord, God of power and might,
heaven and earth are full of your glory.
Hosanna in the highest.

Blessed is he who comes in the name of the Lord.
Hosanna in the highest.

Then, the minister may say:

Holy Father: we thank you for your Son Jesus, who lived with us
sharing joy and sorrow. He told your story, healed the sick, and
was a friend of sinners. Obeying you, he took up his cross and

*According to the church year, some other form may be substituted for this paragraph.
See page 40.

was murdered by men he loved. We praise you that he is not dead, but is risen to rule the world; and that he is still the friend of sinners. We trust him to overcome every power to hurt or divide us, so that, when you bring in your promised kingdom, we will celebrate victory with him.

> **Remembering the Lord Jesus, we break bread and share one cup, announcing his death for the sins of the world, and telling his resurrection to all men and nations.**

Great God: give your Holy Spirit in the breaking of bread, so that we may be drawn together, and, joined to Christ the Lord, receive new life, and remain his glad and faithful people until we feast with him in glory.

> **O God, who called us from death to life: we give ourselves to you; and with the church through all ages, we thank you for your saving love in Jesus Christ our Lord. Amen.**

> **Our Father in heaven,**
> **holy be your name,**
> **your kingdom come,**
> **your will be done,**
> **on earth as in heaven.**
> **Give us today our daily bread.**
> **Forgive us our sins**
> **as we forgive those who sin against us.**
> **Do not bring us to the test**
> **but deliver us from evil.**
> **For the kingdom, the power, and the glory are yours**
> **now and forever. Amen.**

> *The minister shall break bread in the presence of the people, saying:*

The Lord Jesus, on the night of his arrest, took bread, and after giving thanks to God, broke it and said: "This is my body, which is for you; do this, remembering me."

> *The minister shall pour the wine in the presence of the people, saying:*

In the same way, he took the cup after supper, and said: "This cup is the new covenant sealed in my blood. Whenever you drink it, do this, remembering me."

Every time you eat this bread and drink the cup, you proclaim the death of the Lord, until he comes.

> The minister and those assisting him shall themselves partake, and shall distribute the bread and the wine to the people. As the bread and wine are distributed, the people may sing or say psalms, or hymns of praise to Christ.

> As the minister gives the bread and the wine, he may say:

Jesus said: I am the bread of life. He who comes to me will never be hungry; he who believes in me will never thirst.

> And,

Jesus said: I am the vine, you are the branches. Cut off from me you can do nothing.

> When all the people have received, the minister shall say:

The grace of the Lord Jesus Christ be with you all. Amen.

> Then, the minister and the people shall praise God by singing or saying:

Alleluia! For the Lord our God, the Almighty, has come into his kingdom! Let us rejoice, let us be glad with all our hearts. Let us give him the glory forever and ever. Amen.

> Or,

Bless the Lord, O my soul;

And all that is within me, bless his holy name!

Bless the Lord, O my soul,

And forget not all his benefits.

> Or,

Let us pray.

> God our help: we thank you for this supper shared in the Spirit with your Son Jesus, who makes us new and strong,

who brings us life eternal. We praise you for giving us all good gifts in him, and pledge ourselves to serve you, even as in Christ you have served us. Amen.

A hymn may be sung, after which the people shall be dismissed:

Go in peace. Live as free men. Serve the Lord, rejoicing in the power of the Holy Spirit.

Or,

Go out into the world in peace; have courage; hold on to what is good; return no man evil for evil; strengthen the fainthearted; support the weak; help the suffering; honor all men; love and serve the Lord, rejoicing in the power of the Holy Spirit.

And,

The grace of our Lord Jesus Christ and the love of God and the fellowship of the Holy Spirit be with you all.

Let the people say:

Alleluia! Amen.

When the Lord's Supper is omitted, the service shall continue from page 33, and conclude in the following manner:

OFFERING

The minister shall say:

Let us bring our gifts to God.

As the offerings of the people are gathered, an anthem may be sung, or other music provided. When the offerings are brought forward the people may stand to sing a doxology or some other response.

PRAYER OF THANKSGIVING

The following may be sung or said:

Lift up your hearts.

We lift them to the Lord.

Give thanks to God, for he is good.

His love is everlasting.

Or,

Lift up your hearts.

We lift them up to the Lord.

Let us give thanks to the Lord our God.

It is right to give him thanks and praise.

Then, the minister may say:

O God our Father, creator of the world and giver of all good things: we thank you for our home on earth and for the joy of living. We praise you for your love in Jesus Christ, who came to set things right, who died rejected on the cross and rose triumphant from the dead. Because he lives, we live to praise you, Father, Son, and Holy Spirit, our God forever.

O God, who called us from death to life: we give ourselves to you; and with the church through all ages, we thank you for your saving love in Jesus Christ our Lord. Amen.

Let us pray our Lord's Prayer.

Our Father in heaven,
  holy be your name,
  your kingdom come,
  your will be done,
    on earth as in heaven.
Give us today our daily bread.
Forgive us our sins
  as we forgive those who sin against us.
Do not bring us to the test
  but deliver us from evil.
For the kingdom, the power, and the glory are yours
  now and forever. Amen.

*A hymn may be sung, after which the people shall be
dismissed:*

Go in peace. Live as free men. Serve the Lord, rejoicing in the
power of the Holy Spirit.

Or,

Go out into the world in peace; have courage; hold on to what
is good; return no man evil for evil; strengthen the fainthearted;
support the weak; help the suffering; honor all men; love and
serve the Lord, rejoicing in the power of the Holy Spirit.

And,

The grace of our Lord Jesus Christ and the love of God and the
fellowship of the Holy Spirit be with you all.

Let the people say:

Alleluia! Amen.

SEASONAL VARIATIONS FOR THE THANKSGIVING
(see page 35)

Advent

who made this world a place for Jesus Christ, and, before he was
born, promised his coming in the words of the prophets: we
thank you for this holy supper, which is for us a sign of his returning to claim his lands and people.

Christmas

we thank you for the gift of your Son Jesus, light in darkness,
savior of men, who was born in a poor place, who now rules the
world, Lord of lords and King of kings.

Epiphany

who sent a star to guide wise men to where Christ was born, and
whose signs and words in every age lead men to him: we thank
you for showing us our Lord Jesus, the light of the world, by
whom we are saved, and baptized into your service.

Lent

before whose justice no man can stand, yet whose love is so sure we need not hide ourselves: we thank you for your mercy reported by the prophets and shown in Jesus Christ, for the law you give to guide us, and for the promise of new life to live for you and with our neighbors.

Palm Sunday

we thank you for your Son Jesus, who fulfilled the prophets' words, and entered the city of Jerusalem to die for us and all men. We praise you that he enters our world as Savior and King, and calls men to obey him.

Maundy Thursday

who sent Jesus as a servant to wash away our pride, and to feed us with bread of life: we thank you for inviting us to feast with him who died for us, and who teaches us to serve each other in modesty and love.

Good Friday

whose Son Jesus was condemned, forsaken, and hanged on a cross: we are thankful that he obeyed you and died, to show us that we are not forsaken or condemned, but will have a promised paradise with him.

Easter

we thank you for the power which brought our Lord Jesus from death to life, and which is promised to us who believe in him. We praise you that, breaking bread by faith, we know Christ risen, and can trust him to save us from death and from sin.

Ascension

who created this world and raised Christ to rule it: we thank you that because he is lifted in power, he can draw us from weakness into the way of righteousness and truth.

Pentecost

who sent the Holy Spirit to kindle faith and to teach the truth of your Son Jesus: we thank you that you are working in the church to make us brave disciples who will preach Christ the Lord in every nation.

Trinity

Creator of the world, Savior of men, life-giving Spirit: we thank you for baptizing us in your name, Father, Son, and Holy Spirit, and for welcoming us by faith into one holy church.

World Communion

you have formed the universe in your wisdom, and created all things by your power; and you have set us in families on the earth to live with you in faith. We praise you for good gifts of bread and wine, and for the table you spread in the world as a sign of your love for all men in Christ.

Another Optional Form

we thank you for commanding light to shine out of darkness, for stretching out the heavens, and laying the foundations of the earth; for making all things through your Word. We thank you for creating us in your image and for keeping us in your steadfast love. We praise you for calling us to be your people, for revealing your purpose in the law and the prophets, and for dealing patiently with our pride and disobedience.

The Sacrament of Baptism*

The service is designed for the baptism of mature believers,
or for the baptism of infants. When infants are being baptized, the wording should be changed as indicated in the
rubrics.

Ordinarily, baptism is to be administered in the presence of
the worshiping congregation, following the preaching of the
word and the Apostles' Creed.

Then let the minister say:

Hear the words of our Lord Jesus Christ:
All authority in heaven and on earth has been given to me. Go
therefore and make disciples of all nations, baptizing them in
the name of the Father and of the Son and of the Holy Spirit,
teaching them to observe all that I have commanded you; and
lo, I am with you always, to the close of the age.

Obeying the word of our Lord Jesus, and sure of his presence
with us, we baptize those whom he has called to be his own.

In Jesus Christ, God has promised to forgive our sins, and has
joined us together in the family of faith which is his church. He
has delivered us from darkness and transferred us to the kingdom of his beloved Son. In Jesus Christ, God has promised to be
our Father, and to welcome us as brothers and sisters of Christ.

Know that the promises of God are for you. By baptism, God
puts his sign on you to show that you belong to him, and gives
you Holy Spirit as a guarantee that, sharing Christ's reconciling
work, you will also share his victory; that, dying with Christ to
sin, you will be raised with him to new life.

*This book is for three Churches. Questions asked in this service are those used
in The United Presbyterian Church in the United States of America. Other questions
may be required in the Cumberland Presbyterian Church and the Presbyterian Church
in the United States.

The minister shall address the person to be baptized, or the parents presenting a child for baptism, saying those words required by the Constitution of his church (see footnote on page 43).

Friend: In presenting yourself for baptism, you announce your faith in Jesus Christ, and show that you want to study him, know him, love him, and serve him as his chosen disciple.

Or,

Friends: In presenting your *child* for baptism, you announce your faith in Jesus Christ, and show that you want your *child* to study him, know him, love him, and serve him as *his* chosen *disciple*.

And,

Show your purpose by answering these questions.

Who is your Lord and Savior?

Jesus Christ is my Lord and Savior.

Do you trust in him?

I do.

Do you intend (your child) to be his disciple, to obey his word and show his love?

I do.

If the candidate for baptism is to be received as a communicant member of the church, the minister shall ask this additional question:

Will you be a faithful member of this congregation, giving of yourself in every way, and will you seek the fellowship of the church wherever you may be?

I will.

Let the people stand. An elder representing the session shall address the people (and the parents presenting a child for baptism), saying:

Our Lord Jesus Christ ordered us to teach those who are baptized. Do you, the people of the church, promise to tell this new disciple (*this child*) the good news of the gospel, to help *him*

know all that Christ commands, and, by your fellowship, to strengthen *his* family ties with the household of God?
We do.

Let the minister say:
Let us pray.

God our Father: we thank you for your faithfulness, promised in this sacrament, and for the hope we have in your Son Jesus. As we baptize with water, baptize us with Holy Spirit, so that what we say may be your word and what we do may be your work. By your power, may we be made one with Christ our Lord in common faith and purpose.

The minister and the people shall say together:
O God, who called us from death to life: we give ourselves to you, and, with the church through all ages, we thank you for your saving love in Jesus Christ our Lord. Amen.

Let the minister address the candidate (or the parents presenting a child for baptism), saying:
What is your (child's) name?

The minister shall baptize the candidate with water, calling him by his given name or names:
_____, I baptize you in the name of the Father and of the Son and of the Holy Spirit. **Amen.**

This child of God is now received into the holy catholic church. See what love the Father has given us, that we should be called children of God; and we are!

If an infant has been baptized, turn to intercessions on pages 46-47.

If the baptized person is being received into full communicant membership, let the minister or an elder say those words required by the Constitution of his church (see footnote on page 43).

_____, you are a disciple of Jesus Christ. He has commissioned you. Live in his love, and serve him.

Be filled with gratitude. Let the message of Christ dwell among you in all its richness. Whatever you are doing, whether you speak or act, do everything in the name of the Lord Jesus, giving thanks to God the Father through him.

You are no longer aliens, but fellow citizens with God's people, members of God's household. You are built upon the foundation laid by the apostles and prophets, and Christ Jesus himself is the foundation stone. In him you too are being built with all the rest into a spiritual dwelling for God.

> Let a representative of the session lead the people in prayer, saying:

Let us pray.

God our Father: we praise you for calling us to be a servant people, and for gathering us into the body of Christ. We thank you for choosing to add to our number brothers and sisters in faith. Together, may we live in your Spirit and so love one another, that we may have the mind of Jesus Christ our Lord, to whom we give honor and glory forever. Amen.

> Let the minister, and the elder representing the session, welcome the baptized member with a handshake, saying:

Welcome to the ministry of Jesus Christ.

> The baptized member shall be dismissed:

Go now, and serve the Lord.

The grace of the Lord Jesus Christ, and the love of God, and the fellowship of the Holy Spirit, be with you all. **Amen.**

> The following intercessions may be used in the service of baptism:

Let us pray.

Almighty God, giver of life: you have called us by name, and pledged to each of us your faithful love. We pray for your *child*, _____. Watch over *him*. Guide *him* as *he* grows in faith.

Give *him* understanding, and a quick concern for neighbors. Help *him* to be a true disciple of Jesus Christ, who was baptized your Son and servant, who is our risen Lord. **Amen.**

God of grace, Father of us all: we pray for parents, _____ and _____. Help them to know you, to love with your love, to teach your truth, and to tell the story of Jesus to their child, so that your word may be heard, and bring about plans for us you have promised, in Jesus Christ our Lord. **Amen.**

The following prayer may be said in unison:

Holy God: remind us of the promises given in our own baptism, and renew our trust in you. Make us strong to obey your will, and to serve you with joy; for the sake of Jesus Christ our Lord. Amen.

ORDER FOR THE
PUBLIC WORSHIP OF GOD

The Commissioning of Baptized Members; the Order for Their Confirmation; and the Reception of Members from Other Churches

Sections I and II of this service may be used separately; or they may be joined as indicated in the rubrics.

I. THE ORDER FOR CONFIRMATION

After the Sermon has been preached, let an elder representing the session invite the candidate(s) for confirmation to stand before the congregation, saying:

_____ *have* been received by the session into the communicant membership of the church. *They have* studied God's word, and *have* learned the belief and practice of his people. *They are* here to declare *their* faith, and to be joined with us in the service of Jesus Christ.

When those to be confirmed have assembled, let the minister say:

Hear the words of our Lord Jesus Christ.

You did not choose me, but I chose you and appointed you that you should go and bear fruit.

Everyone who acknowledges me before men, I also will acknowledge before my Father who is in heaven.

Friends: Jesus Christ has chosen you, and, in baptism, has joined you to himself. He has called you, together with us, into the church, which is his body. Now, he has brought you to this time and place, so you may confess his name before men, and go out to serve him as faithful disciples.

48

The minister shall address those to be confirmed, asking questions required by the Constitution of his church (see footnote on page 43).

_____, who is your Lord and Savior?

Jesus Christ is my Lord and Savior.

Do you trust in him?

I do.

Do you intend to be his disciple, to obey his word and to show his love?

I do.

Will you be a faithful member of this congregation, giving of yourself in every way, and will you seek the fellowship of the church wherever you may be?

I will.

Those to be confirmed may kneel. Let the minister or an elder give the following charge:

_____, you are a disciple of Jesus Christ. He has commissioned you. Live in his love, and serve him.

And,

Be filled with gratitude. Let the message of Christ dwell among you in all its richness. Whatever you are doing, whether you speak or act, do everything in the name of the Lord Jesus, giving thanks to God the Father through him.

If there are members who have been received by the session from other Christian churches, they may be recognized and made welcome at this time (see section II). Otherwise, let the minister say:

Let us affirm our faith.

I believe in God, the Father almighty,
creator of heaven and earth.

I believe in Jesus Christ, his only Son, our Lord.
He was conceived by the power of the Holy Spirit
and born of the Virgin Mary.

He suffered under Pontius Pilate,
   was crucified, died, and was buried.
He descended to the dead.
On the third day he rose again.
He ascended into heaven,
   and is seated at the right hand of the Father.
He will come again to judge the living and the dead.

I believe in the Holy Spirit,
   the holy catholic church,
   the communion of saints,
   the forgiveness of sins,
   the resurrection of the body,
   and the life everlasting. Amen.

Let the representative of the session lead the people in prayer, saying:

Let us pray.

O God our Father: we praise you for calling us to be a servant people, and for gathering us into the body of Christ. We thank you for choosing to add to our number brothers and sisters in faith. Together, may we live in your Spirit, and so love one another, that we may have the mind of Jesus Christ our Lord, to whom we give honor and glory forever. Amen.

Let the minister and the elder representing the session welcome those confirmed with a handshake, saying:

Welcome to this ministry of Jesus Christ.

Those confirmed shall be dismissed:

Go, and serve the Lord.

The grace of our Lord Jesus Christ, and the love of God, and the fellowship of the Holy Spirit, be with you all. **Amen.**

II. THE RECEPTION OF MEMBERS FROM OTHER CHURCHES

An elder representing the session shall name those who have been received by letter of commendation from other Christian churches, or by reaffirmation of their faith in Jesus Christ. He shall invite them to stand, saying:

_____ *have* been received into the membership of this congregation by letter of commendation from *another* Christian *church*, or by reaffirmation of *their* faith in Jesus Christ.

When those to be received have stood before the congregation, let the minister say:

Friends: As members of the one, holy, catholic, and apostolic church, you do not come to us as strangers, but as brothers and sisters in the Lord. We welcome you to the worship and work of this people of God.

There is one body and one Spirit, one Lord, one faith, one baptism, one God and Father of us all, who is above all, and through all, and in all.

Do you promise to be a faithful member of this congregation, giving of yourself in every way, and so fulfill your calling as a disciple of Jesus Christ the Lord?

I do.

Then, let the minister say:

Let us affirm our faith.

I believe in God, the Father almighty,
    creator of heaven and earth.

I believe in Jesus Christ, his only Son, our Lord.
    He was conceived by the power of the Holy Spirit
        and born of the Virgin Mary.
    He suffered under Pontius Pilate,
        was crucified, died, and was buried.
    He descended to the dead.
    On the third day he rose again.
    He ascended into heaven,
        and is seated at the right hand of the Father.
    He will come again to judge the living and the dead.

I believe in the Holy Spirit,
the holy catholic church,
the communion of saints,
the forgiveness of sins,
the resurrection of the body,
and the life everlasting. Amen.

Let the representative of the session lead the people in prayer, saying:

Let us pray.

O God our Father: we praise you for calling us to be a servant people, and for gathering us into the body of Christ. We thank you for choosing to add to our number brothers and sisters in faith. Together, may we live in your Spirit, and so love one another, that we may have the mind of Jesus Christ our Lord, to whom we give honor and glory forever. Amen.

Let the minister and the elder representing the session welcome the new communicant members with a handshake, saying:

Welcome to this ministry of Jesus Christ.

Then, the new communicant members shall be dismissed:

Go, and serve the Lord.

The grace of our Lord Jesus Christ, and the love of God, and the fellowship of the Holy Spirit, be with you all. **Amen.**

A Brief Order for the Lord's Supper

This brief order for the Lord's Supper is designed for parish use, but is not intended to be a substitute for the Service for the Lord's Day. The order may be adapted for use with the sick. When the service is used with the sick, the minister should be accompanied by elders and, if possible, by other members of the congregation to show the communal character of the Lord's Supper. With members of the congregation present, the minister or an elder shall say:

Hear what Jesus Christ promises:

Happy are those who hunger and thirst for what is right. They shall be satisfied.

I am the bread of life. He who comes to me will never be hungry; he who believes in me will never thirst.

A doxology or a psalm may be sung or said. Then, let the minister or the elder say:

This is the word of the Lord: All those whom I love I correct and discipline. Therefore, shake off your complacency and repent. See, I stand knocking at the door. If anyone listens to my voice and opens the door, I will go into his house and dine with him, and he with me.

Let us open our hearts to the Lord.

God our Father: we have done wrong, and do not deserve to be called your children. We have turned from your way, and been taken in by our own desires. We have not loved neighbors as you commanded. Have mercy on us, Lord, have mercy on us, and forgive us; for the sake of your Son, our Savior, Jesus Christ. Amen.

Friends: Hear and believe the good news of the gospel. In Jesus Christ we are forgiven. Let us forgive one another. The peace of the Lord Jesus Christ be with you.

Amen.

A Scripture lesson may be read and briefly interpreted. A psalm or a hymn of thanksgiving may be sung. Then, let the minister say:

According to Luke, when our risen Lord was at table with his disciples, he took the bread, and blessed and broke it, and gave it to them. And their eyes were opened and they recognized him. Remember the Lord Jesus Christ.

We remember and are thankful.

Lift up your hearts.

We lift them to the Lord.

Let us pray.

Mighty God, good Father: we thank you for the gift of life, and for the world our home. We thank you for your loving-kindness to us and all men. Your works are great and wonderful. Your ways are just and true. You alone are holy.

The following response may be sung or said:

Holy, holy, holy
Is the Lord God, the Almighty;
He was, he is and he is to come.

Holy God: we praise you for your Son Jesus, who shared our weakness, and was tempted in every way as we are; who obeyed you, by suffering and dying for us. You have raised him to rule the world, and given him a name above every name—Lord and Christ. We praise him and we glorify you, great God our Father.

Now give us your Spirit in the breaking of bread, so that by your power we may be drawn together and made one with Jesus Christ, who is the way, the truth, and the life.

The following may be said by all the people:

With Christians through all ages, we lift our hearts to you, giving thanks, and trusting you to use us as your people; for the sake of Jesus Christ our Savior.

The Lord's Prayer may be said. Then, as the minister breaks bread, let him say:

The Lord Jesus, on the night of his arrest, took bread, and after giving thanks to God, broke it and said: "This is my body, which is for you; do this, remembering me."

As the bread is distributed, the minister may say:

I am the bread of life. He who comes to me will never be hungry; he who believes in me will never thirst.

As the minister lifts the cup, let him say:

In the same way, Jesus took the cup after supper, and said: "This cup is the new covenant sealed in my blood. Whenever you drink it, do this, remembering me."

As the cup is passed, the minister may say:

I am the vine, you are the branches. Cut off from me, you can do nothing.

Then, let the minister or an elder pray, saying:

We thank you, Father, for this supper shared in the Spirit with your Son Jesus, who makes us new and strong, and brings us life eternal. We praise you for giving all good gifts in him, and pledge ourselves to serve you, even as you have served us in Jesus Christ the Lord. **Amen.**

And,

Jesus said: I am the light of the world; anyone who follows me will not be walking in the dark; he will have the light of life.

The grace of the Lord Jesus Christ be with you all. **Amen.**

Morning Prayer

(For Daily Use)

The service shall begin with a Call to Worship:

God said: Let there be light; and there was light. And God saw that the light was good.

This is the day which the Lord has made;

Let us rejoice and be glad in it.

Praise the Lord.

The Lord's name be praised!

Or,

Though you were once all darkness, now as Christians you are light. Live like men who are at home in daylight, for where light is, there all goodness springs up, all justice and truth.

God is light:

In him there is no darkness at all.

Praise the Lord.

The Lord's name be praised!

Or,

God, who said, "Let light shine out of darkness," has shone in our hearts to give the light of the knowledge of the glory of God in the face of Christ.

Glory be to God!

Through Jesus Christ our Lord.

A hymn of praise may be sung, a canticle, or a Gloria. Then, one of the following prayers may be said, or some other appropriate prayer:

Let us pray.

God of light, in whom there is no darkness: look to your wayward children. Forgive our sin, and give us such joy

in Jesus that darkness may be driven from us, and your light shine in our lives by faith; through Jesus Christ our Lord. Amen.

Mighty God, who divided light from darkness, and made the sun to shine: wake us from the night of doubt and fear, and let us live this day, and every day, in the light of the truth taught by your Spirit, and revealed in Jesus Christ our Lord, whom we praise forever. Amen.

New every morning is your love, great God of light, and all day long you are working for good in the world. Stir up in us desire to serve you, to live peacefully with our neighbors, and to devote each day to your Son, our Savior, Jesus Christ the Lord. Amen.

A psalm may be said or sung. Then a Scripture lesson may be read and briefly interpreted.

The following prayer, or other prayers, may be said:

Let us pray.

God our Father: you taught us to pray not only for friends in faith, but for those who do not believe, who also stand before your judgment and live in your love. Answer our prayers according to your great plan for us and for all men.

We pray for peace among men and nations, split by ancient pride and wrongs remembered. Disarm us; break the hold of hate on our hearts, and draw us from every race and nation to live together in brotherhood, as children of one Father.

God of peace, bring peace to the world.

We pray for hungry and poor men, for victims of greed or careless gain. Teach us compassion, so that no one may be kept from a share of the world's richness.

God of love, tell us what to do.

We pray for the friendless, the sick and the fearful, for prisoners, for people who are burdened. May this day not pass without words spoken and gifts given to show that you care.

God of mercy, help us to be helpful.

We pray for leaders who serve in the United Nations, in our nation, and in other lands. May they bow to your power and follow your leading.

God of power, rule your lands and peoples.

We pray for the church, your unworthy servant. Speak commands, and give us the faithfulness to do and say what you want said and done, in the world you love so much.

God of prophets, set your word in our lives.

Hear our prayers, God of grace, and help us to enact them, working for your peace and justice, mercy and purpose, in all we do today; through Jesus Christ our Lord.

Amen.

Our Father . . .

> A hymn, or the Doxology, may be sung, after which the people shall be dismissed:

Go in peace.

Serve the Lord.

The grace of our Lord Jesus Christ be with you all. **Amen.**

Evening Prayer

(For Daily Use)

The service shall begin with a Call to Worship:

Lord, your love is better than life itself,

Our lips will recite your praise.

We proclaim your love at daybreak

And your faithfulness all through the night.

Or,

If I asked darkness to cover me,

And light to become night around me,

Darkness would not be dark to you,

Night would be as light as day.

God, examine me and know my heart,

And guide me in the way everlasting.

Or,

God shall come, and there shall be continuous day,

For at evening time there shall be light.

God is light:

In him there is no darkness at all.

Let one of the following prayers be said, or some other appropriate prayer:

Eternal God: you gave your Son Jesus to be light of the world. In his light, help us to face our darkness, to confess our sins, and, trusting your mercy, to rest in peace this night, so that with the coming of the day we may wake in good faith to serve you; through Jesus Christ our Lord. **Amen.**

God our Father: in Jesus Christ you called us to come when we are weary and overburdened. Give us rest from the trials of the day; guard our sleep and speak to our dreaming, so that refreshed we may greet daylight with resolve, and be strong to do your will; through Jesus Christ our Lord. **Amen.**

Morning and evening, for your goodness we praise you, great God of our lives, and pray that awake or asleep we may stay in your care, believing your love for us declared in Jesus Christ your Son, our Lord. **Amen.**

A hymn may be sung, or a canticle. Then, Scripture may be read and briefly interpreted.

The following prayer, or other prayers, may be said:

God of mercy: forgive and correct the wrong we have done this day. We have turned from the way of your Son Jesus and have not cared for neighbors. We have permitted pride to blind and anger to burn, and we have failed to live the new life you have given us. We come to you at night with little to offer except our sins, begging mercy in the name of Jesus Christ, who was always faithful to you, and is always faithful to us. **Amen.**

God of power: you hear our prayers before we speak, yet welcome our praying. Work out plans for us and all men as you know best.

Guide men and nations into peace.

Power the church to be your witness.

Enrich the poor, and show the rich their poverty.

Strengthen those who work nights to make our days brighter.

Watch with the sick who are restless in pain.

Comfort the dying with signs of your presence.

Be close to those who are close to us.

Keep faith with us as you have in the past, and help us to trust your promises, so that we may live expecting goodness and mercy all our days; through Jesus Christ our Lord. **Amen.**

O God our Father, creator of this world and giver of all good things: we thank you for our home on earth and for the joy of living. We praise you for your love in Jesus Christ, who came to set things right, who died rejected on the cross and rose triumphant from the dead; because he lives, we live to praise you, Father, Son, and Holy Spirit, our God forever. Amen.

Our Father . . .

A hymn may be sung, or the Nunc Dimittis, after which the people shall be dismissed:

Go in peace.

Trust the Lord.

The grace of our Lord Jesus Christ be with you. **Amen.**

Order for an Agape

Praise to you, O Lord our God, king of the universe, who causes the earth to yield food for all.

Or,

Give thanks to the Lord, for he is good,

His love is everlasting!

Give thanks to the God of gods,

His love is everlasting!

Give thanks to the Lord of lords,

His love is everlasting!

A hymn of praise or thanksgiving may be sung, after which the leader may greet the people, welcoming them as friends in Christ.

Then, let a reader read Luke 9:12–17. The leader shall pray, saying:

Let us pray.

Great God, our Father, whose Son Jesus broke bread to feed a crowd in Galilee: we thank you for the food you give us. May we enjoy your gifts thankfully, and share what we have with brothers on earth who hunger and thirst, giving praise to Jesus Christ, who has shown your perfect love. **Amen.**

Appropriately, there may be five loaves of bread. The leader may break one of them, and, after taking a piece of bread, may pass the broken halves, one to the left and the other to the right. The remaining loaves may be distributed to all the people.

Then, the people shall eat bread, and pass their dishes of food. People may talk together as neighbors in faith; or the leader may direct their conversations by suggesting matters of mutual concern.

When the meal is ended, a reader may read one or more of the following passages, or some other appropriate lesson from Scripture:

> *Matthew 22:34–40*
> *Luke 14:16–24*
> *I Corinthians, ch. 13*
> *II Corinthians 9:6–15*
> *Philippians 2:5–11*

Then, let the leader say:

Let us pray.

We praise you, God our creator, for your good gifts to us and all mankind. We thank you for the friendship we have in Christ; and for the promise of your coming kingdom, where there will be no more hunger and thirst, and where men will be satisfied by your love. As this bread was once seed scattered on earth to be gathered into one loaf, so may your church be joined together into one holy people, who praise you for your love made known in Jesus Christ the Lord. **Amen.**

My dear people, we are already children of God. His commandments are these: that we believe in his Son Jesus Christ, and that we love one another. Whoever keeps his commandments lives in God and God lives in him. We know he lives in us by the Spirit he has given us.

Or,

My dear people, since God loved us so much, we too should love one another. No one has ever seen God; but as long as we love one another God will live in us, and his love will be complete in us.

The people may sing the Doxology.

Then, the leader shall say:

Let us show our love for neighbors.

The leader may wish to announce a particular need to which the people may give. Baskets may be passed around the table, so that the people may contribute. A hymn may be sung as the collection is taken, or after the collection has been taken.

The Lord's Prayer shall be said:

Our Father . . .

The Agape may conclude with a dismissal:

Go in peace. The grace of the Lord Jesus Christ be with you all
Amen.

ORDER FOR THE
PUBLIC WORSHIP OF GOD
The Marriage Service

The man and the woman to be married may be seated together facing the Lord's table, with their families, friends, and members of the congregation seated with them.

When the people have assembled, let the minister say:

Let us worship God.

There was a marriage at Cana in Galilee; Jesus was invited to the marriage, with his disciples.

Friends: Marriage is established by God. In marriage a man and a woman willingly bind themselves together in love, and become one even as Christ is one with the church, his body.

Let marriage be held in honor among all.

All may join in a hymn of praise and the following prayer:

Let us confess our sin before God.

Almighty God, our Father: you created us for life together. We confess that we have turned from your will. We have not loved one another as you commanded. We have been quick to claim our own rights and careless of the rights of others. We have taken much and given little. Forgive our disobedience, O God, and strengthen us in love, so that we may serve you as a faithful people, and live together in your joy; through Jesus Christ our Lord. Amen.

The minister shall declare God's mercy, saying:

Hear and believe the good news of the gospel.

Nothing can separate us from the love of God in Christ Jesus our Lord!

In Jesus Christ, we are forgiven.

The people may stand to sing a doxology, or some other appropriate response to the good mercy of God.

The minister may offer a Prayer for Illumination.

Before the reading of the Old Testament lesson, the minister shall say:

The lesson is . . .

Listen for the word of God.

The Gloria Patri, or some other response, may be sung.

Before the reading of the New Testament lesson, the minister shall say:

The lesson is . . .

Listen for the word of God.

The minister may deliver a brief Sermon on the lessons from Scripture, concluding with an Ascription of Praise.

Then let the minister address the man and woman, saying:

_____ and _____, you have come together according to God's wonderful plan for creation. Now, before these people, say your vows to each other.

Let the man and the woman stand before the people, facing each other. Then, the minister shall say:

Be subject to one another out of reverence for Christ.

The man shall say to the woman:

_____, *I promise with God's help to be your faithful husband, to love and serve you as Christ commands, as long as we both shall live.*

The woman shall say to the man:

_____, *I promise with God's help to be your faithful wife, to love and serve you as Christ commands, as long as we both shall live.*

A ring, or rings, may be given, with the following words:

I give you this ring as a sign of my promise.

The minister shall address the man and the woman, saying:

As God's picked representatives of the new humanity, purified and beloved of God himself, be merciful in action, kindly in heart, humble in mind. Accept life, and be most patient and tolerant with one another. Forgive as freely as the Lord has forgiven you. And, above everything else, be truly loving. Let the peace of Christ rule in your hearts, remembering that as members of the one body you are called to live in harmony, and never forget to be thankful for what God has done for you.

Or,

Love is slow to lose patience—it looks for a way of being constructive. It is not possessive: it is neither anxious to impress nor does it cherish inflated ideas of its own importance. Love has good manners and does not pursue selfish advantage. It is not touchy. It does not keep account of evil or gloat over the wickedness of other people. On the contrary, it is glad with all good men when truth prevails. Love knows no limit to its endurance, no end to its trust, no fading of its hope; it can outlast anything. It still stands when all else has fallen.

The minister shall call the people to prayer, saying:

Praise the Lord.

The Lord's name be praised.

Lift up your hearts.

We lift them to the Lord.

Let us pray.

Eternal God: without your grace no promise is sure. Strengthen _____ and _____ with the gift of your Spirit, so they may fulfill the vows they have taken. Keep them faithful to each other and to you. Fill them with such love and joy that they may build a home where no one is a stranger. And guide them by your word to serve you all the days of their lives; through Jesus Christ our Lord, to whom be honor and glory forever and ever. **Amen.**

The Lord's Prayer shall be said.

Then, the man and the woman having joined hands, the minister shall say:

_____ and _____, you are now husband and wife according to the witness of the holy catholic church, and the law of the state. Become one. Fulfill your promises. Love and serve the Lord.

What God has united, man must not divide.

Here may be sung a hymn of thanksgiving. Then, let the people be dismissed:

Glory be to him who can keep you from falling and bring you safe to his glorious presence, innocent and happy. To God, the only God, who saves us through Jesus Christ our Lord, be the glory, majesty, authority, and power, which he had before time began, now and forever. **Amen.**

Or,

The grace of the Lord Jesus Christ, the love of God, and the fellowship of the Holy Spirit, be with you all. **Amen.**

A Service for
the Recognition of a Marriage

This service may be used to recognize a civil marriage; or with the deletion of the first paragraph, it may be used as a brief marriage service.

The service may be conducted during public worship on the Lord's Day, when the Sacrament is not celebrated, immediately after the preaching of a sermon; or it may be used at other times. Members of the congregation should be present, in addition to the minister.

Let the minister or an elder say:

_____ and _____ have been married by the law of the state, and they have spoken vows pledging loyalty and love. Now, in faith, they come before the witness of the church to acknowledge their marriage covenant and to tell their common purpose in the Lord.

Then, the minister shall say:

Friends: Marriage is God's gift. In marriage a man and a woman bind themselves in love and become one, even as Christ is one with the church, his body.

_____ and _____, be subject to one another out of reverence for Christ.

The man shall say to the woman:

_____, you are my wife. With God's help I promise to be your faithful husband, to love and serve you as Christ commands, as long as we both shall live.

The woman shall say to the man:

_____, *you are my husband. With God's help I promise to be your faithful wife, to love and serve you as Christ commands, as long as we both shall live.*

A ring, or rings, may be given, with the following words:

I give you this ring as a sign of my promise.

Then, let the minister say:

Hear the words of our Lord Jesus Christ:

Remain in my love. If you keep my commandments you will remain in my love, just as I have kept my Father's commandments and remain in his love. I have told you this so that my own joy may be in you and your joy be complete. This is my commandment: love one another, as I have loved you.

Let us pray.

Eternal God: without your grace no promise is sure. Strengthen _____ and _____ with the gift of your Spirit, so they may fulfill the vows they have taken. Keep them faithful to each other and to you. Fill them with such love and joy that they may build a home where no one is a stranger. And guide them by your word to serve you all the days of their lives; through Jesus Christ our Lord, to whom be honor and glory, forever and ever. **Amen.**

The man and the woman having joined hands, the minister shall say:

_____ and _____, you are husband and wife according to the witness of the holy catholic church. Help each other. Be united; live in peace, and the God of love and peace will be with you.

What God has united, man must not divide.

The following benediction may be said:

The grace of the Lord Jesus Christ, the love of God, and the fellowship of the Holy Spirit, be with you all. **Amen.**

ORDER FOR THE PUBLIC WORSHIP OF GOD

Witness to the Resurrection

Funeral Service

The people shall stand, and the minister shall say:

Jesus said: I am the resurrection and the life. If anyone believes in me, even though he die he will live, and whoever lives and believes in me will never die.

Come to me, all you who labor and are overburdened, and I will give you rest.

Our help is in the name of the Lord,

Who made heaven and earth.

Praise the Lord.

The Lord's name be praised.

All may join in a hymn of praise and the following prayer:

Let us confess our sin, trusting God's promised mercy.

The people may kneel and say together:

Eternal Father, guardian of our lives: we confess that we are children of dust, unworthy of your gracious care. We have not loved as we ought to love, nor have we lived as you command, and our years are soon gone. Lord God, have mercy on us. Forgive our sin and raise us to new life, so that as long as we live we may serve you, until, dying, we enter the joy of your presence; through Jesus Christ our Lord. Amen.

Who is in a position to condemn? Only Christ, and Christ died for us, Christ rose for us, Christ reigns in power for us, Christ prays for us.

Hear and believe the good news of the gospel: God is love. In Jesus Christ, we are forgiven. Be reconciled to God our Father. **Amen.**

> The people may stand to sing a doxology, or some other thankful response to the mercy of God.

> Then, let the minister say:

While we live, we are always being given up to death. Lord, to whom shall we go? You have the words of eternal life!

Let us pray.

Almighty God, whose love never fails, and who can turn the shadow of death into daybreak: help us to receive your word with believing hearts, so that, hearing the promises in Scripture, we may have hope and be lifted out of darkness into the light and peace of your presence; through Jesus Christ our Lord. **Amen.**

> Or,

Almighty God, our refuge and strength, our present help in trouble: give us such trust in you that, holding on to your word, we may be strong in this and every time of need; through Jesus Christ our Lord. **Amen.**

> Let the minister say:

Listen to Scripture read from the Old Testament.

> Several of the following Old Testament lessons may be read:

Lord, you have been
our refuge age after age.

Before the mountains were born,
before the earth or the world came to birth,
you were God from all eternity and forever.

You can turn man back into dust
by saying, "Back to what you were, you sons of men!"
To you, a thousand years are a single day,
a yesterday now over, an hour of the night.

You brush men away like waking dreams,
they are like grass
sprouting and flowering in the morning
withered and dry before dusk.

We too are burnt up by your anger
and terrified by your fury;
having summoned up our sins
you inspect our secrets by your own light.

Our days dwindle under your wrath,
our lives are over in a breath
—our life lasts for seventy years,
eighty with good health,

but they all add up to anxiety and trouble—
over in a trice, and then we are gone.

Teach us to count how few days we have
and so gain wisdom of heart.

Let us wake in the morning filled with your love
and sing and be happy all our days;
make our future as happy as our past was sad,
those years when you were punishing us.

Let your servants see what you can do for them,
let their children see your glory.
May the sweetness of the Lord be on us!
Make all we do succeed.   *From Psalm 90 (Jerusalem)*

Man, born of woman,
   has a short life yet has his fill of sorrow.
He blossoms, and he withers, like a flower;
   fleeting as a shadow, transient.
Since man's days are measured out,
   since his tale of months depends on you,
   since you assign him bounds he cannot pass,
turn your eyes from him, leave him alone,
   like a hired drudge, to finish his day.
There is always hope for a tree:
   when felled, it can start its life again;
   its shoots continue to sprout.

Its roots may be decayed in the earth,
   its stump withering in the soil,
but let it scent the water, and it buds,
   and puts out branches like a plant new set.
But man? He dies, and lifeless he remains;
   man breathes his last, and then where is he?

From Job, ch. 14 (Jerusalem)

Lord, you examine me and know me,
you know if I am standing or sitting,
you read my thoughts from far away,
whether I walk or lie down, you are watching,
you know every detail of my conduct.

The word is not even on my tongue,
Lord, before you know all about it;
close behind and close in front you fence me round,
shielding me with your hand.
Such knowledge is beyond my understanding,
a height to which my mind cannot attain.

Where could I go to escape your spirit?
Where could I flee from your presence?
If I climb the heavens, you are there,
there too, if I lie in Sheol.

If I flew to the point of sunrise,
or westward across the sea,
your hand would still be guiding me,
your right hand holding me.

If I asked darkness to cover me,
and light to become night around me,
that darkness would not be dark to you,
night would be as light as day.

It was you who created my inmost self,
and put me together in my mother's womb;
for all these mysteries I thank you:
for the wonder of myself, for the wonder of your works.

You know me through and through,
from having watched my bones take shape
when I was being formed in secret,
knitted together in the limbo of the womb.

You had scrutinized my every action,
all were recorded in your book,
my days listed and determined,
even before the first of them occurred.

God, how hard it is to grasp your thoughts!
How impossible to count them!
I could no more count them than I could the sand,
and suppose I could, you would still be with me.

God, examine me and know my heart,
probe me and know my thoughts;
make sure I do not follow pernicious ways
and guide me in the way that is everlasting.

From Psalm 139 (*Jerusalem*)

From the depths I call to you,
Lord, listen to my cry for help!
Listen compassionately
   to my pleading!

If you never overlooked our sins,
Lord, could anyone survive?
But you do forgive us:
   and for that we revere you.

I wait for the Lord, my soul waits for him,
   I rely on his promise,
   my soul relies on the Lord
   more than a watchman on the coming of dawn.

Let Israel rely on the Lord
   as much as the watchman on the dawn!
For it is with the Lord that mercy is to be found,
and a generous redemption;
it is he who redeems Israel
   from all their sins.

Psalm 130 (*Jerusalem*)

Bless the Lord, my soul,
bless his holy name, all that is in me!
Bless the Lord, my soul,
and remember all his kindnesses:

in forgiving all your offenses,
in curing all your diseases,
in redeeming your life from the Pit,
in crowning you with love and tenderness,
in filling your years with prosperity,
in renewing your youth like an eagle's.

The Lord, who does what is right,
is always on the side of the oppressed;
he revealed his intentions to Moses,
his prowess to the sons of Israel.

The Lord is tender and compassionate,
slow to anger, most loving;
his indignation does not last forever,
his resentment exists a short time only;
he never treats us, never punishes us,
as our guilt and our sins deserve.

No less than the height of heaven over earth
is the greatness of his love for those who fear him;
he takes our sins farther away
than the east is from the west.

As tenderly as a father treats his children,
so the Lord treats those who fear him;
he knows what we are made of,
he remembers we are dust.

Man lasts no longer than grass,
no longer than a wild flower he lives,
one gust of wind, and he is gone,
never to be seen there again;

yet the Lord's love for those who fear him
lasts from all eternity and forever,
like his goodness too for their children's children,

as long as they keep his covenant
and remember to obey his precepts.

The Lord has fixed his throne in the heavens,
his empire is over all.
Bless the Lord, all his angels,
heroes mighty to enforce his word,
attentive to his word of command.

Bless the Lord, all his armies,
servants to enforce his will.
Bless the Lord, all his creatures
in every part of his empire!

Bless the Lord, my soul.   *Psalm 103* (*Jerusalem*)

If I lift up my eyes to the hills,
    where shall I find help?
Help comes only from the Lord,
    maker of heaven and earth.
How could he let your foot stumble?
    How could he, your guardian, sleep?
The guardian of Israel
    never slumbers, never sleeps.
The Lord is your guardian,
    your defense at your right hand;
the sun will not strike you by day
    nor the moon by night.
The Lord will guard you against all evil;
    he will guard you, body and soul.
The Lord will guard your going and your coming,
    now and for evermore.   *Psalm 121* (*NEB*)

The Lord is my shepherd, I shall not want;
    he makes me lie down in green pastures.
He leads me beside still waters;
    he restores my soul.
He leads me in paths of righteousness
    for his name's sake.

Even though I walk through the valley of the shadow of death,
   I fear no evil;
for you are with me;
   your rod and your staff,
   they comfort me.

You prepare a table before me
   in the presence of my enemies;
you anoint my head with oil,
   my cup overflows.

Surely goodness and mercy shall follow me
   all the days of my life;
and I shall dwell in the house of the Lord
      forever.   *Psalm 23 (based on RSV)*

> The people may stand and sing the Gloria Patri, or some
> other appropriate response. Then, let the minister say:

Listen to Scripture read from the New Testament.

> Several of the following New Testament lessons may be
> read:

Two criminals were also led out with him for execution, and
when they came to the place called The Skull, they crucified him
with the criminals, one on either side of him. But Jesus himself
was saying,
"Father, forgive them; they do not know what they are doing."

One of the criminals hanging there covered him with abuse,
and said,
"Aren't you Christ? Why don't you save yourself—and us?"
But the other one checked him with the words:
"Aren't you afraid of God even when you're getting the same
punishment as he is? And it's fair enough for us, for we've only
got what we deserve, but this man never did anything wrong in
his life."

Then he said,
"Jesus, remember me when you come into your kingdom."
And Jesus answered,
"I tell you truly, this very day you will be with me in paradise."
                              From Luke, ch. 23 (Phillips)

Now when Jesus came, he found that Lazarus had already been in the tomb four days. Bethany was near Jerusalem, about two miles off, and many of the Jews had come to Martha and Mary to console them concerning their brother. When Martha heard that Jesus was coming, she went and met him, while Mary sat in the house. Martha said to Jesus, "Lord, if you had been here, my brother would not have died. And even now I know that whatever you ask from God, God will give you." Jesus said to her, "Your brother will rise again." Martha said to him, "I know that he will rise again in the resurrection at the last day." Jesus said to her, "I am the resurrection and the life; he who believes in me, though he die, yet shall he live, and whoever lives and believes in me shall never die. Do you believe this?" She said to him, "Yes, Lord; I believe that you are the Christ, the Son of God." *From John, ch. 11 (RSV)*

"Set your troubled hearts at rest. Trust in God always; trust also in me. There are many dwelling-places in my Father's house; if it were not so, I should have told you; for I am going there on purpose to prepare a place for you. And if I go and prepare a place for you, I shall come again and receive you to myself, so that where I am you may be also; and my way there is known to you." Thomas said, "Lord, we do not know where you are going, so how can we know the way?" Jesus replied, "I am the way; I am the truth and I am life; no one comes to the Father except by me." *From John, ch. 14 (NEB)*

We want you to be quite certain, brothers, about those who have died, to make sure that you do not grieve about them, like the other people who have no hope. We believe that Jesus died and rose again, and that it will be the same for those who have died in Jesus: God will bring them with him.
From I Thessalonians, ch. 4 (Jerusalem)

For I passed on to you—as among the first to hear it, the message I had myself received—that Christ died for our sins, as the scriptures said he would; that he was buried and rose again on the third day, again as the scriptures foretold. He was seen by Cephas, then by the twelve, and subsequently he was seen simultaneously by over five hundred Christians, of whom the majority are still alive, though some have since died. He was then seen by James, then by all the messengers. And last of all, as if to one born abnormally late, he appeared to me!

Now if the rising of Christ from the dead is the very heart of our message, how can some of you deny that there is any resurrection? For if there is no such thing as the resurrection of the dead, then Christ was never raised. And if Christ was not raised, then neither our preaching nor your faith has any meaning at all. Further it would mean that we are lying in our witness for God, for we have given our solemn testimony that he did raise up Christ—and that is utterly false if it should be true that the dead do not, in fact, rise again! For if the dead do not rise, neither did Christ rise, and if Christ did not rise, your faith is futile and your sins have never been forgiven. Moreover, those who have died believing in Christ are utterly dead and gone. Truly, if our hope in Christ were limited to this life only, we should, of all mankind, be the most to be pitied!

But the glorious fact is that Christ *did* rise from the dead!

But perhaps someone will ask: "How is the resurrection achieved? With what sort of body do the dead arrive?" Now that is talking without using your minds! In your own experience you know that a seed does not germinate without itself "dying." When you sow a seed you do not sow the "body" that will eventually be produced, but bare grain, of wheat, for example, or one of the other seeds. God gives the seed a "body" according to his laws—a different "body" to each kind of seed.

There are illustrations here of the raising of the dead. The body is "sown" in corruption; it is raised beyond the reach of corruption. It is "sown" in dishonor; it is raised in splendor. It is sown in weakness; it is raised in power. It is sown a natural body; it is raised a spiritual body. As there is a natural body so will there be a spiritual body. For I assure you, my brothers, it is utterly impossible for flesh and blood to possess the kingdom of God. The transitory could never possess the everlasting.

From I Corinthians, ch. 15 (Phillips)

We are always facing death, but this means that you know more and more of life. And we know for certain that he who raised the Lord Jesus from death shall also raise us with Jesus. We shall all stand together before him.

We wish you could see how all this is working out for your benefit, and how the more grace God gives, the more thanksgiving will redound to his glory. This is the reason that we never collapse. The outward man does indeed suffer wear and tear, but every day the inward man receives fresh strength. These little troubles (which are really so transitory) are winning for us a permanent, glorious and solid reward out of all proportion to our pain. For we are looking all the time not at the visible things but at the invisible. The visible things are transitory: it is the invisible things that are really permanent.

We know, for instance, that if our earthly dwelling were taken down, like a tent, we have a permanent house in Heaven, made, not by man, but by God. In this present frame we sigh with deep longing for the heavenly house, for we do not want to face utter nakedness when death destroys our present dwelling—these bodies of ours. As long as we are clothed in this temporary dwelling we have a painful longing, not because we want just to get rid of these "clothes" but because we want to know the full cover of the permanent house that will be ours. We want our transitory life to be absorbed into the life that is eternal.

Now the power that has planned this experience for us is God, and he has given us his Spirit as a guarantee of its truth. This makes us confident, whatever happens. We realize that being "at home" in the body means that to some extent we are "away" from the Lord, for we have to live by trusting him without seeing him. We are so sure of this that we would really rather be "away" from the body and be "at home" with the Lord.

It is our aim, therefore, to please him, whether we are "at home" or "away."

From II Corinthians, chs. 4 and 5 (Phillips)

In face of all this, what is there left to say? If God is for us, who can be against us? He who did not hesitate to spare his own

Son but gave him up for us all—can we not trust such a God to give us, with him, everything else that we can need?

Who would dare to accuse us, whom God has chosen? The judge himself has declared us free from sin. Who is in a position to condemn? Only Christ, and Christ died for us, Christ rose for us, Christ reigns in power for us, Christ prays for us!

Who can separate us from the love of Christ? Can trouble, pain or persecution? Can lack of clothes and food, danger to life and limb, the threat of force of arms?

No, in all these things we win an overwhelming victory through him who has proved his love for us.

I have become absolutely convinced that neither death nor life, neither messenger of Heaven nor monarch of earth, neither what happens today nor what may happen tomorrow, neither a power from on high nor a power from below, nor anything else in God's whole world has any power to separate us from the love of God in Christ Jesus our Lord!

From Romans, ch. 8 (Phillips)

Then I saw a new Heaven and a new earth, for the first Heaven and the first earth had disappeared, and the sea was no more. I saw the holy city, the new Jerusalem, descending from God out of Heaven, prepared as a bride dressed in beauty for her husband. Then I heard a great voice from the throne crying:

"See! The home of God is with men, and he will live among them. They shall be his people, and God himself shall be with them, and will wipe away every tear from their eyes. Death shall be no more, and never again shall there be sorrow or crying or pain. For all those former things are past and gone."

I could see no Temple in the city, for the Lord, the Almighty God, and the Lamb are themselves its Temple. The city has no need for the light of sun or moon, for the splendor of God fills it with light, and its radiance is the Lamb. The nations will walk by its light, and the kings of the earth will bring their glory into it. The city's gates shall stand open day after day—and there will be no night there.

Nothing that has cursed mankind shall exist any longer; the throne of God and of the Lamb shall be within the city. His servants shall worship him; they shall see his face, and his name will be upon their foreheads. Night shall be no more, they have no more need for either lamplight or sunlight, for the Lord God will shed his light upon them and they shall reign as kings for timeless ages. *From Revelation, chs. 21; 22 (Phillips)*

Blessed be God the Father of our Lord Jesus Christ, who in his great mercy has given us a new birth as his sons, by raising Jesus Christ from the dead, so that we have a sure hope and the promise of an inheritance that can never be spoilt or soiled and never fade away, because it is being kept for you in the heavens. Through your faith, God's power will guard you until the salvation which has been prepared is revealed at the end of time. This is a cause of great joy for you, even though you may for a short time have to bear being plagued by all sorts of trials; so that, when Jesus Christ is revealed, your faith will have been tested and proved like gold—only it is more precious than gold, which is corruptible even though it bears testing by fire— and then you will have praise and glory and honor. You did not see him, yet you love him; and still without seeing him, you are already filled with a joy so glorious that it cannot be described, because you believe; and you are sure of the end to which your faith looks forward, that is, the salvation of your souls. *From I Peter, ch. 1 (Jerusalem)*

I kneel in prayer to the Father, from whom every family in heaven and on earth takes its name, that out of the treasures of his glory he may grant you strength and power through his Spirit in your inner being, that through faith Christ may dwell in your hearts in love. With deep roots and firm foundations, may you be strong to grasp, with all God's people, what is the breadth and length and height and depth of the love of Christ, and to know it, though it is beyond knowledge. So may you attain to fullness of being, the fullness of God himself.

Now to him who is able to do immeasurably more than all we can ask or conceive, by the power which is at work among us,

to him be glory in the church and in Christ Jesus from generation to generation evermore! Amen.

From Ephesians, ch. 3 (NEB)

After the reading of the Scriptures, the minister may say a
prayer:

Eternal God, our Father: we praise you for your word which is
our light in darkness. Help us to hear and believe the promises
you have spoken; through Jesus Christ our Lord. **Amen.**

A hymn may be sung.

The minister may preach, briefly testifying to the hope that is
found in Scripture. He may conclude with an Ascription of
Praise.

The people may stand to say a creed of the church, and to
pray in unison:

I believe in God, the Father almighty,
creator of heaven and earth.

I believe in Jesus Christ, his only Son, our Lord.
He was conceived by the power of the Holy Spirit
and born of the Virgin Mary.
He suffered under Pontius Pilate,
was crucified, died, and was buried.
He descended to the dead.
On the third day he rose again.
He ascended into heaven,
and is seated at the right hand of the Father.
He will come again to judge the living and the dead.

I believe in the Holy Spirit,
the holy catholic church,
the communion of saints,
the forgiveness of sins,
the resurrection of the body,
and the life everlasting. Amen.

Let us pray.

God of grace: in Jesus Christ you have given a new and
living hope. We thank you that by dying he has con-

quered death; and that by rising again he promises eternal life. Help us to know that because he lives, we shall live also; and that neither death, nor life, nor things present, nor things to come, shall be able to separate us from your love; in Jesus Christ our Lord. Amen.

Instead of the Apostles' Creed, the following affirmation may be used:

We believe there is no condemnation for those who are in Christ Jesus: and we know that in everything God works for good with those who love him, who are called according to his purpose. We are sure that neither death, nor life, nor angels, nor principalities, nor things present, nor things to come, nor powers, nor height, nor depth, nor anything else in all creation, will be able to separate us from the love of God in Christ Jesus our Lord. Amen.

Let us pray.

Heavenly Father: in your Son Jesus you have given us a true faith and a sure hope. Help us to live trusting in the communion of saints, the forgiveness of sins, and the resurrection to life eternal. Strengthen this faith and hope in us, all the days of our life; through the love of your Son, Jesus Christ our Savior. Amen.

The minister may say the following prayers, or other appropriate prayers:

O God, before whom generations rise and pass away: we praise you for all your servants who, having lived this life in faith, now live eternally with you. Especially we thank you for your servant _____, for the gift of *his* life, for the grace you have given *him*, for all in *him* that was good and kind and faithful. (*Here mention may be made of characteristics or service.*) We thank you that for *him* death is past, and pain is ended, and *he* has entered the joy you have prepared; through Jesus Christ our Lord. **Amen.**

And,

Almighty God: in Jesus Christ you promised many homes within your house. Give us faith to see beyond touch and sight some sign of your kingdom, and, where vision fails, to trust your love which never fails. Lift heavy sorrow, and give us good hope in Jesus, so we may bravely walk our earthly way, and look forward to glad heavenly reunion; through Jesus Christ our Lord, who was dead but is risen, to whom be honor and praise, now and forever. **Amen.**

Let the minister and people say:

O God, who called us from death to life: we give ourselves to you; and with the church through all ages, we thank you for your saving love in Jesus Christ our Lord. Amen.

A hymn of praise or thanksgiving may be sung, after which the people may be dismissed:

Hear the words of our Lord Jesus Christ:

Peace I leave with you; my peace I give to you; not as the world gives do I give to you. Let not your hearts be troubled, neither let them be afraid.

The grace of the Lord Jesus Christ, and the love of God, and the fellowship of the Holy Spirit, be with you all. **Amen.**

Witness to the Resurrection

Committal Service

When all are assembled, let the minister say:

Thank God, the God and Father of our Lord Jesus Christ, that in his great mercy we men have been born again into a life full of hope, through Christ's rising from the dead.

Do not be afraid. I am the first and the last. I am the living one; for I was dead and now I am alive for evermore.

Because I live, you shall live also.

Almighty God: we commend to you our neighbor _____, trusting your love and mercy; and believing in the promise of a resurrection to eternal life; through our Lord Jesus Christ. **Amen.**

All thanks to God, who gives us the victory through our Lord Jesus Christ!

Then, let the minister say any of the following prayers:

O Lord: support us all the day long, until the shadows lengthen and the evening comes, and the busy world is hushed, and the fever of life is over, and our work is done. Then, in your mercy, grant us a safe lodging, and a holy rest, and peace at the last; through Jesus Christ our Lord. **Amen.**

O God: you have designed this wonderful world, and know all things good for us. Give us such faith that, by day and by night, in all times and in all places, we may without fear trust those who are dear to us to your never-failing love, in this life and in the life to come; through Jesus Christ our Lord. **Amen.**

Eternal God: our days and years are lived in your mercy. Make us know how frail we are, and how brief our time on earth; and lead us by your Holy Spirit, so that, when we have served you in our generation, we may be gathered into your presence, faithful in the church, and loving toward neighbors; through Jesus Christ our Lord. **Amen.**

Father: you gave your own Son Jesus to die on the cross for us, and raised him from death as a sign of your love. Give us faith, so that, though our child has died, we may believe that you welcome *him* and will care for *him*, until, by your mercy, we are together again in the joy of your promised kingdom; through Jesus Christ our Lord. **Amen.**

Almighty God, Father of the whole family in heaven and on earth: stand by those who sorrow; that, as they lean on your strength, they may be upheld, and believe the good news of life beyond life; through Jesus Christ our Lord. **Amen.**

> The Lord's Prayer may be said. Then, the people may be dismissed with a benediction.

A Service for Ordination and Installation*

This service is designed to be used for the ordination of ministers of the word, elders, and deacons; and also for their installation. When a minister of the word is being ordained but not installed, the congregational questions should be omitted.

The service may take place during public worship, following the preaching of a sermon. Let the moderator lead the people, saying:

There are different gifts,

But it is the same Spirit who gives them.

There are different ways of serving God,

But it is the same Lord who is served.

God works through different men in different ways,

But it is the same God who achieves his purpose through them all.

Each one is given a gift by the Spirit,

To use it for the common good.

Together we are the body of Christ,

And individually members of him.

Though we have different gifts, together we are a ministry of reconciliation led by the risen Christ. We work and pray to

---

*This book is for three Churches. The ordination questions in this service are required in The United Presbyterian Church in the United States of America. Other questions may be required in the Cumberland Presbyterian Church and the Presbyterian Church in the United States.

make his church useful in the world, and we call men and women to faith, so that, in the end, every knee shall bow and every tongue confess that Jesus Christ is Lord, to the glory of God the Father.

Within our common ministry, some members are chosen for particular work as ministers of the word, ruling elders, or deacons. In ordination, we recognize these special ministries, remembering that our Lord Jesus said:

Whoever among you wants to be great must become the servant of all, and if he wants to be first among you, he must be the slave of all men!

Just as the Son of Man came not to be served, but to serve, and to give his life to set others free.

Then, let an elder come forward, bringing the candidate(s). Let the elder say to the moderator:

Mr. Moderator, speaking for the people of the church, I bring _____ to be ordained as _____.

Or,

Mr. Moderator, speaking for the people of the church, I bring _____ to be installed as _____.

Then, the moderator shall ask those questions required by the Constitution of his church (see footnote on page 89).

_____, God has called you by the voice of the church to serve Jesus Christ in a special way. You know who we are and what we believe, and you understand the work for which you have been chosen.

Do you trust in Jesus Christ your Savior, acknowledge him Lord of the world and head of the church, and through him believe in one God, Father, Son, and Holy Spirit?

I do.

Do you accept the scriptures of the Old and New Testaments to be, by the Holy Spirit, the unique and authoritative witness to Jesus Christ in the church universal, and God's word to you?

I do.

Will you be instructed by the Confessions of our church, and led by them as you lead the people of God?

I will.

Will you be _____ (*a* minister of the word, elder*s*, deacon*s*) in obedience to Jesus Christ, under the authority of Scripture, and continually guided by our Confessions?

I will.

Do you endorse our church's government, and will you honor its discipline? Will you be a friend among your comrades in ministry, working with them, subject to the ordering of God's word and Spirit?

I do and I will.

Will you govern the way you live, by following the Lord Jesus Christ, loving neighbors, and working for the reconciliation of the world?

I will.

Will you seek to serve the people with energy, intelligence, imagination, and love?

I will.

FOR A MINISTER OF THE WORD

When a minister of the word is being ordained or installed, the following question shall be asked:

Will you be a faithful minister, proclaiming the good news in word and sacrament, teaching faith, and caring for people? Will you be active in government and discipline, serving in courts of the church, and, in your ministry, will you try to show the love and justice of Jesus Christ?

I will

FOR AN ELDER

When an elder is being ordained, the following question shall be asked:

Will you be a faithful elder, watching over the people, providing for their worship and instruction? Will you share in government and discipline, serving in courts of the church; and, in your ministry, will you try to show the love and justice of Jesus Christ?

I will.

FOR A DEACON

When a deacon is being ordained, the following question shall be asked:

Will you be a faithful deacon, teaching charity, urging concern, and directing the peoples' help to the friendless and those in need? In your ministry, will you try to show the love and justice of Jesus Christ?

I will.

WHEN ORDAINED ELDERS OR DEACONS ARE AGAIN ELECTED

If there are previously ordained elders or deacons to be installed, let an elder present them to the moderator, saying:

Mr. Moderator: (Elder, Deacon) _____ having been elected again to active service by the vote of this congregation, *he* may now be installed to office.

The moderator shall ask those questions required by the Constitution of his church (see footnote on page 89).

_____, you have been called again to a position of special leadership in the church.

Do you welcome the work for which you have been chosen, and will you serve the people with energy, intelligence, imagination, and love, relying on God's mercy and rejoicing in his promises through Jesus Christ our Lord?

I do and I will.

Then, let a designated elder face the congregation with the candidate(s) being installed, and ask those questions required by the Constitution of his church (see footnote on page 89).

Do we, members of the church, accept _____ as _____
(*a* minister of the word, elder*s*, deacon*s*), chosen by God through
the voice of this congregation, to lead us in the way of Jesus
Christ?

We do.

Do we agree to encourage *him*, to respect *his* decisions, and to
follow as *he* guides us, serving Jesus Christ, who alone is head
of the church?

We do.

FOR A MINISTER OF THE WORD

> When a minister of the word is being installed, the following
> question may also be asked:

Do we promise to pay *him* fairly and provide for *his*
welfare as *he* works among us; to stand by *him* in trouble
and share *his* joys? Will we listen to the word *he* preaches,
welcome *his* pastoral care, and honor *his* authority, as
he seeks to honor and obey Jesus Christ our Lord?

We do and we will.

> Candidate(s) for ordination will kneel; ministers of the
> gospel and elders may come forward for the laying on of
> hands.

> In an ordination service all of the following prayers, or
> similar prayers, should be used. When ministers of the word,
> elders, or deacons, previously ordained, are being installed,
> only the unison prayer which follows should be said.

Let us pray.

Almighty God: in every age you have chosen servants to speak
your word and lead your loyal people. We thank you for *this
man* whom you have called to serve you. Give *him* special gifts
to do *his* special work; and fill *him* with Holy Spirit, so *he* may
have the same mind that was in Christ Jesus, and be *a* faithful
disciple as long as *he* shall live.

> The candidate(s) may say the following brief prayer, or a
> similar prayer:

God our Father: you have chosen me. Now give me strength, wisdom, and love to work for the Lord Jesus Christ.

Let all the people join in the following prayer:

God of grace, who called us to a common ministry as ambassadors of Christ, trusting us with the message of reconciliation: give us courage and discipline to follow where your servants rightly lead us; that together we may declare your wonderful deeds and show your love to the world; through Jesus Christ the Lord of all. Amen.

Then, the moderator shall say to the candidate(s):

_____, you are now _____ (*a* minister of the word, elder*s*, deacon*s*) in the church (and for this congregation). Whatever you do, in word or deed, do everything in the name of the Lord Jesus, giving thanks to God the Father through him. **Amen.**

Ministers of the gospel and elders shall welcome the new minister or new elder(s) with a handshake; deacons may join in welcoming the new deacon(s). They shall say:

Welcome to this ministry.

Brief charges may be given. Because the New Testament contains helpful charges, they may be selected and read.

When a minister of the word is ordained or installed, another minister of the word may be appointed to read a passage from Scripture, such as:

II Timothy 4:1–5
II Corinthians 4:1–15

When elders are ordained or installed, another elder may read a passage from Scripture, such as:

I Peter 5:1–4
I Timothy 3:1–7

When deacons are ordained or installed, another deacon may read a passage from Scripture, such as:

I Corinthians, ch. 13
I Timothy 3:8–13

A charge may be given the congregation by reading a passage from Scripture, such as:

I Peter 5:5–13
I Thessalonians 5:12–23
Philippians 2:1–16
I Corinthians 12:12–26

The service shall conclude with a benediction.

The Installation of a Commissioned Church Worker

The installation may be conducted during public worship on the Lord's Day, immediately after the preaching of a sermon. Let the moderator say:

Hear what the apostle Paul has written:

Our gifts differ according to the grace given us. If your gift is prophecy, use it as your faith suggests; if administration, then use it for administration; if teaching, then use it for teaching. Let the preachers deliver sermons, the almsgivers give freely, the officials be diligent, and those who do works of mercy do them cheerfully. Do not let your love be pretense, but sincerely prefer good to evil. Work for the Lord with untiring effort and with great earnestness of spirit.

There are different gifts,

But it is the same Spirit who gives them.

Each one is given a gift by the Spirit,

To use it for the common good.

An elder may come forward with the candidate for installation, and say to the moderator:

Mr. Moderator, speaking for the session of this church, I bring _____ to be installed as _____.

Then, let the moderator address the candidate, saying:

_____, you believe yourself called by Jesus Christ to a special work, and you have studied to prepare yourself for a vocation in the church. Presbytery has approved your qualifications and has commissioned you a church worker.

96

Are you willing to be installed as _____?

> *I am.*

Do you welcome this responsibility because you are determined to follow the Lord Jesus, to love neighbors, and to work for the reconciling of the world?

> *I do.*

Will you serve the people with energy, intelligence, imagination, and love, relying on God's mercy and rejoicing in his promises through Jesus Christ our Lord?

> *I will.*

> Then, let the elder, standing with the candidate, face the congregation, and say:

Do we, members of _____, accept _____ as _____, chosen of God and appointed by the _____, to guide us in the way of Jesus Christ?

> **We do.**

> The candidate may kneel, as the moderator leads the people in prayer, saying:

Let us pray.

> **God of Grace, who called us to a common ministry as ambassadors of Christ, trusting us with the message of reconciliation: give us courage and discipline to follow where your servants rightly lead us; that together we may declare your wonderful deeds and show your love to the world; through Jesus Christ the Lord of all. Amen.**

> The moderator shall declare the commissioned church worker installed into office, saying:

_____, you are now installed as _____ in the church. Whatever you do, in word or deed, do everything in the name of the Lord Jesus, giving thanks to God the Father through him.

> **Amen.**

> Brief charges may be given the commissioned church worker and the congregation by a minister or another commissioned church worker.

ORDER FOR THE
PUBLIC WORSHIP OF GOD

Recognition of Trustees

The recognition of trustees may take place during public worship on the Lord's Day, following the preaching of a sermon.

Let an elder bring forward the elected trustees, and say to the minister:

Mr. Moderator, _____ *are* elected to serve as *trustees* of the church. We wish to recognize the responsibility *they* have accepted.

The minister shall address the elected trustees, saying:

Friends: God has given you special gifts to serve him, and we have chosen you for a special work. Under the law of the state, you will hold and manage properties and, as authorized, conduct business for the church. By your energy, honesty, and fairness you will demonstrate Christian faith to those you deal with on our behalf.

Let the elder address the elected trustees:

Do you promise to give the business affairs of this congregation your devoted attention, to encourage generosity, and, in all your dealings, work to further our service of Christ in the world?

I do.

Then, standing with the elected trustees, facing the congregation, let the elder say:

Do you receive these persons as your trustees, and do you promise to support them in their work for the church?

We do.

The minister will say:

Let us pray.

Holy God: you made this world and called it good, and appointed us to manage things as agents of your love. Guide your servants as they represent us, and direct our business. Help them to be wise children of light, who show your trust by being trustworthy; through Jesus Christ our Lord. **Amen.**

The minister will say to the trustees:

You are now trustees for this church. Be good and faithful servants, who will enter into the joy of our Lord.

The grace of the Lord Jesus Christ be with you. **Amen.**

Recognition of Church School Teachers

Those appointed to teach shall stand among or before the congregation. The minister shall say:

Hear, O Israel: The Lord our God is one Lord; and you shall love the Lord your God with all your heart, and with all your soul, and with all your might. And these words which I command you this day shall be upon your heart; and you shall teach them diligently to your children, and shall talk of them when you sit in your house, and when you walk by the way, and when you lie down, and when you rise.

Jesus said to his disciples: I give you a new commandment: Love one another; just as I have loved you.

Go, therefore, make disciples of all the nations; baptize them in the name of the Father and of the Son and of the Holy Spirit, and teach them to observe all the commands I gave you.

What we have heard and known for ourselves and what our ancestors have told us must not be withheld from their descendants, but be handed on by us to the next generation; these in their turn will tell their own children so that they too put confidence in God, never forgetting God's achievements, and always keeping his commandments.

Then, the minister shall address the teachers, saying:

Friends: You have been chosen by the session of this church to serve as teachers. You will announce God's good law to each new generation, and tell of Jesus Christ, so we may know him, love him, and live his truth in the world.

Do you trust Jesus Christ your Savior, and through him believe in one God, Father, Son, and Holy Spirit?

We do.

Do you promise to study the Scriptures and the teachings of the church, so that with imagination and love you may serve the Holy Spirit, by calling men to faith in Christ and training his disciples?

We do.

By the authority of the session, you are commissioned to teach in the church. Be energetic, honest, and faithful to Christ your Lord!

Let a ruling elder lead the people in prayer:

God of our fathers: in every age you have appointed teachers to tell your power, justice, and love. We thank you for brothers and sisters in faith, who will teach your ways. Give them Holy Spirit, so they may know your Son our Lord, speak his truth, and with us live the new life, serving neighbors, obedient to your commandments; through Jesus Christ our Savior. Amen.

The truth of the Lord Jesus Christ be with you. **Amen.**

Litanies

Litanies

The litany is an ancient form of prayer that predates the New Testament and was in common use among the early Christians.

The litanies that follow are designed for special occasions in the life of the church, but they may be used during public worship on the Lord's Day.

Each of the litanies may be used in entirety, or in separate sections as indicated; or some of the petitions within the litanies may be extended to create brief prayers by adding an "Address" and a "Conclusion."

Litany of the Beatitudes

For use during Lent,
or in services preparing for the Lord's Supper

LEADER: Jesus said: Happy are the poor in spirit; theirs is the kingdom of heaven.

God our Father: help us to know that away from you we have nothing. Save us from pride that mistakes your gifts for possessions; and keep us humble enough to see that we are poor sinners who always need you.

PEOPLE: **Happy are the poor in spirit.**

LEADER: Thank you, God, for your Son Jesus, who, though he was rich, became poor to live among us; who had no place for himself on earth. By his weakness we are made strong, and by his poverty, rich.

Happy are the poor in spirit;

PEOPLE: **Theirs is the kingdom of heaven.**

LEADER: Jesus said: Happy are those who mourn; they shall be comforted.

God our Father: we are discouraged by evil and frightened by dying, and have no word of hope within ourselves. Unless you speak to us, O God, we shall be overcome by grieving and despair.

PEOPLE: **Happy are those who mourn.**

LEADER: Thank you, God, for Jesus Christ, who on the cross faced evil, death, and desertion. You raised him in triumph over every dark power to be our Savior. We give thanks for the hope we have in him.

Happy are those who mourn;

PEOPLE: **They shall be comforted.**

LEADER: Jesus said: Happy are the gentle; they shall have the earth.

God our Father: restrain our arrogance and show us our place on earth. Keep us obedient, for we are your servants, unwise and unworthy, who have no rights and deserve no honors.

PEOPLE: **Happy are the gentle.**

LEADER: Thank you, God, for Jesus Christ our Master, who did not call us slaves, but your true sons. Help us to work with him, ordering all things for joy, according to your will.

Happy are the gentle;

PEOPLE: **They shall have the earth.**

LEADER: Jesus said: Happy are those who hunger and thirst for what is right; they shall be satisfied.

God our Father: stir up in us a desire for justice, and a love of your law. May we never live carelessly or selfishly, but in all our dealing with neighbors may we look for the right and do it.

PEOPLE: **Happy are those who hunger and thirst for what is right.**

LEADER: Thank you, God, for Jesus Christ, who overturned small man-made rules, yet lived your law in perfect love. Give us freedom to live with your Spirit in justice, mercy, and peace.

Happy are those who hunger and thirst for what is right;

PEOPLE: **They shall be satisfied.**

LEADER: Jesus said: Happy are the merciful; they shall have mercy shown them.

God our Father: we do not forgive as you have forgiven us. We nurse old wrongs and let resentments rule us. We tolerate evil in ourselves, yet harshly judge our neighbors. God, forgive us.

PEOPLE: **Happy are the merciful**

LEADER: Thank you, God, for your Son Jesus, who gave his

life for sinners; who on the cross forgave unforgivable things. Receiving his mercy, may we always forgive.

Happy are the merciful;

PEOPLE: **They shall have mercy shown them.**

LEADER: Jesus said: Happy are the pure in heart; they shall see God.

God our Father: we are not pure. We do not live in love. The good we do, we admire too much; we tabulate our virtues. Deliver us, O God, from a divided heart.

PEOPLE: **Happy are the pure in heart.**

LEADER: Thank you, God, for Jesus Christ, whose words and deeds were pure. By his life our lives are justified, and by his death we are redeemed. In him we see you face to face, and praise you for your goodness.

Happy are the pure in heart;

PEOPLE: **They shall see God.**

LEADER: Jesus said: Happy are the peacemakers; they shall be called sons of God.

God our Father: we have not lived in peace. We have spread discord, prejudice, gossip, and fear among neighbors. Help us, for we cannot help ourselves. Show us your way of peace.

PEOPLE: **Happy are the peacemakers.**

LEADER: Thank you, God, for Jesus Christ, who has broken down dividing walls of hate to make one family on earth. As he has reconciled us to you, may we be reconciled to one another, living in peace with all your children everywhere.

Happy are the peacemakers;

PEOPLE: **They shall be called sons of God.**

LEADER: Jesus said: Happy are those who are persecuted in the cause of right; theirs is the kingdom of heaven.

God our Father: we are afraid to risk ourselves for the right. We have grown accustomed to wrong and been silent in the face of injustice. Give us anger without hate, and courage to obey you no matter what may happen.

PEOPLE: **Happy are those who are persecuted in the cause of right.**

LEADER: Thank you, God, for Jesus Christ, who was persecuted for what he said and did; who took the cross upon himself for our sake. May we stand with him in justice and love, and follow where he leads, even to a cross.

Happy are those who are persecuted in the cause of right;

PEOPLE: **Theirs is the kingdom of heaven.**

LEADER: Jesus said: Happy are you when people abuse you and persecute you and speak all kinds of evil against you on my account. Rejoice and be glad, for your reward will be great in heaven.

God our Father: give us a will to live by your commandments. Keep us from slander, cruelty, and mocking talk, so that we may be faithful witnesses to Jesus Christ our Lord.

PEOPLE: **Happy are you when people abuse you and persecute you and speak all kinds of evil against you on my account.**

LEADER: We praise you, O God, for your Son Jesus, who called us to be disciples. Give us grace to confess him before men, and faith to believe he suffered for us. We ask no rewards, only make us brave.

Happy are you when people abuse you and persecute you and speak all kinds of evil against you on my account.

PEOPLE: **Rejoice and be glad, for your reward will be great in heaven.**

LEADER: You are the light of the world. Your light must shine in the sight of men, so that, seeing your good works, they may give praise to your Father in heaven.

PEOPLE: **Amen.**

Litany of Confession

LEADER: Almighty God: you alone are good and holy. Purify our lives and make us brave disciples. We do not ask you to keep us safe, but to keep us loyal, so we may serve Jesus Christ, who, tempted in every way as we are, was faithful to you.

PEOPLE: **Amen.**

LEADER: From lack of reverence for truth and beauty; from a calculating or sentimental mind; from going along with mean and ugly things;

PEOPLE: **O God, deliver us.**

LEADER: From cowardice that dares not face truth; laziness content with half-truth; or arrogance that thinks it knows it all;

PEOPLE: **O God, deliver us.**

LEADER: From artificial life and worship; from all that is hollow or insincere;

PEOPLE: **O God, deliver us.**

LEADER: From trite ideals and cheap pleasures; from mistaking hard vulgarity for humor;

PEOPLE: **O God, deliver us.**

LEADER: From being dull, pompous, or rude; from putting down neighbors;

PEOPLE: **O God, deliver us.**

LEADER: From cynicism about our brothers; from intolerance or cruel indifference;

PEOPLE: **O God, deliver us.**

LEADER: From being satisfied with things as they are, in the church or in the world; from failing to share your indignation;

PEOPLE: **O God, deliver us.**

LEADER: From selfishness, self-indulgence, or self-pity;

PEOPLE: **O God, deliver us.**

LEADER: From token concern for the poor, for lonely or loveless
people; from confusing faith with good feeling, or love
with a wanting to be loved;

PEOPLE: **O God, deliver us.**

LEADER: For everything in us that may hide your light;

PEOPLE: **O God, light of life, forgive us.**

Litany of Intercession

The Litany of Intercession may be said in entirety, or selectively. The response, "Hear our prayer, O Lord," may be used after each petition instead of the variety of responses provided.

LEADER: Great God our Father: you hear our prayers before we speak, and answer before we know our need. Though we cannot pray, may your Spirit pray in us, drawing us to you and toward our neighbors on earth.

PEOPLE: **Amen.**

LEADER: We pray for the whole creation: may all things work together for good, until, by your design, men inherit the earth and order it wisely.

PEOPLE: **Let the whole creation praise you, Lord and God.**

LEADER: We pray for the church of Jesus Christ; that, begun, maintained, and promoted by your Spirit, it may be true, engaging, glad, and active, doing your will.

PEOPLE: **Let the church be always faithful, Lord and God.**

LEADER: We pray for men and women who serve the church in special ways, preaching, ruling, showing charity; that they may never lose heart, but have all hope encouraged.

PEOPLE: **Let leadership be strong, Lord and God.**

LEADER: We pray for people who do not believe, who are shaken by doubt, or have turned against you. Open their eyes to see beyond our broken fellowship the wonders of your love displayed in Jesus, Jew of Nazareth; and to follow when he calls them.

PEOPLE: **Conquer doubt with faith, O God.**

LEADER: We pray for peace in the world. Disarm weapons, silence guns, and put out ancient hate that smolders still, or flames in sudden conflict. Create goodwill among men of every race and nation.

PEOPLE: **Bring peace to earth, O God.**

LEADER: We pray for men who must go to war, and for those who will not go: may they have conviction, and charity toward one another.

PEOPLE: **Guard brave men everywhere, O God.**

LEADER: We pray for enemies, as Christ commanded; for those who oppose us or scheme against us, who are also children of your love. May we be kept from infectious hate or sick desire for vengeance.

PEOPLE: **Make friends of enemies, O God.**

LEADER: We pray for those involved in world government, in agencies of control or compassion, who work for the reconciling of nations: keep them hopeful, and work with them for peace.

PEOPLE: **Unite our broken world, O God.**

LEADER: We pray for those who govern us, who make, administer, or judge our laws. May this country ever be a land of free and able men, who welcome exiles and work for justice.

PEOPLE: **Govern those who govern us, O God.**

LEADER: We pray for poor people who are hungry, or are housed in cramped places. Increase in us, and all who prosper, concern for the disinherited.

PEOPLE: **Care for the poor, O God.**

LEADER: We pray for social outcasts; for those excluded by their own militance or by the harshness of others. Give us grace to accept those our world names unacceptable, and so show your mighty love.

PEOPLE: **Welcome the alienated, O God.**

LEADER: We pray for sick people who suffer pain, or struggle with demons of the mind, who silently cry out for healing: may they be patient, brave, and trusting.

PEOPLE: **Heal sick and troubled men, O God.**

LEADER: We pray for the dying, who face final mystery: may they enjoy light and life intensely, keep dignity, and greet death unafraid, believing in your love.

PEOPLE: **Have mercy on the dying, O God.**

LEADER: We pray for those whose tears are not yet dry, who listen for familiar voices and look for still familiar faces: in loss, may they affirm the gain you promise in Jesus, who prepares a place for us within your spacious love.

PEOPLE: **Comfort those who sorrow, O God.**

LEADER: We pray for people who are alone and lonely, who have no one to call in easy friendship: may they be remembered, befriended, and know your care for them.

PEOPLE: **Visit lonely people, O God.**

LEADER: We pray for families, for parents and children: may they enjoy each other, honor freedoms, and forgive as happily as we are all forgiven in your huge mercy.

PEOPLE: **Keep families in your love, O God.**

LEADER: We pray for young and old: give impatient youth true vision, and experienced age openness to new things. Let both praise your name.

PEOPLE: **Join youth and age together, O God.**

LEADER: We pray for all men everywhere: may they come into their own as sons of God, and inherit the kingdom prepared in Jesus Christ, the Lord of all, and Savior of the world.

PEOPLE: **Hear our prayers, almighty God, in the name of Jesus Christ, who prays with us and for us, to whom be praise forever. Amen.**

Litany of Thanksgiving

LEADER: Give thanks to the Lord, for he is good.

PEOPLE: **His love is everlasting.**

LEADER: Come, let us praise God joyfully.

PEOPLE: **Let us come to him with thanksgiving.**

LEADER: For the good world; for things great and small, beautiful and awesome; for seen and unseen splendors;

PEOPLE: **Thank you, God.**

LEADER: For human life; for talking and moving and thinking together; for common hopes and hardships shared from birth until our dying;

PEOPLE: **Thank you, God.**

LEADER: For work to do and strength to work; for the comradeship of labor; for exchanges of good humor and encouragement;

PEOPLE: **Thank you, God.**

LEADER: For marriage; for the mystery and joy of flesh made one; for mutual forgiveness and burdens shared; for secrets kept in love;

PEOPLE: **Thank you, God.**

LEADER: For family; for living together and eating together; for family amusements and family pleasures;

PEOPLE: **Thank you, God.**

LEADER: For children; for their energy and curiosity; for their brave play and their startling frankness; for their sudden sympathies;

PEOPLE: **Thank you, God.**

LEADER: For the young; for their high hopes; for their irreverence toward worn-out values; their search for freedom; their solemn vows;

PEOPLE: **Thank you, God.**

LEADER: For growing up and growing old; for wisdom deepened by experience; for rest in leisure; and for time made precious by its passing;

PEOPLE: **Thank you, God.**

LEADER: For your help in times of doubt and sorrow; for healing our diseases; for preserving us in temptation and danger;

PEOPLE: **Thank you, God.**

LEADER: For the church into which we have been called; for the good news we receive by word and sacrament; for our life together in the Lord;

PEOPLE: **We praise you, God.**

LEADER: For your Holy Spirit, who guides our steps and brings us gifts of faith and love; who prays in us and prompts our grateful worship;

PEOPLE: **We praise you, God.**

LEADER: Above all, O God, for your Son Jesus Christ, who lived and died and lives again for our salvation; for our hope in him; and for the joy of serving him;

PEOPLE: **We thank and praise you, God our Father, for all your goodness to us.**

LEADER: Give thanks to the Lord, for he is good.

PEOPLE: **His love is everlasting.**

Litany for the Church

A

LEADER: Almighty God: you built your church on the rock of human faith and trust; we praise you for Jesus Christ, the foundation and cornerstone of all we believe.

PEOPLE: **We praise you, God.**

LEADER: For the faith of Abraham, Isaac, and Jacob; and for Moses, who led your people out of slavery, and established the law in their hearts;

PEOPLE: **We praise you, God.**

LEADER: For the prophets who listened for your word and called your people back from disobedience and from the worship of man-made gods;

PEOPLE: **We praise you, God.**

LEADER: For those who foretold the coming of your Son Jesus Christ, and prepared the way for his birth;

PEOPLE: **We praise you, God.**

LEADER: For Mary and Joseph, who taught him to love you and trained him in synagogue and temple to serve you;

PEOPLE: **We praise you, God.**

LEADER: For Christ, our Savior, who loved us and gave himself for us on the cross;

PEOPLE: **We praise you, God.**

LEADER: For the apostles and martyrs of the church, who gave their lives that we, in our day, might receive the good news of grace and forgiveness;

PEOPLE: **We praise you, God.**

LEADER: For the great men of history, whose love for your church made it a willing instrument of your care and mercy; who placed you first in their lives and held to their faith in good times and in bad;

PEOPLE: **We praise you, God.**

B

LEADER: Save us, Father, from living in the past, and from resting on the work of others. Let us find a new beginning and a new vision; that we may know our duty in this place and this world today.

PEOPLE: **O Lord, please hear us.**

LEADER: Keep us from pride that excludes others from the shelter of your love; and from mean prejudice and mass evils that scar the tissues of our common life.

PEOPLE: **O Lord, please hear us.**

LEADER: Spare us from the selfishness that uses your house as a means of getting social position or personal glory, and let us not hold back what we have or what we are when there is so much need.

PEOPLE: **O Lord, please hear us.**

LEADER: Defend us from the ignorance that nourishes injustice and from indifference that causes hearts to break; that, in these times of racial bitterness, we may demonstrate your love and live beyond caste or color as Christ's men and women.

PEOPLE: **O Lord, please hear us.**

LEADER: Help us to avoid isolation in our apartments and our private homes, while others near us do not have a bed of their own or any quiet place; and, as we work to bring a decent life to others, let us know a purer enjoyment of all your blessings.

PEOPLE: **O Lord, please hear us.**

C

LEADER: That we may accept the responsibility of our freedom, the burden of our privilege, and so conduct ourselves as to set an example for those who will follow after;

PEOPLE: **O God, be our strength.**

LEADER: That we may not be content with a secondhand faith, worshiping words rather than the Word;

PEOPLE: **O God, be our strength.**

LEADER: That we may find joy in the study of Scripture, and growth in exposure to new ideas;

PEOPLE: **O God, be our strength.**

LEADER: That we may be part of our presbytery and community, sharing in the great mission which you have set before us, and always seeking the common good;

PEOPLE: **O God, be our strength.**

LEADER: That we may find in your church a prod to our imaginations, a shock to our laziness, and a source of power to do your will;

PEOPLE: **O God, be our strength.**

LEADER: O God, who gave us minds to know you, hearts to love you, and voices to sing your praise: send your Spirit among us; that, confronted by your truth, we may be free to worship you as we should; through Jesus Christ our Lord.

ALL: **Amen.**

Litany for
the Unity of Christ's Church

A

LEADER: O God: you have welcomed us by baptism into one holy church, and joined us by faith to Christian men in every place. May your church on earth be a sign of the communion you promise, where we will all be one with Christ, and joyful in your kingdom.

PEOPLE: **Amen.**

LEADER: From a clinging to power that prevents church union; from thinking forms of government perfect, or courts of the church infallible;

PEOPLE: **Good Lord, deliver us.**

LEADER: From mistaken zeal that will not compromise; from worshiping neat doctrines rather than you;

PEOPLE: **Good Lord, deliver us.**

LEADER: From religious pride that belittles faith of others, or claims true wisdom, but will not love;

PEOPLE: **Good Lord, deliver us.**

LEADER: From a worldly mind that drums up party spirit; from divisiveness; from protecting systems that have seen their day;

PEOPLE: **Good Lord, deliver us.**

B

LEADER: As you sent disciples into every land, O God, gather them now, from the ends of the earth, into one fellowship that chooses your purpose and praises your name, in one faith, hope, and love.

PEOPLE: **Amen.**

LEADER: Make us one, Lord, in our eagerness to speak good news and set all captives free.

PEOPLE: **Give us your Holy Spirit.**

LEADER: Make us one, Lord, in concern for the poor, the hurt, and the downtrodden, to show them your love.

PEOPLE: **Give us your Holy Spirit.**

LEADER: Make us one, Lord, in worship, breaking bread together and singing your praise with single voice.

PEOPLE: **Give us your Holy Spirit.**

LEADER: Make us one, Lord, in faithfulness to Jesus Christ, who never fails us, and who will come again in triumph.

PEOPLE: **Give us your Holy Spirit.**

LEADER: Give us your Holy Spirit, God our Father, so we may have among us the same mind that was in Christ Jesus; and proclaim him to the world. May every knee bow down and every tongue confess him Lord, to the glory of your name.

PEOPLE: **Amen.**

Litany of the Names of the Church

In the New Testament, the church is called by many different names that tell us who we are and what we must be doing for God. This litany uses some of the Scriptural pictures of the church, and urges obedience.

LEADER: God of Abraham and Isaac, of apostles and prophets: in every age you have picked out people to work for you, showing justice, doing mercy, and directing living men. Let the church share Christ's own work as prophet, priest, and king, reconciling the world to your law and your love, and telling your mighty power.

Give thanks to God for the church of Jesus Christ.

PEOPLE: **We are a chosen people.**

LEADER: You have called us out of the world, O God, and chosen us to be a witness to nations. Give us Holy Spirit to show the way, the truth, and the life of our Savior Jesus Christ.

PEOPLE: **Forgive silence and stubbornness. Help us to be your chosen people.**

LEADER: Give thanks to God for the church of Jesus Christ.

PEOPLE: **We are a royal priesthood.**

LEADER: You have appointed us priests, O God, to pray for all men and declare your mercy. Give us Holy Spirit; that, sacrificing ourselves for neighbors in love, they may be drawn to you, and to each other.

PEOPLE: **Forgive hypocrisy and lazy prayers. Help us to be your royal priesthood.**

LEADER: Give thanks to God for the church of Jesus Christ.

PEOPLE: **We are the household of God.**

LEADER: You have baptized us into one family of faith, and named us your children, and brothers of Christ. Give us Holy Spirit to live in peace and serve each other gladly.

PEOPLE: **Forgive pride and unbrotherly divisions. Help us to be your household.**

LEADER: Give thanks to God for the church of Jesus Christ.

PEOPLE: **We are a temple for your Spirit.**

LEADER: You have built us up, O God, into a temple for worship. Give us Holy Spirit to know there is no other foundation for us than Jesus Christ, rock and redeemer.

PEOPLE: **Forgive weakness and lack of reverence. Help us to be a temple for your Spirit.**

LEADER: Give thanks to God for the church of Jesus Christ.

PEOPLE: **We are a colony of heaven.**

LEADER: You have welcomed us as your citizens, O God, to represent our homeland. Give us Holy Spirit to act your laws, speak your language, and to show in life-style your kingdom's courtesy and love.

PEOPLE: **Forgive injustice and going along with the world. Help us to be a colony of heaven.**

LEADER: Give thanks to God for the church of Jesus Christ.

PEOPLE: **We are the body of Christ.**

LEADER: You have joined us in one body, O God, to live for our Lord in the world. Give us Holy Spirit; that, working together without envy or pride, we may serve our Lord and head.

PEOPLE: **Forgive slack faith and separate ways. Help us to be the body of Christ.**

LEADER: O God, we are your church, called, adopted, built up, blessed, and joined to Jesus Christ. Help us to know who we are, and in all we do to be your useful servants.

PEOPLE: We are a chosen people
                a royal priesthood
                a household of God
                a temple for the Spirit
                a colony of heaven
                the body of Christ

LEADER: Give thanks to God.

PEOPLE: For the church of Jesus Christ.

LEADER: Give thanks to God.

PEOPLE: And trust his Holy Spirit. Amen.

Litany for World Peace

A

LEADER: Remember, O Lord, the peoples of the world divided into many nations and tongues. Deliver us from every evil that gets in the way of your saving purpose; and fulfill the promise of peace on earth among men with whom you are pleased; through Jesus Christ our Lord.

PEOPLE: **Amen.**

LEADER: From the curse of war and the sin of man that causes war;

PEOPLE: **O Lord, deliver us.**

LEADER: From pride that turns its back on you, and from unbelief that will not call you Lord;

PEOPLE: **O Lord, deliver us.**

LEADER: From national vanity that poses as patriotism; from loud-mouthed boasting and blind self-worship that admit no guilt;

PEOPLE: **O Lord, deliver us.**

LEADER: From the self-righteousness that will not compromise, and from selfishness that gains by the oppression of others;

PEOPLE: **O Lord, deliver us.**

LEADER: From the lust for money or power that drives men to kill;

PEOPLE: **O Lord, deliver us.**

LEADER: From trusting in the weapons of war, and mistrusting the councils of peace;

PEOPLE: **O Lord, deliver us.**

LEADER: From hearing, believing, and speaking lies about other nations;

PEOPLE: **O Lord, deliver us.**

LEADER: From groundless suspicions and fears that stand in the way of reconciliation;

PEOPLE: **O Lord, deliver us.**

LEADER: From words and deeds that encourage discord, prejudice, and hatred; from everything that prevents the human family from fulfilling your promise of peace;

PEOPLE: **O Lord, deliver us.**

B

LEADER: O God our Father: we pray for all your children on earth, of every nation and of every race; that they may be strong to do your will.

We pray for the church in the world.

PEOPLE: **Give peace in our time, O Lord.**

LEADER: For the United Nations;

PEOPLE: **Give peace in our time, O Lord.**

LEADER: For international federations of labor, industry, and commerce;

PEOPLE: **Give peace in our time, O Lord.**

LEADER: For departments of state, ambassadors, diplomats, and statesmen;

PEOPLE: **Give peace in our time, O Lord.**

LEADER: For worldwide agencies of compassion, which bind wounds and feed the hungry;

PEOPLE: **Give peace in our time, O Lord.**

LEADER: For all who in any way work to further the cause of peace and goodwill;

PEOPLE: **Give peace in our time, O Lord.**

LEADER: For common folk in every land who live in peace;

PEOPLE: **Give peace in our time, O Lord.**

LEADER: Eternal God: use us, even our ignorance and weakness, to bring about your holy will. Hurry the day when people shall live together in your love; for yours is the kingdom, the power, and the glory forever.

PEOPLE: **Amen.**

Litany for the Nation

This litany is designed to be used on days of national celebration, or in times of national crisis.

A

LEADER: Mighty God: the earth is yours and nations are your people. Take away our pride and bring to mind your goodness, so that, living together in this land, we may enjoy your gifts and be thankful.

PEOPLE: **Amen.**

LEADER: For clouded mountains, fields and woodland; for shoreline and running streams; for all that makes our nation good and lovely;

PEOPLE: **We thank you, God.**

LEADER: For farms and villages where food is gathered to feed our people;

PEOPLE: **We thank you, God.**

LEADER: For cities where men talk and work together in factories, shops, or schools to shape those things we need for living;

PEOPLE: **We thank you, God.**

LEADER: For explorers, planners, statesmen; for prophets who speak out, and for silent faithful people; for all who love our land and guard freedom;

PEOPLE: **We thank you, God.**

LEADER: For vision to see your purpose hidden in our nation's history, and courage to seek it in brother-love exchanged;

PEOPLE: **We thank you, God.**

B

LEADER: O God: your justice is like rock, and your mercy like pure flowing water. Judge and forgive us. If we have turned from you, return us to your way; for without you we are lost people.

From brassy patriotism and a blind trust in power;

PEOPLE: **Deliver us, O God.**

LEADER: From public deceptions that weaken trust; from self-seeking in high political places;

PEOPLE: **Deliver us, O God.**

LEADER: From divisions among us of class or race; from wealth that will not share, and poverty that feeds on food of bitterness;

PEOPLE: **Deliver us, O God.**

LEADER: From neglecting rights; from overlooking the hurt, the imprisoned, and the needy among us;

PEOPLE: **Deliver us, O God.**

LEADER: From a lack of concern for other lands and peoples; from narrowness of national purpose; from failure to welcome the peace you promise on earth;

PEOPLE: **Deliver us, O God.**

C

LEADER: Eternal God: before you nations rise and fall; they grow strong or wither by your design. Help us to repent our country's wrong, and to choose your right in reunion and renewal.

PEOPLE: **Amen.**

LEADER: Give us a glimpse of the Holy City you are bringing to earth, where death and pain and crying will be gone away; and nations gather in the light of your presence.

PEOPLE: **Great God, renew this nation.**

LEADER: Teach us peace, so that we may plow up battlefields and pound weapons into building tools, and learn to talk across old boundaries as brothers in your love.

PEOPLE: **Great God, renew this nation.**

LEADER: Talk sense to us, so that we may wisely end all prejudice, and may put a stop to cruelty, which divides or wounds the human family.

PEOPLE: **Great God, renew this nation.**

LEADER: Draw us together as one people who do your will, so that our land may be a light to nations, leading the way to your promised kingdom, which is coming among us.

PEOPLE: **Great God, renew this nation.**

LEADER: Great God, eternal Lord: long years ago you gave our fathers this land as a home for free men. Show us there is no law or liberty apart from you; and let us serve you modestly, as devoted people; through Jesus Christ our Lord.

PEOPLE: **Amen.**

Litany for Those Who Work

LEADER: O Lord God: you are ever at work in the world for us and for all mankind. Guide and protect all who work to get their living.

PEOPLE: **Amen.**

LEADER: For those who plow the earth,
For those who tend machinery;

PEOPLE: **Work with them, O God.**

LEADER: For those who sail deep waters,
For those who venture into space;

PEOPLE: **Work with them, O God.**

LEADER: For those who work in offices and warehouses,
For those who labor in stores or factories;

PEOPLE: **Work with them, O God.**

LEADER: For those who work in mines,
For those who buy and sell;

PEOPLE: **Work with them, O God.**

LEADER: For those who entertain us,
For those who broadcast or publish;

PEOPLE: **Work with them, O God.**

LEADER: For those who keep house,
For those who train children;

PEOPLE: **Work with them, O God.**

LEADER: For all who live by strength of arm,
For all who live by skill of hand;

PEOPLE: **Work with them, O God.**

LEADER: For all who employ or govern;

PEOPLE: **Work with them, O God.**

LEADER: For all who excite our minds with art, science, or
learning;

PEOPLE: **Work with them, O God.**

LEADER: For all who instruct,
For writers and teachers;

PEOPLE: **Work with them, O God.**

LEADER: For all who serve the public good in any way by working;

PEOPLE: **Work with them, O God.**

LEADER: For all who labor without hope,
For all who labor without interest;
For those who have too little leisure,
For those who have too much leisure;
For those who are underpaid,
For those who pay small wages;
For those who cannot work,
For those who look in vain for work;
For those who trade on troubles of others,
For profiteers, extortioners, and greedy people;

PEOPLE: **Great God: we pray your mercy, grace, and saving
power.**

LEADER: Work through us and help us always to work for you;
in Jesus Christ our Lord.

PEOPLE: **Amen.**

The Christian Year

The Christian Year

As they worship, Christians are mindful of the mighty acts of God, especially as they are seen in the birth, the life, the death, and the resurrection of Jesus Christ. The pattern in which worshipers proceed from event to event and from remembrance to remembrance is called the Christian year.

The following prayers and readings are arranged according to the seasons of the Christian year. Calls to worship, readings, and special prayers are provided, as well as collects for each Lord's Day. Congregations are urged to supply Bibles for use in public worship, so that psalms and readings may be sung or said responsively.

For congregations that use color symbolism in connection with the seasons of the Christian year, the following summary of prevailing usage may be helpful:

Advent	Violet
Christmas Eve and Christmastide	White
Epiphany	White
Lent	Violet
Holy Week:	
Monday, Tuesday, Wednesday	Violet
Maundy Thursday	White
Good Friday	Red
Eastertide	White
Pentecost (and week following)	Red
Trinity Sunday (and week following)	White
Sundays After Pentecost (and weekdays)	Green

The Christian Year

ADVENT

CALLS TO WORSHIP

Isaiah 35:3–4	*Mark 1:15*	*Romans 13:11–12*
Isaiah 40:9	*Luke 3:4–6*	*II Corinthians 6:2*
Matthew 25:31–34	*Luke 12:35–37*	*Philippians 4:4–5*

RESPONSIVE READINGS

Psalms 24; 47; 76; 96; 98; Luke 1:46–55 or 68–79

PRAYER OF CONFESSION

God of the future: you are coming in power to bring nations
under your rule. We confess that we have not expected your
kingdom. We have lived casual lives, and ignored your promised
judgment. Judge us, O God, for we have been slow to serve you.
Forgive us, for the sake of your faithful servant Jesus, our
Savior, whose triumph we want and eagerly wait for. **Amen.**

PRAYER OF THANKSGIVING

God our Father: you go before us, drawing us into the future
where you are. We thank you for the hope we have in your word,
the good promises of peace, healing, and justice. For signs of
your patience, we are grateful. For every call to duty, we give
you praise. Help us, O God, to follow where you lead until the
day of our Lord Jesus, when the kingdom will come and you
rule the world; for the sake of Christ our Savior. **Amen.**

COLLECTS

1st Sunday in Advent

O Lord: keep us awake and alert, watching for your kingdom.
Make us strong in faith, so we may greet your Son when he
comes, and joyfully give him praise, with you, and with the
Holy Spirit. **Amen.**

2d Sunday in Advent

God of prophets: in the wilderness of Jordan you sent a messenger to prepare men's hearts for the coming of your Son. Help us to hear good news, to repent, and be ready to welcome the Lord, our Savior, Jesus Christ. **Amen.**

3d Sunday in Advent

Mighty God: you have made us and all things to serve you; now ready the world for your rule. Come quickly to save us, so that violence and crying shall end, and your children shall live in peace, honoring each other with justice and love; through Jesus Christ, who lives in power with you, and with the Holy Spirit, one God, forever. **Amen.**

4th Sunday in Advent

Eternal God: through long generations you prepared a way in our world for the coming of your Son, and by your Spirit you are still bringing the light of the gospel to darkened lives. Renew us, so that we may welcome Jesus Christ to rule our thoughts and claim our love, as Lord of lords and King of kings, to whom be glory always. **Amen.**

Christmas Eve

Give us, O God, such love and wonder, that with shepherds, and wise men, and pilgrims unknown, we may come to adore the holy child, the promised King; and with our gifts worship him, our Lord and Savior Jesus Christ. **Amen.**

As you came in the stillness of night, great God, enter our lives this night. Overcome darkness with the light of Christ's presence, so that we may clearly see the way to walk, the truth to speak, and the life to live for him, our Lord Jesus Christ. **Amen.**

CHRISTMASTIDE

CALLS TO WORSHIP

Isaiah 9:6   Luke 2:10–11   I John 4:9
Micah 5:2–4   Luke 2:13–14

RESPONSIVE READINGS

Psalms 67; 85; 113; 148
Isaiah 9:2–7

PRAYER OF CONFESSION

Almighty God, who sent a star to guide men to the holy child
Jesus: we confess that we have not followed the light of your
word. We have not searched for signs of your love in the world,
or trusted good news to be good. We have failed to praise your
Son's birth, and refused his peace on earth. We have expected
little, and hoped for less. Forgive our doubt, and renew in us
all fine desires, so we may watch and wait and once more hear
the glad story of our Savior, Jesus Christ the Lord. **Amen.**

PRAYER OF THANKSGIVING

Great God of power: we praise you for Jesus Christ, who came
to save us from our sins. We thank you for the prophets' hope,
the angels' song, for the birth in Bethlehem. We thank you that
in Jesus you joined us, sharing human hurts and pleasures.
Glory to you for your wonderful love. Glory to you, eternal
God; through Jesus Christ, Lord of lords, and King of kings,
forever. **Amen.**

COLLECTS

Christmas Day

All glory to you, great God, for the gift of your Son, light in
darkness and hope of the world, whom you sent to save man-
kind. With singing angels, let us praise your name, and tell the
earth his story, so that men may believe, rejoice, and bow down,
acknowledging your love; through Jesus Christ our Lord.
Amen.

Holy Father: you brought peace and goodwill to earth when Christ was born. Fill us with such gladness that, hearing again news of his birth, we may come to worship him, who is Lord of lords, and King of kings, Jesus Christ our Savior. **Amen.**

Almighty God, whose glory angels sang when Christ was born: tell us once more the good news of his coming; that, hearing, we may believe, and live to praise his name, Jesus Christ our Savior. **Amen.**

1st Sunday After Christmas

God our Father: your Son Jesus became a man to claim us men as brothers in faith. Make us one with him, so that we may enjoy your love, and live to serve you as he did, who rules with you and with the Holy Spirit, one God, forever. **Amen.**

2d Sunday After Christmas

Eternal God: to you a thousand years go by as quickly as an evening. You have led us in days past; guide us now and always, that our hearts may turn to choose your will, and new resolves be strengthened; through Jesus Christ our Lord. **Amen.**

EPIPHANY

CALLS TO WORSHIP

Isaiah 60:1–3   *Luke 2:29–32*   *II Corinthians 4:6*
Matthew 2:1–2   *John 1:14*   *Ephesians 2:17–18*

RESPONSIVE READINGS

Psalms 27; 107:1–15
Isaiah 42:1–9
Isaiah, ch. 55

PRAYER OF CONFESSION

Great God our Father: you have given us Jesus, light of the world, but we choose darkness and cling to sins that hide the brightness of your love. We are frightened disciples who are slow to speak your gospel. Immersed in ourselves, we have not risen to new life. Baptize us with Holy Spirit, so that, forgiven and renewed, we may preach your word to nations, and tell your glory shining in the face of Jesus Christ, our Lord and our light forever. **Amen.**

PRAYER OF THANKSGIVING

God of light, Lord of nations: you have shown your glory in Jesus Christ to all mankind. We thank you for the power in him that has drawn us together, and baptized us into one holy church. We praise you for the work you have asked us to do in the world, going before you with good news, so that all people shall know your truth, and praise you; through Jesus Christ the Lord of all. **Amen.**

COLLECTS

Epiphany

God our Father, who by a star led men from far away to see the child Jesus: draw us and all men to him, so that, praising you now, we may in life to come meet you face to face; through Christ our Lord. **Amen.**

God of hope, who sent a star to guide men to where Christ was born: guide us by the light of your word, so we may come to him offering the gift of our lives, and go out into the world glorifying and praising you, for our Savior Jesus Christ. **Amen.**

1st Sunday After Epiphany

Holy God: you sent your Son to be baptized among sinners, to seek and save the lost. May we, who have been baptized in his name, never turn away from the world, but reach out in love to rescue wayward men; by the mercy of Christ our Lord. **Amen.**

2d Sunday After Epiphany

Great God: your mercy is an unexpected miracle. Help us to believe and obey, so that we may be free from the worry of sin, and be filled with the wine of new life, promised in the power of Jesus Christ our Savior. **Amen.**

3d Sunday After Epiphany

Almighty God: your Son our Lord called men to serve him as disciples. May we who have also heard his call rise up to follow where he leads, obedient to your perfect will; through Jesus Christ our Lord. **Amen.**

4th Sunday After Epiphany

Give us, O God, patience to speak good news to those who oppose us, and to help those who may rage against us, so that, following in the way of your Son, we may rejoice even when rejected, trusting in your perfect love which never fails; through Jesus Christ our Lord. **Amen.**

5th Sunday After Epiphany

God our Father: you have appointed us witnesses, to be a light that shines in the world. Let us not hide the bright hope you have given us, but tell all men your love, revealed in Jesus Christ the Lord. **Amen.**

6th Sunday After Epiphany

Almighty God: you gave the law as a good guide for our lives. May we never shrink from your commandments, but, as we are taught by your Son Jesus, fulfill the law in perfect love; through Christ our Lord and Master. **Amen.**

7th Sunday After Epiphany

Almighty God: you have commanded us to love our enemies, and to do good to those who hate us. May we never be content with affection for our friends, but reach out in love to all your children; through Jesus Christ our Lord. **Amen.**

8th Sunday After Epiphany

Gracious God: you know that we are apt to bring back the troubles of yesterday, and to forecast the cares of tomorrow. Give us grace to throw off fears and anxieties, as our Lord commanded, so that today and every day we may live in peace; through Jesus Christ our Lord. **Amen.**

LENT

CALLS TO WORSHIP

Psalm 139:23–24   *Luke 15:18*   *I John 1:8–9*
Isaiah 1:18   *I Corinthians 10:13*
Isaiah 53:6   *Hebrews 4:14–16*

RESPONSIVE READINGS

Psalms 1; 6; 14; 32; 39; 51; 73; 130

PRAYER OF CONFESSION

O God of mercy: you sent Jesus Christ to save lost men. Judge us with love, and lift the burden of our sins. We confess that we are twisted by pride. We see ourselves pure when we are stained, and great when we are small. We have failed in love, forgotten to be just, and have turned away from your truth. Have mercy, O God, and forgive our sin, for the sake of Jesus your Son, our Savior. **Amen.**

PRAYER OF THANKSGIVING

We give thanks to you, God our Father, for mercy that reaches out, for patience that waits our returning, and for your love that is ever ready to welcome sinners. We praise you that in Jesus Christ you came to us with forgiveness, and that, by your Holy Spirit, you move us to repent and receive your love. Though we are sinners, you are faithful and worthy of all praise. We praise you, great God, in Jesus Christ our Lord. **Amen.**

COLLECTS

Ash Wednesday

Almighty God: you love all your children, and do not hate them for their sins. Help us to face up to ourselves, admit we are in the wrong, and reach with confidence for your mercy; in Jesus Christ the Lord. **Amen.**

1st Sunday in Lent

Almighty God: you know that in this world we are under great pressure, so that, at times, we cannot stand. Stiffen our resolve and make faith strong, so we may dig in against temptation and, by your power, overcome; through Jesus Christ the Lord. **Amen.**

2d Sunday in Lent

O God, who revealed glory in Jesus Christ to disciples: help us to listen to your word, so that, seeing the wonders of Christ's love, we may descend with him to a sick and wanting world, and minister as he ministered with compassion for all; for the sake of Jesus, your Son, our Lord. **Amen.**

3d Sunday in Lent

God of holy love: you have poured out living water in the gift of your Son Jesus. Keep us close to him, and loyal to his leading, so that we may never thirst for righteousness, but live eternal life; through our Savior, Christ the Lord. **Amen.**

4th Sunday in Lent

Almighty God, merciful Father: we do not deserve to be called your children, for we have left you, and wasted our gifts. Help us to know that when we repent and turn to you, you are forgiving, and are coming with joy to welcome us; through Jesus Christ our Lord. **Amen.**

5th Sunday in Lent

Great God, whose Son Jesus came as a servant among us: control our wants and restrain our ambitions, so that we may serve you faithfully and fulfill our lives; in Jesus Christ our Lord. **Amen.**

O God: your Son Jesus set his face toward Jerusalem, and did not turn from the cross. Save us from timid minds that shrink from duty, and prepare us to take up our cross, and to follow in the way of Jesus Christ our Lord. **Amen.**

PALM SUNDAY AND HOLY WEEK

CALLS TO WORSHIP

Psalm 24:9–10; Zechariah 9:9; Mark 11:9–10; Revelation 11:15b

RESPONSIVE READINGS

Psalms 24; 118:19–29; 150

PRAYER OF CONFESSION

Eternal God: in Jesus Christ you entered Jerusalem to die for our sins. We confess we have not hailed you as king, or gone before you in the world with praise. For brief faith that fades in trouble, for enthusiasms that fizzle out, for hopes we parade but do not pursue, have mercy on us. Forgive us, God, and give us such trust in your power that, in every city, we may live for justice and tell your loving-kindness; for the sake of our Savior, the Lord Jesus Christ. **Amen.**

PRAYER OF THANKSGIVING

Great God of power: you sent the Lord Jesus to enter our world and save men from sins. We thank you for glad disciples, who greeted him with praise and spread branches in his pathway. We thank you that he comes again to enter our lives by faith, and that, as his new disciples, we too may shout Hosanna, and welcome him, the King of love, Jesus Christ our Savior. **Amen.**

COLLECTS

Palm Sunday

Almighty God: you gave your Son to be the leader of men. As he entered Jerusalem, may we enter our world to follow him, obeying you and trusting your power, willing to suffer or die; through Jesus Christ the Lord. **Amen.**

Monday

Great God: cleanse your church of fake piety, overturn our greed, and let us be a holy people, repentant, prayerful, and

144

ready to worship you in Spirit and in truth; through Jesus Christ our Lord. **Amen.**

Tuesday

Holy Father, whose mercy never ends: even as Jesus came not to judge but to save men, so may we, his believing people, seek to reach men everywhere with your saving word; through Jesus Christ our Lord. **Amen.**

Wednesday

Everlasting God, who delivered the Children of Israel from cruel captivity: may we be delivered from sin and death by your mighty power, and celebrate the hope of life eternal within your promised kingdom; through Jesus Christ our Savior. **Amen.**

MAUNDY THURSDAY

CALLS TO WORSHIP

Luke 22:15–16   *John 6:9*   *I Corinthians 5:7–8*

RESPONSIVE READINGS

Psalms 23; 42; 59:1–4, 14–17; 63:1–9

PRAYER OF CONFESSION

Eternal God, whose covenant with us is never broken: we confess that we have failed to fulfill your will for us. We betray our neighbors and desert our friends, and run in fear when we should be loyal. Though you have bound yourself to us, we will not bind ourselves to you. God, have mercy on us, weak and willful people. Lead us once more to table, and, once more, unite us to Christ, who is bread of life and the vine from which we grow in grace, to whom be praise forever. **Amen.**

PRAYER OF THANKSGIVING

God of grace: you welcome us to the table of our Lord Jesus and give gifts more than we deserve or desire. We are grateful for Christ, who feeds our faith and renews your covenant with us, who by his death gives life to all who trust in him. How can we thank you for his love? Give us a willingness to serve as he has served us, our Lord and Savior, Jesus Christ your Son. **Amen.**

COLLECT

O God: your love lived in Jesus Christ, who washed disciples' feet on the night of his betrayal. Wash from us the stain of sin, so that, in hours of danger, we may not fail, but follow your Son through every trial, and praise him to the world as Lord and Christ, to whom be glory now and forever. **Amen.**

GOOD FRIDAY

Psalm 22:1; Isaiah 53:4; Lamentations 1:12; I Peter 2:24–25

RESPONSIVE READINGS

Psalms 13; 22:1–11; 88; 89:38–52

PRAYER OF CONFESSION

Holy God, Father of our Lord Jesus Christ: your mercy is more than our minds can measure; your love outlasts our sin. Forgive our guilt and fear and angers. We pass by neighbors in distress, and are cruel to needy men. We are quick to blame others, slow making up, and our resentments fester. Have mercy on us, God, have mercy on us, who blindly live our lives, for we do not know what we are doing. Destroy sin and sick pride, and renew us by the love of Christ, who was crucified, and died for us. **Amen.**

PRAYER OF THANKSGIVING

Great God: we thank you for Jesus, who was punished for our sins, and suffered shameful death to rescue us. We praise you for the trust we have in him, for mercy undeserved, and for love you pour out on us and all men. Give us gratitude, O God, and a great desire to serve you, by taking our cross, and following in the way of Jesus Christ the Savior. **Amen.**

COLLECTS

Merciful Father: you gave your Son to suffer the shame of the cross. Save us from hardness of heart, so that, seeing him who died for us, we may repent, confess our sin, and receive your overflowing love, in Jesus Christ our Lord. **Amen.**

How great is your love, O God, for sending Jesus to take up a cross and lay down his life for the world. Work in us such true remorse that we may cast out sin, welcome mercy, and live in wonder, praising the perfect sacrifice of Jesus Christ the Savior. **Amen.**

EASTERTIDE

CALLS TO WORSHIP

John 11:25   *I Corinthians 15:55*   *I Peter 1:3–4*
I Corinthians 15:20–21   *Colossians 3:1–4*

RESPONSIVE READINGS

Psalms 30; 66; 103; 111; 116; 150

PRAYER OF CONFESSION

Mighty God: by your power is Christ raised from death to rule this world with love. We confess that we have not believed in him, but fall into doubt and fear. Gladness has no home in our hearts, and gratitude is slight. Forgive our dread of dying, our hopelessness, and set us free for joy in the victory of Jesus Christ, who was dead but lives, and will put down every power to hurt or destroy, when your promised kingdom comes. **Amen.**

PRAYER OF THANKSGIVING

We give you thanks, great God, for the hope we have in Jesus, who died but is risen, and rules over all. We praise you for his presence with us. Because he lives, we look for eternal life, knowing that nothing past, present, or yet to come can separate us from your great love made known in Jesus Christ our Lord. **Amen.**

COLLECTS

Easter

Almighty God: through the rising of Jesus Christ from the dead you have given us a living hope. Keep us joyful in all our trials, and guard faith, so we may receive the wonderful inheritance of life eternal, which you have prepared for us; through Jesus Christ the Lord. **Amen.**

Mighty God: you raised up Jesus from death to life. Give us such trust in your power that, all our days, we may be glad, looking to

48

that perfect day when we celebrate your victory with Christ the Lord, to whom be praise and glory. **Amen.**

2d Sunday in Eastertide

Mighty God, whose Son Jesus broke bonds of death and scattered the powers of darkness: arm us with such faith in him that, facing evil and death, we may overcome as he overcame, Jesus Christ, our hope and our redeemer. **Amen.**

3d Sunday in Eastertide

Tell us, O God, the mystery of your plans for the world, and show us the power of our risen Lord, so that day by day obeying you, we may look forward to a feast with him within your promised kingdom; by the grace of our Lord Jesus Christ. **Amen.**

4th Sunday in Eastertide

Almighty God, who sent Jesus, the good shepherd, to gather us together: may we not wander from his flock, but follow where he leads us, knowing his voice and staying near him, until we are safely in your fold, to live with you forever; through Jesus Christ our Lord. **Amen.**

5th Sunday in Eastertide

God of hope: you promise many homes within your house where Christ now lives in glory. Help us to take you at your word, so our hearts may not be troubled or afraid, but trust your fatherly love, for this life, and the life to come; through Jesus Christ our Lord. **Amen.**

6th Sunday in Eastertide

O God: your Son Jesus prayed for his disciples, and sent them into the world to preach good news. Hold the church in unity by your Holy Spirit, and keep the church close to your word, so that, breaking bread together, disciples may be one with Christ in faith and love and service. **Amen.**

ASCENSION DAY

CALLS TO WORSHIP

John 17:1–3   *Acts 1:11*   *Hebrews 4:14*
John 20:17   *Colossians 3:1–2*

RESPONSIVE READINGS

Psalms 47; 93; 95:1–7; 97; 113

PRAYER OF CONFESSION

Almighty God: you have lifted up our Lord Jesus from death into life eternal, and set him over men and nations. We confess that we have not bowed before him, or acknowledged his rule in our lives. We have gone along with the way of the world, and been careless of fellowmen. Forgive us, O God, and lift us out of sin. Make us men who live to praise you, and to obey the commands of our Lord Jesus Christ, who is King of the world and head of the church his body. **Amen.**

PRAYER OF THANKSGIVING

Great God, mighty God: by your power is Jesus raised to be Savior of men and ruler of nations. We thank you that he commands our lives, lifts our aims, and leads us into faith. We praise you for his love which embraces the world, and works compassion in us. Glory to you for the gift of his life. Glory to you for his loving death. Glory to you for Jesus Christ, the master of us all. **Amen.**

COLLECTS

Ascension Day

Almighty God: your Son Jesus promised that if he was lifted up, he would draw all men to himself. Draw us to him by faith, so that we may live to serve you, and look toward life eternal; through Jesus Christ the Lord. **Amen.**

7th Sunday in Eastertide

Lord of all times and places: your thoughts are not our thoughts, your ways are not our ways, and you are lifted high above our little lives. Rule our minds, and renew our ways, so that, in mercy, we may be drawn near you; through Jesus Christ our Lord and Master. **Amen.**

PENTECOST

Joel 2:28 *John 14:15–17* *I Corinthians 12:4–7*
Matthew 9:37–38 *Acts 1:8* *I John 4:13*
John 3:6–8 *Romans 5:3–5*

RESPONSIVE READINGS

Psalms 19; 29; 84; 139

PRAYER OF CONFESSION

Almighty God, who sent the promised power of the Holy Spirit
to fill disciples with willing faith: we confess that we have held
back the force of your Spirit among us; that we have been slow
to serve you, and reluctant to spread the good news of your love.
God, have mercy on us. Forgive our divisions, and by your
Spirit draw us together. Fill us with flaming desire to do your
will, and be a faithful people; for the sake of your Son, our Lord,
Jesus Christ. **Amen.**

PRAYER OF THANKSGIVING

Mighty God: you have called us together, and, by your Holy
Spirit, made us one with your Son our Lord. We thank you for
the church, for the power of the word and the sacraments. We
praise you for apostles, martyrs, and brave men who have witnessed for you. We are glad you have joined us in friendship
with all Christian men, and that you sent us into the world full
of Holy Spirit to say that you are love; through Jesus Christ our
Lord. **Amen.**

COLLECTS

Pentecost (Whitsunday)

O God: you sent the promised fire of your Spirit to make saints
of common men. Once more, as we are waiting and together,
may we be enflamed with such love for you that we may speak

boldly in your name, and show your wonderful power to the world; through Jesus Christ our Lord. **Amen.**

Mighty God: by the fire of your Spirit you have welded disciples into one holy church. Help us to show the power of your love to all men, so they may turn, and, with one voice in one faith, call you Lord and Father; through Jesus Christ. **Amen.**

1st Sunday After Pentecost (Trinity Sunday)

Almighty God, Father of our Lord Jesus Christ and giver of the Holy Spirit: keep our minds searching your mystery, and our faith strong to declare that you are one eternal God and Father, revealed by the Spirit, through our Lord Jesus Christ. **Amen.**

2d Sunday After Pentecost

Almighty God: you have commanded us to rise up and walk in righteousness. Help us not only to hear you, but to do what you require; through Jesus Christ, our rock and our redeemer. **Amen.**

3d Sunday After Pentecost

God of power: you work for good in the world, and you want us to work with you. Keep us from being divided, so that when you call, we may follow single-mindedly in the way of Jesus Christ, our Lord and Master. **Amen.**

4th Sunday After Pentecost

Mighty God: your kingdom has come in Jesus of Nazareth, and grows among us day by day. Send us into the world to preach good news, so that men may believe, be rescued from sin, and become your faithful people; through Jesus Christ our Savior. **Amen.**

5th Sunday After Pentecost

Great God: you guard our lives, and put down powers that could overturn us. Help us to trust you, to acknowledge you before men, and to live for Jesus Christ, the Lord of all. **Amen.**

6th Sunday After Pentecost

Holy God: your Son demands complete devotion. Give us courage to take up our cross, and, without turning back, to follow where he leads us, Christ our Lord and Master. **Amen.**

7th Sunday After Pentecost

Almighty God: you have disclosed your purpose in Jesus of Nazareth. May we never reject him, but, hearing his message with childlike faith, praise him, our Lord and Master. **Amen.**

8th Sunday After Pentecost

Great God: your word is seed from which faith grows. As we receive good news, may your love take root in our lives, and bear fruit of compassion; through Jesus Christ our Lord. **Amen.**

9th Sunday After Pentecost

God of compassion: you are patient with evil, and you care for lost men. Teach us to obey you, and to live our lives following the good shepherd, Jesus Christ our Lord. **Amen.**

10th Sunday After Pentecost

Help us to seek you, God of our lives, so that in seeking, we may find the hidden treasure of your love, and rejoice in serving you; through Jesus Christ our Lord. **Amen.**

11th Sunday After Pentecost

God of grace: your Son Jesus fed hungry men with loaves of borrowed bread. May we never hoard what we have, but gratefully share with others good things you provide; through Jesus Christ, the bread of life. **Amen.**

12th Sunday After Pentecost

Mighty God: your Son Jesus came to comfort fearful men. May we never be afraid, but, knowing you are with us, take heart, and faithfully serve Christ the Lord. **Amen.**

13th Sunday After Pentecost

Holy God: we do not deserve crumbs from your table, for we are sinful, dying men. May we have grace to praise you for the bread of life you give in Jesus Christ, the Lord of love, and the Savior of us all. **Amen.**

14th Sunday After Pentecost

God our Father: you sent your Son to be our Savior. Help us to confess his name, to serve him without getting in the way, and to hear words of eternal life through him, Jesus Christ our Lord. **Amen.**

15th Sunday After Pentecost

Holy God: you welcome men who are modest and loving. Help us to give up pride, serve neighbors, and humbly walk with your Son, our Lord, Jesus Christ. **Amen.**

16th Sunday After Pentecost

God our Father: you have promised the Holy Spirit whenever we gather in the name of your Son. Be with us now, so we may hear your word, and believe in Christ, our Lord and Savior. **Amen.**

17th Sunday After Pentecost

Loving Father: whenever we wander, in mercy you find us. Help us to forgive without pride or ill will, as you forgive us, so that your joy may be ours; through Jesus Christ the Lord. **Amen.**

18th Sunday After Pentecost

Almighty God: you call men to serve you, and count desire more than deeds. Keep us from measuring ourselves against neighbors who are slow to serve you; and make us glad whenever men turn to you in faith; through Jesus Christ our Lord. **Amen.**

19th Sunday After Pentecost

Great God, Father of us all: you send us into the world to do your work. May we not only promise to serve you, but do what you command, loving neighbors, and telling the good news of Jesus Christ our Lord. **Amen.**

20th Sunday After Pentecost

Great God: you have put us to work in the world, reaping the harvest of your word. May we be modest servants, who follow orders willingly, in the name of Jesus Christ, your faithful Son, our Lord. **Amen.**

21st Sunday After Pentecost

Gracious God: you have invited us to feast in your promised kingdom. May we never be so busy taking care of things that we cannot turn to you, and thankfully celebrate the power of your Son, our Lord, Jesus Christ. **Amen.**

22d Sunday After Pentecost

Almighty God: in your kingdom the last shall be first, and the least shall be honored. Help us to live with courtesy and love, trusting the wisdom of your rewards, made known in Jesus Christ our Lord. **Amen.**

23d Sunday After Pentecost

Eternal God: you taught us that we shall live, if we love you and our neighbor. Help us to know who our neighbor is, and to serve him, so that we may truly love you; through Jesus Christ our Lord. **Amen.**

24th Sunday After Pentecost

Lord God: open our eyes to see wonderful things in your law, and open our hearts to receive the gift of your saving love; through Jesus Christ the Lord. **Amen.**

25th Sunday After Pentecost

Eternal God: help us to watch and wait for the coming of your Son, so that when he comes, we may be found living in light, ready to celebrate the victory of Jesus Christ the Lord. **Amen.**

26th Sunday After Pentecost

God our Father: you have given us a measure of faith, and told us to be good workmen. Keep us busy, brave, and unashamed, ever ready to greet your Son Jesus Christ, our judge and our redeemer. **Amen.**

27th Sunday After Pentecost

Eternal God: in Jesus Christ you judge the nations. Give us a heart to love the loveless, the lonely, the hungry, and the hurt, without pride or a calculating spirit, so that at last we may bow before you, and be welcomed into joy; through Jesus Christ, King of ages and Lord of all creation. **Amen.**

Special Days

NEW YEAR'S EVE OR DAY

CALLS TO WORSHIP

Isaiah 40:31   *II Peter 3:8–9*   *Revelation 4:8b*

RESPONSIVE READINGS

Psalms 60; 121; 150
Isaiah 65:17–25

PRAYER OF CONFESSION

Eternal God: you make all things new, and forgive old wrongs we can't forget. We confess we have spent time without loving, and years without purpose; and the calendar condemns us. Daily we have done wrong, and failed to do what you demand. Forgive the past; do not let evil cripple or shame us. Lead us into the future, free from sin, free to love, and ready to work for your Son, our Savior, Jesus Christ the Lord. **Amen.**

PRAYER OF THANKSGIVING

God of our lives: you will be faithful in time to come, as in years gone by. We praise you for goodness undeserved, and gifts received we cannot number. For life and health and loving friends; for work and leisure; for all grand things you give, we thank you, Lord and God. Above all, we praise you for Jesus Christ, who lifts our hopes, and leads us in your way. Praise and reverence, honor and glory, to you, great God; through Jesus Christ the Lord. **Amen.**

COLLECT

Judge eternal: in your purpose our lives are lived, and by your grace our hopes are bright. Be with us in the coming year, forgiving, leading, and saving; so that we may walk without fear, in the way of Jesus Christ our Lord. **Amen.**

CHRISTIAN UNITY

(See also Litany for the Unity of Christ's Church)

CALLS TO WORSHIP

Matthew 18:19–20   *Ephesians 2:13–15*   *Ephesians 4:4–6*
Romans 15:5–6

RESPONSIVE READINGS

Psalms 81; 84; 96; 100; 111; 122

PRAYER OF CONFESSION

Great God: your Son called disciples, and prayed for their unity. Forgive divisions. Help us to confess our lack of charity toward people whose customs are different, or whose creeds conflict with what we believe. Forgive arrogance that claims God's truth; that will not listen or learn new ways. Heal broken fellowship in your mercy, and draw the church together in one faith, loyal to one Lord and Savior, Jesus Christ. **Amen.**

PRAYER OF THANKSGIVING

God of prophets and apostles, whose Spirit is working peace among us: you have called us to be your holy people, and invited us to break bread in common faith. We thank you for every word or act that makes unity in the church; for open minds and hearts; for patient understanding. Above all, we thank you for your Son, who prays for us; that we may be one in charity toward each other, serving him who is our head, Christ the Lord and Savior. **Amen.**

COLLECT

Eternal God: you have called us to be members of one body. Bind us to those who in all times and places have called on your name, so that, with one heart and mind, we may display the unity.of the church, and bring glory to your Son, our Savior, Jesus Christ. **Amen.**

WORLD COMMUNION

(See also Litany for the Church, and Litany of the Names of the Church)

CALLS TO WORSHIP

I Corinthians 10:16–17; II Corinthians 5:17–18; Ephesians 4:4–6

RESPONSIVE READINGS

Psalms 23; 65; 84; 116; 130

PRAYER OF CONFESSION

Almighty God: from the ends of the earth you have gathered us around Christ's holy table. Forgive our separate ways. Forgive everything that keeps us apart; the prides that prevent our proper reunion. O God, have mercy on your church, troubled and divided. Renew in us true unity of purpose; that we may break bread together, and, with one voice, praise Jesus Christ our Lord. **Amen.**

PRAYER OF THANKSGIVING

God our Father: we thank you for setting a table before us, and for calling disciples from every place to feast together. We praise you for love that binds, and for faith that makes us brothers. We glorify you for your Spirit at work, building one holy church in the world, to serve Jesus Christ, the true vine and the bread of life, our Lord and living Savior. **Amen.**

COLLECT

O God: your Son prayed for his disciples; that they might be one. Draw us to you, so that we may be united in fellowship with your Spirit, loving one another as in Jesus Christ you have loved us. **Amen.**

REFORMATION SUNDAY

CALLS TO WORSHIP

Psalm 27:4

Hebrews 12:1–2

RESPONSIVE READINGS

Psalms 85; 145; 150

PRAYER OF CONFESSION

God of our Fathers: you raised up brave and able men to reform the church. We confess that we have lost our way again, and need new reformation. We are content with easy religion, with too much money and too little charity; we cultivate indifference. Lord, let your word shake us up, and your Spirit renew us, so that we may repent, have better faith, and never shrink from sacrifice; in the name of Jesus Christ our only Lord and Savior. **Amen.**

PRAYER OF THANKSGIVING

Holy God: you have chosen us to serve you, and appointed us the agents of your love. We thank you for prophets who recall us to your will. We are grateful for every impulse to confess and correct wrongs, to keep faith pure and purposes faithful. We praise you for your Holy Spirit always reforming the church, so we may better serve as disciples of your Son, Jesus Christ the Lord. **Amen.**

COLLECT

God of Abraham, Isaac, and Jacob; God of prophets and martyrs: give us courage to obey your word, and power to renew your church, so that we may live in the Spirit, sharing faith with Jesus Christ our Lord. **Amen.**

THANKSGIVING DAY

(See also Litany of Thanksgiving)

CALLS TO WORSHIP

Psalm 24:1   *Psalm 100:4–5*   *Psalm 107:1*
Psalm 72:18–19

RESPONSIVE READINGS

Psalms 67; 103; 107; 136; 138; 148

PRAYER OF CONFESSION

Almighty God: in love you spread good gifts before us, more than we need or deserve. You feed, heal, teach, and save us. We confess that we always want more; that we never share as freely as you give. We resent what we lack, and are jealous of neighbors. We misuse what you intend for joy. God, forgive our stubborn greed, and our destructiveness. In mercy, help us to take such pleasure in your goodness that we will always be thanking you; through Jesus Christ our Lord. **Amen.**

PRAYER OF THANKSGIVING

Gracious God: by your providence we live and work and join in families; and from your hand receive those things we need, gift on gift, all free. We thank you for the harvest of goodness you supply: for food and shelter, for words and gestures, for all our human friendships. Above all, we praise you for your Son, who came to show mercy, and who names us his own brothers. Glory to you for great kindness to us and all your children; through Jesus Christ our Lord. **Amen.**

COLLECT

Heavenly Father: you have filled the world with beauty. Open our eyes to see love in all your works, so that, enjoying the whole creation, we may serve you with gladness; through Jesus Christ our Lord. **Amen.**

DAY OF CIVIC OR NATIONAL SIGNIFICANCE

(See also Litany for the Nation)

CALLS TO WORSHIP

Psalm 29:11   *Psalm 62:8*   *Matthew 5:9*
Psalm 33:12

RESPONSIVE READINGS

Psalms 2; 33; 46; 47; 98
Isaiah 9:2–7

PRAYER OF CONFESSION

God our Father: you led men to this land, and, out of conflict, created in us a love of peace and liberty. We have failed you by neglecting rights and restricting freedoms. Forgive pride that overlooks national wrong, or justifies injustice. Forgive divisions caused by prejudice or greed. Have mercy, God, on the heart of this land. Make us compassionate, fair, and helpful to each other. Raise up in us a right patriotism, that sees and seeks this nation's good; through Jesus Christ the Lord. **Amen.**

PRAYER OF THANKSGIVING

Great God: we thank you for this land so fair and free; for its worthy aims and charities. We are grateful for people who have come to our shores, with customs and accents to enrich our lives. You have led us in the past, forgiven evil, and will lead us in time to come. Give us a voice to praise your goodness in this land of living men, and a will to serve you, now and always; through Jesus Christ our Lord. **Amen.**

COLLECT

Almighty God, judge of nations: make us brave to seek your will in the land you have given us, lest in our political actions, we neglect those things which belong to your glory; through Jesus Christ our Lord. **Amen.**

Lectionary
for the Christian Year

Lectionary for the Christian Year

A lectionary is a list of Scripture lessons, each lesson assigned to be helpful on a particular Lord's Day within the Christian year. Presbyterian churches seek to be obedient to Holy Scripture. A lectionary not only aids worshipers in the remembering of the events of God but also assures the reading and the hearing of the Old Testament and the New Testament in their fullness.

This lectionary provides readings for a cycle of three years. The designations A, B, and C are used for the first, second, and third years. Each Christian year in the three-year cycle begins, of course, at Advent of one year and continues to the Lord's Day just before the beginning of Advent in the next year.

Because other Christian churches are using this lectionary, congregations may wish to follow the cycle in the same pattern as the others. The general practice is such that those years whose last two digits are divisible by three are years in which the lessons designated B are employed, beginning at Advent. This arithmetical rule is usable from 1969 to 1999. For example: the year 1981 has as its last two digits 81. They are divisible by 3, with the result being 27, and no fraction. Thus a congregation using the lectionary, and wanting to read the Scriptures concurrently with its neighbors, would begin to use the readings for year B at Advent 1981 and would conclude year B just before Advent 1982. Year C would immediately follow and would be followed by Year A.

Lectionary for the Christian Year

ADVENT

A four-week period in which the church joyfully remembers the coming of Christ and eagerly looks forward to his coming again. Beginning with the Sunday nearest November 30, the season is observed for the four Sundays prior to Christmas.

Sunday or Festival	Year	First Lesson	Second Lesson	Gospel
1st Sunday in Advent	A	Isa. 2:1–5	Rom. 13:11–14	Matt. 24:36–44
	B	Isa. 63:16 to 64:4	I Cor. 1:3–9	Mark 13:32–37
	C	Jer. 33:14–16	I Thess. 5:1–6	Luke 21:25–36
2d Sunday in Advent	A	Isa. 11:1–10	Rom. 15:4–9	Matt. 3:1–12
	B	Isa. 40:1–5, 9–11	II Peter 3:8–14	Mark 1:1–8
	C	Isa. 9:2, 6–7	Phil. 1:3–11	Luke 3:1–6
3d Sunday in Advent	A	Isa. 35:1–6, 10	James 5:7–10	Matt. 11:2–11
	B	Isa. 61:1–4, 8–11	I Thess. 5:16–24	John 1:6–8, 19–28
	C	Zeph. 3:14–18	Phil. 4:4–9	Luke 3:10–18
4th Sunday in Advent	A	Isa. 7:10–15	Rom. 1:1–7	Matt. 1:18–25
	B	II Sam. 7:8–16	Rom. 16:25–27	Luke 1:26–38
	C	Micah 5:1–4	Heb. 10:5–10	Luke 1:39–47
Christmas Eve	A	Isa. 62:1–4	Col. 1:15–20	Luke 2:1–14
	B	Isa. 52:7–10	Heb. 1:1–9	John 1:1–14
	C	Zech. 2:10–13	Phil. 4:4–7	Luke 2:15–20

CHRISTMASTIDE

The festival of the birth of Christ, the celebration of the incarnation. A twelve-day period from December 25 to January 5, which may include either one or two Sundays after Christmas.

Sunday or Festival	Year	First Lesson	Second Lesson	Gospel
Christmas Day	A	Isa. 9:2, 6–7	Titus 2:11–15	Luke 2:1–14
	B	Isa. 62:6–12	Col. 1:15–20	Matt. 1:18–25
	C	Isa. 52:6–10	Eph. 1:3–10	John 1:1–14

CHRISTMASTIDE—Continued

Sunday or Festival	Year	First Lesson	Second Lesson	Gospel
1st Sunday After Christmas	A	Eccl. 3:1–9, 14–17	Col. 3:12–17	Matt. 2:13–15, 19–23
	B	Jer. 31:10–13	Heb. 2:10–18	Luke 2:25–35
	C	Isa. 45:18–22	Rom. 11:33 to 12:2	Luke 2:41–52
2d Sunday After Christmas	A	Prov. 8:22–31	Eph. 1:15–23	John 1:1–5, 9–14
	B	Isa. 60:1–5	Rev. 21:22 to 22:2	Luke 2:21–24
	C	Job 28:20–28	I Cor. 1:18–25	Luke 2:36–40

EPIPHANY

A season marking the revelation of God's gift of himself to all men. Beginning with the day of Epiphany (January 6), this season continues until Ash Wednesday, and can include from four to nine Sundays.

Sunday or Festival	Year	First Lesson	Second Lesson	Gospel
Epiphany		Isa. 60:1–6	Eph. 3:1–6	Matt. 2:1–12
1st Sunday After Epiphany	A	Isa. 42:1–7	Acts 10:34–43	Matt. 3:13–17
	B	Isa. 61:1–4	Acts 11:4–18	Mark 1:4–11
	C	Gen. 1:1–5	Eph. 2:11–18	Luke 3:15–17, 21–22

(or the readings for the day of Epiphany, if observed on Sunday)

Sunday or Festival	Year	First Lesson	Second Lesson	Gospel
2d Sunday After Epiphany	A	Isa. 49:3–6	I Cor. 1:1–9	John 1:29–34
	B	I Sam. 3:1–10	I Cor. 6:12–20	John 1:35–42
	C	Isa. 62:2–5	I Cor. 12:4–11	John 2:1–12
3d Sunday After Epiphany	A	Isa. 9:1–4	I Cor. 1:10–17	Matt. 4:12–23
	B	Jonah 3:1–5, 10	I Cor. 7:29–31	Mark 1:14–22
	C	Neh. 8:1–3, 5–6, 8–10	I Cor. 12:12–30	Luke 4:14–21
4th Sunday After Epiphany	A	Zeph. 2:3; 3:11–13	I Cor. 1:26–31	Matt. 5:1–12
	B	Deut. 18:15–22	I Cor. 7:32–35	Mark 1:21–28
	C	Jer. 1:4–10	I Cor. 13:1–13	Luke 4:22–30
5th Sunday After Epiphany	A	Isa. 58:7–10	I Cor. 2:1–5	Matt. 5:13–16
	B	Job 7:1–7	I Cor. 9:16–19, 22–23	Mark 1:29–39
	C	Isa. 6:1–8	I Cor. 15:1–11	Luke 5:1–11

EPIPHANY—Continued

Sunday or Festival	Year	First Lesson	Second Lesson	Gospel
6th Sunday After Epiphany	A	Deut. 30:15–20	I Cor. 2:6–10	Matt. 5:27–37
	B	Lev. 13:1–2, 44–46	I Cor. 10:31 to 11:1	Mark 1:40–45
	C	Jer. 17:5–8	I Cor. 15:12–20	Luke 6:17–26
7th Sunday After Epiphany	A	Lev. 19:1–2, 17–18	I Cor. 3:16–23	Matt. 5:38–48
	B	Isa. 43:18–25	II Cor. 1:18–22	Mark 2:1–12
	C	I Sam. 26:6–12	I Cor. 15:42–50	Luke 6:27–36
8th Sunday After Epiphany	A	Isa. 49:14–18	I Cor. 4:1–5	Matt. 6:24–34
	B	Hos. 2:14–20	II Cor. 3:17 to 4:2	Mark 2:18–22
	C	Job 23:1–7	I Cor. 15:54–58	Luke 6:39–45
9th Sunday After Epiphany		Use readings listed for 27th Sunday after Pentecost.		

LENT

A period of forty weekdays and six Sundays, beginning on Ash Wednesday and culminating in Holy Week. In joy and sorrow during this season, the church proclaims, remembers, and responds to the atoning death of Christ.

Sunday or Day	Year	First Lesson	Second Lesson	Gospel
Ash Wednesday	A	Joel 2:12–18	II Cor. 5:20 to 6:2	Matt. 6:1–6, 16–18
	B	Isa. 58:3–12	James 1:12–18	Mark 2:15–20
	C	Zech. 7:4–10	I Cor. 9:19–27	Luke 5:29–35
1st Sunday in Lent	A	Gen. 2:7–9; 3:1–7	Rom. 5:12–19	Matt. 4:1–11
	B	Gen. 9:8–15	I Peter 3:18–22	Mark 1:12–15
	C	Deut. 26:5–11	Rom. 10:8–13	Luke 4:1–13
2d Sunday in Lent	A	Gen. 12:1–7	II Tim. 1:8–14	Matt. 17:1–9
	B	Gen. 22:1–2, 9–13	Rom. 8:31–39	Mark 9:1–9
	C	Gen. 15:5–12, 17–18	Phil. 3:17 to 4:1	Luke 9:28–36

LENT—Continued

Sunday	Year	First Lesson	Second Lesson	Gospel
3d Sunday in Lent	A	Ex. 24:12–18	Rom. 5:1–5	John 2:13–25
	B	Ex. 20:1–3, 7–8, 12–17	I Cor. 1:22–25	John 4:19–26
	C	Ex. 3:1–8, 13–15	I Cor. 10:1–12	Luke 13:1–9
4th Sunday in Lent	A	II Sam. 5:1–5	Eph. 5:8–14	John 9:1–11
	B	II Chron. 36:14–21	Eph. 2:1–10	John 3:14–21
	C	Josh. 5:9–12	II Cor. 5:16–21	Luke 15:11–32
5th Sunday in Lent	A	Ezek. 37:11–14	Rom. 8:6–11	John 11:1–4, 17, 34–44
	B	Jer. 31:31–34	Heb. 5:7–10	John 12:20–33
	C	Isa. 43:16–21	Phil. 3:8–14	Luke 22:14–30
Palm Sunday	A	Isa. 50:4–7	Phil. 2:5–11	Matt. 21:1–11
	B	Zech. 9:9–12	Heb. 12:1–6	Mark 11:1–11
	C	Isa. 59:14–20	I Tim. 1:12–17	Luke 19:28–40

HOLY WEEK

The week prior to Easter, during which the church gratefully commemorates the passion and death of Jesus Christ.

Day of Holy Week	Year	First Lesson	Second Lesson	Gospel
Monday		Isa. 50:4–10	Heb. 9:11–15	Luke 19:41–48
Tuesday		Isa. 42:1–9	I Tim. 6:11–16	John 12:37–50
Wednesday		Isa. 52:13 to 53:12	Rom. 5:6–11	Luke 22:1–16
Maundy Thursday	A	Ex. 12:1–8, 11–14	I Cor. 11:23–32	John 13:1–15
	B	Deut. 16:1–8	Rev. 1:4–8	Matt. 26:17–30
	C	Num. 9:1–3, 11–12	I Cor. 5:6–8	Mark 14:12–26
Good Friday	A	Isa. 52:13 to 53:12	Heb. 4:14–16; 5:7–9	John 19:17–30
	B	Lam. 1:7–12	Heb. 10:4–18	Luke 23:33–46
	C	Hos. 6:1–6	Rev. 5:6–14	Matt. 27:31–50

EASTERTIDE

A fifty-day period of seven Sundays, beginning with Easter, the festival of Christ's resurrection. Ascension Day, forty days after Easter, is celebrated to affirm that Jesus Christ is Lord of all times and places.

Sunday or Festival	Year	First Lesson	Second Lesson	Gospel
Easter	A	Acts 10:34–43	Col. 3:1–11	John 20:1–9
	B	Isa. 25:6–9	I Peter 1:3–9	Mark 16:1–8
	C	Ex. 15:1–11	I Cor. 15:20–26	Luke 24:13–35
2d Sunday in Eastertide	A	Acts 2:42–47	I Peter 1:3–9	John 20:19–31
	B	Acts 4:32–35	I John 5:1–6	Matt. 28:11–20
	C	Acts 5:12–16	Rev. 1:9–13, 17–19	John 21:1–14
3d Sunday in Eastertide	A	Acts 2:22–28	I Peter 1:17–21	Luke 24:13–35
	B	Acts 3:13–15, 17–19	I John 2:1–6	Luke 24:36–49
	C	Acts 5:27–32	Rev. 5:11–14	John 21:15–19
4th Sunday in Eastertide	A	Acts 2:36–41	I Peter 2:19–25	John 10:1–10
	B	Acts 4:8–12	I John 3:1–3	John 10:11–18
	C	Acts 13:44–52	Rev. 7:9–17	John 10:22–30
5th Sunday in Eastertide	A	Acts 6:1–7	I Peter 2:4–10	John 14:1–12
	B	Acts 9:26–31	I John 3:18–24	John 15:1–8
	C	Acts 14:19–28	Rev. 21:1–5	John 13:31–35
6th Sunday in Eastertide	A	Acts 8:4–8, 14–17	I Peter 3:13–18	John 14:15–21
	B	Acts 10:34–48	I John 4:1–7	John 15:9–17
	C	Acts 15:1–2, 22–29	Rev. 21:10–14, 22–23	John 14:23–29
Ascension Day		Acts 1:1–11	Eph. 1:16–23	Luke 24:44–53
7th Sunday in Eastertide	A	Acts 1:12–14	I Peter 4:12–19	John 17:1–11
	B	Acts 1:15–17, 21–26	I John 4:11–16	John 17:11–19
	C	Acts 7:55–60	Rev. 22:12–14, 16–17, 20	John 17:20–26

(or the readings for Ascension Day, if observed on Sunday)

PENTECOST

The festival commemorating the gift of the Holy Spirit to the church, and an extended season for reflecting on how God's people live under the guidance of his Spirit. The season extends from the seventh Sunday after Easter to the beginning of Advent.

Sunday	Year	First Lesson	Second Lesson	Gospel
Pentecost	A	I Cor. 12:4–13	Acts 2:1–13	John 14:15–26
(Whitsunday)	B	Joel 2:28–32	Acts 2:1–13	John 16:5–15
	C	Isa. 65:17–25	Acts 2:1–13	John 14:25–31
1st Sunday	A	Ezek. 37:1–4	II Cor. 13:5–13	Matt. 28:16–20
After Pentecost	B	Isa. 6:1–8	Rom. 8:12–17	John 3:1–8
(Trinity Sunday)	C	Prov. 8:22–31	I Peter 1:1–9	John 20:19–23
2d Sunday	A	Deut. 11:18–21	Rom. 3:21–28	Matt. 7:21–29
After Pentecost	B	Deut. 5:12–15	II Cor. 4:6–11	Mark 2:23 to 3:6
	C	I Kings 8:41–43	Gal. 1:1–10	Luke 7:1–10
3d Sunday	A	Hos. 6:1–6	Rom. 4:13–25	Matt. 9:9–13
After Pentecost	B	Gen. 3:9–15	II Cor. 4:13 to 5:1	Mark 3:20–35
	C	I Kings 17:17–24	Gal. 1:11–19	Luke 7:11–17
4th Sunday After Pentecost	A	Ex. 19:2–6	Rom. 5:6–11	Matt. 9:36 to 10:8
	B	Ezek. 17:22–24	II Cor. 5:6–10	Mark 4:26–34
	C	II Sam. 12:1–7a	Gal. 2:15–21	Luke 7:36–50
5th Sunday	A	Jer. 20:10–13	Rom. 5:12–15	Matt. 10:26–33
After Pentecost	B	Job 38:1–11	II Cor. 5:16–21	Mark 4:35–41
	C	Zech. 12:7–10	Gal. 3:23–29	Luke 9:18–24
6th Sunday	A	II Kings 4:8–16	Rom. 6:1–11	Matt. 10:37–42
After Pentecost	B	Gen. 4:3–10	II Cor. 8:7–15	Mark 5:21–43
	C	I Kings 19:15–21	Gal. 5:1, 13–18	Luke 9:51–62
7th Sunday	A	Zech. 9:9–13	Rom. 8:6–11	Matt. 11:25–30
After Pentecost	B	Ezek. 2:1–5	II Cor. 12:7–10	Mark 6:1–6
	C	Isa. 66:10–14	Gal. 6:11–18	Luke 10:1–9
8th Sunday	A	Isa. 55:10–13	Rom. 8:12–17	Matt. 13:1–17
After Pentecost	B	Amos 7:12–17	Eph. 1:3–10	Mark 6:7–13
	C	Deut. 30:9–14	Col. 1:15–20	Luke 10:25–37
9th Sunday	A	II Sam. 7:18–22	Rom. 8:18–25	Matt. 13:24–35
After Pentecost	B	Jer. 23:1–6	Eph. 2:11–18	Mark 6:30–34
	C	Gen. 18:1–11	Col. 1:24–28	Luke 10:38–42

PENTECOST—Continued

Sunday	Year	First Lesson	Second Lesson	Gospel
10th Sunday After Pentecost	A	I Kings 3:5–12	Rom. 8:26–30	Matt. 13:44–52
	B	II Kings 4:42–44	Eph. 4:1–6, 11–16	John 6:1–15
	C	Gen. 18:20–33	Col. 2:8–15	Luke 11:1–13
11th Sunday After Pentecost	A	Isa. 55:1–3	Rom. 8:31–39	Matt. 14:13–21
	B	Ex. 16:2–4, 12–15	Eph. 4:17–24	John 6:24–35
	C	Eccl. 2:18–23	Col. 3:1–11	Luke 12:13–21
12th Sunday After Pentecost	A	I Kings 19:9–16	Rom. 9:1–5	Matt. 14:22–33
	B	I Kings 19:4–8	Eph. 4:30 to 5:2	John 6:41–51
	C	II Kings 17:33–40	Heb. 11:1–3, 8–12	Luke 12:35–40
13th Sunday After Pentecost	A	Isa. 56:1–7	Rom. 11:13–16, 29–32	Matt. 15:21–28
	B	Prov. 9:1–6	Eph. 5:15–20	John 6:51–59
	C	Jer. 38:1b–13	Heb. 12:1–6	Luke 12:49–53
14th Sunday After Pentecost	A	Isa. 22:19–23	Rom. 11:33–36	Matt. 16:13–20
	B	Josh. 24:14–18	Eph. 5:21–33	John 6:60–69
	C	Isa. 66:18–23	Heb. 12:7–13	Luke 13:22–30
15th Sunday After Pentecost	A	Jer. 20:7–9	Rom. 12:1–7	Matt. 16:21–28
	B	Deut. 4:1–8	James 1:19–25	Mark 7:1–8, 14–15, 21–23
	C	Prov. 22:1–9	Heb. 12:18–24	Luke 14:1, 7–14
16th Sunday After Pentecost	A	Ezek. 33:7–9	Rom. 13:8–10	Matt. 18:15–20
	B	Isa. 35:4–7	James 2:1–5	Mark 7:31–37
	C	Prov. 9:8–12	Philemon 8–17	Luke 14:25–33
17th Sunday After Pentecost	A	Gen. 4:13–16	Rom. 14:5–9	Matt. 18:21–35
	B	Isa. 50:4–9	James 2:14–18	Mark 8:27–35
	C	Ex. 32:7–14	I Tim. 1:12–17	Luke 15:1–32
18th Sunday After Pentecost	A	Isa. 55:6–11	Phil. 1:21–27	Matt. 20:1–16
	B	Jer. 11:18–20	James 3:13 to 4:3	Mark 9:30–37
	C	Amos 8:4–8	I Tim. 2:1–8	Luke 16:1–13
19th Sunday After Pentecost	A	Ezek. 18:25–29	Phil. 2:1–11	Matt. 21:28–32
	B	Num. 11:24–30	James 5:1–6	Mark 9:38–48
	C	Amos 6:1, 4–7	I Tim. 6:11–16	Luke 16:19–31
20th Sunday After Pentecost	A	Isa. 5:1–7	Phil. 4:4–9	Matt. 21:33–43
	B	Gen. 2:18–24	Heb. 2:9–13	Mark 10:2–16
	C	Hab. 1:1–3; 2:1–4	II Tim. 1:3–12	Luke 17:5–10

PENTECOST—Continued

Sunday	Year	First Lesson	Second Lesson	Gospel
21st Sunday After Pentecost	A	Isa. 25:6–9	Phil. 4:12–20	Matt. 22:1–14
	B	Prov. 3:13–18	Heb. 4:12–16	Mark 10:17–27
	C	II Kings 5:9–17	II Tim. 2:8–13	Luke 17:11–19
22d Sunday After Pentecost	A	Isa. 45:1–6	I Thess. 1:1–5	Matt. 22:15–22
	B	Isa. 53:10–12	Heb. 5:1–10	Mark 10:35–45
	C	Ex. 17:8–13	II Tim. 3:14 to 4:2	Luke 18:1–8
23d Sunday After Pentecost	A	Ex. 22:21–27	I Thess. 1:2–10	Matt. 22:34–40
	B	Jer. 31:7–9	Heb. 5:1–6	Mark 10:46–52
	C	Deut. 10:16–22	II Tim. 4:6–8, 16–18	Luke 18:9–14
24th Sunday After Pentecost	A	Mal. 2:1–10	I Thess. 2:7–13	Matt. 23:1–12
	B	Deut. 6:1–9	Heb. 7:23–28	Mark 12:28–34
	C	Ex. 34:5–9	II Thess. 1:11 to 2:2	Luke 19:1–10
25th Sunday After Pentecost	A	S. of Sol. 3:1–5	I Thess. 4:13–18	Matt. 25:1–13
	B	I Kings 17:8–16	Heb. 9:24–28	Mark 12:38–44
	C	I Chron. 29:10–13	II Thess. 2:16 to 3:5	Luke 20:27–38
26th Sunday After Pentecost	A	Prov. 31:10–13, 19–20, 30–31	I Thess. 5:1–6	Matt. 25:14–30
	B	Dan. 12:1–4	Heb. 10:11–18	Mark 13:24–32
	C	Mal. 3:16 to 4:2	II Thess. 3:6–13	Luke 21:5–19
27th Sunday After Pentecost	A	Ezek. 34:11–17	I Cor. 15:20–28	Matt. 25:31–46
	B	Dan. 7:13–14	Rev. 1:4–8	John 18:33–37
	C	II Sam. 5:1–4	Col. 1:11–20	Luke 23:35–43
28th Sunday After Pentecost		Use readings listed for 8th Sunday after Epiphany.		

SPECIAL DAYS

"It is also fitting that congregations celebrate such other days as recall the heritage of the reformed church, proclaim its mission, and forward its work; and such days as recognize the civic responsibilities of the people." (*Directory for Worship*, 19.04c.)

Special Day	Year	First Lesson	Second Lesson	Gospel
New Year's Eve or	A	Deut. 8:1–10	Rev. 21:1–7	Matt. 25:31–46
Day	B	Eccl. 3:1–13	Col. 2:1–7	Matt. 9:14–17
	C	Isa. 49:1–10	Eph. 3:1–10	Luke 14:16–24
Christian Unity	A	Isa. 11:1–9	Eph. 4:1–16	John 15:1–8
	B	Isa. 35:3–10	I Cor. 3:1–11	Matt. 28:16–20
	C	Isa. 55:1–5	Rev. 5:11–14	John 17:1–11
World Communion	A	Isa. 49:18–23	Rev. 3:17–22	John 10:11–18
	B	Isa. 25:6–9	Rev. 7:9–17	Luke 24:13–35
	C	I Chron. 16:23–34	Acts 2:42–47	Matt. 8:5–13
Reformation Sunday	A	Hab. 2:1–4	Rom. 3:21–28	John 8:31–36
	B	Gen. 12:1–4	II Cor. 5:16–21	Matt. 21:17–22
	C	Ex. 33:12–17	Heb. 11:1–10	Luke 18:9–14
Thanksgiving Day	A	Isa. 61:10–11	I Tim. 2:1–8	Luke 12:22–31
	B	Deut. 26:1–11	Gal. 6:6–10	Luke 17:11–19
	C	Deut. 8:6–17	II Cor. 9:6–15	John 6:24–35
Day of civic or	A	Deut. 28:1–9	Rom. 13:1–8	Luke 1:68–79
national significance	B	Isa. 26:1–8	I Thess. 5:12–23	Mark 12:13–17
	C	Dan. 9:3–10	I Peter 2:11–17	Luke 20:21–26

Other Prayers for Christian Worship

Other Prayers for Christian Worship

In a Time of International Crisis

Eternal God, our only hope, our help in times of trouble: get nations to work out differences. Do not let threats multiply or power be used without compassion. May your word rule the words of men, so that they may agree and settle claims peacefully. Hold back impulsive persons, lest desire for vengeance overwhelm our common welfare. Bring peace to earth right now, through Jesus Christ, the Prince of peace and Savior of us all. **Amen.**

For World Community

God our Father: in Jesus Christ you have ordered us to live as loving neighbors. Though we are scattered in different places, speak different words, or descend from different races, give us brotherly concern, so that we may be one people, who share the governing of the world under your guiding purpose. May greed, war, and lust for power be curbed, and all men enter the community of love promised in Jesus Christ our Lord. **Amen.**

For Racial Peace

Great God and Father of us all: destroy prejudice that turns us against our brothers. Teach us that we are all children of your love, whether we are black or red or white or yellow. Encourage us to live together, loving one another in peace, so that someday a golden race of men may have the world, giving praise to Jesus Christ our Lord. **Amen.**

When There Has Been a Natural Disaster

God of earthquake, wind, and fire: tame natural forces that defy control, or shock us by their fury. Keep us from calling disaster your justice; and help us, in good times or in calamity, to trust your mercy, which never ends, and your power, which in Jesus Christ stilled storms, raised the dead, and put down demonic powers. **Amen.**

In a Time of Social Change

All things are new in your grace, Lord God, and old things pass away. Break our hold on familiar things that you discard, and give us forward-looking courage to reach toward wiser ways. Lead us beyond ourselves to the new life promised in Jesus Christ, who is first and last, the beginning and the end. **Amen.**

During a National Crisis

God of ages, eternal Father: in your sight nations rise and fall, and pass through times of peril. Now when our land is troubled, be near to judge and save. May leaders be led by your wisdom; may they search your will and see it clearly. If we have turned from your way, reverse our ways and help us to repent. Give us your light and your truth; let them guide us; through Jesus Christ, who is Lord of this world, and our Savior. **Amen.**

For a Right Use of Nature's Power

Mighty God: your power fills heaven and earth, is hidden in atoms and flung from the sun. Control us so that we may never turn natural forces to destruction, or arm nations with cosmic energy; but guide us with wisdom and love, so that we may tame power to good purpose, for the building of human brotherhood and the bettering of our common lives; through Jesus Christ the Lord. **Amen.**

During an Election

Under your law we live, great God, and by your will we govern ourselves. Help us as good citizens to respect neighbors whose views differ from ours, so that without partisan anger, we may work out issues that divide us, and elect candidates to serve the welfare of mankind in freedom; through Jesus Christ the Lord. **Amen.**

For Conserving Natural Resources

Almighty God: you made the world and named it good and gave it to our management. Make us wise enough to keep air clear and

water pure and natural beauty beautiful. Prevent us from
destroying land and fouling streams. Let us treat lovely things
with love and courtesy, so that all men may enjoy the earth;
through Jesus Christ our Lord. **Amen.**

When There Is Tragedy

God of compassion: you watch the ways of men, and weave out
of terrible happenings wonders of goodness and grace. Surround
those who have been shaken by tragedy with a sense of your
present love, and hold them in faith. Though they are lost in
grief, may they find you and be comforted; through Jesus Christ,
who was dead, but lives, and rules this world with you. **Amen.**

For Victims of Oppression

Great God: with justice you watch over the ways of men, and in
love know each one by name. Lift those who are put down by
poverty, hurt by war, or scorned by neighbors. Do not let us
forget people you remember. Prevent us from oppressing, and
make us do something to show helpful love; for the sake of
Jesus Christ, a victim of cruelty, who is now our Lord and
Savior. **Amen.**

For the Handicapped

God of compassion: in Jesus Christ you cared for men who were
blind or deaf, crippled or slow to learn. Though all of us need
help, give special attention to those who are handicapped. Make
us care, so they may know the great regard you have for them,
and believe in your love; through Jesus Christ our Lord. **Amen.**

For Those in Mental Distress

Mighty God: in Jesus Christ you dealt with spirits that darken
minds or set men against themselves. Give peace to people who
are torn by conflict, are cast down, or dream deceiving dreams.
By your power, drive from our minds demons that shake confidence and wreck love. Tame unruly forces in us, and bring us
to your truth, so that we may accept ourselves as good, glad
children of your love, known in Jesus Christ. **Amen.**

For the Lonely

God of comfort, companion of the lonely: be with those who by neglect or willful separation are left alone. Fill empty places with present love, and long times of solitude with lively thoughts of you. Encourage us to visit lonely men and women, so they may be cheered by the Spirit of Jesus Christ, who walked among us as a friend, and is our Lord forever. **Amen.**

For Prisoners

God our Father: your Son Jesus was condemned to death, held captive, and hung on a cross with criminals. Never let us forget that our laws are not your law, that those we punish are still children of your love. Keep us from condemning men whose crimes are seen, in order to cover up our unseen sins. Move us to care for prisoners, and to visit them in unpleasant places, so they may know they are still loved brothers of Jesus Christ your Son. **Amen.**

For Social Misfits

In Jesus Christ, O God, you were despised and rejected by men. Watch over people who are different, who cannot copy well-worn customs, or put on popular styles of life. If they are left out because narrow men fear different ways, help us to welcome them into the wider love of Jesus Christ, brother of us all. **Amen.**

For Addicts

Faithful God: you have power to set men free from harmful habits and weakness of the will. May those who are hooked on drugs, or gripped by cravings too strong to control, be given freedom. Keep us from condemning the weakness of others while we overlook our own ungoverned desires. Enable us to help those who can no longer help themselves, so that they may see your power and believe in Jesus Christ, the liberator. **Amen.**

For the Unemployed

Lord God: you have made us co-workers with you in the world. May we never neglect the unemployed, or name them lazy if they have no work. Help us to help them, to train them, and to open doors, so that they may find employment. Working together with one another and with you, may we shape a world in which no child goes hungry, and every man contributes to the good of all; through Jesus Christ our Lord. **Amen.**

For Travelers

The world is yours, mighty God, and all men live by your faithfulness. Watch over people who are traveling, who drive or fly, or speed through space. May they be careful, but not afraid, and safely reach their destinations. Wherever we wander in your spacious world, teach us that we never journey beyond your loving care, revealed in Jesus Christ our Lord. **Amen.**

For Healing

By your power, great God, our Lord Jesus healed the sick and gave new hope to hopeless men. Though we cannot command or possess your power, we pray for those who want to be healed (especially for _____). Close wounds, cure sickness, make broken people whole again, so they may live to rejoice in your love. Help us to welcome every healing as a sign that, though death is against us, you are for us, and have promised renewed and risen life in Jesus Christ the Lord. **Amen.**

For Rejoicing in Childbirth

Mighty God: by your love we are given children through the miracle of birth. May we greet each new son and daughter with joy, and surround them all with faith, so they may know who you are and want to be your disciples. Never let us neglect children, but help us to enjoy them, showing them the welcome you have shown us all; through Jesus Christ the Lord. **Amen.**

For Little Children

Great God our Father, Father of families: guard the laughter of children. Bring them safely through injury and illness, so they may live the promises you give. Do not let us be so preoccupied with our purposes that we fail to hear their voices, or pay attention to their special vision of the truth; but keep us with them, ready to listen and to love, even as in Jesus Christ you have loved us, your grown-up, wayward children. **Amen.**

For the Young

Almighty God: again and again you have called on young people to force change or fire human hopes. Never let us be so set in our ways that we refuse to hear young voices, or so firm in our grip on power that we reject them. Let the young be candid, but not cruel. Keep them dreaming dreams that you approve, and living in the Spirit of the young man Jesus, who was crucified, who now rules the world. **Amen.**

For Graduates

Father: in your will our lives are lived, and by your wisdom truth is found. We pray for graduates who finish a course of study, and now move on to something new. Take away anxiety, or confusion of purpose; and give them a confidence in the future you plan, where energies may be gathered up and given to neighbors in love; for the sake of Jesus Christ our Lord. **Amen.**

For Those Engaged to Marry

Almighty God: in the beginning you made man and woman to join themselves in shared affection. May those who engage to marry be filled with joy. Let them be so sure of each other that no fear or disrespect may shake their vows. Though their eyes may be bright with love for each other, keep in sight a wider world, where neighbors want and strangers beg, and where service is a joyful duty; through Jesus Christ the Lord. **Amen.**

For the Newly Married

God of grace: in your wisdom you made man and woman to be one flesh in love. As in Jesus Christ you came to serve us, let newlyweds serve each other, putting aside selfishness and separate rights. May they build homes where there is free welcome. At work or in leisure, let them enjoy each other, forgive each other, and embrace each other faithfully, serving the Lord of love, Jesus Christ. **Amen.**

For Those in Middle Years

Eternal God: you have led us through our days and years, made wisdom ripe and faith mature. Show men and women your purpose for them, so that, when youth is spent, they may not find life empty or labor stale, but may devote themselves to dear loves and worthy tasks, with undiminished strength; for the sake of Jesus Christ the Lord. **Amen.**

For Retired People

Your love for us never ends, eternal God, even when by age or weakness we can no longer work. When we retire, keep us awake to your will for us. Give us energy to enjoy the world, to attend to neighbors busy men neglect, and to contribute wisely to the life of the church. If we can offer nothing but our prayers, remind us that our prayers are a useful work you want, so that we may live always serving Jesus Christ, our hope and our true joy. **Amen.**

For the Dying

Almighty God: by your power Jesus Christ was raised from death. Watch over dying men and women. Fill eyes with light, to see beyond human sight a home within your love, where pain is gone and frail flesh turns to glory. Banish fear. Brush tears away. Let death be gentle as nightfall, promising a day when songs of joy shall make us glad to be together with Jesus Christ, who lives in triumph, the Lord of life eternal. **Amen.**

For Those Who Suffer Sexual Confusion

God of creation: you made men and women to find in love fulfillment as your creatures. We pray for those who deny love between man and woman, who are repelled by flesh, or frightened by their daydreams. Straighten us all out, O Lord, and show us who we are, so that we may affirm each other bodily in covenants of love, approved by Jesus Christ our Lord. **Amen**

For Those in Marital Difficulty

Lord God, who set us in families, where we learn to live together in charity and truth: strengthen weak bonds of love. Where separation threatens, move in with forgiving power. Melt hard hearts, free fixed minds, break the hold of stubborn pride. Lay claim on us, so that our separate claims may be set aside in love; through Jesus Christ our Lord. **Amen.**

For the Divorced or Separated

God of grace: you are always working to hold us together, to heal division, and make love strong. Help men and women whose marriages break up to know that you are faithful. Restore confidence, bring understanding, and ease the hurt of separation. If they marry others, instruct them in better love, so that vows may be said and kept with new resolve; through Jesus Christ our Lord. **Amen.**

For Families Where There is Only One Parent

God our Father: we are never away from your care, and what we lack you give in love. Watch over families where, by death or separation, a parent is left alone with children. Lift bitterness, or too great a sense of lonely obligation. Show them that they live under your protection, so that they have not less love, but more; through Jesus Christ, your Son and our eternal brother.
Amen.

For Orphans

Gracious God: you care for all your children. Pay attention to orphans. May they be free from unprotected fears or secret bitterness. Enroll them in the human family as special children of your love. By our concern, may we welcome them into the brotherhood of your church, showing them by word and deed your great concern for them; through Jesus Christ our Lord. **Amen.**

For City People

Eternal God: you are bringing your holy city to earth, where death and pain shall be no more, and men shall live together in your light. We pray for cities, where, in high towers or close-built houses, people work and live. Ease tensions and break down separation, so that every stranger may know himself to be a citizen among citizens, governed by Jesus Christ, who came to Jerusalem as a Savior. **Amen.**

For People in Rural Areas

O God, your Son Jesus grew up in a small town and walked the hills of Galilee. We pray for people who live on farms or in little villages. May they take pleasure in nature's natural beauty, and watch over growing things with love. Help them to keep neighborhoods wide open to your world, so that they may be in touch with the whole human family; through Jesus Christ the Lord. **Amen.**

For Agreement Between Labor and Management

O God: you have made a world where men may join to get things done according to your will. Bring understanding between those who labor and those who manage. Do not let greed blind us to basic needs, or make men careless of one another. May wages be fair and work be worthy. Where there are grievances, help us to talk them out, so that name-calling may end, and we may work together as comrades; through Jesus Christ our Master. **Amen.**

For Those in Military Service

Righteous God: you rule the nations. Guard brave men who risk themselves in battle for their country. Give them compassion for enemies who also fight for patriotic causes. Keep our sons from hate that hardens, or from scorekeeping with human lives. Though they must be men of war, let them live for peace, as eager for agreement as for victory. Encourage them as they encourage one another, and never let hard duty separate them from loyalty to your Son, our Lord, Jesus Christ.
Amen.

For Those Who Refuse Military Service

God of peace, whose Son Jesus Christ came preaching goodwill among men: guard brave people among us who refuse military service because of conviction. May they never confuse conscience with cowardice, but, in good faith, withstand all public opposition. Save them from self-righteousness. Give them charity to love brothers who fight, but courage to speak the call to peace, heard in Jesus Christ, your Son our Lord. **Amen.**

For Play

God our Father: you made the world for sane and cheerful pleasures. Show us how to live free from false restraint or the terror of aimless craving, so that we may enjoy good times together, like guiltless children who play within the safety of your love, known in Jesus Christ, who set us free for joy. **Amen.**

For Those Who Do Not Believe

God of love, who sent Jesus Christ to seek and save lost men: may we who have been found by him value those who do not believe, and never shun neighbors who reject you. Remembering how our faith was given, may we preach good news with goodwill, trusting you to follow up your word, so that men may hear and believe and come to you; through Jesus Christ our Lord. **Amen.**

For Those We May Forget in Prayer

We do not know how to pray, O God, unless your Spirit guides us. Help us to pray for neighbors on earth, who wait for us to care, whose needs we have neglected, whose names we do not know. Make us want to know and name and care. Through our prayers draw us toward forgotten men and women, who are children of your love and our brothers in Jesus Christ, the Lord of all. **Amen.**

For Criminals and Racketeers

Holy God, your Son Jesus visited a crooked tax collector, and died between criminals. Never let us pretend to be pure while neglecting those who live in evil, but send us out with the friendliness of Christ to those our world condemns, so they may turn to you, restored and forgiven, to live as loyal children by your law, revealed in Jesus Christ our Lord. **Amen.**

For Prostitutes

God of compassion: your Son Jesus showed mercy to a woman condemned by harsh judgment, and gave her new life. We pray for prostitutes, who are victims of lovelessness, or of a craving to be loved. Keep us from easy blame or cruel dismissal. May our church seek them out, and show such genuine friendship that they may know your welcome, and live among us, as sisters of Jesus Christ our Lord. **Amen.**

For Those Who Work in International Government

High God, holy God: you rule the ways of men, and govern every earthly government. Work with those who work for peace. Make every diplomat an agent of your reconciliation, and every statesman an ambassador of hope. Bring peace and goodwill among men, fulfilling among us the promise made in Jesus Christ, who was born to save the world. **Amen.**

For Those Who Fight for Social Justice

You give us prophets, holy God, to cry out for justice and mercy. Open our ears to hear them, and to follow the truth they speak, lest we support injustice to secure our own well-being. Give prophets the fire of your word, but love as well. Though they speak for you, may they know that they stand with us before you, and have no Messiah other than your Son, Jesus Christ, the Lord of all. **Amen.**

For Scientists

God of wisdom: you have given us a world filled with hidden holy meaning. Thank you for scientists who search for truth, who use their minds to better life on earth. Give them patience, moral judgment, and curiosity to grope through great mysteries. May their work be constructive, building community among men and nations; through Jesus Christ our Lord. **Amen.**

For Those Who Grow, Prepare, and Distribute Food

God of grace: in your world there are fields to seed and harvest. We thank you for men who farm the land, and for workers who prepare or distribute food. Give them joy in the miracle of growth, and trust in your provision. May no one starve because of greed, but let men hunger for righteousness alone; through Jesus Christ the Lord. **Amen.**

For Migrant Workers

Eternal God: your Son Jesus had no place to lay his head, and no home to call his own. We pray for men and women who follow seasons and go where the work is, who harvest crops or do part-time jobs. Follow them around with love, so they may believe in you, and be pilgrim people, trusting Jesus Christ the Lord. **Amen.**

For Communication Workers

God of grace: you have taught us that faith comes from hearing the good news, and that we fulfill our lives by sending messages of love. Thank you for those who work to speed words between us, who enable us to converse with neighbors. May their skill draw close ties between us all, so that in our words your word may sound; through Jesus Christ our Lord and living Master. **Amen.**

For Transportation Workers

God almighty: you scattered us throughout the earth, yet bound us in a brotherhood of need and service. Thank you for those who move us through the world, who speed deliveries, or take us to and from our homes. May they see themselves as workmen who help us to share ourselves with neighbors; through Jesus Christ the Lord. **Amen.**

For Those Who Manufacture and Sell

Great God: you keep us going and give us energy to get things done. Thank you for men and women in industry, who work in factories and offices, or cover territories. Though they may do routine tasks or run machines, keep them free and thoughtful, so that their work may contribute to a better world, where neighbors will take time to love one another; through Jesus Christ, who lived and worked among us. **Amen.**

For Those in Business or Commerce

God of the covenant: you give love without return, and lavish gifts without looking for gain. Watch over the ways of business, so that those who buy or sell, get or lend, may live justly and show mercy and walk in your ways. May profits be fair and contracts kept. In our dealings with each other may we display true charity; through Jesus Christ, who has loved us with mercy. **Amen.**

For Those in Medical Services

Merciful God: by your power people are healed. Give strength to doctors, nurses, and technicians, who staff hospitals and homes for the sick. Make them brave to battle our last enemy, trusting your power to overcome death and pain and crying. May they be thankful for every sign of health you give, and humble before the mystery of mending grace; through Jesus Christ our Lord. **Amen.**

For Journalists, Publishers, and Printers

By your word, Lord God, the earth was created, and by our words we serve your will. Thank you for men and women who write, print, and publish, who bring us news and help us to think things out. Keep them in touch with all that you are doing in the world, so that their printed words may tell good news, to reconcile nations and renew the minds of men; through Jesus Christ the Lord. **Amen.**

For Janitors, Maintenance Men, and Refuse Collectors

Great God: you have made the world a home for us, and surrounded us with beauty. Thank you for those who take pride in keeping air fresh and streets clean; who make corridors and working spaces clear and safe for us. May they labor faithfully to maintain your world; for the sake of Jesus Christ our Lord.
Amen.

For Those in Legal Work

God of justice: you gave us law by Moses, and in Jesus Christ interpreted the law in selfless love. Give to those who make, administer, or defend our laws love for mercy and truth. May we never confuse our paper laws with the tablets of your eternal will, but have courage to repeal wrong rules. May our laws set men free for righteousness, revealed in Jesus Christ, the Judge and Savior of us all. **Amen.**

For Secretaries and Clerical Workers

Almighty God: your word has come to us copied by scribes with loving care. Guard those who record words, and keep files, without whose work we would lose track of ourselves, or slip into sad confusion. Help them to be alert and accurate; to rule machines they use and not be run by them. May they know that they are your servants, who speed messages within the broken world you love; through Jesus Christ our Lord. **Amen.**

For Architects, Builders, and Decorators

Great God: you gave Jesus Christ to be the foundation on which our lives are built. Thank you for men and women who build shelters, order space, and decorate rooms where our lives are lived. Help them to provide hospitable places where men may be free for one another, in the love of Jesus Christ our Lord. **Amen.**

For Entertainers

God our Father: you have made us for each other, to live by glad exchanges of love and skill. Thank you for men and women who work to entertain us, who deepen understanding, make laughter, or give us songs to sing. May they desire truth more than profit, and art more than applause. In all they do, may they celebrate good humanity, revealed in your man Jesus Christ, the Lord of all creation. **Amen.**

For Those in the Arts

God of life: you filled the world with beauty. Thank you for artists who see clearly, who with trained skill can paint, shape, or sing your truth to us. Keep them attentive, and ready to applaud the wonder of your works, finding in the world signs of the love revealed in Jesus Christ our Lord. **Amen.**

For Counselors

God of wisdom, God of love: when we are perplexed you give
light to go by. Thank you for those who work out problems
with us. May they have respect for our struggles, and never
fail to marvel at the mystery of human minds. Guide them
with your Holy Spirit, so they may guide us into the way of
Jesus Christ, our truth and our new life. **Amen.**

For Government Workers

Almighty God: you have plans for us, and power to make them
happen. Give legislators, executives, and government workers
a knowledge of your will for the world. Let them remember
that they serve a public trust, beyond personal gain or glory.
May they see that no nation lives for itself alone, but is responsible to you for peace, and for the well-being of all your
children; through Jesus Christ our Lord. **Amen.**

For Those Who Wait on Others

Great God and Father of mankind: you have taught us that if
we want to be great, we must be servants of all. We thank you
for those who help with household chores or wait on tables,
whose work gives ease and comfort to others. Help them to
know that their work is specially valued by Jesus Christ, who
came as a servant with humility and love. **Amen.**

For Those Who Work in Education

Holy Father: you have led us in each new generation to dis-
coveries of the truth. Thank you for men and women who
teach, administer, and work in schools and colleges. Make
them eager to explore your world, searching mysteries. Never
let them neglect students who are slow to learn. Keep teachers
young in mind, resilient, exciting, and devoted to human welfare; through the love of Jesus Christ our Lord. **Amen.**

For Students

Eternal God: your wisdom is greater than our small minds can
contain, and your truth shows up our little learning. To those

who study, give curiosity, imagination, and patience enough to wait and work for insight. Help them to doubt with courage, but to hold all their doubts in the larger faith of Jesus Christ our Lord. **Amen.**

For Those Who Work in Social Service or Charitable Agencies

As you have given yourself to us, O God, help us to give ourselves to one another in perfect charity. Thank you for men and women who work for the welfare of others. Fill them with energetic love to show friendship and compassion with no strings attached, so that men may believe you care; through Jesus Christ our Lord. **Amen.**

For Mechanics, Repairmen, and Those in Skilled Trades

Almighty God: you have given us intelligence, and skillful hands to work with. Thank you for those who provide, maintain, and repair things we use. Help them to know that neighbors depend on them, and to be worthy workmen; for the sake of Jesus Christ our Lord. **Amen.**

For Those in Dangerous Occupations

God of earth and air, height and depth: we pray for those who work in danger above, below, or on the earth. Give them caution and a concern for one another, so that in safety they may do what must be done, under your watchful love, in Jesus Christ our Lord. **Amen.**

For the Mission of the Church

The whole world lives in your love, holy God, and we are your people. Send us out in faith to tell your story and to demonstrate your truth to men of every race and nation, so that, won by your powerful word, the world of men may join together giving you praise, and living to serve you in Jesus Christ the Lord. **Amen.**

For a Particular Mission of the Church

By your will, O God, we go out into the world with good news of your undying love, and minister among men to show wonders of your grace. We pray for _____, where there are men and women who minister for you. May they be strengthened by our concern, and supported by our gifts. Do not let them be discouraged, but make them brave and glad and hopeful in your word; through Jesus Christ the Lord. **Amen.**

For Evangelists and Fraternal Workers

Great God: in every age you have picked out people to spread good news, and to light your light in darkness. Guard those who witness to you in far-off places, in crowded cities or in open fields. Keep them sure of your power, so that they may work without fear of failure. Help them tell your wonderful story until all men turn to you, even as you have turned to us with love, in Jesus Christ our Savior. **Amen.**

For Teachers in the Church

Almighty God: you have given your law to lead us in a life of love, and you have appointed teachers to interpret your will. Create in those who instruct your people a mind to study your word, and good understanding, so that we may learn your truth and do it gladly; for the sake of Jesus Christ our Master. **Amen.**

For Ministers of the Word

In every age, O God, you have appointed spokesmen, prophets and priests, to lead your faithful people. May ministers of the gospel tell the truth in love. Keep them from mouthing pieties they do not mean. Make them humble men and women without pretense or pride, who bring light to darkness, showing the way of Jesus Christ, to whom be praise forever. **Amen.**

For Chaplains

O God: you have ordered men and women to serve the church, and given them special gifts by your Spirit. May those who serve as chaplains be strong in faith. Keep them from being discouraged. Let us bring them hope and friendship wherever they may serve; through Jesus Christ our Lord and Savior. **Amen.**

For a Moderator

Almighty God: you called us into the church, and from among us chose leaders to direct us in your way. We thank you for _____, our Moderator. Enlarge *his* gifts and help *him* to obey you, so that we may enjoy good work under *his* guidance, loyally serving Jesus Christ the Lord. **Amen.**

For Those Who Intend Christian Service

God of prophets and apostles: you have chosen leaders to train your people in the way of Jesus Christ. We thank you that in our day you are still claiming men and women for special work within the church. As _____ has dedicated *himself* to you, let us pledge ourselves to *him*, so that, surrounded by affection and hope, *he* may grow in wisdom, mature in love, and become a faithful worker, approved by Jesus Christ our Lord. **Amen.**

For Church Workers

How many are the ways we serve within your church, O God. Watch over those who work for boards or in agencies of the church, who promote the gospel. Do not let them think themselves lesser or greater than those who preach or teach; but show them that their gifts are needed in the one ministry of the Lord Jesus Christ, who is head of the church. **Amen.**

When a Minister Is Leaving or Retiring

You have bound us together in the church, great God, and built up the Spirit of love among us. Though we must go separate ways in working for your kingdom, help us to know that we are joined forever in your loving care. We thank you for years together, for mutual support and mutual forgiveness. Never let friendship fade, but keep us remembering one another, and grateful for the life we have shared, in Jesus Christ our Lord.
Amen.

For a Meeting of the General Assembly, Synod, or Presbytery

Almighty God: in Jesus Christ you called disciples and, by the Holy Spirit, made them one church to serve you. Be with

members of our *General Assembly*. Help them to welcome new
things you are doing in the world, and to respect old things you
keep and use. Save them from empty slogans or senseless con-
troversy. In their deciding, determine what is good for us and
all men. As the *General Assembly* meets, let your Spirit rule,
so that our church may be joined in love and service to Jesus
Christ, who, having gone before us, is coming to meet us in the
promise of your kingdom. **Amen.**

For Church Schools and Colleges

God of light: your truth makes every dark place bright, and sets
men free from foolishness to live in wisdom. Build up schools
and colleges where men and women may grow in the knowledge
of your Son. Keep them from becoming sheltered groves away
from human agony. Draw faculty, staff, and students together
in your Spirit, so they may know that you alone are good and
true; through Jesus Christ our Lord. **Amen.**

For Seminaries

Almighty God: in Jesus Christ you called ordinary men to be
disciples and sent them out to teach and preach your truth.
Bring to seminaries men and women who are honest and eager
to serve you. Give them tender hearts to care for fellowmen,
and tough minds to wrestle with your word, so that, as they
speak and act for you, men may repent and return to love, believing in Jesus Christ, who is our Lord and Master. **Amen.**

For a Church Meeting

Eternal God: you called us to be a special people, to preach the
gospel and show mercy. Keep your Spirit with us as we meet
together, so that in everything we may do your will. Guide us
lest we stumble or be misguided by our own desires. May all
we do be done for the reconciling of the world, for the upbuild-
ing of the church, and for the greater glory of Jesus Christ our
Lord. **Amen.**

For a Church Supper

God our companion: in Jesus Christ you ate and drank with
sinners, broke bread with disciples, and joined your Spirit with

Christian men at table. As we meet and eat together, be among us to bring love, so that as we go out into the world, your Spirit may go with us, spreading the fellow-feeling we find at table here; through Jesus Christ our Lord. **Amen.**

When New Members Are Received by the Session

Almighty God: by the love of Jesus Christ you draw men to faith, and welcome them into the church family. May we show your joy by embracing new brothers and sisters, who with us believe and with us will work to serve you. Keep us close together in your Spirit, breaking bread in faith and love, one with Jesus Christ our Lord and Master. **Amen.**

For Founders and Previous Leaders of a Congregation

We thank you, Lord God, for brave and believing men who brought your message to this place. Let us not forget them (*names may be named*). By their energies this church was gathered, given order, and continued. Remembering all those Christians who have gone before us, may we follow as they followed in the way, truth, and life of Jesus Christ, the head of the church. **Amen.**

For the Acknowledgment of Special Gifts

God of goodness: from your love we have received all that we need or can rightly desire, and by your grace we are prompted to grateful generosity. Thank you for the special gift we now receive. May we use everything to spread word of your deeds and proclaim your faithful love. Let those who have given this gift live in our affection. With them, may we do all things to honor your name; through Jesus Christ our Lord. **Amen.**

For a New Church Building

Eternal God, high and holy: no building can contain your glory or display the wonders of your love. May this space be used as a gathering place for men of goodwill. If we worship, let us worship gladly; if we study, let us learn your truth. May every meeting held here meet with your approval, so that this building may stand as a sign of your Spirit at work in the world, and as a witness to our Lord and Savior, Jesus Christ. **Amen.**

For a Right Use of Church Money and Property

Righteous God: you have taught us that the poor shall have your kingdom, and that the gentle-minded shall inherit the earth. Keep the church poor enough to preach to poor people, and humble enough to walk with the despised. Never weigh us down with real estate or too much cash on hand. Save your church from vain display or lavish comforts, so that, traveling light, we may move through the world showing your generous love, made known in Jesus Christ our Lord. **Amen.**

When the Church Faces a Decision

O God: you are always forcing us to face decisions, so that in choosing, we will choose your will. Now that we must decide what to do, guide us with your word and Spirit. Prevent us from clinging to old strategies, and show new ways for us to follow and obey; through Jesus Christ, the pioneer of faith. **Amen.**

For the Authority of Scripture in the Church

We thank you, Lord God, for men of old who preserved your word for us, who recorded your law, copied the prophets, and remembered the gospel message. May your church never neglect the study of Scripture, but with lively and persistent interest read, recite, interpret, and teach the news declared in Jesus Christ your living Word, and the Savior of us all. **Amen.**

For the Holy Spirit in the Church

Almighty God: you poured out the Holy Spirit on believers at Pentecost, drawing them together in the mission of the church. Give us great enthusiasm for your work, and keep your Spirit with us, so that, united and in peace with one another, we may live new lives as ambassadors of Jesus Christ, who is head of the church, our Savior and our strength. **Amen.**

For Worship in the Church

Holy God: you call us to worship, and by your Spirit prompt prayers and praise. Keep us from saying words or singing hymns with ritual disinterest. Fill us with such wonder that we may worship you, grateful for the mystery of your unfailing love for us, in Jesus Christ the Lord. **Amen.**

For an Inclusive Church

How great is your love, Lord God, how wide is your mercy! Never let us board up the narrow gate that leads to life with rules or doctrines that you dismiss; but give us a Spirit to welcome all people with brotherly affection, so that your church may never exclude secret friends of yours, who are included in the love of Jesus Christ, who came to save us all. **Amen.**

For Peace in the Church

God of our lives: by the power of your Holy Spirit, we have been drawn together by one baptism into one faith, serving one Lord and Savior. Do not let us tear away from one another through division or hard argument. May your peace embrace our differences, preserving us in unity, as one body of Jesus Christ our Lord. **Amen.**

When There Is Division in the Church

Holy God, giver of peace, author of truth: we confess that we are divided and at odds with one another, that a bad spirit has risen among us, and set us against your Holy Spirit of peace and love. Take from this congregation mistrust, party spirit, contention, and all evil that now divides us. Work in us a desire for reconciliation, so that, putting aside personal grievances, we may go about your business with a single mind, devoted to our Lord and Savior, Jesus Christ. **Amen.**

For Courage by the Church

Strong God of truth: your Son Jesus was arrested and killed for outspoken faith. Save us from shrinking back in the face of opposition or from trembling when conflicts flare. Do not let us fall in love with martyrdom, but make us brave to speak your word and do your truth with courage, obeying Jesus Christ, whose disciples we are, whose commands we serve. **Amen.**

For Jewish Friends of the Church

God of Abraham, Isaac, and Jacob, Father of us all, whose Son Jesus was born a Jew, was circumcised, and was dedicated in the Temple: thank you for patriarchs and prophets and righteous rabbis, whose teaching we revere, whose law is our law fulfilled in Jesus Christ. Never let us forget that we, who are your people, are by faith children of Abraham, bound in one family with Jewish brothers, who also serve your purpose; through Jesus Christ, our Master and Messiah. **Amen.**

For Other Christian Churches

Almighty God: in Jesus Christ you called disciples and prayed for them to be joined in faith. We pray for Christian churches from which we are separated. Never let us be so sure of ourselves that we condemn the faith of others or refuse reunion with them, but make us ever ready to reach out for more truth, so that your church may be one in the Spirit; through Jesus Christ our Lord. **Amen.**

By Women in the Church

God of love: you chose the woman Mary to bring your Son to the world, and on Easter Day sent women from his empty tomb with news of resurrection. Show us the special work you have for us. Give us a desire to follow worthy women who, in every age, brought life to earth, spread your word, and witnessed to the risen power of Jesus Christ, a woman's child, who is now the Lord of all. **Amen.**

By Men in the Church

Mighty God: your Son Jesus picked out disciples from ordinary men, and told them to follow him. Keep us, who are his disciples now, unafraid and faithful, so that, with manly courage, we may say and do what you want said and done in the world; through Jesus Christ, a man among men, who is the Lord forever. **Amen.**

For Families of the Church

Lord God, holy Father: you set us in families to teach one another and practice ways of love. Oversee families in the church, so that, fed by your word and held in your Spirit, they may forgive one another, and give one another gifts of joy and courage. Join families day by day to the wider family of mankind as friends and neighbors in Jesus Christ, the Lord of all. **Amen.**

For Enemies of the Church

Strong God, God of love: your Son Jesus told us that his church would be persecuted as he was persecuted. If we should suffer for righteousness' sake, save us from self-righteousness. Give us grace to pray for enemies, and to forgive them, even as you have forgiven us; through Jesus Christ, who was crucified but is risen, whom we praise forever. **Amen.**

For Those Who Write Prayers

Almighty God: you have no patience with solemn assemblies, or heaped-up prayers to be heard by men. Forgive those who have written prayers for congregations. Remind them that their foolish words will pass away, but that your word will last and be fulfilled, in Jesus Christ our Lord. **Amen.**

Prayers for Use at Home

Prayers for Use at Home

Parents' Prayer

God our Father: you have brought children out of our love, and put us in charge of them for a little while. Keep us from doing damage. May love be strong, but not possessive; liberating, but never careless. Help us to remember that we are also your children, willful and foolish, in need of patient grace; through Jesus Christ our Lord. **Amen.**

A Family Prayer

Our Father: we are your children. You know us better than we know ourselves, or can know each other. Help us to love, so that we can learn to love our neighbors. May we forgive, hold no grudges, and put up with being hurt. Let there be laughter as we enjoy each other. Serving, may we practice serving you; through Jesus Christ our Lord. **Amen.**

Morning Prayers

God: be with us all day, in streets or buildings where we work, so that everything we do may be for you, and your Son, our Lord, Jesus Christ. **Amen.**

May we wake thinking of your love, great God, and trusting your plans for us. Give us your Spirit today, so we may do what you want done in the world; through Jesus Christ our Lord. **Amen.**

Evening Prayers

As darkness comes, Father, forgive wrong things we have said or done. Renew our love for one another, and give us quiet minds to sleep, so when morning comes, we may be glad to serve you; for the sake of Jesus Christ. **Amen.**

Strong God: you made day and night. As we sleep, tell us your love, so that when light comes we may wake happy, forgiven, and ready to live for you; through Jesus Christ our Lord. **Amen.**

Grace at Table

Father: we thank you for good things you give us. May we enjoy, share, and give thanks; through Jesus Christ our Lord. **Amen.**

FATHER: Praise the Lord.

FAMILY: **The Lord's name be praised.**

FATHER: Let us thank God.

FAMILY: **For he is good.**

God: we thank you for home, family, and friends. May your love be with us as we break bread in Jesus' name. **Amen.**

Thank you, God, for food, and all your gifts; through Jesus Christ our Lord. **Amen.**

When a Family Is Separated

Lord God: watch over us while we are apart. Keep us in your love, and bring us together again to praise you; through Jesus Christ our Lord. **Amen.**

Musical Responses and Hymns

Musical Responses—Contents

Each musical response is listed by its first line. The numbers in parentheses refer to the page or pages in the Service for the Lord's Day on which the words appear. The numbers that follow are page numbers of the several musical settings included in this book. A number in brackets indicates a page in the Service for the Lord's Day on which the given response does not appear, but where its use would be appropriate. Further guidance will be found in the outlines for the Service, pp. 21–23.

Praise the Lord (25), 211, 234, 253
You are the Lord, giver of mercy! (27), 212, 234, 253
   Or, Lord, have mercy upon us [27], 213, 235
Glory to the Father (Gloria Patri) [27], 214, 236, 254, 272
Glory to God in the highest (Gloria in Excelsis) [27], 215, 237, 255
I believe in God, the Father almighty (30), 259
This is the good news (30), 219, 241, 263
The Lord is risen (31), 223, 243, 265
Praise God, from whom all blessings flow! (Doxology) [34, 38], 224, 244,
   266, 272; *also hymn* 292, *stanza* 4
Lift up your hearts (first) (34, 38), 225, 245, 267
Lift up your hearts (second) (35, 39), 226, 246, 268
Holy, holy, holy, God of power and majesty (35), 227, 247, 268
Holy, holy, holy, Lord, God of power and might (35), 228, 248, 269
Alleluia! For the Lord our God (37), 230, 250, 270
Bless the Lord, O my soul (37), 232, 252, 271

Preface to the Musical Responses
and Hymns

The musical responses and hymns on the following pages complete *The Worshipbook—Services and Hymns*. This volume provides Presbyterian churches in North America with precisely the sort of liturgical book that was first produced at the time, and under the influence, of the Protestant Reformation of the sixteenth century. It is a *people's* book, including texts and music for song, spoken prayer, and proclamation. This book is in harmony with the Reformed tradition in that it envisions a high level of vocal participation as well as personal comprehension of public worship. Its provision for the careful integration of liturgical and musical materials follows the best theology and practice of Reformed worship. The latter point may require explanation, and a brief description of the structure and use of this book is offered here.

As stated in the general Preface, page 7, the Joint Committee on Worship, in planning for the compilation of musical responses and hymns, did not have as its intention "to create a general hymnal." Rather, through The Committee on Selection of Hymns, it sought to provide musical materials which, when thoughtfully chosen, would complete and fulfill the structure and style of worship embodied in the services here, especially the Service for the Lord's Day. The Joint Committee envisioned a style of worship marked by a careful integration of varied elements, among them musical responses and hymns. Hence the fitness of the aphorism, "Music is a part of worship, not apart from worship."

In order to provide adequate resources for the kind of worship envisioned here, the compilers of the musical section have drawn material from many traditions. The quality, variety, and organization of this musical material will facilitate more frequent celebration of the Lord's Supper, regular observance of the Christian year, and the employment of texts which originate from, and apply to, the contemporary situation. Congregations will wish to supplement these musical materials with some of their own. To do so is recommended and is in accordance with the familiar Reformed principle of freedom in all things liturgical.

Underlying the unity of *The Worshipbook* is the Bible, the basic source and resource for worship. The Lectionary for the Christian Year, a three-year cycle of Bible readings, is the cornerstone of this Scriptural foundation. The **Index of Scripture and Scriptural Allusions** can be used to locate related prayers, hymns, and liturgical materials for completion of the structure of a service. The **Guide for the Use of Prayers** and the **Guide for the Use of Hymns** will assist the worship planner in selection by topic or by worship-related category. The usual alphabetical index of first lines has been omitted, since the hymns in this book are arranged in *alphabetical order*. An **Index of Familiar Hymns with Unfamiliar First Lines** has been prepared to help the user find hymns whose first lines have been extensively altered.

In keeping with the general use of modern translations of the Bible in the services and modern expression in the prayers, changes have been made where possible in the language of song. Thus in some familiar hymns, the contemporary familiar form *you* rather than the archaic familiar form *thee* is used in address to the Deity. Because the music in this book is meant to be an integral part of corporate worship, some hymns that refer to the people, the singers, now use *we* rather than *I*. An asterisk (*) before a stanza indicates that the stanza may be omitted without impairing the remaining text, if the situation so requires. Chord symbols for guitar and other folk-type instruments have been added above the music of appropriate hymns and responses to encourage the use of a diversity of instruments for accompaniment of the singing.

Reformed worship can be described as bringing together the people of God and the Word of God. This book is intended to provide a context for that encounter, in its structure and in its content, in word and in music.

Musical Responses—Setting One

by David N. Johnson

Praise the Lord

Praise the Lord.

The Lord's name be praised.

*May be sung by minister, choir, or everyone.

You Are the Lord, Giver of Mercy!

You are the Lord, giv - er of

mer - cy! You are the Christ, giv - er of mer - cy!

You are the Lord, giv - er of mer - - - cy!

Setting One (cont.)

Lord, have mer - cy up - on us.

Christ, have mer - cy up - on us.

Lord, have mer - cy up - on us.

Setting One (cont.)

Glory to the Father

Glo-ry to the Fa - ther, and to the Son,

and to the Ho - ly Spir - it: as in the be - gin-ning, so

now, and for - ev - - er. A - men.

Moderately fast (♩ =c. 132) *f*

Glo - ry to God in the high - est,— and peace to his peo - ple on earth. Lord God, heav-enly King, Al - might-y God and Fa - ther, we wor-ship you, we

See following page.
Setting One (cont.)

give you thanks, we praise you for your glo - ry.   Lord Je-sus   Christ, on-ly

Son   of the   Fa - ther,   Lord   God,   Lamb   of

p subdued

God,   you   take a - way the   sin   of the   world: Have

Setting One (cont.)

mer - cy on us; you are seat-ed at the right hand of the

f with vigor

Fa - ther: re - ceive our prayer. For you a -

lone are the Ho - ly One, you a - lone are the Lord, you a-

See following page.
Setting One (cont.)

lone are the Most High, Je - sus   Christ,   with the   Ho - ly

Spir - it,   in   the   glo - ry   of   God,   the

Fa - ther.   A - men,   A - - men.

This Is the Good News

Moderately fast (♩=c. 63)

This is the good news which we re-ceived, in which we stand, and by which we are saved: that Christ died for our sins, that Christ died ac - cord-ing to the

See following page.
Setting One (cont.)

Scrip - tures,   that | he was bur - ied   and that he was   raised,_____

_____ that he was rais - ed   on the third   day;   and that

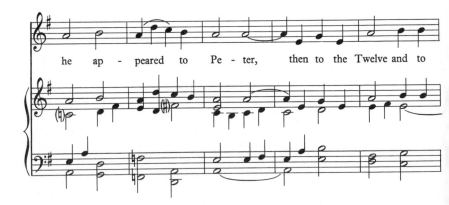

he   ap - peared to Pe - ter,   then to the Twelve and to

Setting One (cont.)

man-y faith-ful wit-ness-es. We be - lieve he is the

Christ, the Son of the liv - ing God.

He is the first and the last, the be - gin-ning and the end,

See following page.
Setting One (cont.)

he   is   our   Lord and our   God.   He   is   our

Lord   and   our   God.   A –   –   –   men.

*May be sung by minister, choir, or everyone.

224   Praise God, from Whom All Blessings Flow

Thomas Ken, 1693, 1709

Praise God, from whom all bless-ings flow; Praise him, all crea-tures here be-low; Praise him a-bove, ye heav-enly host: Praise Fa-ther, Son, and Ho-ly Ghost. A - men, A - men.

Setting One (cont.)

Lift up your hearts. We lift them to the Lord. Give thanks to God, for he is good. His love is ev - er - last - ing.

*May be sung by minister, choir, or everyone.

Setting One (cont.)

Lift Up Your Hearts (2)

Lift up your hearts. We lift them up to the

Lord. Let us give thanks to the Lord our

God. It is right to give him thanks and praise.

*May be sung by minister, choir, or everyone.

Setting One (cont.)

Ho - ly, ho - ly, ho - ly,

God of power and maj - es - ty, heaven and earth are

full of your glo - ry, O God most high!

Holy, Holy, Holy Lord

Ho - ly, ho - ly, ho - ly

Lord, God of power and might, heaven and earth are

full of your glo - ry. Ho - san - na in the

Setting One (cont.)

Alleluia!

let us be glad with all our hearts. Let us give him the glo - ry for - ev - er and ev - er. A - men, A - men, A - men!

Bless the Lord, O My Soul

Moderately slowly (♩=c. 80)

p

Bless the Lord, O my soul; And
all that is with - in me, bless his ho - ly
name! Bless the Lord, O my soul, And for-get not all his

R.H. R.H.

Setting One (cont.)

ben - e - fits, his ben - e - fits.

Bless the Lord, O my soul.

Musical Responses—Setting Two
by Joseph Goodman

Praise the Lord

Praise the Lord. The Lord's name be praised.

*May be sung by minister, choir, or everyone.

You Are the Lord, Giver of Mercy!

You are the Lord, giv-er of mer - cy! You are the Christ,

giv - er of mer - cy! You are the Lord, giv-er of mer - cy!

Lord, Have Mercy Upon Us

235

Setting Two (cont.)

Glory to the Father

(♩ = c. 132)

Glo - ry to the Fa - ther, and to the Son,

and to the Ho - ly Spir - it: as in the be - gin - ning,

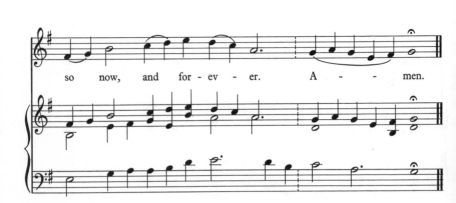

so now, and for - ev - er. A - - men.

Setting Two (cont.)

Glo-ry to God in the high-est, and peace to his peo-ple on earth. Lord God, heav-enly King, al-might-y God and Fa-ther, we wor-ship you, we give you

See following page.
Setting Two (cont.)

thanks,   we   praise   you   for   your   glo - ry.   Lord   Je - sus   Christ,

on - ly   Son   of   the   Fa - ther,   Lord   God,

Lamb   of   God,   you   take   a - way   the   sin   of   the

Setting Two (cont.)

world: have mer - cy on us; you are seat - ed at the

right hand of the Fa - ther: re - ceive our prayer.

For you a - lone are the Ho - ly One, you a - lone

See following page.
Setting Two (cont.)

are the Lord,   you   a - lone   are   the   Most   High,

Je - sus   Christ,   with   the   Ho - ly   Spir - it,

in   the   glo - ry   of   God   the   Fa - ther.   A - men.

Setting Two (cont.)

This is the good news which we re-ceived; in which we stand, and by which we are saved: that Christ died for our sins ac-cord-ing to the Scrip-tures, that he was bur-ied,

See following page.
Setting Two (cont.)

that he was raised on the third day; and that he ap-peared to Pe - ter,

then   to   the Twelve and   to   man - y   faith - ful   wit - ness - es.

We   be - lieve he   is   the Christ, the   Son   of   the liv - ing God.

Setting Two (cont.)

He is the first and the last, the be-gin-ning and the end,

he is our Lord and our God. A - men.

The Lord Is Risen

(♩ = 92)

f (Soloist*) (All)

The Lord is ris - en. He is ris - en in - deed.

*May be sung by minister, choir, or everyone.

Setting Two (cont.)

Praise God, from Whom All Blessings Flow!

Thomas Ken, 1693, 1709

Praise God, from whom all bless-ings flow! Praise

him, all crea-tures here be - low! Praise him a - bove, ye

heav-enly host! Praise Fa - ther, Son, and Ho - ly Ghost. A - men.

Setting Two (cont.)

*May be sung by minister, choir, or everyone.

Setting Two (cont.)

Lift Up Your Hearts (2)

Lift up your hearts. We lift them

up to the Lord. Let us give thanks to the Lord our

God. It is right to give him thanks and praise.

*May be sung by minister, choir, or everyone.

Setting Two (cont.)

Ho - ly, ho - ly, ho - ly Lord,

God of pow - er and might, heav - en and earth are

full of your glo - ry. Ho - san - na in the high - est.

Setting Two (cont.)

Bless - ed is he who comes in the name of the Lord.

Ho - san - na in the

high - est.

poco rit.

Alleluia!

Al – le – lu – ia!

For the Lord our God, the Al – might – y, has

come in – to his king – dom!

Setting Two (cont.)

Let us re - joice, let us be glad with all our

hearts. Let us give him the glo - ry for - ev -

er and ev - - - er. A - men.

poco rit.

Bless the Lord, O My Soul

Bless the Lord, O my soul; And all

that is with-in me, bless his ho-ly name! Bless the Lord,

O my soul, And for-get not all his ben-e-fits.

*May be sung by minister, choir, or everyone.

Setting Two (cont.)

Praise the Lord

Praise the Lord. The Lord's name be praised.

You Are the Lord, Giver of Mercy!

You are the Lord, giv-er of mer-cy!

You are the Christ, giv-er of mer-cy!

You are the Lord, giv-er of mer-cy!

Glory to the Father

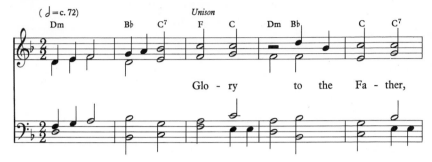

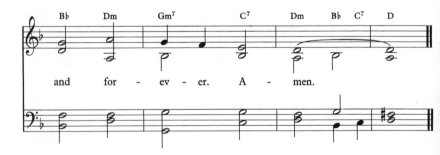

Setting Three (cont.)

Glory to God in the Highest

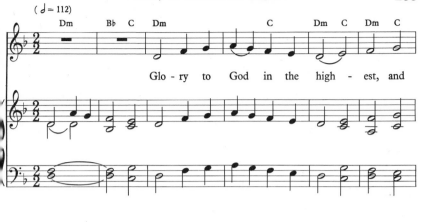

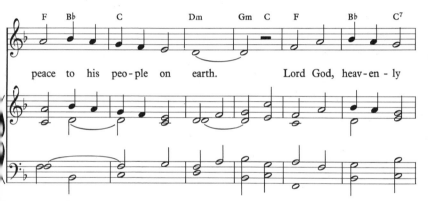

See following page.
Setting Three (cont.)

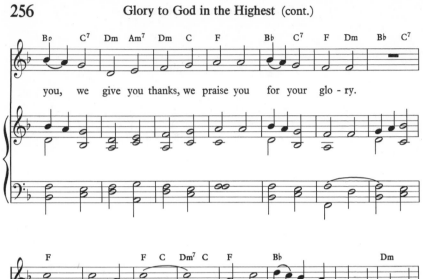

you, we give you thanks, we praise you for your glo - ry.

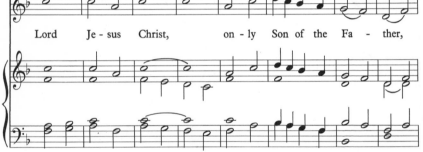

Lord Je - sus Christ, on - ly Son of the Fa - ther,

Lord God, Lamb of God, you take a - way the sin of the

See following page.
Setting Three (cont.)

Lord, you a - lone are the Most High,

Je - sus Christ, with the Ho - ly Spir - it,

in the glo - ry of God the Fa - ther. A - men.

Setting Three (cont.)

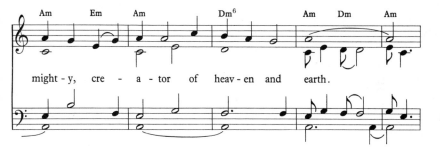

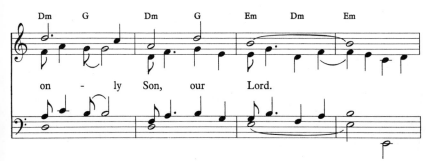

See following page.
Setting Three (cont.)

He was con-ceived by the pow-er of the Ho-ly Spir-it and born of the Vir-gin Mar-y. He suf-fered un-der Pon-tius Pi-late, was cru-ci-fied, died, and was bur-ied. He de-scend-ed to the dead.

Setting Three (cont.)

On the third day he rose a - gain. He a - scend - ed

in - to heav - en, and is seat - ed at the right hand of the

Fa - ther. He will come a - gain to judge the

liv - ing and the dead. I be - lieve in the Ho - ly

See following page.
Setting Three (cont.)

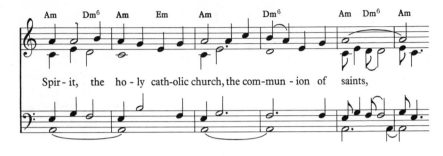

Spir-it, the ho-ly cath-olic church, the com-mun-ion of saints,

the for-give - ness of sins, the res-ur-rec-tion of the

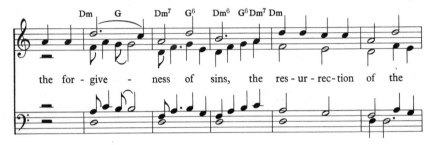

bod-y,   and the life   ev - er - last -

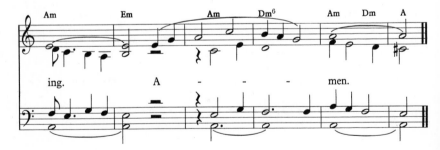

ing.   A - - - men.

Setting Three (cont.)

This Is the Good News

See following page.
Setting Three (cont.)

raised on the third day; and that he ap-peared to Pe-ter,

then to the Twelve and to man-y faith-ful wit-ness-es.

We be-lieve he is the Christ, the Son of the

liv-ing God. He is the first and the

last, the be - gin - ning and the end,

he is our Lord and our God. A - - men.

The Lord Is Risen

The Lord is ris - en. He is risen in - deed.

*May be sung by minister, choir, or everyone.

266 Praise God, from Whom All Blessings Flow

Thomas Ken, 1693, 1709

Setting Three (cont.)

Lift Up Your Hearts (1)

Based on Southern mountain melody

Lift up your hearts. We lift them to the

Lord. Give thanks to God, for he is good.

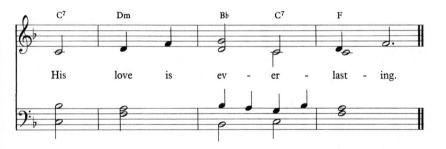

His love is ev - er - last - ing.

Setting Three (cont.)

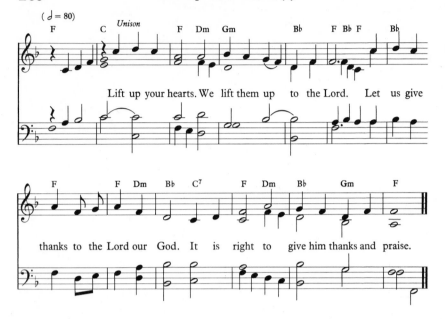

Lift up your hearts. We lift them up to the Lord. Let us give

thanks to the Lord our God. It is right to give him thanks and praise.

Holy, Holy, Holy

Based on Russian folk melody

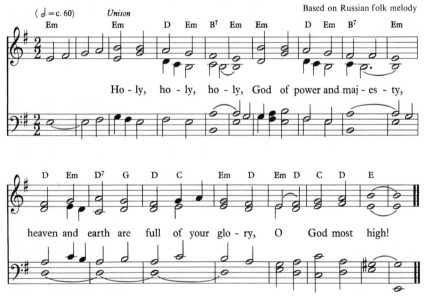

Ho - ly, ho - ly, ho - ly, God of power and maj - es - ty,

heaven and earth are full of your glo - ry, O God most high!

Setting Three (cont.)

Based on Russian folk melody

Ho - ly, ho - ly, ho - ly Lord, God of power and might,

heaven and earth are full of your glo - ry. Ho - san - na

in the high - est. Bless - ed is he who comes in the

name of the Lord. Ho - san - na in the high - est.

Setting Three (cont.)

270

Alleluia!

Based on Appalachian folk melody

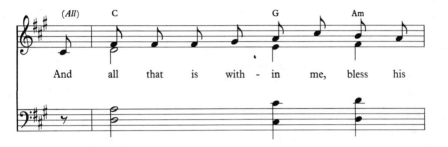

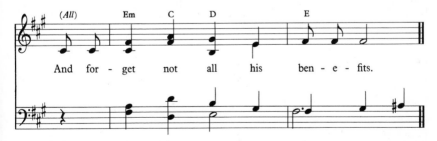

*May be sung by minister, choir, or everyone.

Setting Three (cont.)

Glory to the Father

Old Scottish chant

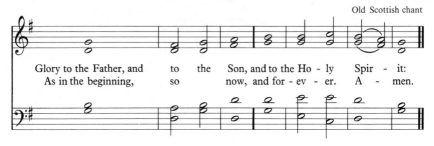

Glory to the Father, and to the Son, and to the Ho - ly Spir - it:
As in the beginning, so now, and for - ev - er. A - men.

Praise God, from Whom All Blessings Flow

OLD HUNDREDTH L.M.

Thomas Ken, 1693, 1709

Comp. or adapted by Louis Bourgeois, 1551

Praise God, from whom all bless - ings flow; Praise him, all crea - tures

here be - low; Praise him a - bove, ye heav - enly host:

Praise Fa - ther, Son, and Ho - ly Ghost. A - men.

A Hymn of Glory Let Us Sing

DEO GRACIAS L.M.

273

The Venerable Bede (ca. 672-735)
Sts. 1, 2 trans. by Elizabeth Rundle Charles,
1858; alt., 1972
St. 3 trans. by Benjamin Webb, 1854; alt., 1972

"The Agincourt Song," England, ca. 1415
Arr. in *Hymnal for Colleges and Schools*, 1956

1. A hymn of glo - ry let us sing, New hymns through-
out the world shall ring; By a new way none
ev - er trod Christ takes his place—the throne of God!

2. You are a pres - ent joy, O Lord; You will be
ev - er our re - ward; And great the light in
you we see To guide us to e - ter - ni - ty.

3. O ris - en Christ, as - cend - ed Lord, All praise to
you let earth ac - cord, Who are, while end - less
ag - es run, With Fa - ther and with Spir - it, One. A-men.

274   A Mighty Fortress Is Our God

EIN' FESTE BURG P.M.

Martin Luther, 1529
Trans. by Frederick H. Hedge, 1853; alt., 1972

Martin Luther, 1529

1. A might-y for-tress is our God, A bul-wark nev-er
2. Did we in our own strength con-fide, Our striv-ing would be
3. And though this world, with dev-ils filled, Should threat-en to un-
4. That word a-bove all earth-ly powers, No thanks to them, is

fail - ing; Our help-er he a-mid the flood Of
los - ing, Were not the right Man on our side, The
do us, We will not fear, for God has willed His
stand - ing; The Spir-it and his gifts are ours— We

mor-tal ills pre-vail - ing: For still our an-cient foe Does
Man of God's own choos - ing: You ask who that may be? Christ
truth to tri-umph through us: The prince of dark-ness grim, We
an-swer his com-mand - ing. Let goods and kin-dred go, This

seek to work us woe; His craft and power are great, And,
Je - sus, it is he; The Lord of Hosts his name, From
trem - ble not for him; His rage we can en - dure, For
mor - tal life al - so; The bod - y they may kill: God's

armed with cru - el hate, On earth is not his e - qual.
age to age the same, And he must win the bat - tle.
lo! his doom is sure, One lit - tle word shall fell him.
truth is rul - ing still— His king - dom is for - ev - er! A-men.

276 A Mighty Fortress Is Our God
EIN' FESTE BURG P.M.

Based on Psalm 46
J. Clifford Evers, 1964
Lines 1, 2, Martin Luther, 1529; trans.
by Frederick H. Hedge, 1853

Martin Luther, 1529

1. A might-y for-tress is our God, A bul-wark nev-er
2. The wa-ters of his good-ness flow Through-out his ho-ly
3. Be-hold his won-drous deeds of peace, The God of our sal-

fail - ing, Pro-tect-ing us with staff and rod, His
cit - y, And glad-den hearts of those who know His
va - tion; He knows our wars and makes them cease In

pow-er all-pre-vail - ing. What if the na - tions
ten-der-ness and pit - y. Though na-tions stand un-
ev-ery land and na - tion. The war-rior's spear and

Words reprinted by permission of World Library Publications, Inc., Cincinnati, Ohio. Harmonization from *The Lutheran Hymnal*, copyright 1941 by Concordia Publishing House; used by permission.

rage And surg-ing seas ram - page; What though the moun-tains fall, The
sure, God's king-dom shall en - dure; His pow - er shall re - main, His
lance Are splin-tered by his glance; The guns and nu - clear might Stand

Lord is God of all; On earth is not his e - qual.
peace shall ev - er reign, Our God, the God of Ja - cob.
with - ered in his sight; The Lord of hosts is with us. A-men.

278 Abide with Me: Fast Falls the Eventide

EVENTIDE 10.10.10.10.

Henry Francis Lyte, 1847; alt.

William Henry Monk, 1861

1. A - bide with me: fast falls the e - ven - tide;
2. I need your pres - ence ev - ery pass - ing hour.
3. I fear no foe, with you at hand to bless;
4. Hold now the cross be - fore my clos - ing eyes;

The dark - ness deep - ens; Lord, with me a - bide.
What but your grace can foil the tempt - er's power?
Ills have no weight, and tears no bit - ter - ness.
Shine through the gloom, and point me to the skies:

When oth - er help - ers fail and com - forts flee,
Who like your - self my guide and stay can be?
Where is death's sting? Where, grave, your vic - to - ry?
Heaven's morn - ing breaks, and earth's vain shad - ows flee:

Help of the help - less, O a - bide with me.
Through cloud and sun - shine, O a - bide with me.
I tri - umph still, if you a - bide with me.
In life, in death, O Lord, a - bide with me. A - men.

Ah, Dearest Jesus, Holy Child

VOM HIMMEL HOCH L.M.

279

Martin Luther, 1535
Trans. by Catherine Winkworth, 1855; alt.

Geystliche Lieder, Leipzig, 1539

1. Ah, dear-est Je-sus, ho-ly Child, Make thee a bed, soft, un-de-filed, With-in our hearts, that they may be All qui-et cham-bers kept for thee.

2. Our hearts for ver-y joy do leap, Our lips no more can si-lence keep; We, too, must sing with joy-ful tongue That sweet-est an-cient cra-dle song.

3. Glo-ry to God in high-est heaven, Who un-to man his Son hath given, While an-gels sing with ten-der mirth A glad new year to all the earth. A-men.

280 Ah, Holy Jesus, How Have You Offended

HERZLIEBSTER JESU 11.11.11.5.

Latin, attr. to Jean de Fécamp (d. 1078)
Para. by Johann Heermann, 1630
Repara. by Robert Bridges, 1899; alt., 1972

Johann Crüger, 1640

1. Ah, ho - ly Je - sus, how have you of - fend - ed, That man to judge you has in hate pre - tend - ed? By foes de - rid - ed, by your own re - ject - ed, O most af - flict - ed!

2. Who was the guilt - y? Who brought this up - on you? A - las, my trea - son, Je - sus, has un - done you! 'Twas I, Lord Je - sus, I it was de - nied you; I cru - ci - fied you.

3. For me, kind Je - sus, was your in - car - na - tion, Your mor - tal sor - row, and your life's ob - la - tion; Your death of an - guish and your bit - ter pas - sion, For my sal - va - tion.

4. There - fore, kind Je - sus, since I can - not pay you, I do a - dore you, and will ev - er pray you, Think on your pit - y and your love un - swerv - ing, Not my de - serv - ing. A - men.

Words altered from *The Yattendon Hymnal*; used by permission of Oxford University Press.

All Beautiful the March of Days

FOREST GREEN C.M.D.

281

Frances Whitmarsh Wile, 1911; alt., 1972

Traditional English melody, collected and
harm. by Ralph Vaughan Williams, 1906

1. All beau-ti-ful the march of days, As sea-sons come and go;
2. O'er white ex-pans-es spar-kling pure The ra-diant morns un-fold;
3. O God, from whose un-fath-omed law The year in beau-ty flows,

The hand that shaped the rose has wrought The crys-tal of the snow,
The sol-emn splen-dors of the night Burn bright-er through the cold.
Your-self the vi-sion pass-ing by In crys-tal and in rose,

Has sent the hoar-y frost of heaven, The flow-ing wa-ters sealed,
Life mounts in ev-ery throb-bing vein, Love deep-ens round the hearth,
Day un-to day does ut-ter speech, And night to night pro-claim,

And laid a si-lent love-li-ness On hill and wood and field.
And clear-er sounds the an-gel hymn, "Good will to men on earth."
In ev-er-chang-ing words of light, The won-der of your name. A-men.

282   All Creatures of Our God and King

LASST UNS ERFREUEN 8.8.8.8.8.8. with Alleluias

Francis of Assisi, ca. 1225
Para. by William H. Draper (1855-1933)

Geistliche Kirchengesäng, Cologne, 1623
Arr. and harm. by Ralph Vaughan Williams, 1906

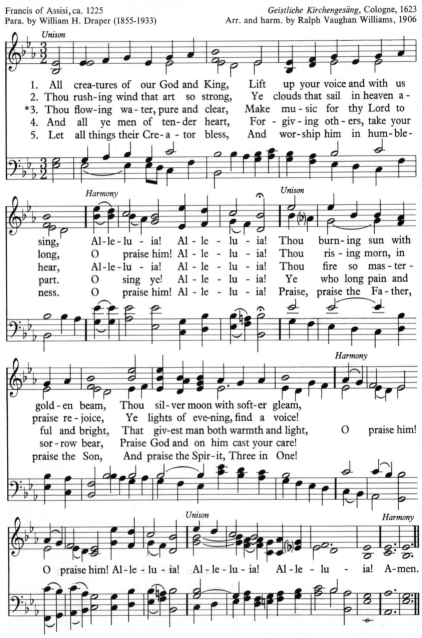

1. All crea-tures of our God and King, Lift up your voice and with us
2. Thou rush-ing wind that art so strong, Ye clouds that sail in heaven a-
*3. Thou flow-ing wa-ter, pure and clear, Make mu-sic for thy Lord to
4. And all ye men of ten-der heart, For - giv-ing oth - ers, take your
5. Let all things their Cre-a - tor bless, And wor-ship him in hum-ble-

sing, Al-le-lu - ia! Al - le - lu - ia! Thou burn-ing sun with
long, O praise him! Al - le - lu - ia! Thou ris - ing morn, in
hear, Al-le-lu-ia! Al - le - lu - ia! Thou fire so mas-ter-
part. O sing ye! Al - le - lu - ia! Ye who long pain and
ness. O praise him! Al - le - lu - ia! Praise, praise the Fa - ther,

gold - en beam, Thou sil - ver moon with soft-er gleam,
praise re - joice, Ye lights of eve-ning, find a voice!
ful and bright, That giv-est man both warmth and light, O praise him!
sor - row bear, Praise God and on him cast your care!
praise the Son, And praise the Spir-it, Three in One!

O praise him! Al-le - lu - ia! Al-le-lu-ia! Al-le - lu - ia! A-men.

Words copyright by J. Curwen & Sons, Ltd.; used by permission of
G. Schirmer, Inc. Music from *The English Hymnal*; used by permission of Oxford University Press.

For lower key, see "From All That
Dwell Below the Skies."

All Glory Be to God on High

ALLEIN GOTT IN DER HÖH' 8.7.8.7.8.8.7.

Based on Gloria in excelsis
Attr. to Nikolaus Decius, 1525
Trans. by Catherine Winkworth, 1863; alt.

Based on plainsong melody
Attr. to Nikolaus Decius, 1539
As in *Service Book and Hymnal*, 1958

283

1. All glo-ry be to God on high, Who has our race be-friend-ed!
2. We praise, we wor-ship you, we trust And give you thanks for-ev-er,
3. O Je-sus Christ, our God and Lord, Be-got-ten of the Fa-ther,
4. O Ho-ly Spir-it, pre-cious gift, O Com-fort-er un-fail-ing,

To us no harm shall now come nigh, The strife at last is end-ed;
O Fa-ther, that your rule is just And wise, and chang-es nev-er;
O Sav-ior, who our peace re-stored, And who lost sheep did gath-er,
Do you our trou-bled souls up-lift, A-gainst the foe pre-vail-ing;

God his good-will dis-plays to men, And peace shall reign on
Your bound-less power o'er all things reigns, You do what-e'er your
O Lamb of God, en-throned on high, Be-hold our need and
A-vert our woes and calm our dread: For us the Sav-ior's

earth a-gain; O thank him for his good-ness!
will or-dains; 'Tis well you are our rul-er!
hear our cry; Have mer-cy on us, Je-sus!
blood was shed; Do you in faith sus-tain us! A-men.

284 All Glory, Laud, and Honor

ST. THEODULPH 7.6.7.6.D.

Theodulph of Orleans, ca. 820
Trans. by John Mason Neale, 1851; alt., 1859

Melchior Teschner, 1615

1. All glo - ry, laud, and hon - or To thee, Re - deem - er, King,
2. Thou art the King of Is - rael, Thou Da - vid's roy - al son,
3. Thou didst ac - cept their prais - es; Ac - cept the prayers we bring,

To whom the lips of chil - dren Made sweet ho - san - nas ring!
Who in the Lord's name com - est, The King and bless - ed One;
Who in all good de - light - est, Thou good and gra - cious King.

The peo - ple of the He - brews With palms be - fore thee went;
To thee, be - fore thy pas - sion, They sang their hymns of praise;
All glo - ry, laud, and hon - or To thee, Re - deem - er, King,

Our praise and prayer and an - thems Be - fore thee we pre - sent.
To thee, now high ex - alt - ed, Our mel - o - dy we raise.
To whom the lips of chil - dren Made sweet ho - san - nas ring! A - men.

All Hail the Power of Jesus' Name! 285

CORONATION C.M.

(First Tune)

Sts. 1,2, Edward Perronet, 1779, 1780; alt.
Sts. 3,4, John Rippon, 1787

Oliver Holden, 1793

1. All hail the power of Je-sus' name! Let an-gels pros-trate fall;
2. Hail him, the heir of Da-vid's line, Whom Da-vid Lord did call;
3. Let ev-ery kin-dred, ev-ery tribe, On this ter-res-trial ball
4. O that with yon-der sa-cred throng We at his feet may fall!

Bring forth the roy - al di - a - dem,
The God in - car - nate, man di - vine,
To him all maj - es - ty as - cribe,
We'll join the ev - er - last - ing song,

And crown him Lord of all! Bring forth the roy - al
And crown him Lord of all! The God in - car - nate,
And crown him Lord of all! To him all maj - es -
And crown him Lord of all! We'll join the ev - er -

di - a - dem, And crown him Lord of all!
man di - vine, And crown him Lord of all!
ty as - cribe, And crown him Lord of all!
last - ing song, And crown him Lord of all! A - men.

286 All Hail the Power of Jesus' Name!

MILES LANE C.M.
(Second Tune)

Sts. 1,2, Edward Perronet, 1779, 1780; alt.
Sts. 3,4, John Rippon, 1787

William Shrubsole, 1779
Melody alt., ca. 1861

1. All hail the power of Je - sus' name! Let an - gels
2. Hail him, the heir of Da - vid's line, Whom Da - vid
3. Let ev - ery kin - dred, ev - ery tribe, On this ter -
4. O that with yon - der sa - cred throng We at his

pros - trate fall; Bring forth the roy - al di - a - dem,
Lord did call; The God in - car - nate, man di - vine,
res - trial ball To him all maj - es - ty as - cribe,
feet may fall! We'll join the ev - er - last - ing song,

And crown him, crown him, crown him, crown him Lord of all! A-men.

All My Heart Today Rejoices

287

WARUM SOLLT ICH (EBELING) 8.3.3.6.D.

Paul Gerhardt, 1653
Trans. by Catherine Winkworth, 1858; alt.

Johann Georg Ebeling, 1666

1. All my heart to-day re-joic-es, As I hear,
Far and near, Sweet-est an-gel voic-es:
"Christ is born," their choirs are sing-ing, Till the air,
Ev-ery-where, Now with joy is ring-ing.

2. Hark! a voice from yon-der man-ger, Soft and sweet,
Does en-treat: "Flee from woe and dan-ger;
Broth-ers, come; from all that grieves you You are freed;
All you need I will sure-ly give you."

3. Come, then, let us has-ten yon-der; Here let all,
Great and small, Kneel in awe and won-der;
Love him, who with love is yearn-ing; Hail the star
That from far Bright with hope is burn-ing!

4. You, dear Lord, with heed I'll cher-ish; Live to you,
And, with you Dy-ing, shall not per-ish;
But shall dwell with you for-ev-er, Far on high,
In the joy That shall al-ter nev-er. A-men.

288 All People That on Earth Do Dwell

OLD HUNDREDTH L.M.

Psalm 100
Para. by William Kethe, 1561; alt., 1650

Comp. or adapted by Louis Bourgeois, 1551
Rhythm, English Psalters

1. All peo-ple that on earth do dwell, Sing to the
2. Know that the Lord is God in - deed; With - out our
3. O en - ter then his gates with praise, Ap - proach with
4. For why? the Lord our God is good, His mer - cy

Lord with cheer - ful voice; Him serve with mirth, His
aid he did us make; We are his folk, he
joy his courts un - to; Praise, laud, and bless his
is for - ev - er sure; His truth at all times

praise forth tell, Come ye be-fore him and re - joice.
doth us feed, And for his sheep he doth us take.
name al - ways, For it is seem-ly so to do.
firm - ly stood, And shall from age to age en - dure. A-men.

All Poor Men and Humble

289

OLWEN 6.6.8.D.

Welsh carol
Para. by Katherine E. Roberts, 1928

Welsh carol
Arr. by Caradog Roberts (1879-1935)

1. All poor men and hum-ble, All lame men who stum-ble, Come
   For Je-sus, our trea-sure, With love past all mea-sure, In

haste ye, nor feel ye a-fraid; 2. Though Wise Men who found him Laid
low-ly poor man-ger was laid. 3. Then haste we to show him The

rich gifts a-round him, Yet ox-en they gave him their hay:
prais-es we owe him; Our serv-ice he ne'er can de-spise:

And Je-sus in beau-ty Ac-cept-ed their
Whose love still is a-ble To show us that

du-ty; Con-tent-ed in man-ger he lay.
sta-ble Where soft-ly in man-ger he lies.

Words from *The Oxford Book of Carols*; used by permission of Oxford University Press. Music used by permission of the Union of Welsh Independents.

290 All Praise Be Yours; for You, O King Divine

NATIONAL CITY 10.10.10. with Alleluia

F. Bland Tucker, 1938, 1972

Lawrence P. Schreiber, 1967

1. All praise be yours; for you, O King di-
2. You came to us in low - li - ness of
3. O Je - sus, let your mind with - in us
4. There - fore you are, by God's e - ter - nal
5. Let ev - ery tongue con - fess with one ac -

vine, Your right - ful glo - ry free - ly did re -
thought; By you the out - cast and the poor were
be; For you were serv - ant that we might be
vow, Most high ex - alt - ed o'er all crea - tures
cord In heaven and earth that Je - sus Christ is

sign, That in our dark - ened hearts your
sought; And by your death was God's sal -
free, And hum - bly stooped to death on
now, And given the name to which all
Lord; And God the Fa - ther be by

grace might shine.
va - tion wrought.
Cal - va - ry. Al - le - lu - ia!
knees shall bow.
all a - dored. A - men.

All Praise to God in Highest Heaven 291

GELOBT SEI GOTT 8.8.8. with Alleluias

Michael Weisse, 1531
Sts. 1,2,4-6 trans. by Margaret Barclay, 1950; alt., 1972
St. 3 trans. by Dalton E. McDonald, 1972

Attr. to Melchior Vulpius, 1609
As in *Pilgrim Hymnal*, 1958

1. All praise to God in high-est heaven And his in-car-nate
2. On the third morn at break of day, While still the stone a-
3. Three wom-en came their grief to share And, fright-ened, saw an
4. Then spoke the an-gel, "O fear naught! I know why you are
5. "He is a-ris-en from the dead, And all tra-vail has
6. Sav-ior and Lord, grant us to see You in your ris-en

Son be given, Who glo-rious-ly for us has striven.
bove him lay, Free he a-rose, to go his way.
an-gel there — A heav-enly light shone ev-ery-where!
thus dis-traught: You can-not find the Lord you sought."
con-quer-ed. Lo, where he lay, his shroud is spread."
maj-es-ty; Grant us to live right bless-ed-ly.

Al-le-lu-ia! Al-le-lu-ia! Al-le-lu-ia! A-men.

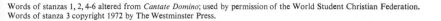

292 All Praise to Thee, Our God, This Night

TALLIS' CANON L.M.

Thomas Ken, 1693, 1709; alt., 1972

Thomas Tallis, ca. 1567

1. All praise to thee, our God, this night, For all the bless - ings of the light; Keep us, O keep us, King of kings, Be - neath thine own al - might - y wings.

2. For - give us, Lord, for thy dear Son, The ill that we this day have done; That with the world, our - selves, and thee We, ere we sleep, at peace may be.

3. O may our souls on thee re - pose, And with sweet sleep our eye - lids close; Sleep that may us more vig - orous make To serve our God when we a - wake.

4. Praise God, from whom all bless - ings flow; Praise him, all crea - tures here be - low; Praise him a - bove, ye heav - enly host: Praise Fa - ther, Son, and Ho - ly Ghost. A - men.

*May be sung as a canon.

All Who Love and Serve Your City

293

CHARLESTOWN 8.7.8.7.

The United States Sacred Harmony, 1799
Harm. by Carlton R. Young, 1965

Erik Routley, 1967

1. All who love and serve your cit - y, All who
2. In your day of loss and sor - row, In your
3. In your day of wealth and plen - ty, Wast - ed
4. For all days are days of judg-ment, And the
5. Ris - en Lord, shall yet the cit - y Be the

bear its dai - ly stress, All who cry for peace and
day of help - less strife, Hon - or, peace, and love re -
work and wast - ed play, Call to mind the word of
Lord is wait - ing still, Draw - ing near to men who
cit - y of de - spair? Come to - day, our Judge, our

jus - tice, All who curse and all who bless,
treat - ing, Seek the Lord, who is your life.
Je - sus, "Work ye yet while it is day."
spurn him, Of - fering peace from Cal - vary's hill.
Glo - ry. Be its name "The Lord is there!" A - men.

294
Alone You Journey Forth, O Lord
BANGOR C.M.

Peter Abelard (1079-1142)
Trans. by F. Bland Tucker, 1938, 1972

Comp. or arr. by William Tans'ur, 1734

1. A - lone you jour - ney forth, O Lord, In
2. Our sins, not yours, O Lord, you bear; Make
3. This is earth's dark - est hour, but you Both
4. Give us com - pas - sion for you, Lord, That,

sac - ri - fice to die; Is this your sor - row
us your sor - row feel, Till through our pit - y
light and life re - store; Then let all praise to
as we share this hour, Your cross may bring us

naught to us Who pass un - heed - ing by?
and our shame Love an - swers love's ap - peal.
you be given Who live for - ev - er - more.
to your joy And res - ur - rec - tion power. A - men.

"Am I My Brother's Keeper?"   295

WHITFORD 7.6.7.6.D.

Ian Ferguson, 1967

John Ambrose Lloyd, Sr., 1870

1. "Am I my broth-er's keep-er?" The mut-tered cry was drowned
2. The rul - er called for wa - ter And thought his hands were clean.
3. As long as peo - ple hun - ger, As long as peo - ple thirst,

By A - bel's life-blood shout-ing In si - lence from the ground.
Christ count-ed less than or - der, The man than the ma - chine.
And ig - no - rance and ill - ness And war-fare do their worst,

For no man is an is - land Di - vid - ed from the main—
The crowd cried, "Cru - ci - fy him," Their mal - ice would-n't budge,
As long as there's in - jus - tice In an - y of God's lands,

The bell which tolled for A - bel Tolled e - qual-ly for Cain.
So Pi - late called for wa - ter, And his - to - ry's his judge.
I am my broth-er's keep-er, I dare not wash my hands. A-men.

296   Amazing Grace! How Sweet the Sound

AMAZING GRACE C.M.

John Newton, 1779

American folk hymn
Arr. by Edwin O. Excell, 1900

1. A - maz - ing grace! How sweet the sound That
2. 'Twas grace that taught my heart to fear, And
3. Through man - y dan - gers, toils, and snares I
4. The Lord has prom - ised good to me, His

saved a wretch like me! I once was lost, but
grace my fears re - lieved; How pre - cious did that
have al - read - y come; 'Tis grace has brought me
word my hope se - cures; He will my shield and

now am found, Was blind, but now I see.
grace ap - pear The hour I first be - lieved!
safe thus far, And grace will lead me home.
por - tion be As long as life en - dures. A-men.

Ancient of Days, Who Sit Enthroned in Glory 297

L'OMNIPOTENT 11.10.11.10.

William C. Doane, 1886; alt., 1972

Comp. or adapted by Louis Bourgeois, 1551
As in *Pilgrim Hymnal*, 1958

1. An - cient of Days, who sit en-throned in glo - ry,
2. O Ho - ly Fa - ther, you have led your chil - dren
3. O Ho - ly Je - sus, Prince of Peace and Sav - ior,
4. O Ho - ly Ghost, the Lord and the Life - giv - er,
5. O Tri - une God, with heart and voice a - dor - ing,

To you all knees are bent, all voic - es pray;
In all the ag - es, with the fire and cloud,
To you we owe the peace that still pre - vails,
Yours is the quick - ening power that gives in - crease;
Praise we the good - ness that does crown our days;

Your love has blest the wide world's won - drous sto - ry
Through seas dry - shod, through wea - ry wastes be - wil - dering;
Still - ing the rude wills of men's wild be - hav - ior,
From you have flowed, as from a pleas - ant riv - er,
Pray we that you will hear us, still im - plor - ing

With light and life since E - den's dawn - ing day.
To you, in rev - erent love, our hearts are bowed.
And calm - ing pas - sion's fierce and storm - y gales.
Our her - i - tage, our bless - ings, and our peace.
Your love and fa - vor, given to us al - ways. A - men.

298 Angels, from the Realms of Glory

REGENT SQUARE 8.7.8.7.8.7.

James Montgomery, 1816, 1825; alt., 1972

Henry Smart, 1867

1. An - gels, from the realms of glo - ry, Wing your flight o'er
2. Shep - herds, in the fields a - bid - ing, Watch - ing o'er your
3. Sag - es, leave your con - tem - pla - tions, Bright - er vi - sions
4. Saints, be - fore the al - tar bend - ing, Watch - ing long in

all the earth; As you sang cre - a - tion's sto - ry,
flocks by night, God with man is now re - sid - ing,
beam a - far; Seek the great De - sire of na - tions;
hope and fear, Sud - den - ly the Lord, de - scend - ing,

Now pro - claim Mes - si - ah's birth:
Yon - der shines the in - fant Light:
You have seen his na - tal star: Come and wor - ship,
In his tem - ple shall ap - pear:

Come and wor - ship, Wor - ship Christ, the new - born King! A - men.

Angels We Have Heard on High

299

GLORIA 7.7.7.7. with Refrain

French carol
Trans. in *Crown of Jesus*, 1862; alt.
Adapted by Earl Marlatt, 1937

French carol
As in *Pilgrim Hymnal*, 1958

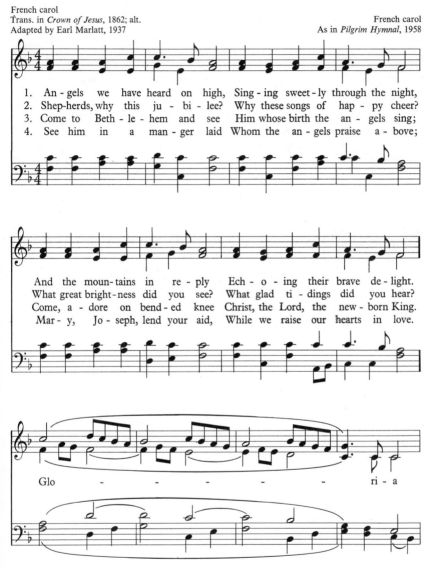

1. An - gels we have heard on high, Sing - ing sweet - ly through the night,
2. Shep-herds, why this ju - bi - lee? Why these songs of hap - py cheer?
3. Come to Beth - le - hem and see Him whose birth the an - gels sing;
4. See him in a man - ger laid Whom the an - gels praise a - bove;

And the moun-tains in re - ply Ech - o - ing their brave de - light.
What great bright-ness did you see? What glad ti - dings did you hear?
Come, a - dore on bend - ed knee Christ, the Lord, the new - born King.
Mar - y, Jo - seph, lend your aid, While we raise our hearts in love.

Glo - - - - - ri - a

Words from *The New Church Hymnal*; used by permission of
Fleming H. Revell Company, publisher.

See following page.

in ex - cel - sis De - o,   Glo -   -   -   -

-     -   -   ri - a in ex - cel - sis De -   o. A - men.

As Men of Old Their Firstfruits Brought

HIGH POPPLES C.M.D.

Frank von Christierson, 1960, 1972

Samuel Walter, 1964

1. As men of old their first-fruits brought Of or - chard, flock, and field
2. A world in need now sum - mons us To la - bor, love, and give;
3. In grat - i - tude and hum - ble trust We bring our best to - day,

To God, the giv - er of all good, The source of boun-teous yield;
To make our life an of - fer - ing To God, that man may live;
To serve your cause and share your love With all a - long life's way.

So we to - day first-fruits would bring, The wealth of this good land,
The church of Christ is call - ing us To make the dream come true:
O God, who gave your - self to us In Christ, your on - ly Son,

Of farm and mar-ket, shop and home, Of mind and heart and hand.
A world re-deemed by Christ-like love, All life in Christ made new.
Teach us to give our-selves each day Un - til life's work is done. A - men.

Alternative Tune: FOREST GREEN

302
As with Gladness Men of Old
DIX 7.7.7.7.7.7.

William Chatterton Dix, ca. 1858

Conrad Kocher, 1838
Abr. by William Henry Monk, 1861

1. As with glad-ness men of old Did the guid-ing
2. As with joy-ful steps they sped To that low-ly
3. As they of-fered gifts most rare At that man-ger
4. Ho-ly Je-sus, ev-ery day Keep us in the

star be-hold; As with joy they hailed its light,
man-ger bed, There to bend the knee be-fore
rude and bare, So may we with ho-ly joy,
nar-row way; And, when earth-ly things are past,

Lead-ing on-ward, beam-ing bright; So, most gra-cious
Him whom heaven and earth a-dore, So may we with
Pure, and free from sin's al-loy, All our cost-liest
Bring our ran-somed souls at last Where they need no

Lord, may we Ev-er-more be led to thee.
will-ing feet Ev-er seek thy mer-cy seat.
trea-sures bring, Christ, to thee, our heav-enly King.
star to guide, Where no clouds thy glo-ry hide. A-men.

At the Name of Jesus

KING'S WESTON 6.5.6.5.D.

Caroline Maria Noel, 1870; alt., 1931

Ralph Vaughan Williams, 1925
Arr. for *The Hymnbook*, 1955

1. At the name of Je - sus Ev - ery knee shall bow,
2. Hum-bled for a sea - son, To re - ceive a name
3. Bore it up tri - um - phant, With its hu - man light,
4. Broth-ers, this Lord Je - sus Shall re - turn a - gain,

Ev - ery tongue con - fess him King of glo - ry now:
From the lips of sin - ners, Un - to whom he came,
Through all ranks of crea - tures, To the cen - tral height,
With his Fa - ther's glo - ry O'er the earth to reign;

'Tis the Fa - ther's plea - sure We should call him Lord,
Faith - ful - ly he bore it Spot - less to the last,
To the throne of God - head, To the Fa - ther's breast;
For all wreaths of em - pire Meet up - on his brow,

Who from the be - gin - ning Was the might - y Word.
Brought it back vic - to - rious, When from death he passed;
Filled it with the glo - ry Of that per - fect rest.
And our hearts con - fess him King of glo - ry now. A - men.

Music arranged from *Songs of Praise*, Enlarged Edition; used by permission of Oxford University Press.

304
Be Thou My Vision
SLANE 10.10.9.10.

Ancient Irish
Trans. by Mary Byrne, 1905
Versified by Eleanor Hull, 1912; alt.

Traditional Irish melody
Harm. by David Evans, 1927

1. Be thou my vi - sion, O Lord of my heart;
2. Be thou my wis - dom, and thou my true word;
3. Rich - es I heed not, nor man's emp - ty praise,
4. High King of heav - en, my vic - to - ry won,

Naught be all else to me, save that thou art —
I ev - er with thee and thou with me, Lord;
Thou mine in - her - i - tance, now and al - ways;
May I reach heav - en's joys, O bright heaven's Sun!

Thou my best thought, by day or by night,
Thou my great Fa - ther, I thy true son;
Thou and thou on - ly, first in my heart,
Heart of my own heart, what - ev - er be - fall,

Wak - ing or sleep - ing, thy pres - ence my light.
Thou in me dwell - ing, and I with thee one.
High King of heav - en, my trea - sure thou art.
Still be my vi - sion, O Rul - er of all. A - men.

Words used by permission of Eleanor Hull's Estate and Chatto & Windus, Ltd. Music altered from *The Church Hymnary*, Revised Edition, 1927; used by permission of Oxford University Press.

Become to Us the Living Bread

O FILII ET FILIAE 8.8.8. with Alleluia

Miriam Drury, 1970

Probably French, ca. 15th century
As in *Pilgrim Hymnal*, 1958

305

1. Be - come to us the liv - ing bread By which the
2. Be - come the nev - er - fail - ing wine, The spring of
3. May Chris - tians all with one ac - cord U - nite a -

Chris - tian life is fed, Re - newed, and great - ly
joy that shall in - cline Our hearts to bear the
round the sa - cred board To praise your ho - ly

Unison

com - fort - ed, Al - le - lu - ia!
cov - enant sign, Al - le - lu - ia!
name, O Lord, Al - le - lu - ia! A - men.

306 Before the Lord Jehovah's Throne

PARK STREET L.M.

Based on Psalm 100
Isaac Watts, 1719
Alt. by John Wesley, 1737, and others

Frédéric M.-A. Venua, ca. 1810

1. Be - fore the Lord Je - ho - vah's throne, All na - tions, bow with sa - cred joy; Know that the Lord is God a - lone, He can cre - ate, and he de - stroy; He can cre - ate, and he de - stroy.

2. His sov - ereign power, with - out our aid, Made us of clay, and formed us men; And when like wan - dering sheep we strayed, He brought us to his fold a - gain, He brought us to his fold a - gain.

3. We'll crowd his gates with thank - ful songs, High as the heavens our voic - es raise; And earth, with her ten thou - sand tongues, Shall fill his courts with sound - ing praise, Shall fill his courts with sound - ing praise.

4. Wide as the world is his com - mand, Vast as e - ter - ni - ty his love; Firm as a rock his truth shall stand, When roll - ing years shall cease to move, When roll - ing years shall cease to move. A - men.

Behold the Lamb of God!

WIGAN 6.6.6.4.8.8.4.

Matthew Bridges, 1848; alt.

Samuel S. Wesley, 1872

1. Be - hold the Lamb of God! O thou for sin - ners slain,
2. Be - hold the Lamb of God! All hail, in - car - nate Word!
3. Be - hold the Lamb of God! Wor - thy is he a - lone

Let it not be in vain That thou hast died.
Thou ev - er - last - ing Lord, Sav - ior most blest!
To sit up - on the throne Of God a - bove,

Thee for my Sav - ior let me take. My on - ly ref - uge
Fill us with love that nev - er faints. Grant us, with all thy
One with the An - cient of all days, One with the Com - fort -

let me make Thy pierc - ed side!
bless - ed saints, E - ter - nal rest.
er in praise, All Light, all Love! A - men.

308 Beneath the Cross of Jesus

ST. CHRISTOPHER 7.6.8.6.8.6.8.6.

Sts. 1,2, Elizabeth C. Clephane, 1872
St. 3, Dalton E. McDonald
and Donald D. Kettring, 1972

Frederick C. Maker, 1881

1. Be - neath the cross of Je - sus I fain would take my stand—
2. Up - on the cross of Je - sus Mine eye at times can see
3. "Take up your cross," said Je - sus, "And fol - low af - ter me."

The shad - ow of a might - y rock With - in a wea - ry land;
The ver - y dy - ing form of one Who suf - fered there for me:
I take your cross to learn your will, What - e'er the cost may be;

A home with - in the wil - der - ness, A rest up - on the way,
And from my strick - en heart with tears Two won - ders I con - fess—
We share the vi - sion of a world Which puts an end to strife,

From the burn - ing of the noon - tide heat, And the bur - den of the day.
The won - ders of re - deem - ing love And my un - worth - i - ness.
And work that all man - kind shall know Your way, your truth, your life. A - men.

Blessed Jesus, at Your Word

LIEBSTER JESU 7.8.7.8.8.8.

Tobias Clausnitzer, 1663
Trans. by Catherine Winkworth, 1858; alt., 1972

Johann Rudolph Ahle, 1664
Arr. by J. S. Bach, 1769

309

1. Bless-ed Je-sus, at your word We are gath-ered
2. All our knowl-edge, sense, and sight Lie in deep-est
3. Glo-rious Lord, your-self im-part! Light of light, from

all to hear you; Let our hearts and souls be stirred
dark-ness shroud-ed, Till your Spir-it breaks our night
God pro-ceed-ing, O-pen now our ears and heart,

Now to seek and love and fear you; By your teach-ings
With the beams of truth un-cloud-ed; You a-lone to
Help us by your Spir-it's plead-ing; Hear the cry that

true and ho-ly, Drawn from earth to love you sole-ly.
God can win us, You must work all good with-in us.
we are rais-ing; Hear, and bless our prayers and prais-ing. A-men.

310 Blessed Jesus, We Are Here

LIEBSTER JESU 7.8.7.8.8.8.

Benjamin Schmolck, 1706
Trans. by C. Winfred Douglas, 1939; alt., 1972

Johann Rudolph Ahle, 1664
Arr. by J. S. Bach, 1769

Bless - ed Je - sus, we are here, Your be - lov - ed word o - bey - ing. With {these chil - dren we / this child we now} draw near As you bid us in your say - ing, "Let the lit - tle ones be giv - en Un - to me; of such is heav - en." A - men.

Blessing and Honor and Glory and Power 311

O QUANTA QUALIA 10.10.10.10.

Horatius Bonar, 1866; alt., 1972

Paris Antiphoner, 1681
Harm. by David Evans, 1927

1. Bless - ing and hon - or and glo - ry and power,
2. Hear through the heav - ens the sound of his name,
3. Ev - er as - cend - ing the song and the prayer;
4. Give we the glo - ry and praise to the Lamb;

Wis - dom and rich - es and strength ev - er - more,
While rings the earth with his glo - ry and fame;
Ev - er de - scend - ing the love that we share;
Take we the robe and the harp and the palm;

Give we to him who our bat - tle has won,
O - cean and moun - tain, stream, for - est, and flower
Bless - ing and hon - or and glo - ry and praise —
Sing we the song of the Lamb that was slain,

Whose are the king - dom, the crown, and the throne.
Ech - o his prais - es and tell of his power.
This is the theme of the hymns that we raise.
Dy - ing in weak - ness, but ris - ing to reign. A - men.

312 Born in the Night, Mary's Child

(Mary's Child)

Geoffrey Ainger, 1964

Geoffrey Ainger, 1964
Harm. by Richard D. Wetzel, 1972

1. Born in the night, Mar-y's Child, A long way from your home; Com-ing in need, Mar-y's Child, Born in a bor-rowed room.
2. Clear shin-ing light, Mar-y's Child, Your face lights up our way; Light of the world, Mar-y's Child, Dawn on our dark-ened day.
3. Truth of our life, Mar-y's Child, You tell us God is good; Prove it is true, Mar-y's Child, Go to your cross of wood.
4. Hope of the world, Mar-y's Child, You're com-ing soon to reign; King of the earth, Mar-y's Child, Walk in our streets a-gain.

Bread of Heaven, on Thee We Feed

ARFON 7.7.7.7.7.7.

Josiah Conder, 1824; alt.

Traditional melody, France and Wales
Adapted by Hugh Davies, ca. 1906

313

1. Bread of heaven, on thee we feed, For thou art our
food in - deed; Ev - er may our souls be fed
With this true and liv - ing Bread, Day by day with
strength sup - plied Through the life of him who died.

2. Vine of heaven, thy love sup - plies This blest cup of
sac - ri - fice; 'Tis thy wounds our heal - ing give;
To thy cross we look and live: Thou our life! O
let us be Root - ed, graft - ed, built on thee. A - men.

314   Break Forth, O Beauteous Heavenly Light

ERMUNTRE DICH 8.7.8.7.8.8.7.7.

St. 1, Johann von Rist, 1641;
trans. by John Troutbeck, 1873; alt., 1972
St. 2, Dalton E. McDonald, 1972

Johann Schop, 1641
Alt. by Johann Crüger, 1648
Harm. by J. S. Bach, 1734

1. Break forth, O beau-teous heav-enly light, And ush - er in the morn - ing. You shep-herds, shrink not with af-fright, But hear the an - gel's warn - ing. This child, now weak in

2. He comes to rec - on - cile all men, And men to God for - ev - er; He comes to mend the cords of love Wher - ev - er sin does sev - er. He is the light up -

in - fan - cy, Our con - fi - dence and joy shall be, The
on   our way To bring us   to   the   prom-ised day–This

power of Sa - tan break - ing, Our peace e - ter-nal mak - ing.
child, God's in - car - na - tion, Our hope and our sal - va - tion! A-men.

316 Break Forth, O Living Light of God

ST. PETER C.M.

Frank von Christierson, 1952; alt., 1972

Alexander R. Reinagle, ca. 1836

1. Break forth, O liv - ing light of God, Up -
2. Re - move the veil of an - cient words, With
*3. Show us the proph - ets and the priests, The
4. O let your Word be light a - new To
5. O may one Lord, one faith, one Word, One

on the world's dark hour! Show us the way the
mes - sage long ob - scure; Re - store to us your
kings, the com - mon men, Who kept the faith and
ev - ery na - tion's life; U - nite us in your
Spir - it lead us still: And one great church go

Mas - ter trod; Re - veal his sav - ing power.
truth, O God, And make its mean - ing sure.
walked with you; O make them live a - gain!
will, O Lord, And end all sin - ful strife.
forth in might To work God's per - fect will. A - men.

Break Thou the Bread of Life

BREAD OF LIFE 6.4.6.4.D.

Mary Ann Lathbury, 1877   William F. Sherwin, 1877

1. Break thou the bread of life, Dear Lord, to me,
2. Bless thou the truth, dear Lord, To me— to me,

As thou didst break the loaves Be - side the sea.
As thou didst bless the bread By Gal - i - lee.

Be - yond the sa - cred page I seek thee, Lord;
Then shall all bond - age cease, All fet - ters fall,

My spir - it pants for thee, O liv - ing Word.
And I shall find my peace, My all in all. A - men.

318 Brightest and Best of the Sons of the Morning

WALKER 11.10.11.10.

Reginald Heber, 1811; alt., 1972

Southern Harmony, 1835
Harm. by Richard M. Peek, 1972

1. Bright - est and best of the sons of the morn - ing,
2. Cold on his cra - dle the dew - drops are shin - ing;
3. Say, shall we yield him, in cost - ly de - vo - tion,
4. Vain - ly we of - fer each am - ple ob - la - tion,

Dawn on our dark - ness and lend us your aid;
Low lies his head with the beasts of the stall;
O - dors of E - dom and of - ferings di - vine,
Vain - ly with gifts would his fa - vor se - cure;

Star of the East, the ho - ri - zon a - dorn - ing,
An - gels a - dore him in slum - ber re - clin - ing,
Gems of the moun - tain and pearls of the o - cean,
Rich - er by far is the heart's ad - o - ra - tion,

Guide where our in - fant Re - deem - er is laid.
Mak - er and Mon - arch and Sav - ior of all.
Myrrh from the for - est, or gold from the mine?
Dear - er to God are the prayers of the poor. A - men.

Music copyright 1972 by The Westminster Press.

Bring a Torch, Jeannette, Isabella

BRING A TORCH Irregular

Traditional French carol (?)
Trans. by E. Cuthbert Nunn (1868-1914); alt., 1972

Traditional French carol (?)
Harm. by E. Cuthbert Nunn (1868-1914)
Alt. in *Pilgrim Hymnal*, 1958

319

1. Bring a torch, Jean-nette, Is - a - bel - la! Bring a torch, to the
cra - dle run! It is Je - sus, good folk of the vil - lage;
Christ is born and Mar - y's call - ing. Ah! ah! beau - ti - ful
is the moth - er! Ah! ah! beau - ti - ful is her Son!

2. It is wrong when the child is sleep - ing, It is wrong to
talk so loud; Si - lence, all, as you gath - er a - round,
Lest your noise should wak - en Je - sus. Hush! hush! see how
fast he slum - bers; Hush! hush! see how fast he sleeps!

3. Soft - ly to the lit - tle sta - ble, Soft - ly for a
mo - ment come; Look and see how charm - ing is Je - sus,
How he is warm, his cheeks are ros - y. Hush! hush! see how the
child is sleep - ing; Hush! hush! see how he smiles in dreams.

320 Built on the Rock

KIRKEN (BUILT ON THE ROCK) 8.8.8.8.8.8.8.8.

Nicolai F. S. Grundtvig, 1837
Trans. by Carl Döving, 1909; alt., 1972

Ludvig M. Lindeman, 1840

1. Built on the rock the church does stand, E - ven when stee - ples are
2. Sure - ly in tem - ples made with hands God, the most high, is not
3. We are God's house of liv - ing stones, Build - ed for his hab - i -
4. Now we may gath - er with our King, E'en in the low - li - est

fall - ing; Crum-bled have spires in ev - ery land, Bells still are
dwell - ing; High a - bove earth his tem - ple stands, All earth - ly
ta - tion; He through bap - tis - mal grace us owns, Heirs of his
dwell - ing; Prais - es to him we there may bring, His won-drous

chim - ing and call - ing; Call-ing the young and old to rest, But a-bove
tem - ples ex - cell - ing; Yet he whom heavens can-not con-tain Chose to a -
won-drous sal - va - tion; Were we but two his name to tell, Yet he would
mer - cy forth - tell - ing; Je - sus his grace to us ac-cords, Spir-it and

all the soul dis-tressed, Long-ing for rest ev - er - last - ing.
bide on earth with men, Built in our bod-ies his tem - ple.
deign with us to dwell, With all his grace and his fa - vor.
life are all his words, His truth does hal-low the tem - ple. A - men.

NOTE: Stanza 3 may be used for Baptism.

By the Babylonian Rivers

(Hymn for Those in Captivity)

321

Based on Psalm 137:1-4
Ewald Bash, 1964

Latvian melody
Arr. by Ewald Bash, 1964
Harm. by Paul Abels, 1966

1. By the Bab - y - lo - nian riv - ers We sat
2. There our cap - tors in de - ri - sion Did re -
3. How shall we sing the Lord's song In a
4. Let thy cross be ben - e - dic - tion For men

down in grief and wept; Hanged our harps up - on a
quire of us a song; So we sat with star - ing
strange and bit - ter land? Can our voic - es veil the
bound in tyr - an - ny; By the power of res - ur -

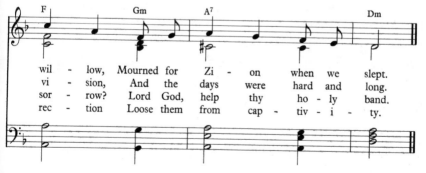

wil - low, Mourned for Zi - on when we slept.
vi - sion, And the days were hard and long.
sor - row? Lord God, help thy ho - ly band.
rec - tion Loose them from cap - tiv - i - ty.

322 Call Jehovah Your Salvation

HYFRYDOL 8.7.8.7.D.

Based on Psalm 91
James Montgomery, 1822; alt., 1972

Rowland Hugh Prichard, 1855

1. Call Je-ho-vah your sal-va-tion, Rest be-neath th'Al-might-y's shade,
2. From the sword at noon-day wast-ing, From the noi-some pes-ti-lence,
3. Since, with pure and firm af-fec-tion, You on God have set your love,

In his se-cret hab-i-ta-tion Dwell, nor ev-er be dis-mayed:
In the depth of mid-night blast-ing, God shall be your sure de-fense:
With the wings of his pro-tec-tion He will shield you from a-bove:

There no tu-mult can a-larm you, You shall dread no hid-den snare;
He shall charge his an-gel le-gions Watch and ward o'er you to keep;
You shall call on him in trou-ble, He will heark-en, he will save;

Guile nor vi-o-lence can harm you, In e-ter-nal safe-guard there.
Though you walk through hos-tile re-gions, Though in des-ert wilds you sleep.
Here for grief re-ward you dou-ble, Crown with life be-yond the grave. A-men.

Cast Your Burden on the Lord

SAVANNAH 7.7.7.7.

Based on Psalm 55:22
Rowland Hill's Psalms and Hymns, 1783; alt., 1972

Foundery Collection, 1742

323

1. Cast your bur-den on the Lord; On-ly lean up-on his word. You will soon have cause to bless His e-ter-nal faith-ful-ness.

2. He sus-tains you by his hand; He en-a-bles you to stand. Those whom Je-sus once has loved From his grace are nev-er moved.

3. Hu-man coun-sels come to naught; That shall stand which God has wrought. His com-pas-sion, love, and power Are the same for-ev-er-more.

4. Heaven and earth may pass a-way; God's free grace shall not de-cay. He has prom-ised to ful-fill All the plea-sure of his will.

5. Je-sus, guard-ian of your flock, Be your-self our con-stant rock. Make us, by your power-ful hand, Strong as Zi-on's moun-tain stand. A-men.

324 Christ, Above All Glory Seated

IN BABILONE 8.7.8.7.D.

Latin hymn, ca. 9th century
Trans. by James Russell Woodford, 1852; alt., 1972

Traditional Dutch melody
Harm. by Julius Röntgen, ca. 1906

1. Christ, a - bove all glo - ry seat - ed! King e - ter - nal, strong to save!
2. There your king-doms all a - dore you, Heaven a - bove and earth be - low,
3. So when you a - gain in glo - ry On the clouds of heaven ap - pear,

Dy - ing, you have death de - feat - ed, Bur - ied, you have doomed the grave.
While the depths of hell be - fore you, Trem - bling and de - feat they know.
We, your flock, may stand be - fore you, Faith - ful fol - lowers, with - out fear.

You are gone, where now is giv - en What no mor - tal might could gain:
We, O Lord! with hearts a - dor - ing, Fol - low you a - bove the sky:
Hail! all hail! In you con - fid - ing, Je - sus, all shall you a - dore,

On th'e - ter - nal throne of heav-en, In your Fa - ther's power to reign.
Hear our prayers your grace im-plor-ing, Lift our souls to you on high.
In your Fa - ther's might a - bid - ing With one spir - it ev - er-more! A-men.

Words copyright 1972 by The Westminster Press. Music used by permission of F. E. Röntgen.

Christ Is Made the Sure Foundation

325

REGENT SQUARE 8.7.8.7.8.7.

Latin hymn, ca. 7th century
Trans. by John Mason Neale, 1851; alt., 1861, 1972

Henry Smart, 1867

1. Christ is made the sure foun-da-tion, Christ the head and cor-ner-stone,
2. To this tem-ple, where we call you, Come, O Lord of Hosts, to-day!
3. Here be-stow on all your serv-ants What they ask of you to gain:
4. Laud and hon-or to the Fa-ther, Laud and hon-or to the Son,

Cho-sen of the Lord and pre-cious, Bind-ing all the church in one;
With your wont-ed lov-ing-kind-ness Hear your peo-ple as they pray,
What they gain from you for-ev-er With the bless-ed to re-tain,
Laud and hon-or to the Spir-it, Ev-er Three and ev-er One;

Ho-ly Zi-on's help for-ev-er, And her con-fi-dence a-lone.
And your full-est ben-e-dic-tion Shed with-in its walls al-way.
And here-af-ter in your glo-ry Ev-er-more with you to reign.
One in might, and One in glo-ry, While un-end-ing ag-es run. A-men.

326 Christn Is the World's True Light

ST. JOAN 6.7.6.7.6.6.6.6.

George Wallace Briggs, 1931; alt., 1972

Percy E. B. Coller, 1941

1. Christ is the world's true Light, Its Cap-tain of sal - va - tion,
2. In Christ all rac - es meet, Their an-cient feuds for - get - ting,
3. One Lord, in one great name, U - nite us all who own you;

The Day-star clear and bright Of ev - ery man and na - tion.
The whole round world com - plete, From sun-rise to its set - ting.
Cast out our pride and shame That hin-der to en - throne you.

New life, new hope, a - wakes Wher - e'er men own his sway:
When Christ is throned as Lord, Men shall for - sake their fear,
The world has wait - ed long, Has tra - vailed long in pain:

Free-dom her bond - age breaks, And night is turned to day.
To plow-share beat the sword, To prun-ing hook the spear.
To heal its an - cient wrong, Come, Prince of Peace, and reign. A - men.

Christ Jesus Lay in Death's Strong Bands

CHRIST LAG P.M.

Martin Luther, 1524
Trans. by Richard Massie, 1854; alt.

Johann Walther's *Geystliche gesangk Buchleyn*, 1524
As in *The Methodist Hymnal*, 1966

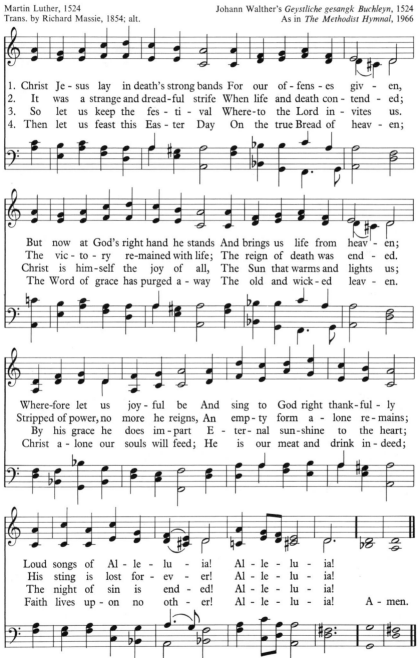

1. Christ Je - sus lay in death's strong bands For our of - fens - es giv - en,
2. It was a strange and dread-ful strife When life and death con - tend - ed;
3. So let us keep the fes - ti - val Where-to the Lord in - vites us.
4. Then let us feast this Eas - ter Day On the true Bread of heav - en;

But now at God's right hand he stands And brings us life from heav' - en;
The vic - to - ry re - mained with life; The reign of death was end - ed.
Christ is him-self the joy of all, The Sun that warms and lights us;
The Word of grace has purged a - way The old and wick - ed leav - en.

Where-fore let us joy - ful be And sing to God right thank-ful - ly
Stripped of power, no more he reigns, An emp - ty form a - lone re - mains;
By his grace he does im - part E - ter - nal sun-shine to the heart;
Christ a - lone our souls will feed; He is our meat and drink in - deed;

Loud songs of Al - le - lu - ia! Al - le - lu - ia!
His sting is lost for - ev - er! Al - le - lu - ia!
The night of sin is end - ed! Al - le - lu - ia!
Faith lives up - on no oth - er! Al - le - lu - ia! A - men.

327

328   # Christ the Lord Is Risen Again

CHRIST IST ERSTANDEN 7.7.7.7. with Alleluias

Michael Weisse, 1531
Trans. by Catherine Winkworth, 1858

German folk hymn, 12th century
Arr. by Ethel Porter, 1958

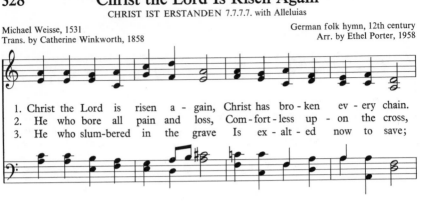

1. Christ the Lord is risen a - gain, Christ has bro - ken ev - ery chain.
2. He who bore all pain and loss, Com - fort - less up - on the cross,
3. He who slum-bered in the grave Is ex - alt - ed now to save;

Hark, the an - gels shout for joy, Sing-ing ev - er - more on high:
Lives in glo - ry now on high, Pleads for us and hears our cry:
Now through Chris-ten - dom it rings That the Lamb is King of kings:

Al - le - lu - ia! Al - le - lu - ia! Al - le -

lu - ia! Al - le - lu - ia! Hark, the an - gels shout for joy,
Lives in glo - ry now on high,
Now through Chris-ten - dom it rings

Sing - ing ev - er - more on high:
Pleads for us and hears our cry: Al - le - lu - ia!
That the Lamb is King of kings: A - men.

330   "Christ the Lord Is Risen Today"

LLANFAIR 7.7.7.7. with Alleluias

Charles Wesley, 1739; alt., 1760,1972

Robert Williams, 1817
Harm. by David Evans, 1927

May be sung in unison

1. "Christ the Lord is risen to - day,"
2. Vain the stone, the watch, the seal;
3. Lives a - gain our glo - rious King; Al - le - lu - ia!
4. Soar we now where Christ has led,
5. Hail, the Lord of earth and heaven!

Sons of men and an - gels say;
Christ has burst the gates of hell;
Where, O death, is now your sting? Al - le - lu - ia!
Fol - lowing our ex - alt - ed Head;
Praise to thee by both be given;

Raise your joys and tri - umphs high;
Death in vain for - bids his rise;
Once he died, our souls to save; Al - le - lu - ia!
Made like him, like him we rise;
You we greet tri - um - phant now;

Sing, you heavens, and earth re - ply,
Christ has o - pened par - a - dise.
Where your vic - to - ry, O grave? Al - le - lu - ia!
Ours the cross, the grave, the skies.
Hail, the res - ur - rec - tion Thou!

A - men.

Music from *The Church Hymnary*, Revised Edition, 1927;
used by permission of Oxford University Press.

Alternative Tune: EASTER HYMN

Christ Was the Word

CLAY COURT 7.7.7.7.

Attr. to Elizabeth I (1533-1603)

Richard Hillert, 1969

Christ was the Word who spake it: He took the

bread and brake it: And what his word doth

make it, That I be-lieve and take it.

332 Christ, Whose Glory Fills the Skies

RATISBON 7.7.7.7.7.7.

Charles Wesley, 1740

German melody, adapted in
J. G. Werner's *Choralbuch*, 1815

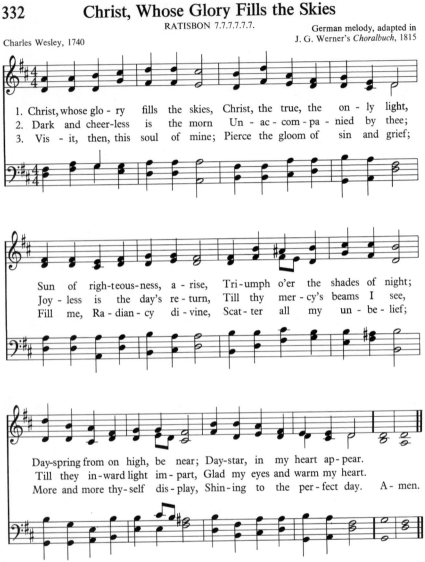

1. Christ, whose glo - ry fills the skies, Christ, the true, the on - ly light,
Sun of righ-teous-ness, a - rise, Tri-umph o'er the shades of night;
Day-spring from on high, be near; Day-star, in my heart ap - pear.

2. Dark and cheer-less is the morn Un - ac - com - pa - nied by thee;
Joy - less is the day's re - turn, Till thy mer - cy's beams I see,
Till they in-ward light im - part, Glad my eyes and warm my heart.

3. Vis - it, then, this soul of mine; Pierce the gloom of sin and grief;
Fill me, Ra - dian - cy di - vine, Scat - ter all my un - be - lief;
More and more thy-self dis - play, Shin-ing to the per - fect day. A - men.

Come, Christians, Join to Sing

MADRID 6.6.6.6.D.

Christian Henry Bateman, 1843; alt.

Source unknown
Harm. by David Evans, 1927

333

1. Come, Chris-tians, join to sing
2. Come, lift your hearts on high; Al - le - lu - ia! A - men!
3. Praise yet our Christ a - gain;

Loud praise to Christ our King;
Let prais - es fill the sky; Al - le - lu - ia! A - men!
Life shall not end the strain;

Let all, with heart and voice, Be - fore his throne re - joice;
He is our guide and friend; To us he'll con - de - scend;
On heav - en's bliss - ful shore His good - ness we'll a - dore,

Praise is his gra-cious choice.
His love shall nev - er end. Al - le - lu - ia! A - men!
Sing - ing for - ev - er-more, A-men.

Music used by permission of the Executors of the late Professor Evans.

334 Come Down, O Love Divine

DOWN AMPNEY 6.6.11.D.

Bianco da Siena, ca. 1367
Trans. by Richard F. Littledale, 1867; alt., 1972

Ralph Vaughan Williams, 1906

1. Come down, O Love di - vine, Seek out this soul of
2. O let it free - ly burn, Till earth - ly pas - sions
3. And so the yearn - ing strong With which the soul will

mine, And vis - it it with your own ar - dor glow - ing;
turn To dust and ash - es in its heat con - sum - ing;
long Shall far out - pass the power of hu - man tell - ing;

O Com-fort - er, draw near, With - in my heart ap - pear,
And let your glo - rious light Shine ev - er on my sight,
For none can guess its grace Till he be - come the place

And kin - dle it, your ho - ly flame be - stow - ing.
And clothe me round, the while my path il - lum - ing.
Where - in the Ho - ly Spir - it makes his dwell - ing. A - men.

Come, Holy Ghost, Our Souls Inspire 335

VENI CREATOR SPIRITUS L.M.

Latin hymn, ca. 9th century
Trans. by John Cosin, 1627

Plainsong melody, Mechlin form
As in *Pilgrim Hymnal*, 1958

1. Come, Ho - ly Ghost, our souls in - spire And light-en with ce -
2. Thy bless - ed unc - tion from a - bove Is com-fort, life, and
3. A - noint and cheer our soil - ed face With the a - bun - dance
4. Teach us to know the Fa - ther, Son, And thee, of both, to

les - tial fire; Thou the a - noint - ing Spir - it art
fire of love; En - a - ble with per - pet - ual light
of thy grace; Keep far our foes, give peace at home;
be but One; That through the ag - es all a - long

After last stanza

Who dost thy seven - fold gifts im - part.
The dull-ness of our blind - ed sight.
Where thou art guide no ill can come.
This may be our end - less song: Praise to thy e -

ter - nal mer - it, Fa - ther, Son, and Ho - ly Spir - it. A - men.

336 Come, Holy Spirit, God and Lord!

DAS NEUGEBORNE KINDELEIN L.M.

Based on medieval Latin antiphon
Martin Luther, 1524
Trans. by Catherine Winkworth, 1855, and others

Melchior Vulpius, 1609
Harm. by J. S. Bach, 1724

1. Come, Ho - ly Spir - it, God and Lord! Let all your
2. Lord, by the bright-ness of your light, You in the
3. From ev - ery er - ror keep us free; Let none but
4. Lord, by your power pre - pare each heart And to our

grac - es be out - poured On each be - liev - er's
faith do men u - nite Of ev - ery land and
Christ our Mas - ter be, That we in liv - ing
weak - ness strength im - part, That brave - ly here we

mind and heart; Your fer - vent love to us im - part.
ev - ery tongue; This to your praise, O Lord, be sung.
faith a - bide, In him with all our might con - fide.
may con - tend, Through life and death to you as - cend. A- men.

Come, My Soul, You Must Be Waking   337

MEINE ARMUTH 8.4.7.D.

Friedrich R. L. von Canitz (1654-1699)
Trans. attr. to Thomas Arnold
and Henry J. Buckoll, 1838, 1841; alt.

Freylinghausen's *Geistreiches Gesangbuch*, 1704
As in *Songs of Syon*, 1910

1. Come, my soul, you must be wak - ing. Now is break - ing O'er the earth an - oth - er day. Come to him who made this splen - dor; May you ren - der All your fee - ble strength can pay.

2. Glad - ly hail the sun re - turn - ing; Read - y burn - ing Be the in - cense of your powers. For the night is safe - ly end - ed; God has tend - ed With his care your help - less hours.

3. Pray that he may pros - per ev - er Each en - deav - or When your aim is good and true; But that he may ev - er thwart you, And con - vert you, When you e - vil would pur - sue.

4. On - ly God's free gifts a - buse not, Light re - fuse not, But his Spir - it's voice o - bey; You with him shall dwell, be - hold - ing Light en - fold - ing All things in un - cloud - ed day. A - men.

Music used by permission of Mrs. J. Meredith Tatton.

338 Come, O Come, Great Quickening Spirit

KOMM, O KOMM, DU GEIST DES LEBENS 8.7.8.7.7.7.

Heinrich Held, ca. 1658
Trans. by Edward Traill Horn III, 1958; alt., 1972

Attr. to Johann Christoph Bach, ca. 1680
Arr. by Ulrich S. Leupold, 1958

1. Come, O come, great quick - ening Spir - it, God be -
2. May your will and your de - sir - ing Be our
3. Bless - ed Spir - it, bring re - new - al To all
4. Help us keep the faith for - ev - er; Let not

fore the dawn of time! Fire our hearts with ho - ly
ob - ject; with your hand Lead our ev - ery thought and
dwell - ing on the earth, When the e - vil one as -
Sa - tan, death, or shame Draw us from you, or de -

ar - dor, Bless - ed Com - fort - er sub - lime! Let your
ac - tion That they be what you com - mand. All our
sails us Help us prove our heav - enly birth; Arm us
prive us Of the hon - or of your name. With your

ra - diance fill our night, Turn- ing dark- ness in - to light.
sin - ful - ness e - rase With the in - crease of your grace.
with your might- y sword In the le - gions of the Lord.
Word and sac - ra - ments Be, our God, the sure de - fense. A - men.

Words and music from *Service Book and Hymnal*; used by permission of the Commission on the Liturgy and Hymnal.

Come, O Thou God of Grace

TRINITY (ITALIAN HYMN) 6.6.4.6.6.6.4.

William E. Evans, 1886

Felice de Giardini, 1769
Arr. by Robert Carwithen, 1972

339

1. Come, O thou God of grace, Dwell in this ho - ly place, E'en now de - scend! This tem - ple, reared to thee, O may it ev - er be Filled with thy maj - es - ty, Till time shall end!
2. Be in each song of praise Which here thy peo - ple raise With hearts a - flame! Let ev - ery an - them rise Like in - cense to the skies, A joy - ful sac - ri - fice, To thy blest name!
3. Speak, O e - ter - nal Lord, Out of thy liv - ing Word, O give suc - cess! Do thou the truth im - part Un - to each wait - ing heart; Source of all strength thou art, Thy gos - pel bless!
4. To the great One in Three Glo - ry and prais - es be In love now given! Glad songs to thee we sing, Glad hearts to thee we bring, Till we our God and King Shall praise in heaven! A - men.

340 Come, Risen Lord, and Deign to Be Our Guest

SURSUM CORDA (Smith) 10.10.10.10.

George Wallace Briggs, 1931

Alfred M. Smith, 1941

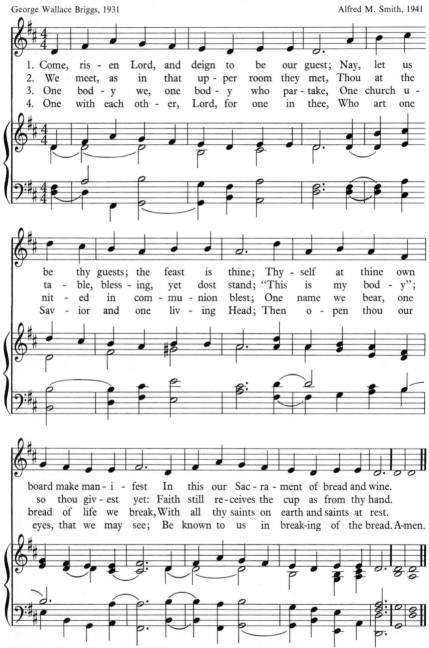

1. Come, ris - en Lord, and deign to be our guest; Nay, let us
2. We meet, as in that up - per room they met, Thou at the
3. One bod - y we, one bod - y who par - take, One church u -
4. One with each oth - er, Lord, for one in thee, Who art one

be thy guests; the feast is thine; Thy - self at thine own
ta - ble, bless - ing, yet dost stand; "This is my bod - y";
nit - ed in com - mu - nion blest; One name we bear, one
Sav - ior and one liv - ing Head; Then o - pen thou our

board make man - i - fest In this our Sac - ra - ment of bread and wine.
so thou giv - est yet: Faith still re - ceives the cup as from thy hand.
bread of life we break, With all thy saints on earth and saints at rest.
eyes, that we may see; Be known to us in break - ing of the bread. A-men.

Come, Thou Fount of Every Blessing

NETTLETON 8.7.8.7.D.

American folk hymn

Robert Robinson, 1758

Wyeth's *A Repository of Sacred Music*, 2d part, 1813

1. Come, thou fount of ev-ery bless-ing, Tune my heart to sing thy grace;
2. Je - sus sought me when a stran-ger, Wan-dering from the fold of God:

Streams of mer - cy, nev-er ceas-ing, Call for songs of loud-est praise.
He, to res - cue me from dan-ger, In-ter-posed his pre-cious blood.

Teach me some me - lo-dious son - net, Sung by flam-ing tongues a-bove;
O to grace how great a debt - or Dai-ly I'm con-strained to be!

Praise the mount! I'm fixed up-on it, Mount of God's un-chang-ing love.
Let that grace now, like a fet - ter, Bind my wan-dering heart to thee. A-men.

Come, Thou Long-expected Jesus

STUTTGART 8.7.8.7.

Charles Wesley, 1744

Psalmodia Sacra, 1715
Adapted in *Hymns Ancient & Modern*, 1861

1. Come, thou long - ex - pect - ed Je - sus, Born to
2. Is - rael's Strength and Con - so - la - tion, Hope of
3. Born thy peo - ple to de - liv - er, Born a
4. By thine own e - ter - nal Spir - it Rule in

set thy peo - ple free; From our fears and sins re -
all the earth thou art; Dear De - sire of ev - ery
child, and yet a King, Born to reign in us for -
all our hearts a - lone; By thine all - suf - fi - cient

lease us; Let us find our rest in thee.
na - tion, Joy of ev - ery long - ing heart.
ev - er, Now thy gra - cious king - dom bring.
mer - it Raise us to thy glo - rious throne. A - men.

Alternative Tune: HYFRYDOL

Come to Us, Mighty King

343

TRINITY (ITALIAN HYMN) 6.6.4.6.6.6.4.

Anonymous tract, 1757; alt., 1972

Felice de Giardini, 1769
Arr. by Robert Carwithen, 1972

1. Come to us, might - y King, Help us your
   name to sing, Help us to praise: Fa - ther, all -
   glo - ri - ous, O'er all vic - to - ri - ous, Come, and reign
   o - ver us, An - cient of Days.

2. Come now, In - car - nate Word, Gird on your
   might - y sword, Our prayer at - tend: Come, and your
   peo - ple bless, And give your word suc - cess; Spir - it of
   ho - li - ness, On us de - scend.

3. Come, Ho - ly Com - fort - er, Your sa - cred
   wit - ness bear In this glad hour: To all your
   grace im - part, Now rule in ev - ery heart, And nev - er
   from us part, Spir - it of power.

4. To the great One in Three The high - est
   prais - es be, For - ev - er - more! His sov - ereign
   maj - es - ty May we in glo - ry see, And to e -
   ter - ni - ty Love and a - dore. A - men.

Music copyright 1972 by The Westminster Press.

344 Come, You Faithful, Raise the Strain

AVE VIRGO VIRGINUM 7.6.7.6.D.

Attr. to John of Damascus (675?-749?)
Trans. by John Mason Neale, 1859; alt., 1972

Bohemian Brethren Hymnal, 1544
As in *Pilgrim Hymnal*, 1958

1. Come, you faith - ful, raise the strain Of tri - um-phant glad - ness;
2. 'Tis the spring of souls to - day; Christ has burst his pris - on,
3. Now the queen of sea - sons, bright With the day of splen - dor,
4. Nei - ther might the gates of death, Nor the tomb's dark por - tal,
*5. "Al - le - lu - ia!" now we cry To our King im - mor - tal,

God has brought his Is - ra - el In - to joy from sad - ness;
And from three days' sleep in death As a sun has ris - en;
With the roy - al feast of feasts, Comes its joy to ren - der;
Nor the watch-ers, nor the seal Hold you as a mor - tal;
Who, tri - um-phant, burst the bars Of the tomb's dark por - tal;

Loosed from Phar-aoh's bit - ter yoke Ja - cob's sons and daugh - ters;
All the win - ter of our sins, Long and dark, is fly - ing
Comes to glad Je - ru - sa - lem Who with true af - fec - tion
But to - day a - mid the twelve You did stand, be - stow - ing
"Al - le - lu - ia," with the Son God the Fa - ther prais - ing;

Led them with un - moist-ened foot Through the Red Sea wa - ters.
From his light, to whom we give Laud and praise un - dy - ing.
Wel - comes in un - wea-ried strains Je - sus' res - ur - rec - tion.
That your peace which ev - er-more Pass - es hu - man know - ing.
"Al - le - lu - ia!" yet a - gain To the Spir - it rais - ing. A-men.

Come, You People, Rise and Sing

345

BOUNDLESS MERCY 7.6.7.6.D.

Cyril A. Alington (1872-1955); alt., 1972

Southern folk hymn
Harm. by Donald D. Kettring, 1965

1. Come, you peo-ple, rise and sing Hymns of ad - o - ra - tion,
2. Praise we God the Fa - ther's name For our world's cre - a - tion,
3. Praise we God the on - ly Son, Who in mer - cy sought us;
4. Grant us, Ho - ly Ghost, we pray, More and more to know him,

And to heaven's e - ter - nal King Of - fer ded - i - ca - tion;
And his sav - ing health pro - claim Un - to ev - ery na - tion;
Born to save a world un - done, Out of death he brought us;
More and more and ev - ery day In our lives to show him,

Bring your praise for mer - cies past, All his love con - fess - ing,
Till, his name by all con - fessed, Ev - ery heart en - throne him,
Here a - while he showed his love, Suf - fered un - com - plain - ing,
That with hearts by you made brave, Strong and wise and ten - der,

And on life, while life shall last, Ask your Fa - ther's bless - ing.
And from far - thest east and west All his chil - dren own him.
Now he pleads for us a - bove, Risen, as - cend - ed, reign - ing!
We, with all the powers we have, Serv - ice fit may ren - der. A - men.

Words used by permission of the family of the late Dean Alington. Music copyright 1968 by The Westminster Press.

346   Come, You Thankful People, Come

ST. GEORGE'S, WINDSOR 7.7.7.7.D.

Henry Alford, 1844, 1865; alt., 1972

George J. Elvey, 1859

1. Come, you thank-ful peo - ple, come, Raise the song of har - vest home:
2. All the world is God's own field, Fruit un - to his praise to yield;
3. For the Lord our God shall come, And shall take his har - vest home,
4. E - ven so, Lord, quick - ly come To your fi - nal har - vest home;

All is safe - ly gath - ered in, Ere the win - ter storms be - gin;
Wheat and tares to - geth - er sown, Un - to joy or sor - row grown;
From his field shall in that day All of - fens - es purge a - way,
Gath - er all your peo - ple in, Free from sor - row, free from sin;

God, our mak - er, does pro - vide For our wants to be sup - plied:
First the blade, and then the ear, Then the full corn shall ap - pear:
Give his an - gels charge at last In the fire the tares to cast,
There, for - ev - er pu - ri - fied, In your pres-ence to a - bide:

Come to God's own tem - ple, come, Raise the song of har - vest home.
Lord of har - vest, grant that we Whole-some grain and pure may be.
But the fruit - ful ears to store In his gar - ner ev - er - more.
Come, with all your an - gels, come, Raise the glo-rious har - vest home. A-men.

Comfort, Comfort You My People

347

PSALM 42 8.7.8.7.7.7.8.8.

Isaiah 40:1-8
Para. by Johannes Olearius, 1671
Trans. by Catherine Winkworth, 1863; alt.

Comp. or adapted by Louis Bourgeois, 1551
As in *Pilgrim Hymnal*, 1958

1. Com - fort, com - fort you my peo - ple, Tell of peace, thus says our God;
2. Hark, the her - ald voice is cry - ing In the des - ert far and near,
3. Make you straight what long was crook - ed, Make the rough - er plac - es plain;

Com - fort those who sit in dark - ness Mourn - ing 'neath their sor - rows' load.
Bid - ding all men to re - pent - ance Since the king - dom now is here.
Let your hearts be true and hum - ble, As be - fits his ho - ly reign.

Speak you to Je - ru - sa - lem Of the peace that waits for them;
Oh, that warn - ing cry o - bey! Now pre - pare for God a way;
For the glo - ry of the Lord Now o'er earth is shed a - broad;

Tell her that her sins I cov - er, And her war - fare now is o - ver.
Let the val - leys rise to meet him And the hills bow down to greet him.
And all flesh shall see the to - ken That his word is nev - er bro - ken. A - men.

348

Creator of the Stars of Night

CONDITOR ALME L.M.

Medieval Latin hymn
Trans. by John Mason Neale, 1851
The Hymnal 1940 version; alt., 1972

Plainsong, Mode IV, Sarum form
Harm. by C. Winfred Douglas, 1940

1. Cre - a - tor of the stars of night, The peo - ple's ev - er -
2. At the great name of Je - sus, now All knees must bend, all
3. Come in all ho - ly might, we pray; Re - deem us for e -
4. To God the Fa - ther, God the Son, And God the Spir - it,

last - ing light, O Christ, the Sav - ior of us all,
hearts must bow; And things ce - les - tial him shall own,
ter - nal day From ev - ery power of dark - ness, when
Three in One, Laud, hon - or, might, and glo - ry be

We pray now, hear us when we call.
And things ter - res - trial, Lord a - lone.
Your judg - ment comes for sons of men.
From age to age e - ter - nal - ly. A - men.

Words and music used by permission of The Church Pension Fund.

Crown Him with Many Crowns

DIADEMATA S.M.D.

Sts. 1, 2, 4, Matthew Bridges, 1851; alt., 1972
St. 3, Godfrey Thring, 1874

George J. Elvey, 1868; alt.

1. Crown him with man - y crowns, The Lamb up - on his . throne;
2. Crown him the Lord of peace, Whose power a scep - ter sways
3. Crown him the Lord of life, Who tri - umphed o'er the grave,
4. Crown him the Lord of years, The Po - ten - tate of time,

Hark! how the heav-enly an - them drowns All mu - sic but its own!
From pole to pole, that wars may cease, Ab-sorbed in prayer and praise.
And rose vic - to - rious in the strife For those he came to save.
Cre - a - tor of the roll - ing spheres, In - ef - fa - bly sub - lime.

A - wake, my soul, and sing Of him who died for you,
His reign shall know no end; And round his pierc - ed feet
His glo - ries now we sing Who died and rose on high,
All hail, Re - deem - er, hail! For you have died for me;

And hail him as your match-less King With wor-ship as his due.
Fair flowers of par - a - dise ex - tend Their fra-grance ev - er sweet.
Who died, e - ter - nal life to bring, And lives that death may die.
Your praise shall nev-er, nev - er fail Through-out e - ter - ni - ty. A - men.

350 Dear Lord and Father of Mankind

REST 8.6.8.8.6.

John Greenleaf Whittier, 1872

Frederick C. Maker, 1887

1. Dear Lord and Fa-ther of man-kind, For-give our fool-ish ways;
2. In sim-ple trust like theirs who heard, Be-side the Syr-ian sea,
3. O Sab-bath rest by Gal-i-lee! O calm of hills a-bove,
4. Drop thy still dews of qui-et-ness, Till all our striv-ings cease;
5. Breathe through the heats of our de-sire Thy cool-ness and thy balm;

Re-clothe us in our right-ful mind, In pur-er lives thy
The gra-cious call-ing of the Lord, Let us, like them, with-
Where Je-sus knelt to share with thee The si-lence of e-
Take from our souls the strain and stress, And let our or-dered
Let sense be dumb, let flesh re-tire; Speak through the earth-quake,

serv-ice find, In deep-er rev-er-ence, praise.
out a word Rise up and fol-low thee.
ter-ni-ty, In-ter-pret-ed by love!
lives con-fess The beau-ty of thy peace.
wind, and fire, O still, small voice of calm! A-men.

Deck Yourself, My Soul, with Gladness 351

SCHMÜCKE DICH L.M.D.

Johann Franck, 1649, 1653
Trans. by Catherine Winkworth, 1863; alt.;
and John Caspar Mattes, 1913
Composite alt., 1972

Johann Crüger, 1649
Harm. by J. S. Bach, 1724

1. Deck your-self, my soul, with glad - ness, Leave be-hind all gloom and
2. Sun, who all my life does bright - en; Light, who does my soul en -
*3. Je - sus, source of life and plea - sure, Tru-est friend and dear - est

sad - ness; Come in - to the day-light's splen - dor, There with
light - en; Joy, your won-drous gift be - stow - ing; Fount, from
trea - sure, By your love I am in - vit - ed, Be your

joy your prais-es ren - der Un - to him whose grace un - bound -
which all good is flow - ing: At your feet I cry, my Mak -
love with love re - quit - ed. From this ban - quet let me mea -

See following page.

ed Has this won-drous ban - quet found - ed; Come, for now the
er, Let me be a fit par - tak - er Of this bless-ed
sure, Lord, how vast and deep its trea - sure; Through the gifts that

King most ho - ly Stoops to you in like-ness low - ly.
food from heav - en, For our good, your glo - ry, giv - en.
here you give me, As your guest in heaven re - ceive me. A - men.

Descend, O Spirit, Purging Flame

LLEF L.M.

353

Scott Francis Brenner, 1969

Griffith Hugh Jones, 1890
Arr. by Donald D. Kettring, 1972

1. De - scend, O Spir - it, purg - ing flame, Brand us this day with Je - sus' name! Con - firm our faith, con - sume our doubt; Sign us as Christ's, with - in, with - out.

2. Wash us with wa - ter, make us pure; Thrust us in mis - sion to en - dure. Let now your heal - ing wa - ters win New life, new hope, re - lease from sin.

3. For - bid us not this sec - ond birth; Grant un - to us the great - er worth! Con - script us in your serv - ice, Lord; Bap - tize all na - tions with your Word. A - men.

354   Earth and All Stars

Herbert Brokering, 1968

David N. Johnson, 1968

1. Earth and all stars, Loud rush - ing plan - ets
2. Steel and ma - chines, Loud pound - ing ham - mers
3. Class - rooms and labs, Loud boil - ing test tubes
4. Knowl - edge and truth, Loud sound - ing wis - dom

Sing to the Lord a new song!
Sing to the Lord a new song!
Sing to the Lord a new song!
Sing to the Lord a new song!

Hail, wind, and rain, Loud blow - ing snow - storm
Lime - stone and beams, Loud build - ing work - men
Ath - lete and band, Loud cheer - ing peo - ple
Daugh - ter and son, Loud pray - ing mem - bers

Sing to the Lord a new song!
Sing to the Lord a new song!
Sing to the Lord a new song!
Sing to the Lord a new song!

He hath done mar - - - vel - ous things.

I, too, will praise him with a new song! A - men.

356 Eternal Father, Strong to Save

MELITA 8.8.8.8.8.8.

Sts. 1, 4, William Whiting, 1860; alt., 1861, 1937, 1972
Sts. 2, 3, Robert Nelson Spencer, 1937; alt., 1972

John B. Dykes, 1861

1. E - ter - nal Fa - ther, strong to save, Whose arm has bound the
2. O Christ, the Lord of hill and plain O'er which our traf - fic
3. O Spir - it, whom the Fa - ther sent To spread a - broad the
4. O Trin - i - ty of love and power, Our broth - ers shield in

rest - less wave, Who bids the might - y o - cean deep Its
runs a - main By moun - tain pass or val - ley low; Wher-
fir - ma - ment; O Wind of heav - en, by your might Save
dan - ger's hour; From rock and tem - pest, fire and foe, Pro -

own ap - point - ed lim - its keep: To you we pray most
ev - er, Lord, your peo - ple go, Pro - tect them by your
all who dare the ea - gle's flight, And keep them by your
tect them where - so - e'er they go; Thus ev - er - more with

ear - nest - ly For those in per - il on the sea.
guard - ing hand From ev - ery per - il on the land.
watch - ful care From ev - ery per - il in the air.
thanks shall we Give praise from air and land and sea. A - men.

Stanzas 2 and 3 used by permission of The Church Pension Fund.

Eternal God, Whose Power Upholds

357

FOREST GREEN C.M.D.

Henry Hallam Tweedy, 1929; alt., 1972

Traditional English melody, collected and
harm. by Ralph Vaughan Williams, 1906

1. E - ter - nal God, whose power up-holds Both flower and flam-ing star,
2. O God of truth, whom sci - ence seeks And rev - erent souls a - dore,
3. O God of beau - ty, oft re-vealed In dreams of hu - man art,
4. O God of righ - teous-ness and grace, Seen in the Christ, your Son,

To whom there is no here nor there, No time, no near nor far,
Il - lu - mine ev - ery ear - nest mind Of ev - ery clime and shore:
In speech that flows to mel - o - dy, In ho - li - ness of heart:
Whose life and death re - veal your face, By whom your will was done;

No a - lien race, no for - eign shore, No child un-sought, un - known:
Dis - pel the gloom of er - ror's night, Of ig - no - rance and fear,
Teach us to ban all ug - li - ness, And all dis - har - mo - ny,
Help us to spread your gra - cious reign Till greed and hate shall cease,

O send us forth, your proph-ets true, To make all lands your own!
Un - til true wis - dom from a - bove Shall make life's path-way clear!
Till all shall know the love - li - ness Of lives made fair and free!
And kind-ness dwell in hu - man hearts, And all the earth find peace! A-men.

358   Eternal Ruler of the Ceaseless Round

SONG 1 10.10.10.10.10.10.

John W. Chadwick, 1864

Orlando Gibbons, 1623

1. E - ter - nal Rul - er of the cease-less round Of cir - cling plan-ets sing-ing
2. We are of thee, the chil-dren of thy love, The broth-ers of thy well-be-
*3. We would be one in ha - tred of all wrong, One in our love of all things
4. O clothe us with thy heav-enly ar - mor, Lord, Thy trust-y shield, thy sword of

on their way, Guide of the na - tions from the night pro - found
lov - ed Son; De - scend, O Ho - ly Spir - it, like a dove
sweet and fair, One with the joy that break-eth in - to song,
love di - vine; Our in - spi - ra - tion be thy con - stant word;

In - to the glo - ry of the per - fect day, Rule in our hearts, that
In - to our hearts, that we may be as one: As one with thee, to
One with the grief that trem-bleth in - to prayer, One in the power that
We ask no vic - to - ries that are not thine; Give or with-hold, let

we may ev - er be Guid - ed and strength-ened and up-held by thee.
whom we ev - er tend; As one with him our broth-er and our friend.
makes thy chil-dren free To fol - low truth, and thus to fol - low thee.
pain or plea-sure be, E - nough to know that we are serv - ing thee. A - men.

Every Star Shall Sing a Carol

Sydney Carter, 1961
Arr. by Richard D. Wetzel, 1972

Sydney Carter, 1961

1. Ev - ery star shall sing a car - ol,
2. When the King of all cre - a - tion
3. Who can tell what oth - er cra - dle
4. Who can count how man - y cross - es
5. Who can tell what oth - er bod - y
6. Ev - ery star and ev - ery plan - et,

Ev - ery crea - ture, high or low, Come and praise the
Had a cra - dle on the earth, Ho - ly was the
High a - bove the milk - y way Still may rock the
Still to come or long a - go, Cru - ci - fy the
He will hal - low for his own? I will praise the
Ev - ery crea - ture high and low, Come and praise the

King of heav - en By what - ev - er name you know.
hu - man bod - y, Ho - ly was the hu - man birth.
King of heav - en On an - oth - er Christ - mas Day?
King of heav - en? Ho - ly is the name I know.
son of Mar - y, Broth - er of my blood and bone.
King of heav - en By what - ev - er name you know.

God a - bove, Man be - low, Ho - ly is the name I know.

360 Fairest Lord Jesus

CRUSADERS' HYMN 5.6.8.5.5.8.

MS., Münster, 1662; alt.
Sts. 1-3 trans. in *Church Chorals
and Choir Studies*, 1850
St. 4 trans. by Joseph A. Seiss, 1873

Silesian folk melody
In *Schlesische Volkslieder*, 1842

1. Fair - est Lord Je - sus, Rul - er of all na - ture,
   O thou of God and man the Son, Thee will I cher - ish,
   Thee will I hon - or, Thou, my soul's glo - ry, joy, and crown.

2. Fair are the mead - ows, Fair - er still the wood - lands,
   Robed in the bloom - ing garb of spring: Je - sus is fair - er,
   Je - sus is pur - er, Who makes the woe - ful heart to sing.

3. Fair is the sun - shine, Fair - er still the moon - light,
   And all the twin - kling, star - ry host: Je - sus shines bright - er,
   Je - sus shines pur - er, Than all the an - gels heaven can boast.

4. Beau - ti - ful Sav - ior, Lord of the na - tions,
   Son of God and Son of Man! Glo - ry and hon - or,
   Praise, ad - o - ra - tion, Now and for - ev - er - more be thine! A-men.

Faith of Our Fathers

361

ST. CATHERINE 8.8.8.8.8.8.

Frederick W. Faber, 1849; alt.

Henri F. Hemy, 1864
Refrain, James G. Walton, 1874

1. Faith of our fa-thers! liv-ing still In spite of dun-geon,
fire, and sword, O how our hearts beat high with joy
When-e'er we hear that glo-rious word:

2. Faith of our fa-thers! God's great power Shall win all na-tions
un-to thee; And through the truth that comes from God
Man-kind shall then be tru-ly free: Faith of our fa-thers,

3. Faith of our fa-thers! we will love Both friend and foe in
all our strife, And preach thee, too, as love knows how,
By kind-ly words and vir-tuous life:

ho-ly faith! We will be true to thee till death. A-men.

362 Father Eternal, Ruler of Creation

LANGHAM 11.10.11.10.10.

Laurence Housman, 1919; alt.

Geoffrey Shaw, 1921

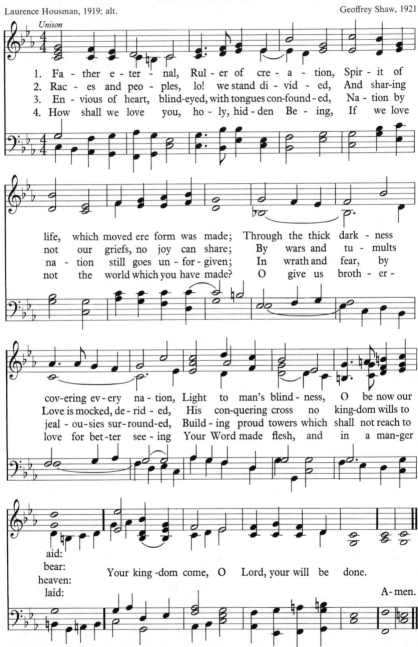

1. Fa - ther e - ter - nal, Rul - er of cre - a - tion, Spir - it of life, which moved ere form was made; Through the thick dark - ness cov - ering ev - ery na - tion, Light to man's blind - ness, O be now our aid:
2. Rac - es and peo - ples, lo! we stand di - vid - ed, And shar - ing not our griefs, no joy can share; By wars and tu - mults Love is mocked, de - rid - ed, His con - quering cross no king - dom wills to bear:
3. En - vious of heart, blind-eyed, with tongues con-found - ed, Na - tion by na - tion still goes un - for - given; In wrath and fear, by jeal - ou - sies sur - round - ed, Build - ing proud towers which shall not reach to heaven:
4. How shall we love you, ho - ly, hid - den Be - ing, If we love not the world which you have made? O give us broth - er - love for bet - ter see - ing Your Word made flesh, and in a man - ger laid:

Your king - dom come, O Lord, your will be done.

A - men.

Words altered from *Songs of Praise*, Enlarged Edition; used by permission of Oxford University Press. Music used by permission of the League of Nations Union.

Father, in Your Mysterious Presence

DONNE SECOURS 11.10.11.10.

363

Samuel Johnson, 1846; alt., 1972

Comp. or adapted by Louis Bourgeois, 1551

1. Fa - ther, in your mys - te - rious pres - ence kneel - ing,
2. Lord, we have wan - dered forth through doubt and sor - row,
3. Now, Fa - ther, now, in your dear pres - ence kneel - ing,

Now would our souls feel all your kin - dling
And you have made each step an on - ward
Our spir - its yearn to feel your kin - dling

love, For we are weak and need some deep re - veal - ing
one, And we will ev - er trust each un - known mor - row;
love; Now make us strong, we need your deep re - veal - ing

Of trust and strength and calm - ness from a - bove.
You will sus - tain us till its work is done.
Of trust and strength and calm - ness from a - bove. A - men.

364 Father, We Greet You

DONNE SECOURS 11.10.11.10.

James G. Adderley, 1924; alt., 1972   Comp. or adapted by Louis Bourgeois, 1551

1. Fa - ther, we greet you, God of love, whose glo - ry
2. Fa - ther, we dare, by our great Broth - er bid - den,
3. Here we pre - sent our - selves, our souls and bod - ies,
4. Friends at his ta - ble, priests a - round his al - tar,

Shines mir - rored in the face of Je - sus
Take up the cross and hum - bly fol - low
Strength - ened with bread, the food of ev - ery
Sol - diers of Christ, dis - ci - ples of your

Christ, Who by his per - fect life of love and la - bor
him: Send out your light and truth that they may lead us;
man, Read - y to love and work, but yet con - fess - ing
Son, Fa - ther, we stand, pre - pared to do your bid - ding;

And in his per - fect death was sac - ri - ficed.
Show us the way a - mid the dark - ness dim.
Lone - ly we can - not, by his grace we can.
Come, God's own king - dom, and God's will be done. A - men.

Father, We Praise You

365

CHRISTE SANCTORUM 11.11.11.5.

Attr. to Gregory I (540-604)
Trans. by Percy Dearmer, 1906; alt., 1972

Paris Antiphoner, 1681
Harm. by David Evans, 1927

1. Fa - ther, we praise you, now the night is o - ver;
2. Mon - arch of all things, fit us for your man - sions;
3. All - ho - ly Fa - ther, Son, and e - qual Spir - it,

Ac - tive and watch - ful, stand we all be - fore you;
Ban - ish our weak - ness, health and whole-ness send - ing;
Trin - i - ty bless - ed, send us your sal - va - tion;

Sing - ing, we of - fer prayer and med - i -
Bring us to heav - en, where your saints u -
Yours is the glo - ry, gleam - ing and re -

ta - tion: Thus we a - dore you.
nit - ed Joy with - out end - ing.
sound - ing Through all cre - a - tion. A - men.

Words altered from *The English Hymnal*; music from *The Church Hymnary*, Revised Edition, 1927; used by permission of Oxford University Press.

366 Father, We Thank You that You Planted

RENDEZ À DIEU 9.8.9.8.D.

Greek, 1st or 2d century
Para. by F. Bland Tucker, 1939; alt., 1972

Comp. or adapted by Louis Bourgeois, 1543, 1551

1. Fa - ther, we thank you that you plant - ed Your ho - ly
2. Watch o'er the church, O Lord, in mer - cy, Save it from

name with-in our hearts. Knowl-edge and faith and life im - mor - tal
e - vil, guard it still; Per - fect it in your love, u - nite it,

Je - sus your Son to us im - parts. You, Lord, have made all for your
Cleansed and con-formed un - to your will. As grain, once scat - tered on the

plea - sure And given man food for all his days, Giv - ing in
hill - sides, Was in this bro - ken bread made one, So from all

Christ the Bread e - ter - nal; Yours is the power, be yours the praise.
lands your church be gath - ered In - to your king -dom by your Son. A - men.

368 Father, Whose Will Is Life and Good

NUN DANKET ALL' (GRÄFENBERG) C.M.

Hardwicke D. Rawnsley, 1922; alt.

Crüger's *Praxis Pietatis Melica*, 1653

1. Fa - ther, whose will is life and good For all of
2. Em - power the hands and hearts and wills Of friends both
3. Wher - e'er they heal the maimed and blind, Let love of
4. O Fa - ther, look from heaven and bless What-e'er your

mor - tal breath, Bind strong the bond of
near and far, Who bat - tle with the
Christ at - tend: Pro - claim the good Phy -
serv - ants do, Their works of pure un -

broth - er - hood Of those who fight with death.
bod - y's ills And wage your ho - ly war.
si - cian's mind, And prove the Sav - ior friend.
self - ish - ness, Made con - se - crate to you. A - men.

For All the Saints

369

SINE NOMINE 10.10.10. with Alleluias

William Walsham How, 1864; alt.

Ralph Vaughan Williams, 1906; alt., 1927

1. For all the saints who from their la-bors rest, All who by faith be-fore the world con-fessed, Your name, O Je-sus, be for-ev-er blest.
2. You were their rock, their for-tress, and their might; Je-sus, their cap-tain in the well-fought fight; You in the dark-ness drear, their one true Light.
3. O may your sol-diers, faith-ful, true, and bold, Fight as the saints who no-bly fought of old, And win with them the vic-tor's crown of gold.
4. O blest com-mu-nion, fel-low-ship di-vine! We fee-bly strug-gle, they in glo-ry shine; all are one with-in your great de-sign.
5. And when the strife is fierce, the war-fare long, Steals on the ear the dis-tant tri-umph song, And hearts are brave a-gain, and arms are strong.
6. From earth's wide bounds, from o-cean's far-thest coast, Through gates of pearl streams in the count-less host, Sing-ing to Fa-ther, Son, and Ho-ly Ghost,

Music from *The English Hymnal Service Book*;
used by permission of Oxford University Press.

See following page.

Al - le-lu - ia! Al - le-lu - ia!

Harmony

A - men.

Harmony, stanzas 3, 4

3. O may your sol - diers, faith-ful, true, and bold, Fight as the saints who
4. O blest com - mu - nion, fel - low-ship di - vine! We fee - bly strug - gle,

no - bly fought of old, And win with them the vic - tor's crown of
they in glo - ry shine; Yet all are one with - in your great de -

D.C. for stanza 5

Al - le - lu - ia!

gold. Al - le - lu - ia! Al - le - lu - ia!
sign.

For Perfect Love So Freely Spent

CHESHIRE C.M.

Louise Marshall McDowell, 1965

Este's Psalter, 1592
As in *Songs of Syon*, 1910

1. For per - fect love so free - ly spent, For
2. We come, by sin dis - qui - et - ed, And
3. A - bide with us; in all our ways Your

fel - low - ship re - stored, We cel - e - brate the
find our lives made whole; A - round this ta - ble
sav - ing love be shown. So may our lives be

sac - ra - ment And sing your praise, O Lord.
we are fed Re - fresh - ment for the soul.
hymns of praise, O Christ, to you a - lone. A - men.

372 For the Beauty of the Earth

DIX 7.7.7.7.7.7.

Sts. 1-4, Folliott S. Pierpoint, 1864; alt.
St. 5, composite

Conrad Kocher, 1838
Abr. by William Henry Monk, 1861

1. For the beau-ty of the earth, For the glo-ry of the skies,
2. For the won-der of each hour Of the day and of the night,
3. For the joy of ear and eye, For the heart and mind's de-light,
4. For the joy of hu-man love, Broth-er, sis-ter, par-ent, child,
5. For your-self, best gift di-vine, To all men so free-ly given,

For the love which from our birth O - ver and a - round us lies,
Hill and vale, and tree and flower, Sun and moon, and stars of light,
For the mys-tic har-mo-ny Link-ing sense to sound and sight,
Friends on earth, and friends a - bove, For all gen - tle thoughts and mild,
For your great, great love's de - sign— Peace on earth and joy in heaven

Lord of all, to you we raise This our hymn of grate-ful praise. A-men.

From All That Dwell Below the Skies 373

LASST UNS ERFREUEN L.M. with Alleluias

Based on Psalm 117
Isaac Watts, 1719

Geistliche Kirchengesäng, Cologne, 1623
Arr. and harm. by Ralph Vaughan Williams, 1906

1. From all that dwell be-low the skies Let the Cre-a-tor's praise a-
2. In ev-ery land be-gin the song, To ev-ery land the strains be-
3. E-ter-nal are your mer-cies, Lord; E-ter-nal truth at-tends your

rise: Al-le-lu-ia! Al-le-lu-ia! Let the Re-deem-er's
long: Al-le-lu-ia! Al-le-lu-ia! In cheer-ful sound all
word: Al-le-lu-ia! Al-le-lu-ia! Your praise shall sound from

name be sung Through ev-ery land, in ev-ery tongue.
voic-es raise And fill the world with joy-ful praise. Al-le-lu-ia!
shore to shore, Till suns shall rise and set no more.

Al-le-lu-ia! Al-le-lu-ia! Al-le-lu-ia! Al-le-lu-ia! A-men.

Music from *The English Hymnal*;
used by permission of Oxford University Press.

For higher key, see "All Creatures of Our God and King."

374 From Shepherding of Stars

SHEPHERDING C.M.

F. Samuel Janzow, 1963

Richard Hillert, 1963

1. From shep-herd-ing of stars that gaze Toward heav-enly fields of
2. Your Shep-herd-King from star-lit hall Bends down to wea-ry
3. This night your King brings from a-far The Vir-gin's lull-a-
4. He shep-herds from the this-tled place The flock by thick-ets
5. Cra-dle the Christ-child, and with songs Bind up the hearts of

light, I come with ti-dings to a-maze You
lands, Lies man-gered low in cat-tle stall. Go
by, The Wise Men's faith, a guid-ing star, And
torn, His pierc-ed hand heals all your race— Sore
men: To Shep-herd-Heal-er-King let throngs Sing

watch-ers in the night, You watch-ers in the night.
touch his in-fant hands, Go touch his in-fant hands.
love from God most high, And love from God most high.
wound-ed by the thorn, Sore wound-ed by the thorn.
glo-ri-as a-gain, Sing glo-ri-as a-gain.

Gentle Mary Laid Her Child

375

TEMPUS ADEST FLORIDUM 7.6.7.6.D.

Joseph Simpson Cook, 1919

Piae Cantiones, 1582
Harm. by Ernest MacMillan, 1930

1. Gen - tle Mar - y laid her child Low - ly in a man - ger;
2. An - gels sang a - bout his birth; Wise Men sought and found him;
3. Gen - tle Mar - y laid her child Low - ly in a man - ger;

There he lay, the un - de - filed, To the world a stran - ger.
Heav - en's star shone bright - ly forth, Glo - ry all a - round him.
He is still the un - de - filed, But no more a stran - ger.

Such a babe in such a place, Can he be the Sav - ior?
Shep - herds saw the won - drous sight, Heard the an - gels sing - ing;
Son of God, of hum - ble birth, Beau - ti - ful the sto - ry;

Ask the saved of all the race Who have found his fa - vor.
All the plains were lit that night; All the hills were ring - ing.
Praise his name in all the earth; Hail the King of glo - ry! A - men.

376 Give to Our God Immortal Praise

ELTON L.M.

Isaac Watts, 1719

Lowell Mason, 1854

1. Give to our God im - mor - tal praise; Mer - cy and
2. He built the earth, he spread the sky, And fixed the
3. He sent his Son with power to save From guilt and

truth are all his ways;
star - ry lights on high; Won - ders of grace to God be - long,
dark - ness and the grave;

Re - peat his mer - cies in your song. A - men.

Give to the Winds Your Fears

ST. BRIDE S.M.

377

Paul Gerhardt, 1653
Trans. by John Wesley, 1739; alt.

Samuel Howard, 1762

1. Give to the winds your fears; In hope be
2. To him com-mit your griefs; Your ways put
3. O put your trust in God; In du-ty's
4. Leave to his sov-ereign sway To choose and

un-dis-mayed: God hears your sighs and
in his hands— To his sure truth and
path go on. Walk in his strength with
to com-mand; So you shall, faith-ful,

counts your tears, God shall lift up your head.
ten-der care Who earth and heaven com-mands.
faith and hope, So shall your work be done.
seek his way— How wise, how strong his hand! A-men.

378 Glorious Is Your Name, Most Holy

AUSTRIAN HYMN 8.7.8.7.D.

Ruth Elliot, 1960; alt., 1972

Franz Joseph Haydn, 1797

1. Glo-rious is your name, Most Ho-ly, God and Fa-ther of us all;
2. For our world of need and an-guish We would lift to you our prayer.
3. In the midst of time we jour-ney; From your hand comes each new day:

We, your ser-vants, bow be-fore you, Strive to an-swer ev-ery call.
Faith-ful stew-ards of your boun-ty, May we with our broth-ers share.
We would use it in your serv-ice, Hum-bly, wise-ly, while we may.

You with life's great good have blest us, Cared for us from ear-liest years;
In the name of Christ our Sav-ior, Who re-deems and sets us free,
So to you, Lord and Cre-a-tor, Praise and hon-or we ac-cord!

Un-to you our thanks we ren-der; Your deep love o'er-comes all fears.
Gifts we bring of heart and trea-sure, That our lives may wor-thier be.
Yours the earth and yours the heav-ens, Through all time the e-ter-nal Word. A-men.

Glorious Things of You Are Spoken

AUSTRIAN HYMN 8.7.8.7.D.

John Newton, 1779; alt., 1972

Franz Joseph Haydn, 1797

379

1. Glo-rious things of you are spo-ken, Zi-on, cit-y of our God;
2. See, the streams of liv-ing wa-ters, Spring-ing from e-ter-nal Love,
3. Round each hab-i-ta-tion hov-ering, See the cloud and fire ap-pear

He whose word can-not be bro-ken Formed you for his own a-bode.
Well sup-ply your sons and daugh-ters, And all fears of want re-move:
For a glo-ry and a cov-ering, Show-ing that the Lord is near:

On the Rock of Ag-es found-ed, What can shake your sure re-pose?
Who can faint, while such a riv-er Flows their thirst to sat-is-fy?
Thus de-riv-ing from their ban-ner Light by night and shade by day,

With sal-va-tion's walls sur-round-ed, You may smile at all your foes.
Grace, which, like the Lord the giv-er, Nev-er fails; he does sup-ply.
Safe they feed up-on the man-na Which he gives them when they pray. A-men.

380 Go, Tell It on the Mountain
GO TELL IT P.M.

Refrain, Negro spiritual
Stanzas, John W. Work, Jr. (1871-1925); alt.

Negro spiritual
Arr. by Hugh Porter, 1958

Unison

Go, tell it on the moun-tain, O-ver the hills and ev-ery-where;

Go, tell it on the moun-tain That Je-sus Christ is born!

Harmony

1. While shep-herds kept their watch-ing O'er si-lent flocks by night, Be-
2. The shep-herds feared and trem-bled When lo! a-bove the earth Rang
3. Down in a low-ly man-ger The hum-ble Christ was born, And

hold through-out the heav-ens There shone a ho-ly light.
out the an-gel cho-rus That hailed our Sav-ior's birth.
God sent us sal-va-tion That bless-ed Christ-mas morn.

God Gives His People Strength

Miriam Therese Winter, 1965

Miriam Therese Winter, 1965
Arr. by Richard D. Wetzel, 1972

1. God gives his peo-ple strength. If we be-
2. God gives his peo-ple hope. If we but
3. God gives his peo-ple love. If we but
4. God gives his peo-ple peace. When sor-row

lieve in his way, He's swift to re-
trust in his word, Our prayers are al-ways
o - pen wide our heart, He's sure to do his
fills us to the brim, And cour - age grows

pay. All those who bear the bur - den of the
heard. He warm - ly wel - comes an - y - one who's
part; He's al - ways the first to make a
dim, He lays to rest our rest - less - ness in

day. God gives his peo - ple strength.
erred. God gives his peo - ple hope.
start. God gives his peo - ple love.
him. God gives his peo - ple peace.

382 God Has Spoken—by His Prophets

EBENEZER (TON-Y-BOTEL) 8.7.8.7.D.

George Wallace Briggs, 1952; alt., 1972

Thomas John Williams, 1890

1. God has spo - ken— by his proph-ets, Spo - ken his un -
2. God has spo - ken— by Christ Je - sus, Christ, the ev - er -
3. God yet speaks— by his own Spir - it Speak - ing to the

chang - ing Word, Each from age to age pro - claim - ing
last - ing Son, Bright - ness of the Fa - ther's glo - ry,
hearts of men, In the age - long Word ex - pound - ing

God, the one, the righ-teous Lord. Mid the world's de - spair and
With the Fa - ther ev - er one; Spo - ken by the Word in -
God's own mes-sage, now as then; Through the rise and fall of

tur - moil, One firm an - chor hold - ing fast; God is King, his
car - nate, God of God, ere time be - gan, Light of Light, to
na - tions One sure faith yet stand - ing fast, God is King, his

throne e - ter - nal, God the first, and God the last.
earth de - scend-ing, Man, re - veal - ing God to man.
Word un - chang-ing, God the first, and God the last. A - men.

God Himself Is with Us

ARNSBERG P.M.

Gerhard Tersteegen, 1729
Trans. composite, as in *The Hymnal*, 1941; alt., 1972

Attr. to Joachim Neander, 1680
Harm. by David Evans, 1927

1. God him-self is with us: Let us now a - dore him
2. God him-self is with us: Whom an - gel - ic le - gions
3. Lord, come dwell with - in us, While on earth we tar - ry;

And with awe ap - pear be - fore him. God is in his
Serve with awe in heav - enly re - gions. "Ho - ly, Ho - ly,
Make us your blest sanc - tu - ar - y. Grant us now your

tem - ple, All with - in keep si - lence, And be - fore him
Ho - ly," Sing the hosts of heav - en, Praise to God be
pres - ence, Un - to us draw near - er, And re - veal your-

Music from *The Church Hymnary*, Revised Edition, 1927; used by permission of Oxford University Press.

bow with rev - erence. Him a - lone, God we own;
ev - er giv - en. O give ear To us here:
self still clear - er. Where we are, Near or far,

To our Lord and Sav - ior Prais - es sing for - ev - er.
Hear, O Christ, the prais - es That your church now rais - es.
Let us see your pow - er, Ev - ery day and hour. A - men.

386 God Is Love: Let Heaven Adore Him

ABBOT'S LEIGH 8.7.8.7.D.

Timothy Rees (1874-1939); alt.

Cyril V. Taylor, 1951

1. God is love: let heaven a - dore him; God is love: let
2. God is love: he is en - fold - ing All the world in
3. God is love: and though with blind-ness Sin af - flicts the

earth re - joice; Let cre - a - tion sing be - fore him,
one em - brace; With un - fail - ing grasp he's hold - ing
souls of men, God's e - ter - nal lov - ing - kind-ness

And ex - alt him with one voice. He who laid the
Ev - ery child of ev - ery race. And when hu - man
Holds and guides them e - ven then. Sin and death and

Words altered from *Sermons and Hymns*, by Timothy Rees; used by permission of A. R. Mowbray & Co. Limited. Music from *The BBC Hymn Book*; used by permission of Oxford University Press.

earth's foun-da-tion, He who spread the heavens a-bove, He who
hearts are break-ing Un-der sor-row's i - ron rod, All the
hell shall nev-er O'er us fi - nal tri - umph gain; God is

breathes through all cre - a - tion, He is love, e - ter - nal love.
sor - row, all the ach - ing, Wrings with pain the heart of God.
love, so love for - ev - er O'er the u - ni - verse must reign. A-men.

388 God Is Our Strong Salvation

WEDLOCK 7.6.7.6.D.

From Psalm 27
Para. by James Montgomery, 1822; alt., 1972

Folk song melody
Collected by Cecil J. Sharp, 1918
Harm. by Richard D. Wetzel, 1972

1. God is our strong sal - va - tion; What foe have we to fear?
2. Place on the Lord re - li - ance; Have faith, with cour - age wait;

In dark - ness and temp - ta - tion Our light, our help is near.
His truth be your af - fi - ance, When faint and des - o - late.

Though hosts en - camp a - round us, Firm to the fight we stand;
His might your heart shall strength - en, His love your joy in - crease;

What ter - ror can con - found us, With God at our right hand?
Your days shall mer - cy length - en; The Lord will give you peace. A - men.

Melody from *English Folk Songs from the Southern Appalachians*; used by permission of Oxford University Press. Harmonization copyright 1972 by The Westminster Press.

God Is Working His Purpose Out

389

PURPOSE Irregular

Arthur Campbell Ainger, 1894

Martin Shaw, 1931

1. God is work-ing his pur-pose out As year suc-
2. What can we do to work God's work, To pros - per
3. March we forth in the strength of God, With the ban-ner of
4. All we can do is noth-ing worth Un - less God

ceeds to year: God is work-ing his
and in - crease The broth - er - hood of
Christ un - furled, That the light of the glo - rious
bless - es the deed; Vain - ly we hope for the

pur - pose out, And the time is draw-ing near; Near - er and
all man - kind, The reign of the Prince of Peace? What can we
gos - pel of truth May shine through-out the world: Fight we the
har - vest - tide Till God gives life to the seed; Yet near - er and

near - er draws the time, The time that shall sure-ly be,
do to has-ten the time, The time that shall sure-ly be,
fight with sor-row and sin To set their cap-tives free,
near - er draws the time, The time that shall sure-ly be,

Music from *Songs of Praise*, Enlarged Edition; used by permission of Oxford University Press. *See following page.*

When the earth shall be filled with the glo - ry of God
When the earth shall be filled with the glo - ry of God
That the earth shall be filled with the glo - ry of God
When the earth shall be filled with the glo - ry of God

Sts. 1-3 | St. 4

As the wa - ters cov - er the sea.
As the wa - ters cov - er the sea.
As the wa - ters cov - er the sea.
As the wa - ters cov - er the   sea.   A-men.

God Moves in a Mysterious Way

DUNDEE (FRENCH) C.M.

William Cowper, 1774; alt., 1972

Scottish Psalter, 1615

391

1. God moves in a mys - te - rious way His
   won - ders to per - form; He plants his foot - steps
   in the sea, And rides up - on the storm.

2. Deep in un - fath - om - a - ble mines Of
   nev - er - fail - ing skill He trea - sures up his
   bright de - signs, And works his sov - ereign will.

3. You fear - ful saints, fresh cour - age take; The
   clouds you so much dread Are big with mer - cy,
   and shall break In bless - ings on your head.

4. Blind un - be - lief is sure to err, And
   scan his work in vain; God is his own In -
   ter - pret - er, And he will make it plain. A - men.

392 God of Compassion, in Mercy Befriend Us

O QUANTA QUALIA 11.11.11.11.

John J. Moment, 1933(?); alt., 1972

Paris Antiphoner, 1681
Harm. by David Evans, 1927

1. God of com-pas-sion, in mer-cy be-friend us;
Giv-er of grace for our needs all-a-vail-ing.
Wis-dom and strength for each day you will send us,
Pa-tience un-tir-ing and cour-age un-fail-ing.

2. Wan-dering and lost, you have sought us and found us,
Stilled our rude hearts with your word of con-sol-ing;
Wrap now your peace, like a man-tle, a-round us,
Guard-ing our thoughts and our pas-sions con-trol-ling.

3. How shall we stray, with the hand to di-rect us
That all the stars in their cours-es is guid-ing?
What shall we fear, with your power to pro-tect us,
We who walk forth in your great-ness con-fid-ing? A-men.

Music from *The Church Hymnary*, Revised Edition, 1927; used by permission of Oxford University Press.

God of Grace and God of Glory

393

CWM RHONDDA 8.7.8.7.8.7.

Harry Emerson Fosdick, 1930; alt., 1972

John Hughes, 1907

1. God of grace and God of glo - ry, On your peo - ple
2. Lo! the hosts of e - vil round us Scorn the Christ, as -
3. Cure your chil - dren's war - ring mad - ness, Bend our pride to
4. Save us from weak res - ig - na - tion To the e - vils

pour your power; Crown the an - cient church's sto - ry; Bring her bud to
sail his ways! From the fears that long have bound us, Free our hearts to
your con - trol; Shame our wan - ton, self - ish glad - ness, Rich in things and
we de - plore; Let the search for your sal - va - tion Be our glo - ry

glo - rious flower. Grant us wis - dom, grant us cour - age,
faith and praise. Grant us wis - dom, grant us cour - age,
poor in soul. Grant us wis - dom, grant us cour - age,
ev - er - more. Grant us wis - dom, grant us cour - age,

For the fac - ing of this hour, For the fac - ing of this hour.
For the liv - ing of these days, For the liv - ing of these days.
Lest we miss the king-dom's goal, Lest we miss the king-dom's goal.
Serv - ing God whom we a-dore, Serv - ing God whom we a - dore. A - men.

Words used by permission of Elinor F. Downs. Music © by Mrs. Dilys Webb, c/o Mechanical-Copyright Protection Society Ltd., and reproduced by permission of the legal representatives of the composer who reserve all rights therein.

394 God of Our Fathers, Whose Almighty Hand

NATIONAL HYMN 10.10.10.10.

Daniel C. Roberts, 1876

George William Warren, 1892

Trumpets (with each stanza)

1. God of our fa - thers, whose al - might - y hand
2. Thy love di - vine hath led us in the past;
3. From war's a - larms, from dead - ly pes - ti - lence,
4. Re - fresh thy peo - ple on their toil - some way,

Leads forth in beau - ty all the star - ry band
In this free land by thee our lot is cast;
Be thy strong arm our ev - er sure de - fense;
Lead us from night to nev - er - end - ing day;

Of shin - ing worlds in splen - dor through the skies,
Be thou our rul - er, guard - ian, guide, and stay;
Thy true re - li - gion in our hearts in - crease;
Fill all our lives with love and grace di - vine,

Our grate - ful songs be - fore thy throne a - rise.
Thy word our law, thy paths our cho - sen way.
Thy boun - teous good - ness nour - ish us in peace.
And glo - ry, laud, and praise be ev - er thine. A - men.

God of Our Life, Through All the Circling Years 395

WITMER 10.4.10.4.10.10.

Hugh T. Kerr, 1916; alt., 1928, 1972   Richard D. Wetzel, 1969

1. God of our life, through all the cir-cling years, We trust in you;
2. God of the past, our times are in your hand; With us a - bide.
3. God of the com - ing years, through paths un-known We fol - low you;

In all the past, through all our hopes and fears, Your hand we view.
Lead us by faith to hope's true Prom-ised Land; Be now our guide.
When we are strong, Lord, leave us not a - lone; Our faith re - new.

With each new day, when morn - ing lifts the veil,
With you to bless, the dark - ness shines as light,
Be now for us in life our dai - ly bread,

We own your mer - cies, Lord, which nev - er fail.
And faith's fair vi - sion chang - es in - to sight.
Our heart's true home when all our years have sped. A - men.

396 God of the Ages, by Whose Hand

GOD OF THE AGES L.M.

Elisabeth Burrowes, 1956, 1971

David N. Johnson, 1964

1. God of the ag - es, by whose hand Through years long past our
2. You are the thought be - yond all thought, The gift be - yond our
3. Lift up our hearts and set us free From wild a - larms and
4. Though there be dark, un - chart - ed space With worlds on worlds be -

lives were led, Give us new cour - age now to
ut - most prayer; No far - thest reach where you are
trem - bling fears; In your strong hand e - ter - nal -
yond our sight, Still may we trust your love and

stand, New faith to find the paths a - head.
not, No height but we may find you there.
ly Rests the un - fold - ing of the years.
grace And wait your word, "Let there be light." A - men.

God of the Living, in Whose Eyes 397

GOTTLOB, ES GEHT 8.8.8.8.8.8.8.

John Ellerton, 1859, 1862; alt., 1972

Comp. or arr. by J. S. Bach, 1769
As in *The Harvard University Hymn Book*, 1926

1. God of the liv - ing, in whose eyes Un-veiled your
2. Re - leased from earth - ly toil and strife, With you is
3. Your word is true, your will is just; To you we

whole cre - a - tion lies, All souls are yours; we must not say
hid - den still their life; Yours are their thoughts, their works, their powers,
leave them, Lord, in trust, And bless you for the love which gave

That those are dead who pass a - way; From this our
All yours, and yet most tru - ly ours, For well we
Your Son to fill a hu - man grave, That none might

world of flesh set free, We know they live e - ter - nal - ly.
know, wher-e'er they be, Our dead now live e - ter - nal - ly.
fear that world to see Where all do live e - ter - nal - ly. A - men.

398 God of the Prophets! Bless the Prophets' Sons

TOULON 10.10.10.10.

Denis Wortman, 1884; alt.

Comp. or adapted by Louis Bourgeois, 1551
Abr. in English Psalters

1. God of the proph - ets! Bless the proph - ets' sons,
2. A - noint them proph - ets! Make their ears at - tent
3. A - noint them priests! Strong in - ter - ces - sors they
4. Make them a - pos - tles! Her - alds of the cross,

Elijah's mantle o'er Elisha cast;
To your divinest speech; their hearts a - wake
For pardon, and for charity and peace!
Forth may they go to tell all realms your grace;

Each age its solemn task may claim but once;
To human need; their lips make eloquent
O that with them might pass the world, a - stray,
In - spired of God, may they count all but loss,

Make each one nobler, stronger, than the last.
To gird the right and every evil break.
In - to the dear Christ's life of sacrifice!
And stand at last with joy before your face. A - men.

God Our Father, You Our Maker

399

BAKER 8.9.8.9.D.

Robert W. McClellan, 1950, 1969   Mary Elizabeth Caldwell, 1950, 1969

1. God our Fa - ther, you our Mak - er, We your peo - ple heed your sov-ereign call; Bow be - fore you, pay - ing hom - age, Own - ing you a - lone as Lord of all. May your wis - dom be our por - tion,

2. Christ our Lead - er, Lord and Sav - ior, You the on - ly Way and Truth and Life; Make your pres - ence known a - mong us, Giv - ing peace to each and set - tling strife. May we learn from you our Teach - er,

3. Ho - ly Spir - it, good com - pan - ion, You the lov - ing Guide the Fa - ther sends; Gent - ly urge us; ev - er stir us To up - hold the Truth toward ho - ly ends. Light of God, dis - pel our dark - ness,

4. Church of Je - sus, church with vi - sion, Built with liv - ing faith and hope to stand; May your peo - ple, now re - joic - ing, Raise your song of praise through - out the land. May your walls be strong and stur - dy;

See following page.

And with - in our hearts your love in - still.
God - ly du - ty as your love de - mands.
And to wait - ing hearts make par - don known.
And your tow - er point to God on high.

Lead us for - ward, ev - er up - ward.
Live with - in us, gra - cious Mas - ter;
Grant your com - fort, now be - friend us;
Let these sym - bols, ev - er pres - ent,

Give us grace to do your ho - ly will.
Grant us strength to fol - low your com - mands.
Then shall qui - et cour - age be our own.
Help us know that God is al - ways nigh. A - men.

God Rest You Merry, Gentlemen

GOD REST YOU MERRY Irregular with Refrain

English carol, 18th century

English carol, 18th century
Harm. by John Stainer, 1871

May be sung in unison

1. God rest you mer - ry, gen - tle - men, Let noth - ing you dis - may;
2. From God, our heav - enly Fa - ther, A bless - ed an - gel came;
3. "Fear not, then," said the an - gel, "Let noth - ing you af - fright;
4. Now to the Lord sing prais - es, All you with - in this place,

Re - mem - ber Christ, our Sav - ior, Was born on Christ - mas Day,
And un - to cer - tain shep - herds Brought ti - dings of the same:
This day is born a Sav - ior, Of a pure vir - gin bright,
And with true love and broth - er - hood Each oth - er now em - brace;

To save us all from Sa - tan's power When we were gone a - stray.
How that in Beth - le - hem was born The Son of God by name.
To free all those who trust in him From Sa - tan's power and might."
This ho - ly tide of Christ - mas Doth bring re - deem - ing grace.

See following page.

God, the Lord, a King Remaineth

BRYN CALFARIA 8.7.8.7.4.7.

Based on Psalm 93
John Keble, 1839; alt.

William Owen (1814-1893)

1. God, the Lord, a King re-main-eth, Robed in his own glo-rious light;
2. In her ev - er - last-ing sta - tion Earth is poised, to swerve no more;
*3. With all tones of wa-ters blend-ing, Glo-rious is the break-ing deep;
4. Lord, the words thy lips are tell - ing Are the per - fect ver - i - ty;

God hath robed him - self and reign-eth; He hath girt him - self with might.
Thou hast laid thy throne's foun-da - tion From all time where thought can soar.
Glo-rious, beau-teous, with-out end - ing, God, who reigns on heaven's high steep.
Of thy high e - ter - nal dwell-ing, Ho - li - ness shall in - mate be:

Al - le - lu - ia! Al - le - lu - ia! Al - le - lu - ia!

God is King in depth and height! God is King in depth and height!
Lord, thou art for - ev - er - more! Lord, thou art for - ev - er - more!
Songs of o - cean nev - er sleep. Songs of o - cean nev - er sleep.
Pure is all that lives with thee. Pure is all that lives with thee. A-men.

404 God, Who Made the Earth and Heaven

AR HYD Y NOS 8.4.8.4.8.4.8.8.8.4.

St. 1, Reginald Heber, 1827; alt., 1972
St. 2, Frederick Lucian Hosmer, 1912; alt., 1972

Traditional Welsh melody
Harm. attr. to L. O. Emerson, 1906

1. God, who made the earth and heav-en, Dark-ness and light,
2. When the con-stant sun re-turn-ing Un-seals our eyes,

Who the day for toil has giv-en, For rest the night,
May we, re-born like the morn-ing, To la-bor rise;

May your lov-ing care de-fend us, Slum-ber sweet your mer-cy send us;
Gird us for the tasks that call us, Let not ease and self en-thrall us.

Ho-ly dreams and hopes at-tend us, This live-long night.
Make us strong what-e'er be-fall us, O God most wise! A-men.

God's Word Is like a Flaming Sword

OLD 107th C.M.D.

Carl Bernhard Garve, 1825
Trans. by Catherine Winkworth, 1855; alt., 1972

Comp. or adapted by Louis Bourgeois, 1543
As in Scottish Psalter, 1635

405

1. God's word is like a flam-ing sword, A wedge that cleaves the stone;
2. God's word, a won-drous guid-ing star, On pil-grim hearts does rise,

Keen as a fire, so burns his word, And pierc-es flesh and bone.
Leads those to God who dwell a-far, And makes the sim-ple wise.

Let it go forth o'er all the earth To cleanse our hearts with-in,
Let not its light e'er sink in night, But in each spir-it shine,

To show God's power in Sa-tan's hour, And break the might of sin.
That none may miss heaven's fi-nal bliss, Led by God's light di-vine. A-men.

406
Good Christian Men, Rejoice
IN DULCI JUBILO P.M.

Based on medieval carol
John Mason Neale, 1853

German carol, 14th century
Harm. by John Stainer, 1871

1. Good Chris-tian men, re - joice   With heart, and soul, and   voice;
2. Good Chris-tian men, re - joice   With heart, and soul, and   voice;
3. Good Chris-tian men, re - joice   With heart, and soul, and   voice;

Give ye heed to what we say: News! news! Je - sus Christ is born to - day.
Now ye hear of end - less bliss: Joy! joy! Je - sus Christ was born for this!
Now ye need not fear the grave: Peace! peace! Je - sus Christ was born to save!

Ox and ass be - fore him bow, And he   is   in   the man - ger now.
He has oped the heav - enly door, And man is bless - ed ev - er-more.
Calls you one and calls you all,   To gain his ev - er - last - ing hall.

Christ is born to - day!   Christ is born to - day!
Christ was born for   this!   Christ was born for   this!
Christ was born to   save!   Christ was born to   save!   A - men.

Good Christian Men, Rejoice and Sing

GELOBT SEI GOTT 8.8.8. with Alleluias

Cyril A. Alington, 1931; alt., 1972

Attr. to Melchior Vulpius, 1609
As in *Pilgrim Hymnal*, 1958

407

1. Good Chris-tian men, re - joice and sing! Now is the tri - umph
2. The Lord of life is risen to - day! Sing songs of praise a -
3. Praise we in songs of vic - to - ry That love, that life which
4. Your name we bless, O ris - en Lord, And sing to - day with

of our King! To all the world glad news we bring:
long his way; Let all man - kind re - joice and say:
can - not die, And sing with hearts up - lift - ed high:
one ac - cord The life laid down, the life re - stored:

Al - le - lu - ia! Al - le - lu - ia! Al - le - lu - ia! A - men.

408 Great God, We Sing That Mighty Hand

WAREHAM L.M.

Philip Doddridge, 1755; alt., 1972

William Knapp, 1738

1. Great God, we sing that mighty hand
By which sup - port - ed still we stand
The o - pening year your mer - cy shows;
That mer - cy crowns it till it close.

2. By day, by night, at home, a - broad,
Still are we guard - ed by our God;
By his in - ces - sant boun - ty fed,
By his un - err - ing coun - sel led.

3. With grate - ful hearts the past we own;
The fu - ture, all to us un - known,
We to your guard - ian care com - mit,
And peace - ful leave be - fore your feet.

4. In scenes ex - alt - ed or de - pressed,
You are our joy, and you our rest;
Your good - ness all our hopes shall raise,
A - dored through all our chang - ing days. A - men.

Guide Me, O Thou Great Jehovah

409

CWM RHONDDA 8.7.8.7.8.7.

William Williams, 1745
St. 1 trans. by Peter Williams, 1771
Sts. 2, 3 trans. by William or John Williams, ca. 1772

John Hughes, 1907

1. Guide me, O thou great Je - ho - vah, Pil - grim through this bar - ren land; I am weak, but thou art might - y; Hold me with thy power - ful hand; Bread of heav - en, Bread of heav - en, Feed me till I want no more, Feed me till I want no more.

2. O - pen now the crys - tal foun - tain, Whence the heal - ing stream doth flow; Let the fire and cloud - y pil - lar Lead me all my jour - ney through; Strong De - liv - erer, strong De - liv - erer, Be thou still my strength and shield, Be thou still my strength and shield.

3. When I tread the verge of Jor - dan, Bid my anx - ious fears sub - side; Death of deaths, and hell's De - struc - tion, Land me safe on Ca - naan's side; Songs of prais - es, songs of prais - es I will ev - er give to thee, I will ev - er give to thee. A - men.

410   Hark! the Glad Sound, the Savior Comes

RICHMOND C.M.

Based on Luke 4: 18-19
Philip Doddridge, 1735; alt., 1972

Thomas Haweis, 1792
Abr. by Samuel Webbe, Jr, (ca.1770-1843)

1. Hark! the glad sound, the Sav - ior comes, The Sav - ior
2. He comes the pris - oners to re - lease In Sa - tan's
3. He comes the bro - ken heart to bind, The bleed - ing
4. Our glad ho - san - nas, Prince of Peace, Your wel - come

prom - ised long! Let ev - ery heart pre - pare a
bond - age held; The gates of brass be - fore him
soul to cure; And with the trea - sures of his
shall pro - claim; And heaven's e - ter - nal arch - es

throne, And ev - ery voice a song.
burst, The i - ron fet - ters yield.
grace To en - rich the hum - ble poor.
ring With your be - lov - ed name. A - men.

Hark! the Herald Angels Sing

MENDELSSOHN 7.7.7.7.D. with Refrain

Charles Wesley, 1739; alt.

Felix Mendelssohn, 1840
Arr. by William H. Cummings, 1855

1. Hark! the her - ald an - gels sing, "Glo - ry to the new-born King;
2. Christ, by high - est heaven a - dored; Christ, the ev - er - last - ing Lord!
3. Hail the heaven-born Prince of Peace! Hail the Sun of Righ-teous-ness!

Peace on earth, and mer - cy mild, God and sin - ners rec - on - ciled!"
Late in time be - hold him come, Off-spring of the Vir - gin's womb:
Light and life to all he brings, Risen with heal - ing in his wings.

Joy - ful, all ye na - tions, rise, Join the tri - umph of the skies;
Veiled in flesh the God-head see; Hail th'in - car - nate De - i - ty,
Mild he lays his glo - ry by, Born that man no more may die,

With th'an - gel - ic host pro - claim, "Christ is born in Beth - le - hem!"
Pleased as man with men to dwell, Je - sus, our Em - man - u - el.
Born to raise the sons of earth, Born to give them sec - ond birth.

Hark! the her - ald an - gels sing, "Glo - ry to the new-born King!" A - men.

412   He Did Not Want to Be Far

Huub Oosterhuis
Trans. by C. Michael de Vries, 1966; alt., 1972

Bernard Huijbers; alt; 1972
Harm. by Richard D. Wetzel, 1972

1. He did not want to be far, Near - ness he in - tend - ed,
2. Ev - ery-where he's at our side, Hu - man 'mongst the hu - man;
3. God of God and Light of Light, Keep - er of cre - a - tion,
4. There-fore, that the world may know, Christ be-came our broth - er;
5. Let's re - joice and sing and cheer: God, to whom be giv - en

There-fore in - to what we are Christ the Lord de - scend - ed.
No-where is he rec - og-nized, No one sees the New Man.
He as-sumed the hu - man plight, Joined our gen - er - a - tion.
No man an - y - thing we owe But to love each oth - er.
Praise, is in - fi - nite - ly near, Dwells where we are liv - ing.

A - mong you is stand - ing He whom you don't know.

A - mong you is stand - ing He whom you don't know.

He Is the Way

413

NEW DANCE P.M.

W. H. Auden, 1944

Richard D. Wetzel, 1972

1. He is the Way. Fol-low him through the Land of Un-like-ness; You will see rare beasts, and have u-nique ad-ven-tures.
2. He is the Truth. Seek him in the King-dom of Anx-i-e-ty; You will come to a great cit-y that has ex-pect-ed your re-turn for years.
3. He is the Life. Love him in the World of the Flesh; And at your mar-riage all its oc-ca-sions shall dance for joy. A-men.

414 He Who Would Valiant Be

ST. DUNSTAN'S 6.5.6.5.6.6.6.5.

John Bunyan, 1684
Adapted by Percy Dearmer, 1906

C. Winfred Douglas, 1917

1. He who would val - iant be 'Gainst all dis - as - ter,
2. Who so be - set him round With dis - mal sto - ries
3. Since, Lord, thou dost de - fend Us with thy Spir - it,

Let him in con - stan - cy Fol - low the Mas - ter.
Do but them - selves con - found— His strength the more is.
We know we at the end Shall life in - her - it.

There's no dis - cour - age - ment Shall make him once re - lent
No foes shall stay his might; Though he with gi - ants fight,
Then, fan - cies, flee a - way! I'll fear not what men say,

His first a - vowed in - tent To be a pil - grim.
He will make good his right To be a pil - grim.
I'll la - bor night and day To be a pil - grim. A - men.

Heaven and Earth, and Sea and Air

GOTT SEI DANK 7.7.7.7.

Joachim Neander, 1680
Trans. composite; *Church Book*, 1868

Freylinghausen's *Geistreiches Gesangbuch*, 1704; alt.

415

1. Heaven and earth, and sea and air, All their Mak - er's praise de - clare; Wake, my soul, a - wake and sing: Now thy grate - ful prais - es bring.
2. See the glo - rious orb of day Break - ing through the clouds his way; Moon and stars with sil - very light Praise him through the si - lent night.
3. See how he hath ev - ery - where Made this earth so rich and fair; Hill and vale and fruit - ful land, All things liv - ing, show his hand.
4. Lord, great won - ders work - est thou! To thy sway all crea - tures bow; Write thou deep - ly in my heart What I am, and what thou art. A - men.

416 Heralds of Christ, Who Bear the King's Commands

NATIONAL HYMN 10.10.10.10.

Laura S. Copenhaver, 1894; alt., 1972　　　　　　　　　　　　George William Warren, 1892

Trumpets (with each stanza)

1. Her - alds of Christ, who bear the King's com-mands,
2. Through des - ert ways, dark fen, and deep mo - rass,
3. Where once the crook - ed trail in dark - ness wound
4. Lord, give us faith and strength the road to build,

Im - mor - tal ti - dings in your mor - tal hands,
Through jun - gles, slug - gish seas, and moun - tain pass,
Let march-ing feet and joy - ous song re - sound,
To see the prom - ise of the day ful - filled,

Pass on and car - ry swift the news you bring:
Build you the road, and fal - ter not, nor stay;
Where burn the fu - neral pyres, and cen - sers swing,
When war shall be no more and strife shall cease

Make straight, make straight the high - way of the King.
Pre - pare a - cross the earth the King's high - way.
Make straight, make straight the high - way of the King.
Up - on the high - way of the Prince of Peace. A - men.

Here, O Lord, Your Servants Gather

TŌKYŌ 7.5.7.5.D.

Tokuo Yamaguchi, 1958
Para. by Everett M. Stowe, 1958; alt., 1972

Japanese gagaku mode
Isau Koizumi, 1958

1. Here, O Lord, your serv-ants gath-er, Hand we link with hand;
2. Man-y are the tongues we speak, Scat-tered are the lands,
3. Na-ture's se-crets o-pen wide, Chang-es nev-er cease;
4. Grant, O God, an age re-newed, Filled with death-less love,

Look-ing toward our Sav-ior's cross, Joined in love we stand.
Yet our hearts are one in God And his love's de-mands.
Where, O where, can wea-ry men Find the source of peace?
Help us as we work and pray, Send us from a-bove

As we seek the realm of God, We u-nite to pray:
E'en in dark-ness hope ap-pears, Call-ing age and youth:
Un-to all those sore dis-tressed, Torn by end-less strife:
Truth and cour-age, faith and power Need-ed in our strife:

Je-sus, Sav-ior, guide our steps, For you are the Way.
Je-sus, teach-er, dwell with us, For you are the Truth.
Je-sus, heal-er, bring your balm, For you are the Life.
Je-sus, Mas-ter, be our way, Be our truth, our life.

417

418 Here, O Our Lord, We See You Face to Face

ERFYNIAD 10.10.10.10.

Horatius Bonar, 1855; alt., 1972

Welsh hymn melody
Harm. by David Evans, 1920

1. Here, O our Lord, we see you face to face;
2. We have no help but yours, nor do we need
3. This is the hour of ban - quet and of song;
4. Too soon we rise; the sym - bols dis - ap - pear.

Here would we touch and han - dle things un - seen,
An - oth - er arm save yours to lean up - on;
This is the heav - enly ta - ble for us spread;
The feast, though not the love, is past and gone;

Here grasp with firm - er hand e - ter - nal grace,
It is e - nough, O Lord, e - nough in - deed;
Here let us feast, and, feast - ing, still pro - long
The bread and wine re move, but you are here,

And all our wea - ri - ness up - on you lean.
Our strength is in your might, your might a - lone.
The fel - low - ship of liv - ing wine and bread.
Near - er than ev - er, still our shield and sun. A - men.

Music used by permission of the Executors of the late Professor Evans.

Holy Ghost, Dispel Our Sadness

HYFRYDOL 8.7.8.7.D.

Paul Gerhardt, 1648
Trans. by J. C. Jacobi, ca. 1725
Alt. by Augustus M. Toplady, 1776, and others

Rowland H. Prichard, 1855

419

1. Ho - ly Ghost, dis - pel our sad - ness; Pierce the clouds of na - ture's night;
2. Au - thor of the new cre - a - tion, Come with bless-ing and with power.

Come, great source of joy and glad - ness, Breathe your life, and spread your light.
Make our hearts your hab - i - ta - tion; On our souls your grac - es shower.

From the height which knows no mea-sure, As a gra - cious shower de - scend,
Hear, O hear our sup - pli - ca - tion, Bless - ed Spir - it, God of peace!

Bring-ing down the rich - est trea - sure Man can wish, or God can send.
Rest up - on this con - gre - ga - tion, With the full - ness of your grace. A - men.

420 Holy God, We Praise Your Name

GROSSER GOTT, WIR LOBEN DICH 7.8.7.8.7.7.

Allgemeines Katholisches Gesangbuch, ca. 1774
Trans. by Clarence A. Walworth, 1853; alt., 1972

Allgemeines Katholisches Gesangbuch, ca. 1774
Alt. in Schicht's *Choral-Buch*, 1819

1. Ho - ly God, we praise your name; Lord of all, we
2. Hark, the glad ce - les - tial hymn An - gel choirs a -
3. All a - pos - tles join the strain As your sa - cred
4. Ho - ly Fa - ther, Ho - ly Son, Ho - ly Spir - it:

bow be - fore you; All on earth your scep - ter claim,
bove are rais - ing; Cher - u - bim and ser - a - phim,
name they hal - low; Proph - ets swell the glad re - frain,
Three we name you While in es - sence on - ly One;

All in heaven a - bove a - dore you. In - fi - nite your
In un - ceas - ing cho - rus prais - ing, Fill the heavens with
And the bless - ed mar - tyrs fol - low, And from morn to
Un - di - vid - ed God we claim you, And a - dor - ing

vast do - main, Ev - er - last - ing is your reign.
sweet ac - cord: Ho - ly, ho - ly, ho - ly Lord.
set of sun, Through the church the song goes on.
bend the knee While we own the mys - ter - y. A - men.

Holy, Holy, Holy! Lord God Almighty!   421

NICAEA 11.12.12.10.

Reginald Heber, 1826   John B. Dykes, 1861

1. Ho - ly, ho - ly, ho - ly! Lord God Al - might - y!
2. Ho - ly, ho - ly, ho - ly! all the saints a - dore thee,
3. Ho - ly, ho - ly, ho - ly! though the dark - ness hide thee,
4. Ho - ly, ho - ly, ho - ly! Lord God Al - might - y!

Ear - ly in the morn - ing our song shall rise to thee;
Cast - ing down their gold - en crowns a - round the glass - y sea;
Though the eye of sin - ful man thy glo - ry may not see,
All thy works shall praise thy name, in earth and sky and sea;

Ho - ly, ho - ly, ho - ly! Mer - ci - ful and might - y!
Cher - u - bim and ser - a - phim fall - ing down be - fore thee,
On - ly thou art ho - ly; there is none be - side thee
Ho - ly, ho - ly, ho - ly! Mer - ci - ful and might - y!

God in three Per - sons, bless - ed Trin - i - ty!
Who wert, and art, and ev - er - more shalt be.
Per - fect in power, in love, and pu - ri - ty.
God in three Per - sons, bless - ed Trin - i - ty! A - men.

422 Holy Spirit, Truth Divine

SONG 13 7.7.7.7.

Samuel Longfellow, 1864; alt., 1972   Orlando Gibbons, 1623

1. Ho - ly Spir - it, truth di - vine, Dawn up - on this
2. Ho - ly Spir - it, love di - vine, Glow with - in this
3. Ho - ly Spir - it, power di - vine, Fill and nerve this
4. Ho - ly Spir - it, peace di - vine, Still this rest - less
5. Ho - ly Spir - it, right di - vine, King with - in my

soul of mine; Word of God, and in - ward light,
heart of mine; Kin - dle ev - ery high de - sire;
will of mine; By you may I strong - ly live,
heart of mine; Speak to calm this toss - ing sea,
con - science reign; Be my law, and I shall be

Wake my spir - it, clear my sight.
Per - ish self in your pure fire.
Brave - ly bear, and no - bly strive.
Stayed in your tran - quil - li - ty.
Firm - ly bound, for - ev - er free. A - men.

Hope of the World

423

DONNE SECOURS 11.10.11.10.

Georgia Harkness, 1953; alt., 1972

Comp. or adapted by Louis Bourgeois, 1551

1. Hope of the world, O Christ of great com - pas - sion,
2. Hope of the world, God's gift from high - est heav - en,
3. Hope of the world, a - foot on dust - y high - ways,
4. Hope of the world, who by your cross did save us
*5. Hope of the world, O Christ, o'er death vic - to - rious,

Speak to our fear - ful hearts by con - flict
Bring - ing to hun - gry souls the bread of
Show - ing to wan - dering souls the path of
From death and dark de - spair, from guilt and
Who by this sign did con - quer grief and

rent. Save us, your peo - ple, from con - sum - ing pas - sion,
life, Still let your Spir - it un - to us be giv - en,
light, Walk close be - side us, lest the tempt - ing by - ways
sin, We ren - der back the love your mer - cy gave us;
pain, We would be faith - ful to your gos - pel glo - rious.

Who by our own false hopes and aims are spent.
To heal earth's wounds and end her bit - ter strife.
Lure us from you and in - to end - less night.
O bless our lives that we may oth - ers win!
Our sov - ereign Lord, now and for - ev - er reign! A - men.

Words copyright 1954 by The Hymn Society of America; altered from *Eleven Ecumenical Hymns*; used by permission.

424

Hosanna, Loud Hosanna

ELLACOMBE 7.6.7.6.D.

Gesangbuch der herzogl. Wirtembergischen Katholischen Hofkapelle, 1784

Jennette Threlfall, 1873

1. Ho - san - na, loud ho - san - na, The lit - tle chil - dren sang;
2. From Ol - i - vet they fol - lowed Mid an ex - ult - ant crowd,
3. "Ho - san - na in the high - est!" That an - cient song we sing,

Through pil - lared court and tem - ple The love - ly an - them rang;
The vic - tor palm branch wav - ing, And chant - ing clear and loud;
For Christ is our Re - deem - er, The Lord of heaven our King.

To Je - sus, who had blessed them Close fold - ed to his breast,
The Lord of men and an - gels Rode on in low - ly state,
O may we ev - er praise him With heart and life and voice,

The chil - dren sang their prais - es, The sim - plest and the best.
Nor scorned that lit - tle chil - dren Should on his bid - ding wait.
And in his bliss - ful pres - ence E - ter - nal - ly re - joice. A - men.

How Firm a Foundation

FOUNDATION 11.11.11.11.

"K"
Rippon's *A Selection of Hymns*, 1787; alt.

American folk hymn

425

1. How firm a foun - da - tion, O saints of the Lord,
2. "Fear not, I am with you, O be not dis - mayed,
3. "When through the deep wa - ters I call you to go,
4. "The soul that on Je - sus has leaned for re - pose,

Is laid for your faith in his ex - cel - lent Word!
For I am your God, and will still give you aid;
The riv - ers of sor - row shall not o - ver - flow;
I will not, I will not de - sert to his foes;

What more can he say than to you he has said,
I'll strength - en you, help you, and cause you to stand,
For I will be near you, your trou - bles to bless,
That soul, though all hell should en - deav - or to shake,

To you who for ref - uge to Je - sus have fled?
Up - held by my righ - teous, om - nip - o - tent hand.
And sanc - ti - fy to you your deep - est dis - tress.
I'll nev - er, no, nev - er, no, nev - er for - sake." A - men.

426 I Danced in the Morning

(Lord of the Dance)

Sydney Carter, 1963

Based on a Shaker tune
Arr. and adapted by Sydney Carter, 1963

1. I danced in the morn-ing when the world was be-gun, And I danced in the moon and the stars and the sun And I came down from heav-en and I danced on the earth— At Beth-le-hem I had my birth.

2. I danced for the scribe and the Phar-i-see, But they would not dance and they would-n't fol-low me; I danced for the fish-er-men, for James and John— They came with me and the dance went on.

3. I danced on the Sab-bath and I cured the lame; The ho-ly peo-ple said it was a shame; They whipped and they stripped and they hung me high, And they left me there on a cross to die.

4. I danced on a Fri-day and the sky turned black. It's hard to dance with the dev-il on your back; They bur-ied my bod-y and they thought I'd gone. But I am the dance and I still go on.

Dance, then, wher-ev-er you may be, I am the Lord of the
Dance, said he, And I'll lead you all, wher-ev-er you may be, And I'll
lead you all in the dance, said he. dance, said he.

5. They cut me down and I leap up high— I am the life that-'ll
nev-er, nev-er die; I'll live in you if you'll
live in me— I am the Lord of the Dance, said he.

428

I Sing as I Arise Today

ST. PATRICK and DEIRDRE P.M.

Attr. to St. Patrick (ca. 389-ca. 461)
Para. by Joseph W. Clokey, 1964

Ancient Irish melodies
Harm. by Donald D. Kettring, 1972

1. I sing as I a - rise to - day; I call up - on the
2. I sing as I a - rise to - day; I call up - on the

Trin - i - ty; I now in - voke the Fa - ther, Son, And
Fa - ther's might; The will of God to be my guide, The

Ho - ly Spir - it, One in Three, In whom cre - a - tion
eye of God to be my sight, The word of God to

now is joined, The vault - ed sky, the sun so bright, The shin - ing
be my speech, The hand of God to be my stay, The shield of

stars, the sea so deep, The rush-ing wind, the snow so white.
God to be my strength, The path of God to be my way.

Christ with-in me, Christ be-side me, Christ be-
Christ in heart of all who love me, Christ in

fore me, Christ to guide me, Christ in ris - ing, Christ in
mouth of neigh-bors near me, Christ in eye of all who

sleep - ing, Christ in work - ing, Christ in speak - ing.
see me, Christ in ear of all who hear me. A - men.

430   I to the Hills Will Lift My Eyes

DUNDEE (FRENCH) C.M.

From Psalm 121
The Psalter, 1912; alt., 1972

Scottish Psalter, 1615

1. I to the hills will lift my eyes; From whence shall come our aid? Our help is from the Lord alone, Who heaven and earth has made.
2. He will not let your foot be moved, Your guardian never sleeps; With watchful and unslumbering care His own he safely keeps.
3. Your faithful keeper is the Lord, Your Shelter and your Shade; 'Neath sun or moon, by day or night, You shall not be afraid.
4. From evil he will keep you safe, For you he will provide; Your going out, your coming in, Forever he will guide. A-men.

If You Will Only Let God Guide You

NEUMARK 9.8.9.8.8.8.

431

Georg Neumark, 1657
Trans. by Catherine Winkworth, 1855, 1863; alt., 1972

Georg Neumark, 1657

1. If you will on - ly let God guide you, And hope in him through all your ways, What-ev - er comes, he'll stand be - side you, To bear you through the e - vil days; Who trusts in God's un - chang - ing love Builds on the rock that can - not move.

2. On - ly be still, and wait his lei - sure In cheer - ful hope, with heart con - tent To take what-e'er the Fa - ther's plea - sure And all dis - cern - ing love have sent; Nor doubt our in - most wants are known To him who chose us for his own.

3. Sing, pray, and swerve not from his ways, But do your part in con-science true; Trust his rich prom - is - es of grace, So shall they be ful - filled in you; God hears the call of those in need, The souls that trust in him in - deed. A - men.

432 I'm So Glad Troubles Don't Last Always

Negro spiritual
Harm. by Joan M. Salmon, 1972

Negro spiritual

NOTE: Additional stanzas may be improvised.

Immortal, Invisible, God Only Wise

ST. DENIO 11.11.11.11.

Walter Chalmers Smith, 1867, 1884; alt.

Welsh folk song
Adapted as hymn tune, 1839

433

1. Im - mor - tal, in - vis - i - ble, God on - ly wise,
2. Un - rest - ing, un - hast - ing, and si - lent as light,
3. To all, life thou giv - est— to both great and small;
4. Great Fa - ther of glo - ry, pure Fa - ther of light,

In light in - ac - ces - si - ble hid from our eyes,
Nor want - ing, nor wast - ing, thou rul - est in might;
In all life thou liv - est, the true life of all;
Thine an - gels a - dore thee, all veil - ing their sight;

Most bless - ed, most glo - rious, the An - cient of Days,
Thy jus - tice like moun - tains high soar - ing a - bove
We blos - som and flour - ish as leaves on the tree,
All praise we would ren - der; O help us to see

Al - might - y, vic - to - rious, thy great name we praise.
Thy clouds which are foun - tains of good - ness and love.
And with - er and per - ish— but naught chang - eth thee.
'Tis on - ly the splen - dor of light hid - eth thee! A - men.

434 Immortal Love, Forever Full

SERENITY C.M.

William V. Wallace, 1856
Arr. by Uzziah C. Burnap, 1869

John Greenleaf Whittier, 1866

1. Im - mor - tal Love, for - ev - er full, For-
2. We may not climb the heav - enly steeps To
3. But warm, sweet, ten - der, e - ven yet A
4. The heal - ing of his seam - less dress Is
5. O Lord and Mas - ter of us all, What-

ev - er flow - ing free, For - ev - er shared, for-
bring the Lord Christ down; In vain we search the
pres - ent help is he; And faith has still its
by our beds of pain; We touch him in life's
e'er our name or sign, We own thy sway, we

ev - er whole, A nev - er - ebb - ing sea!
low - est deeps, For him no depths can drown.
Ol - i - vet, And love its Gal - i - lee.
throng and press, And we are whole a - gain.
hear thy call, We test our lives by thine. A - men.

In Christ There Is No East or West

ST. PETER C.M.
(First Tune)

John Oxenham, 1908

Alexander R. Reinagle, ca. 1836

435

1. In Christ there is no East or West, In him no South or North; But one great fel-low-ship of love Through-out the whole wide earth.

2. In him shall true hearts ev-ery-where Their high com-mu-nion find; His serv-ice is the gold-en cord Close-bind-ing all man-kind.

3. Join hands, then, broth-ers of the faith, What-e'er your race may be! Who serves my Fa-ther as a son Is sure-ly kin to me.

4. In Christ now meet both East and West, In him meet South and North; All Christ-ly souls are one in him Through-out the whole wide earth. A-men.

436 In Christ There Is No East or West

MCKEE C.M.
(Second Tune)

John Oxenham, 1908

Negro spiritual
Adapted by Harry T. Burleigh, 1939

1. In Christ there is no East or West, In
2. In him shall true hearts ev - ery - where Their
3. Join hands, then, broth - ers of the faith, What -
4. In Christ now meet both East and West, In

him no South or North; But one great fel - low -
high com - mu - nion find; His serv - ice is the
e'er your race may be! Who serves my Fa - ther
him meet South and North; All Christ - ly souls are

ship of love Through - out the whole wide earth.
gold - en cord Close - bind - ing all man - kind.
as a son Is sure - ly kin to me.
one in him Through - out the whole wide earth. A - men.

Words from *Bees in Amber*, by John Oxenham; used by permission.

In the Cross of Christ I Glory

RATHBUN 8.7.8.7.

John Bowring, 1825

Ithamar Conkey, 1851

1. In the cross of Christ I glo - ry, Tow - ering
2. When the woes of life o'er - take me, Hopes de -
3. When the sun of bliss is beam - ing Light and
4. Bane and bless - ing, pain and plea - sure, By the
5. In the cross of Christ I glo - ry, Tow - ering

o'er the wrecks of time; All the light of sa - cred
ceive, and fears an - noy, Nev - er shall the cross for -
love up - on my way, From the cross the ra - diance
cross are sanc - ti - fied; Peace is there that knows no
o'er the wrecks of time; All the light of sa - cred

sto - ry Gath - ers round its head sub - lime.
sake me: Lo! it glows with peace and joy.
stream - ing Adds more lus - ter to the day.
mea - sure, Joys that through all time a - bide.
sto - ry Gath - ers round its head sub - lime. A - men.

438 It Came Upon the Midnight Clear

CAROL C.M.D.

Edmund H. Sears, 1849; alt.   Richard Storrs Willis, 1850

1. It came up-on the mid-night clear, That glo-rious song of old,
2. Still through the clo-ven skies they come, With peace-ful wings un-furled,
3. And ye, be-neath life's crush-ing load, Whose forms are bend-ing low,
4. For lo, the days are has-tening on, By proph-et bards fore-told,

From an-gels bend-ing near the earth, To touch their harps of gold:
And still their heav-enly mu-sic floats O'er all the wea-ry world:
Who toil a-long the climb-ing way With pain-ful steps and slow,
When with the ev-er-cir-cling years Comes round the age of gold;

"Peace on the earth, good will to men, From heaven's all-gra-cious King":
A-bove its sad and low-ly plains They bend on hov-ering wing,
Look now! for glad and gold-en hours Come swift-ly on the wing:
When peace shall o-ver all the earth Its an-cient splen-dors fling,

The world in sol-emn still-ness lay, To hear the an-gels sing.
And ev-er o'er its Ba-bel sounds The bless-ed an-gels sing.
O rest be-side the wea-ry road, And hear the an-gels sing.
And the whole world give back the song Which now the an-gels sing. A-men.

Jesus Calls Us

GALILEE 8.7.8.7.

Cecil Frances Alexander, 1852; alt., 1972   William H. Jude, 1887

439

1. Je - sus calls us: o'er the tu - mult Of our
2. As of old, Saint An - drew heard it By the
3. Je - sus calls us from the wor - ship Of the
4. In our joys and in our sor - rows, Days of
5. Je - sus calls us; by your mer - cies, Sav - ior,

life's wild, rest - less sea, Day by day his voice is
Gal - i - le - an lake, Turned from home and toil and
vain world's gold - en store, From each i - dol that would
toil and hours of ease, Still he calls, in cares and
may we hear your call, Give our hearts to your o -

sound - ing, Say - ing, "Chris - tian, fol - low me."
kin - dred, Leav - ing all for his dear sake.
keep us, Say - ing, "Chris - tian, love me more."
plea - sures, "Chris - tian, love me more than these."
be - dience, Serve and love you best of all. A - men.

440 Jesus Christ Is Risen Today

EASTER HYMN 7.7.7.7. with Alleluias

St. 1, Latin carol, 14th century
Para. in *Lyra Davidica*, 1708; alt.
Sts. 2, 3, *The Compleat Psalmodist*, ca. 1750; alt.
St. 4, Charles Wesley, 1740; alt., 1972

Lyra Davidica, 1708
Alt. in *The Compleat Psalmodist*, ca. 1750

1. Je - sus Christ is risen to - day, Al - le - lu - ia!
2. Hymns of praise then let us sing,
3. But the pains which he en - dured,
4. Sing we to our God a - bove,

Our tri - um - phant ho - ly day, Al - le - lu - ia!
Un - to Christ, our heav-enly King,
Our sal - va - tion have pro - cured;
Praise e - ter - nal as his love;

Who did once, up - on the cross, Al - le - lu - ia!
Who en - dured the cross and grave,
Now a - bove the sky he's King,
Praise him, all you heav-enly host,

Suf - fer to re - deem our loss. Al - le - lu - ia!
Sin - ners to re - deem and save.
Where the an - gels ev - er sing.
Fa - ther, Son, and Ho - ly Ghost. A - men.

Alternative Tune: LLANFAIR

Jesus, Lead the Way

441

SEELENBRÄUTIGAM 5.5.8.8.5.5.

Nicolaus L. von Zinzendorf, 1721
Recast by Christian Gregor, 1778
Trans. by Arthur W. Farlander, 1939; alt., 1972

Adam Drese, 1698

1. Je - sus, lead the way Through our life's long
2. Should our lot be hard, Keep us on our
3. When we need re - lief From an in - ner
4. Or - der then our ways, Sav - ior, all our

day, And with faith - ful foot - step stead - y,
guard; Ev - en through se - ver - est tri - al
grief, Or when e - vils come al - lur - ing,
days. If you lead us through rough plac - es,

We will fol - low, al - ways read - y. Guide us
Make us brave in self - de - ni - al: Tran - sient
Make us pa - tient and en - dur - ing: Let us
Grant us your sus - tain - ing grac - es. When our

by your hand To the heav - enly land.
pain may come But your will be done.
fol - low still Your most ho - ly will.
course is o'er, O - pen heav - en's door. A - men.

442 Jesus, Priceless Treasure

JESU, MEINE FREUDE P.M.

Johann Franck, 1653
Trans. by Catherine Winkworth, 1863; alt.

Crüger's *Praxis Pietatis Melica*, 1653
Harm. by J. S. Bach, 1723

1. Je - sus, price - less trea - sure, Source of pur - est plea - sure,
2. In thine arm I rest me; Foes who would mo - lest me
3. Hence, all thoughts of sad - ness! For the Lord of glad - ness,

Tru-est friend to me; Long my heart hath pant - ed, Till it well-nigh
Can-not reach me here. Though the earth be shak - ing, Ev - ery heart be
Je - sus, en - ters in: Those who love the Fa - ther, Though the storms may

faint - ed, Thirst-ing af - ter thee. Thine I am, O spot - less Lamb,
quak - ing, God dis - pels our fear; Sin and hell in con - flict fell
gath - er, Still have peace with - in; Yea, what-e'er we here must bear,

I will suf - fer naught to hide thee, Ask for naught be - side thee.
With their heav-iest storms as - sail us: Je-sus will not fail us.
Still in thee lies pur - est plea - sure, Je-sus, price-less trea - sure! A-men.

Jesus Shall Reign

DUKE STREET L.M.

443

Based on Psalm 72
Isaac Watts, 1719

John Hatton, 1793

1. Je - sus shall reign wher - e'er the sun Does his suc -
2. For him shall end - less prayer be made, And prais - es
3. Peo - ple and realms of ev - ery tongue Dwell on his
4. Bless - ings a - bound wher - e'er he reigns, The pris - oner
5. Let ev - ery crea - ture rise and bring Pe - cu - liar

ces - sive jour - neys run, His king-dom stretch from shore to
throng to crown his head; His name, like sweet per - fume, shall
love with sweet - est song, And in - fant voic - es shall pro -
leaps to lose his chains, The wea - ry find e - ter - nal
hon - ors to our King; An - gels de - scend with songs a -

shore, Till moons shall wax and wane no more.
rise With ev - ery morn - ing sac - ri - fice.
claim Their ear - ly bless - ings on his name.
rest, And all the sons of want are blest.
gain, And earth re - peat the loud A - men! A - men.

444

Joy to the World!

ANTIOCH C.M.

Based on Psalm 98: 5-9
Isaac Watts, 1719

Attr. to George Frederick Handel, 1742
Mason's *The Modern Psalmist*, 1839
Arr. by Robert Carwithen, 1972

1. Joy to the world! the Lord is come: Let earth receive her King; Let ev-ery heart pre-pare him room, And heaven and na-ture sing, And heaven and na-ture sing, And heaven and na-ture sing, And

2. Joy to the earth! the Sav-ior reigns: Let men their songs em-ploy; While fields and floods, rocks, hills, and plains Re-peat the sound-ing joy, Re-peat the sound-ing joy, Re-peat the sound-ing joy, Re-

3. No more let sins and sor-rows grow, Nor thorns in-fest the ground; He comes to make his bless-ings flow Far as the curse is found, Far as the curse is found, Far as the curse is found, Far

4. He rules the world with truth and grace, And makes the na-tions prove The glo-ries of his righ-teous-ness, And won-ders of his love, And won-ders of his love, And won-ders of his love, And

sing, And heaven, and heaven and na - ture sing.
joy, Re - peat, re - peat the sound - ing joy.
found, Far as, far as the curse is found.
love, And won - ders, won - ders of his love. A - men.

heaven and na - ture sing, And
peat the sound-ing joy, Re -
as the curse is found, Far
won-ders of his love, And

446 Joyful, Joyful, We Adore Thee

HYMN TO JOY 8.7.8.7.D.

Henry van Dyke, 1907

Ludwig van Beethoven, 1824
Arr. as hymn tune, 1846

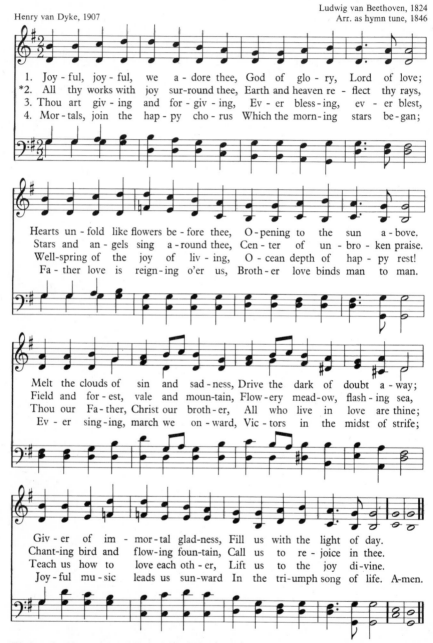

1. Joy - ful, joy - ful, we a - dore thee, God of glo - ry, Lord of love;
*2. All thy works with joy sur - round thee, Earth and heaven re - flect thy rays,
3. Thou art giv - ing and for - giv - ing, Ev - er bless - ing, ev - er blest,
4. Mor - tals, join the hap - py cho - rus Which the morn - ing stars be - gan;

Hearts un - fold like flowers be - fore thee, O - pening to the sun a - bove,
Stars and an - gels sing a - round thee, Cen - ter of un - bro - ken praise.
Well - spring of the joy of liv - ing, O - cean depth of hap - py rest!
Fa - ther love is reign - ing o'er us, Broth - er love binds man to man.

Melt the clouds of sin and sad - ness, Drive the dark of doubt a - way;
Field and for - est, vale and moun - tain, Flow - ery mead - ow, flash - ing sea,
Thou our Fa - ther, Christ our broth - er, All who live in love are thine;
Ev - er sing - ing, march we on - ward, Vic - tors in the midst of strife;

Giv - er of im - mor - tal glad - ness, Fill us with the light of day.
Chant - ing bird and flow - ing foun - tain, Call us to re - joice in thee.
Teach us how to love each oth - er, Lift us to the joy di - vine.
Joy - ful mu - sic leads us sun - ward In the tri - umph song of life. A - men.

Judge Eternal, Throned in Splendor

RHUDDLAN 8.7.8.7.8.7.

Henry Scott Holland, 1902; alt.

Traditional Welsh melody
Adapted in *The English Hymnal*, 1906

1. Judge e - ter - nal, throned in splen - dor, Lord of lords and
2. Still the wea - ry folk are pin - ing For the hour that
3. Crown, O God, your own en - deav - or: Cleave our dark - ness

King of kings, With the liv - ing fire of judg - ment
brings re - lease; And the cit - y's crowd - ed clang - or
with your sword; Feed the faint and hun - gry peo - ples

Purge this realm of bit - ter things: Sol - ace all its
Cries a - loud for sin to cease; And the home - steads
With the rich - ness of your Word; Cleanse the bod - y

wide do - min - ion With the heal - ing of your wings.
and the wood - lands Plead in si - lence for their peace.
of this na - tion Through the glo - ry of the Lord. A - men.

448 Lead On, O King Eternal

LLANGLOFFAN 7.6.7.6.D.

Ernest W. Shurtleff, 1888; alt., 1972

Welsh hymn melody
Evans' *Hymnau a Thonau*, 1865

1. Lead on, O King e - ter - nal, The day of march has come;
2. Lead on, O King e - ter - nal, Till sin's fierce war shall cease,
3. Lead on, O King e - ter - nal: We fol - low, not with fears;

Hence-forth in fields of con - quest Your tents shall be our home:
And Ho - li - ness shall whis - per The sweet A - men of peace;
For glad - ness breaks like morn - ing Wher-e'er your face ap - pears;

Through days of prep - a - ra - tion Your grace has made us strong,
For not with swords' loud clash - ing, Nor roll of stir - ring drums,
Your cross is lift - ed o'er us; We jour - ney in its light:

And now, O King e - ter - nal, We lift our bat - tle song.
But deeds of love and mer - cy, The heav-enly king-dom comes.
The crown a - waits the con - quest; Lead on, O God of might. A - men.

Alternative Tune: LANCASHIRE

Let All Mortal Flesh Keep Silence

PICARDY 8.7.8.7.8.7.

From the Liturgy of St. James
Trans. by Gerard Moultrie, 1864

French carol, 17th century (?)
Arr. in *The English Hymnal*, 1906

1. Let all mor-tal flesh keep si-lence And with fear and trem-bling stand;
2. King of kings, yet born of Mar-y, As of old on earth he stood,
3. Rank on rank the host of heav-en Spreads its van-guard on the way,
4. At his feet the six-winged ser-aph; Cher-u-bim, with sleep-less eye,

Pon-der noth-ing earth-ly-mind-ed, For with bless-ing in his hand
Lord of lords, in hu-man ves-ture— In the bod-y and the blood:
As the Light of light de-scend-eth From the realms of end-less day,
Veil their fac-es to the pres-ence, As with cease-less voice they cry,

Christ our God to earth de-scend — eth, Our full hom-age to de - mand.
He will give to all the faith — ful His own self for heav-enly food.
That the powers of hell may van — ish As the dark-ness clears a - way.
"Al - le-lu - ia, Al - le-lu — ia, Al - le-lu - ia, Lord Most High!" A-men.

450 Let All Together Praise Our God

LOBT GOTT, IHR CHRISTEN C.M.

Nikolaus Herman, 1560
Trans. by Arthur Tozer Russell, 1851; alt.

Nikolaus Herman, 1554
Harm. by Austin C. Lovelace, 1965

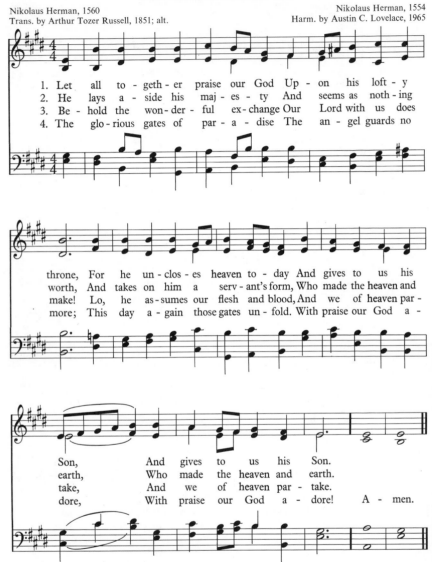

1. Let all to - geth - er praise our God Up - on his loft - y throne, For he un - clos - es heaven to - day And gives to us his Son, And gives to us his Son.

2. He lays a - side his maj - es - ty And seems as noth - ing worth, And takes on him a serv - ant's form, Who made the heaven and earth, Who made the heaven and earth.

3. Be - hold the won - der - ful ex - change Our Lord with us does make! Lo, he as - sumes our flesh and blood, And we of heaven par - take, And we of heaven par - take.

4. The glo - rious gates of par - a - dise The an - gel guards no more; This day a - gain those gates un - fold. With praise our God a - dore, With praise our God a - dore! A - men.

Let There Be Light, Lord God of Hosts

SONG 34 L.M.

William Merrell Vories, 1908; alt., 1972

Orlando Gibbons, 1623
As in *Hymnal for Colleges and Schools*, 1956

1. Let there be light, Lord God of hosts, Let there be wis-dom on the earth! Let broad hu-man-i-ty have birth! Let there be deeds in-stead of boasts!

2. With-in our pas-sioned hearts in-still The calm that ends all strain and strife; Make us your min-is-ters of life; Purge us from lusts that curse and kill!

3. Give us the peace of vi-sion clear To see our broth-ers' good our own, To joy and suf-fer not a-lone — The love that casts a-way all fear!

4. Let woe and waste of war-fare cease, That use-ful la-bor yet may build Its homes with love and laugh-ter filled! God, give your way-ward chil-dren peace! A-men.

451

Let Us Break Bread Together

452

Negro spiritual
Arr. for *The Hymnbook*, 1955

Negro spiritual

1. Let us break bread to-geth-er on our knees;
2. Let us drink wine to-geth-er on our knees; (on our knees;)
3. Let us praise God to-geth-er on our knees;

Let us break bread to-geth-er on our knees.
Let us drink wine to-geth-er on our knees. (on our knees.)
Let us praise God to-geth-er on our knees.

When I fall on my knees, with my face to the ris-ing

sun, O Lord, have mer-cy on me. A - men.

Let Us with a Gladsome Mind

MONKLAND 7.7.7.7.

453

Psalm 136:1, 2, 7, 25
Para. by John Milton, ca. 1624; alt.

John Antes (1740-1811)
Arr. by John B. Wilkes, 1861

1. Let us with a glad - some mind Praise the Lord, for
2. Let us sound his name a - broad, For of gods he
3. He, with all - com - mand - ing might, Filled the new - made
4. All things liv - ing he does feed; His full hand sup -
5. Let us then with glad - some mind Praise the Lord, for

he is kind:
is the God:
world with light: For his mer - cies shall en - dure,
plies their need:
he is kind:

Ev - er faith - ful, ev - er sure. A - men.

454 Lift Up Your Heads, O Mighty Gates

TRURO L.M.

Georg Weissel, 1642
Trans. by Catherine Winkworth, 1855; alt.

Psalmodia Evangelica, 1789

1. Lift up your heads, O might - y gates; Be - hold, the
2. O blest the land, the cit - y blest, Where Christ the
3. Fling wide the por - tals of your heart; Make it a
4. Re - deem - er, come! We o - pen wide Our hearts to

King of glo - ry waits; The King of kings is
rul - er is con - fessed! O hap - py hearts and
tem - ple set a - part From self - ish use for
you; here, Lord, a - bide. Let us your in - ner

draw - ing near; The Sav - ior of the world is here!
hap - py homes To whom this King in tri - umph comes!
his em - ploy, A - dorned with prayer, and love, and joy.
pres - ence feel; Your grace and love in us re - veal. A-men.

Lo, How a Rose E'er Blooming

ES IST EIN' ROS' 7.6.7.6.6.7.6.

455

Attr. to Brother Conrad of Mainz, 1588
Trans. by Theodore Baker, 1894; alt., 1972

Rhineland folk melody
Harm. by Michael Praetorius, 1609

1. Lo, how a Rose e'er bloom-ing From ten-der stem has sprung!
2. I - sa-iah 'twas fore-told it, The Rose I have in mind,

Of Jes-se's lin-eage com-ing As men of old have sung.
With Mar-y we be-hold it, The Vir-gin Moth - er kind.

It came, a flow-eret bright, A - mid the cold of
To show God's love a - right, She bore to men a

win - ter, When half spent was the night.
Sav - ior, When half spent was the night. A-men.

was the

456

Lord, Bless and Pity Us

ST. MICHAEL S.M.

Comp. or adapted by Louis Bourgeois, 1551
Adapted by William Crotch, 1836
As in *Pilgrim Hymnal*, 1958

From Psalm 67
The Psalter, 1912; alt., 1972

1. Lord, bless and pit - y us, Shine on us
2. Your praise, O gra - cious God, Let all the
3. The na - tions you will judge And lead them
4. The earth her fruit shall yield, For God, our

with your face, That all the earth your way may
na - tions sing; Let all men wor - ship you with
in your ways; Let all men praise your name, O
God, will bless; We shall be blest, and all the

know And men may see your grace.
joy And songs of glad - ness bring.
God, Let all the peo - ple praise.
world His glo - ry shall con - fess. A - men.

Lord, by Whose Breath All Souls and Seeds 457

ZU MEINEM HERRN 11.10.11.10.

Andrew Young, 1960; alt., 1972

Johann Gottfried Schicht, 1819

1. Lord, by whose breath all souls and seeds are liv - ing
2. Lord of the earth, ac - cept these gifts in to - ken;
3. Poor is our praise, but these shall be our psal - ter;

With life that is and life that is to
You in your works are to be all a -
Lo, like your - self they rose up from the

be, First - fruits of earth, we of - fer with thanks -
dored, From whom the light as dai - ly bread is
dead; Lord, give them back when at your ho - ly

giv - ing For fields in flood with sum-mer's gold-en sea.
bro - ken, Sun - set and dawn as wine and milk are poured.
al - tar We feed on you, who are the liv - ing bread. A - men.

458 Lord, Dismiss Us with Your Blessing

SICILIAN MARINERS 8.7.8.7.8.7.

Attr. to John Fawcett, 1773; alt.
St. 3 alt. by Godfrey Thring (1823-1903)

Sicilian folk song (?)

1. Lord, dis - miss us with your bless - ing; Fill our hearts with
2. Thanks we give and ad - o - ra - tion For your gos - pel's
3. So that when your love shall call us, Sav - ior, from the

joy and peace; Let us each, your love pos - sess - ing,
joy - ful sound; May the fruits of your sal - va - tion
world a - way, Let no fear of death ap - pall us,

Tri - umph in re - deem - ing grace. O re - fresh us,
In our hearts and lives a - bound. Ev - er faith - ful,
Glad your sum - mons to o - bey. May we ev - er,

O re - fresh us, Trav - eling through this wil - der - ness.
Ev - er faith - ful, To the truth may we be found;
May we ev - er Reign with you in end - less day. A - men.

Lord, from the Depths to You I Cry

SONG 67 C.M.

Psalm 130
Para. in the Scottish Psalter, 1650; alt.

Prys's Welsh Psalter, 1621

459

1. Lord, from the depths to you I cry; My
2. Lord, who shall stand, if you, O Lord, Should
3. I wait for God, my soul does wait; My
4. I say, more than all they who watch The
5. Re - demp - tion al - so plen - te - ous Is

call, Lord, you will hear: Un - to my sup - pli -
mark in - iq - ui - ty? But yet with you for -
hope is in his word. More than they who for
morn - ing light to see. Let Is - ra - el hope
ev - er found with him: And from all his in -

ca - tion's voice Give an at - ten - tive ear.
give - ness is, That feared you still may be.
morn - ing watch, My soul waits for the Lord;
in the Lord, For with him mer - cies be.
iq - ui - ties He Is - rael shall re - deem. A - men.

460 Lord God of Hosts, Whose Purpose

WELWYN 11.10.11.10.

Shepherd Knapp, 1907; alt., 1972

Alfred Scott-Gatty, 1900
As in *The English Hymnal*, 1906

1. Lord God of hosts, whose pur-pose, nev-er swerv-ing,
2. Strong Son of God, whose work was his that sent you,
3. O Prince of Peace, the bring-er of good ti-dings,
4. Lord God, whose grace has called us to your serv-ice,

Leads toward the day of Je-sus Christ your Son,
One with the Fa-ther, thought and deed and word,
Teach us to speak your word of hope and cheer—
How good your thoughts toward us, how great their sum!

Grant us to march a-mong your faith-ful le-gions,
One make us all, true com-rades in your serv-ice,
Rest for the soul, and strength for all man's striv-ing,
We work with you, we go where you will lead us,

Armed with your cour-age, till the world is won.
And make us one in you with God the Lord.
Light for the path of life, and God brought near.
Un-til in all the earth your king-dom come. A-men.

Lord Jesus Christ, Our Lord Most Dear

VOM HIMMEL HOCH L.M.

461

Heinrich von Laufenberg, 1429(?)
Trans. by Catherine Winkworth, 1869; alt.

Geystliche Lieder, Leipzig, 1539

Lord Je - sus Christ, our Lord most dear,

As you were once an in - fant here,

So give this child of yours, we pray,

Your grace and bless - ing day by day. A - men.

462 Lord, Look Upon Our Working Days

AUDREY L.M.

Ian M. Fraser, 1964; alt., 1972   Donald D. Kettring, 1972

1. Lord, look up-on our work-ing days, Bus - ied in fac-tory,
2. Bent to the lot our crafts as - sign, Swayed by deep tides of
3. You are the work-man, Lord, not we: All worlds were made at
4. Our part to do what he'll com - mit, Who strides the world, and
5. Cov - er our faults with par - don full, Shield those who suf - fer

of - fice, store; May word - less work your name a -
need and fear, In loy - al - ties torn, the truth un -
your com - mand. Christ, their sus - tain - er, bared his
calls men all Part - ners in pain and car - ni -
when we shirk; Take what is wor - thy in our

dore, The com - mon round spell out your praise?
clear, How may we build to your de - sign?
hand, Res - cued them from fu - til - i - ty.
val, To grasp the hope he won for it.
work, Give it due por - tion in your rule. A - men.

Lord of All Being, Throned Afar

463

LOUVAN L.M.

Oliver Wendell Holmes, 1859; alt., 1972

Virgil C. Taylor, 1846; alt., 1931, 1958

1. Lord of all be - ing, throned a - far, Your glo - ry
2. Sun of our life, your quick - ening ray Sheds on our
3. Lord of all life, be - low, a - bove, Whose light is
4. Grant us your truth for which we yearn, And kin - dling

flames from sun and star; Cen - ter and soul of ev - ery
path the glow of day; Star of our hope, your soft - ened
truth, whose warmth is love, Be - fore your ev - er - blaz - ing
hearts that for you burn, Till all your liv - ing al - tars

sphere, Yet to each lov - ing heart how near!
light Cheers the long watch - es of the night.
throne We ask no lus - ter of our own.
claim One ho - ly light, one heav - enly flame. A - men.

Lord of All Majesty and Might

VATER UNSER 8.8.8.8.8.8.

George Wallace Briggs, 1931

Geystliche Lieder, Leipzig, 1539
Harm. by J. S. Bach (1685-1750)

1. Lord of all maj - es - ty and might, Whose pres - ence fills th'un-
2. Be - yond all knowl - edge thou art wise, With wis - dom that tran-
*3. Frail though our form, and brief our day, Our mind has bridged the
4. For, when thy won - drous works we scan, And mind gives an - swer
5. We know in part: e - nough we know To walk with thee, and

fath - omed deep, Where - in un - count - ed worlds of light Through
scends all thought: Yet still we seek with strain - ing eyes, Yea,
gulf of years, Our pu - ny bal - anc - es can weigh The
back to mind, Thine im - age stands re - vealed in man; And,
walk a - right; And thou shalt guide us as we go, And

count - less ag - es vig - il keep; E - ter - nal God, can
seek thee as our fa - thers sought; Nor will we from the
mag - ni - tude of star - ry spheres: With - in us is e -
seek - ing, he shall sure - ly find. Thy sons, our her - i -
lead us in - to full - er light, Till, when we stand be -

such as we, Frail mor - tal men, know aught of thee?
quest de - part Till we shall know thee as thou art.
ter - ni - ty; Whence comes it, Fa - ther, but from thee?
tage we claim: Shall not thy chil - dren know thy name?
fore thy throne, We know at last as we are known. A - men.

Words from *Songs of Praise*, Enlarged Edition; used by permission of Oxford University Press.

Lord of All Nations, Grant Me Grace

465

BEATUS VIR L.M.

Olive Wise Spannaus, 1960; alt., 1972

Slovak melody, 16th century
Arr. by Richard Hillert, 1967

1. Lord of all na - tions, grant me grace To love all
2. Break down the wall that would di - vide Your chil - dren,
3. For - give me, Lord, where I have erred By love - less
4. Give me your cour - age, Lord, to speak When - ev - er
5. With your own love may I be filled And by your

men of ev - ery race, And in each fel - low - man to
Lord, on ev - ery side. Let me seek first my neigh - bor's
act and thought - less word. Make me to see the wrong I
strong op - press the weak. Should I my - self the vic - tim
Ho - ly Spir - it willed, That all I touch what - e'er I

view My broth - er, loved, re - deemed by you.
good In bonds of Chris - tian broth - er - hood.
do Will cru - ci - fy my Lord a - new.
be, Help me for - give, from an - ger free.
do May be di - vine - ly touched by you. A - men.

466   Lord of the Strong, When Earth You Trod

CHARLOTTE 8.8.8.8.8.6.

Donald Hankey (1884-1916)   Richard M. Peek, 1972

1. Lord of the strong, when earth you trod, You calm-ly faced the
2. Lord of the weak, when earth you trod, Op-pres-sors writhed be-
3. Lord of the rich, when earth you trod, To Mam-mon's power you
4. Lord of the poor, when earth you trod, The lot you chose was
*5. Lord of us all, when earth you trod, The life you led was

an-gry sea, The fierce un-masked hy-poc-ri-sy, The
neath your scorn; The weak, de-spised, de-praved, for-lorn, You
nev-er bowed, But taught how men with wealth en-dowed In
hard and poor; You taught us hard-ness to en-dure, And
per-fect, free, De-fi-ant of all tyr-an-ny: Now

trai-tor's kiss, the rab-ble's hiss, The aw-ful death up-
taught to hope and know the scope Of love di-vine for
meek-ness' school might learn to rule The de-mon that en-
so to gain through hurt and pain The wealth that lasts forgive us grace that we may face Our foes with like te-

on the tree,
all who mourn:
slaves the proud: All glo-ry be to God.
ev-er-more:
mer-i-ty,   A-men.

Music copyright 1972 by The Westminster Press.

Lord Our God, with Praise We Come

GUD ER GUD P.M.

467

Petter Dass (1647-1707)
Trans. by Peter A. Sveeggen, 1951; alt., 1972

Leland B. Sateren, 1951, 1970

1. Lord our God, with praise we come be-fore you! Let all na-tions
2. God is God, though lands were all for-sak-en. God is God, though
3. Vales and hills shall move from their foun-da-tions; Heaven and earth shall

hum-bly now im-plore you! All en-deav-or to praise you ev-er!
death had all men tak-en. Though all rac-es had left no trac-es—
crash in con-ster-na-tion; Mounts tran-scend-ing will have their end-ing.

And ceas-ing nev-er, may we for-ev-er a-dore you!
In star-ry spac-es God's love em-brac-es cre-a-tion.
Then morn as-cend-ing shall bring un-end-ing sal-va-tion. A-men.

468   Lord, We Thank You for Our Brothers

BLAENHAFREN 8.7.8.7.D.

Roger K. Powell, 1948; alt., 1965

Traditional Welsh melody
As in *Hymns of the Kingdom of God*, 1923

1. Lord, we thank you for our broth-ers Keep-ing
faith with us and you, Join-ing heart to heart with
oth-ers, Thus our one-ness to re-new. With the

2. God be praised for con-gre-ga-tions Join-ing
now in char-i-ty; Man-y tongues of man-y
na-tions, Sing the great-er u-ni-ty. Wel-come

3. May your name be praised for-ev-er! Heal our
dif-ferenc-es of old; Bless your church's new en-
deav-or; For your king-dom make us bold. One our

Words used by permission of Roger K. Powell.

cross our on - ly stan - dard Let us sing with
sound of psalm and car - ol When our song is
Christ and one our gos - pel, Make us one, we

one great voice, Glo - ry, glo - ry, yours the
raised as one. Glo - ry, glo - ry, yours the
now im - plore. Glo - ry, glo - ry, yours the

king - dom; Church - es in your church re - joice.
pow - er, As in heaven your will be done.
glo - ry Through the ag - es ev - er - more. A - men.

470   Lord, Who Throughout These Forty Days

ST. FLAVIAN C.M.

Claudia F. Hernaman, 1873; alt., 1972

Day's Psalter, 1562
Adapted in *Church Hymn Tunes*, 1853

1. Lord, who through-out these for-ty days For
2. As you with Sa-tan did con-tend, And
3. And through these days of pen-i-tence, And
4. A-bide with us, so when this course Of

us did fast and pray, Teach us with you to
did the vic-tory win, O give us strength in
through your Pas-sion-tide, Yes, ev-er-more, in
life on earth is past, An Eas-ter of un-

mourn our sins, And close by you to stay.
you to fight, In you to con-quer sin.
life and death, O Lord, with us a-bide.
end-ing joy We may at-tain at last! A-men.

Love Divine, All Loves Excelling 471

HYFRYDOL 8.7.8.7.D.

Charles Wesley, 1747; alt.

Rowland Hugh Prichard, 1855
Harm. by Ralph Vaughan Williams, 1906

1. Love di - vine, all loves ex - cel - ling, Joy of
2. Breathe, O breathe thy lov - ing Spir - it In - to
3. Come, Al - might - y to de - liv - er, Let us
4. Fin - ish, then, thy new cre - a - tion; Pure and

heaven, to earth come down, Fix in us thy hum - ble
ev - ery trou - bled breast! Let us all in thee in -
all thy life re - ceive; Sud - den - ly re - turn, and
spot - less let us be; Let us see thy great sal -

dwell - ing, All thy faith - ful mer - cies crown! Je - sus,
her - it, Let us find the prom - ised rest; Take a -
nev - er, Nev - er - more thy tem - ples leave. Thee we
va - tion Per - fect - ly re - stored in thee; Changed from

See following page.

thou art all com - pas - sion, Pure, un - bound - ed
way the love of sin - ning; Al - pha and O -
would be al - ways bless - ing, Serve thee as thy
glo - ry in - to glo - ry, Till in heaven we

love thou art; Vis - it us with thy sal -
meg - a be; End of faith, as its Be -
hosts a - bove, Pray, and praise thee with - out
take our place, Till we cast our crowns be -

va - tion, En - ter ev - ery trem - bling heart.
gin - ning, Set our hearts at lib - er - ty.
ceas - ing, Glo - ry in thy per - fect love.
fore thee, Lost in won - der, love, and praise. A - men.

Lovely Child, Holy Child

473

BETHLEHEM 6.6.6.7. with Alleluias

Folk carol

David N. Johnson, 1968

Adapted by David N. Johnson, 1968

1. Love - ly Child, ho - ly Child, Gen - tle, mild, un - de - filed;
2. Child of light, born to - night, Our de - light, prom - ise bright;
3. Rest thy head, sweet - est head; Gifts we'll spread at thy bed.
4. To this Boy, our great joy, We em - ploy hymns of joy;

In - fant King, fair - est King, Gifts we'll bring and an - thems sing:
Child so fair: see him there; Now de - clare him ev - ery - where:
Je - sus Lord, be a - dored, May this word now be out - poured:
Child so fair: see him there; Now de - clare him ev - ery - where:

Al - le - lu - ia, al - le - lu - ia.

Al - le - lu - ia, al - le - lu - ia! A - men.

474 Mine Eyes Have Seen the Glory

BATTLE HYMN OF THE REPUBLIC P.M.

Julia Ward Howe, 1861

Arr. from camp meeting song

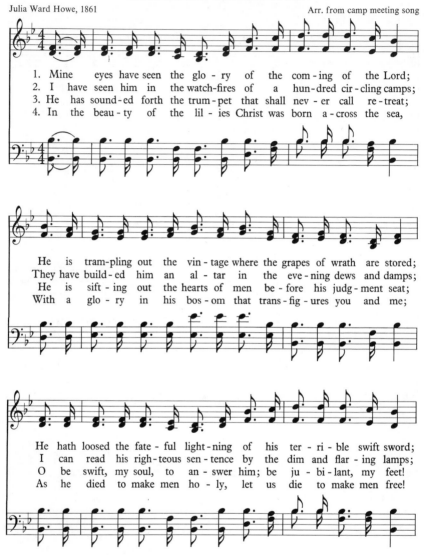

1. Mine eyes have seen the glo - ry of the com - ing of the Lord;
2. I have seen him in the watch-fires of a hun - dred cir - cling camps;
3. He has sound - ed forth the trum - pet that shall nev - er call re - treat;
4. In the beau - ty of the lil - ies Christ was born a - cross the sea,

He is tram-pling out the vin - tage where the grapes of wrath are stored;
They have build - ed him an al - tar in the eve - ning dews and damps;
He is sift - ing out the hearts of men be - fore his judg - ment seat;
With a glo - ry in his bos - om that trans - fig - ures you and me;

He hath loosed the fate - ful light - ning of his ter - ri - ble swift sword;
I can read his righ - teous sen - tence by the dim and flar - ing lamps;
O be swift, my soul, to an - swer him; be ju - bi - lant, my feet!
As he died to make men ho - ly, let us die to make men free!

His truth is march - ing on.
His day is march - ing on.
Our God is march - ing on.
While God is march - ing on.

Glo - ry! glo - ry! Hal - le -

lu - jah! Glo - ry! glo - ry! Hal - le - lu - jah!

Glo - ry! glo - ry! Hal - le - lu - jah! His truth is march-ing on. A-men.

476 My Country, 'Tis of Thee

AMERICA 6.6.4.6.6.6.4.

Samuel F. Smith, 1831   Source unknown

1. My coun-try, 'tis of thee, Sweet land of lib-er-ty, Of thee I sing; Land where my fa-thers died, Land of the pil-grims' pride, From ev-ery moun-tain-side Let free-dom ring.

2. My na-tive coun-try, thee, Land of the no-ble free, Thy name I love; I love thy rocks and rills, Thy woods and tem-pled hills; My heart with rap-ture thrills Like that a-bove.

3. Let mu-sic swell the breeze, And ring from all the trees Sweet free-dom's song: Let mor-tal tongues a-wake; Let all that breathe par-take; Let rocks their si-lence break, The sound pro-long.

4. Our fa-thers' God, to thee, Au-thor of lib-er-ty, To thee we sing: Long may our land be bright With free-dom's ho-ly light; Pro-tect us by thy might, Great God, our King. A-men.

My Shepherd Will Supply My Need

RESIGNATION C.M.D.

Psalm 23
Para. by Isaac Watts, 1719; alt., 1972

Southern Harmony, 1835
Harm. in *Hymnal for Colleges and Schools*, 1956

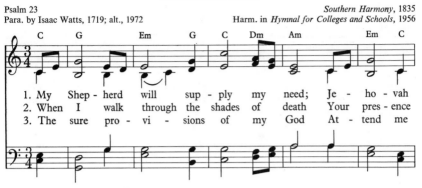

1. My Shep - herd will sup - ply my need; Je - ho - vah
2. When I walk through the shades of death Your pres - ence
3. The sure pro - vi - sions of my God At - tend me

is his name: In pas - tures fresh he makes me feed, Be -
is my stay; One word of your sup - port - ing breath Drives
all my days; O may your house be my a - bode, And

side the liv - ing stream. He brings my wan - dering spir - it
all my fears a - way. Your hand, in sight of all my
all my work be praise. There would I find a set - tled

Music from *Hymnal for Colleges and Schools*, edited by E. Harold Geer;
used by permission of Yale University Press.

See following page.

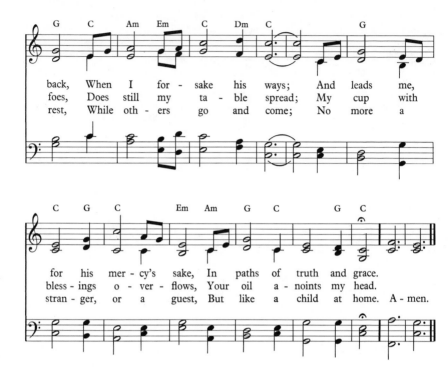

back, When I for - sake his ways; And leads me,
foes, Does still my ta - ble spread; My cup with
rest, While oth - ers go and come; No more a

for his mer - cy's sake, In paths of truth and grace.
bless - ings o - ver - flows, Your oil a - noints my head.
stran - ger, or a guest, But like a child at home. A - men.

Not Alone for Mighty Empire

479

GENEVA 8.7.8.7.D.

William Pierson Merrill, 1909, 1910; alt., 1972

George Henry Day, 1940

Unison

1. Not a - lone for might-y em - pire Stretch-ing far be - yond our view,
*2. Not for bat - tle - ship and for-tress, Not for con-quests of the sword,
3. For the ar - mies of the faith-ful, Souls that passed and left no name;
4. God of jus-tice, save the peo - ple From the clash of race and creed,

Not a - lone for boun-teous har-vests, Lift we up our hearts to you.
But for con-quests of the spir - it Give we thanks to you, O Lord;
For the glo - ry that il - lu-mines Pa - triot lives of death-less fame;
From the strife of class and fac - tion: Make our na - tion free in-deed.

Stand-ing in the liv - ing pres-ent, Mem-o - ry and hope be - tween,
For the price-less gift of free-dom, For the home, the church, the school,
For our proph-ets and a - pos-tles, Loy-al to the liv - ing Word,
Keep her faith in sim - ple man-hood Strong as when her life be - gan,

Lord, we would with deep thanks-giv - ing Praise you most for things un-seen.
For the o - pen door to man-hood In a land the peo-ple rule.
For all he - roes of the spir - it, Give we thanks to you, O Lord.
Till it find its full fru - i - tion In the broth-er - hood of man. A-men.

Music used by permission of The Church Pension Fund.

Alternative Tune: HYFRYDOL

480 Now, on Land and Sea Descending

VESPER HYMN 8.7.8.7.8.6.8.7.

Samuel Longfellow, 1859
Refrain added

Russian melody (?)
Arr. by John A. Stevenson, 1818

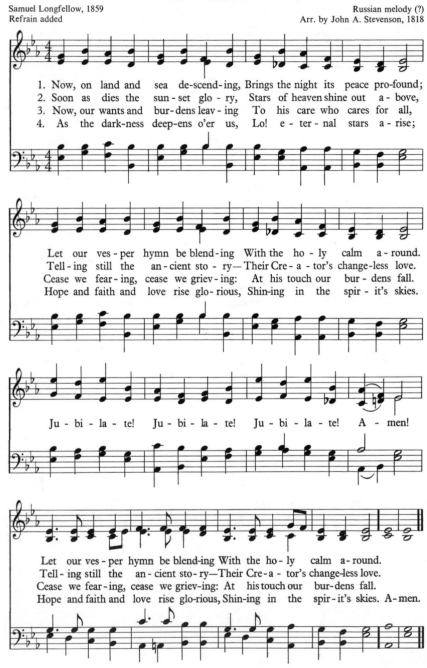

1. Now, on land and sea de-scend-ing, Brings the night its peace pro-found;
2. Soon as dies the sun-set glo-ry, Stars of heaven shine out a-bove,
3. Now, our wants and bur-dens leav-ing To his care who cares for all,
4. As the dark-ness deep-ens o'er us, Lo! e-ter-nal stars a-rise;

Let our ves-per hymn be blend-ing With the ho-ly calm a-round.
Tell-ing still the an-cient sto-ry—Their Cre-a-tor's change-less love.
Cease we fear-ing, cease we griev-ing: At his touch our bur-dens fall.
Hope and faith and love rise glo-rious, Shin-ing in the spir-it's skies.

Ju-bi-la-te! Ju-bi-la-te! Ju-bi-la-te! A-men!

Let our ves-per hymn be blend-ing With the ho-ly calm a-round.
Tell-ing still the an-cient sto-ry—Their Cre-a-tor's change-less love.
Cease we fear-ing, cease we griev-ing: At his touch our bur-dens fall.
Hope and faith and love rise glo-rious, Shin-ing in the spir-it's skies. A-men.

Now Thank We All Our God

NUN DANKET 6.7.6.7.6.6.6.6.

481

Martin Rinkart, 1636
Trans. by Catherine Winkworth, 1858; alt., 1972

Johann Crüger, 1647
As alt. by Felix Mendelssohn, 1840

1. Now thank we all our God With heart and hands and voic - es,
2. O may this boun - teous God Through all our life be near us,
3. All praise and thanks to God The Fa - ther now be giv - en,

Who won-drous things has done, In whom his world re - joic - es;
With ev - er - joy - ful hearts And bless - ed peace to cheer us;
The Son, and him who reigns With them in high - est heav - en,

Who, from our moth - ers' arms Has blessed us on our way
And keep us in his grace, And guide us when per - plexed,
The one e - ter - nal God, Whom earth and heaven a - dore;

With count-less gifts of love, And still is ours to - day.
And free us from all ills In this world and the next.
For thus it was, is now, And shall be ev - er - more. A - men.

482 O Be Joyful in the Lord!

ROCK OF AGES (MOOZ TSUR) 7.7.7.7.5.7.6.7.

Based on Psalm 100
Curtis Beach, 1958; alt., 1972

Traditional Hebrew melody
As in *Pilgrim Hymnal*, 1958

1. O be joy - ful in the Lord! Sing be - fore him, all the earth!
2. Know then that the Lord is King! All his works his wis - dom prove!
3. En - ter now his ho - ly gate; Let our bur-dened hearts be still;
4. For the Lord our God is kind, And his love shall con - stant be;

Praise him with a glad ac - cord And with lives of no - blest worth.
By his might the heav - ens ring; In his love we live and move.
In the sa - cred si - lence wait, As we seek to know his will.
In his will our peace we find; In his serv - ice, lib - er - ty.

Sons of ev - ery land, Hum - bly now be - fore him stand!
By him we are made, So we trust him un - a - fraid.
Let our lives ex - press Our a - bun - dant thank-ful - ness;
Yea, his law is sure; In his light we walk se - cure;

Raise your voice and re - joice In the boun - ty of his hand.
Stand - ing fast to the last, By his hand our lives are stayed.
All our days, all our ways, Shall our Fa - ther's love con - fess.
Ev - er - more, as of yore, Shall his change-less truth en - dure. A - men.

O Beautiful for Spacious Skies

MATERNA C.M.D.

Katharine Lee Bates, 1893, 1904

Samuel A. Ward, 1882

1. O beau - ti - ful for spa - cious skies, For am - ber waves of grain,
2. O beau - ti - ful for pil - grim feet, Whose stern, im - pas - sioned stress
3. O beau - ti - ful for he - roes proved In lib - er - at - ing strife,
4. O beau - ti - ful for pa - triot dream That sees be - yond the years

For pur - ple moun - tain maj - es - ties A - bove the fruit - ed plain!
A thor - ough - fare for free - dom beat A - cross the wil - der - ness!
Who more than self their coun - try loved, And mer - cy more than life!
Thine al - a - bas - ter cit - ies gleam, Un - dimmed by hu - man tears!

A - mer - i - ca! A - mer - i - ca! God shed his grace on thee
A - mer - i - ca! A - mer - i - ca! God mend thine ev - ery flaw,
A - mer - i - ca! A - mer - i - ca! May God thy gold re - fine
A - mer - i - ca! A - mer - i - ca! God shed his grace on thee

And crown thy good with broth - er - hood From sea to shin - ing sea!
Con - firm thy soul in self - con - trol, Thy lib - er - ty in law!
Till all suc - cess be no - ble - ness And ev - ery gain di - vine!
And crown thy good with broth - er - hood From sea to shin - ing sea! A - men!

484   O Brother Man, Fold to Your Heart

WELWYN 11.10.11.10.

John Greenleaf Whittier, 1848; alt., 1972

Alfred Scott-Gatty, 1900
As in *The English Hymnal*, 1906

1. O broth - er man, fold to your heart your broth - er;
2. For he whom Je - sus loved has tru - ly spo - ken:
3. Fol - low with rev - erent steps the great ex - am - ple
4. Then shall all shack - les fall; the storm - y clang - or

Where pit - y dwells, the peace of God is there;
The ho - lier wor - ship which he deigns to bless
Of him whose ho - ly work was do - ing good;
Of wild war mu - sic o'er the earth shall cease;

To wor - ship right - ly is to love each oth - er,
Re - stores the lost, and binds the spir - it bro - ken,
So shall the wide earth seem our Fa - ther's tem - ple,
Love shall tread out the bale - ful fire of an - ger,

Each smile a hymn, each kind - ly deed a prayer.
And feeds the wid - ow and the fa - ther - less.
Each lov - ing life a psalm of grat - i - tude.
And in its ash - es plant the tree of peace. A - men.

O Christ, Whose Love Has Sought Us Out 485

DAS NEUGEBORNE KINDELEIN L.M.

John Edgar Park, 1953; alt., 1972

Melchior Vulpius, 1609
Harm. by J. S. Bach, 1724

1. O Christ, whose love has sought us out
   A - lone and lost in des - ert ways;
   We gath - er round your cross a - gain
   In won - der and u - nit - ed praise.

2. Your life is still the mir - a - cle,
   Our way of liv - ing far a - bove,
   Be yond the reach - es of our minds:
   We can - not un - der - stand; we love.

3. An - ces - tral gifts with - in our hands,
   The cher - ished trea - sures from the past,
   We lay be - fore your feet, O Lord:
   Cleanse, use them, make them yours at last.

4. So may we all be one in you,
   Whose rev - e - la - tions nev - er cease,
   Whose love and truth are ev - er new,
   And in whose serv - ice is our peace. A - men.

Words altered from *Eleven Ecumenical Hymns*; copyright 1954 by The Hymn Society of America; used by permission.

486 O Come, All Ye Faithful

ADESTE FIDELES Irregular

Attr. to John Francis Wade, ca. 1743
Trans. by Frederick Oakeley, 1841; alt.

Attr. to John Francis Wade, ca. 1743

1. O come, all ye faith - ful, Joy - ful and tri - um - phant, O
2. The Bright-ness of glo - ry, Light of light e - ter - nal, Our
3. O sing, choirs of an - gels, Sing in ex - ul - ta - tion! O
4. A - men, Lord, we greet thee, Born this hap - py morn - ing, O

come ye, O come ye to Beth - le - hem!
low - ly na - ture he hath not ab - horred:
sing, all ye cit - i - zens of heaven a - bove!
Je - sus, to thee be all glo - ry given;

Come and be - hold him, Born the King of an - gels!
Son of the Fa - ther, Word of God in - car - nate!
Glo - ry to God, all glo - ry in the high - est!
Word of the Fa - ther, Now in flesh ap - pear - ing!

488   O Come and Sing Unto the Lord

IRISH C.M.

From Psalm 95:1-6
The Psalter, 1912; alt., 1955

A Collection of Hymns and Sacred Poems, 1749

1. O come and sing un-to the Lord, To
2. Be-fore his pres-ence let us come With
3. The Lord our God is King of kings, A-
4. To him the spa-cious sea be-longs, He
5. O come, and bow-ing down to him Our

him our voic-es raise; Let us in our most
praise and thank-ful voice; Let us sing psalms to
bove all gods his throne; The depths of earth are
made its waves and tides; And by his hand the
wor-ship let us bring; Yea, let us kneel be-

joy-ful songs The Lord, our Sav-ior, praise.
him with grace, With grate-ful hearts re-joice.
in his hand, The moun-tains are his own.
ris-ing land Was formed, and still a-bides.
fore the Lord, Our Mak-er and our King. A-men.

O Come, O Come, Emmanuel

VENI EMMANUEL 8.8.8.8.8.8.

Psalteriolum Cantionum Catholicarum, 1710
Sts. 1, 2 trans. by John Mason Neale, 1851, 1854; alt.
Sts. 3, 4 trans. by Henry Sloane Coffin, 1916

French Processional, 15th century
Adapted by Thomas Helmore, 1854
As in *Hymnal for Colleges and Schools*, 1956

May be sung in unison

1. O come, O come, Em - man - u - el, And ran - som cap - tive
2. O come, thou Day-spring, come and cheer Our spir - its by thine
3. O come, thou Wis - dom from on high, And or - der all things,
4. O come, De - sire of na - tions, bind All peo - ples in one

Is - ra - el, That mourns in lone - ly ex - ile here, Un -
ad - vent here; Dis - perse the gloom-y clouds of night, And
far and nigh; To us the path of knowl - edge show, And
heart and mind; Bid en - vy, strife, and quar - rels cease; Fill

til the Son of God ap - pear.
death's dark shad-ows put to flight. Re - joice! Re - joice! Em -
cause us in her ways to go.
the whole world with heav - en's peace.

man - u - el Shall come to thee, O Is - ra - el! A - men.

Music from *Hymnal for Colleges and Schools*, edited by E. Harold Geer; used by permission of Yale University Press.

490   O Come, O Come, Emmanuel

Psalteriolum Cantionum Catholicarum, 1710
Trans. by T. A. Lacey, 1906

James Minchin, 1964

(Solo instrument ad lib.)

1. O come, O come, Em-man-u-el! Re-deem thy cap-tive Is-ra-el, That in-to ex-ile drear has gone Far from the face of God's dear Son.

2. O come, O come, thou Day-spring bright! Pour on our souls thy heal-ing light; Dis-pel the long night's lin-gering gloom, And pierce the shad-ows of the tomb. Re-

3. O come, thou Lord of Da-vid's Key! The roy-al door fling wide and free; Safe-guard for us the heav-enward road, And bar the way to death's a-bode.

joice! Re - joice! Em - man - u -

el Shall come to thee, O

Sts. 1, 2

Is - - - ra - el.

St. 3

el.

492   O Day of God, Draw Nigh

ST. MICHAEL S.M.

Comp. or adapted by Louis Bourgeois, 1551
Adapted by William Crotch, 1836
R. B. Y. Scott, 1937, 1939; alt., 1972
As in *Pilgrim Hymnal*, 1958

1. O Day of God, draw nigh In beau-ty and in power, Come with your time-less judg-ment now To match our pres-ent hour.

2. Bring to our trou-bled minds, Un-cer-tain and a-fraid, The qui-et of a stead-fast faith, Calm of a call o-beyed.

3. Bring jus-tice to our land, That all may dwell se-cure, And fine-ly build for days to come Foun-da-tions that en-dure.

4. Bring to our world of strife Your sov-ereign word of peace, That war may haunt the earth no more And des-o-la-tion cease.

5. O Day of God, draw nigh As at cre-a-tion's birth; Let there be light a-gain, and set Your judg-ments in the earth. A-men.

O for a Thousand Tongues to Sing

AZMON C.M.

Charles Wesley, 1739; alt., 1972

Carl G. Gläser, 1828
Arr. by Lowell Mason, 1839

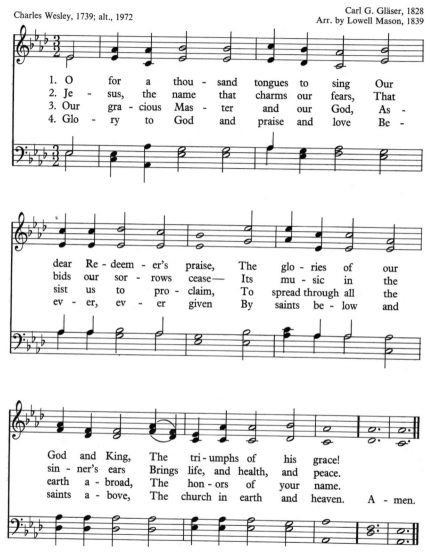

1. O for a thou - sand tongues to sing Our
2. Je - sus, the name that charms our fears, That
3. Our gra - cious Mas - ter and our God, As -
4. Glo - ry to God and praise and love Be -

dear Re - deem - er's praise, The glo - ries of our
bids our sor - rows cease— Its mu - sic in the
sist us to pro - claim, To spread through all the
ev - er, ev - er given By saints be - low and

God and King, The tri - umphs of his grace!
sin - ner's ears Brings life, and health, and peace.
earth a - broad, The hon - ors of your name.
saints a - bove, The church in earth and heaven. A - men.

494   O Gladsome Light, O Grace

NUNC DIMITTIS 6.6.7.D.

Greek hymn, 3d century or earlier
Trans. by Robert Bridges, 1899

Comp. or adapted by Louis Bourgeois, 1549

1. O glad-some Light, O Grace Of God the Fa-ther's
2. Now, ere day fad - eth quite, We see the eve - ning
3. To thee of right be - longs All praise of ho - ly

face, Th'e - ter - nal splen - dor wear - ing; Ce -
light, Our wont - ed hymn out - pour - ing; Fa -
songs, O Son of God, Life - giv - er; Thee,

les - tial, ho - ly, blest, Our Sav - ior Je - sus
ther of might un - known, Thee, his in - car - nate
there - fore, O Most High, The world doth glo - ri -

Christ, Joy - ful in thine ap - pear - ing!
Son, And Ho - ly Spirit a - dor - ing.
fy And shall ex - alt for - ev - er. A - men.

Words from *The Yattendon Hymnal*; used by permission of Oxford University Press.

O God, Beneath Your Guiding Hand

DUKE STREET L.M.

Leonard Bacon, 1833, 1845; alt., 1972

John Hatton, 1793

1. O God, be - neath your guid - ing hand Our ex - iled
2. You heard, well - pleased, the song, the prayer; Your bless - ing
3. Laws, free - dom, truth, and faith in God Came with those
4. And here your name, O God of love, Their chil-dren's

fa - thers crossed the sea; And ech - oed o'er the
came, and still its power Shall on - ward through all
ex - iles o'er the waves, And where their pil - grim
chil - dren shall a - dore, Till these e - ter - nal

win - try strand Their psalms and prayers in wor - ship free.
ag - es bear The mem-ory of that ho - ly hour.
feet have trod, The God they trust - ed guards their graves.
hills re - move, And spring a - dorns the earth no more. A - men.

496   O God of Bethel, by Whose Hand

DUNDEE (FRENCH) C.M.

Philip Doddridge, 1736, and others
As in Scottish Paraphrases, 1781; alt., 1972

Scottish Psalter, 1615

1. O God of Beth - el, by whose hand Your
2. Our vows, our prayers, we now pre - sent Be -
3. Through each per - plex - ing path of life Our
4. O spread your cov - ering wings a - round Till
5. Such bless - ings from your gra - cious hand Our

peo - ple still are fed, Who through this wea - ry
fore your throne of grace; God of our fa - thers,
wan - dering foot - steps guide; Give us each day our
all our wan - derings cease, And at our Fa - ther's
hum - ble prayers im - plore; And you shall be our

pil - grim - age Have all our fa - thers led,
be the God Of their suc - ceed - ing race.
dai - ly bread, And rai - ment fit pro - vide.
loved a - bode Our souls ar - rive in peace.
cho - sen God And por - tion ev - er - more. A - men.

O God of Earth and Altar

497

LLANGLOFFAN 7.6.7.6.D.

Gilbert K. Chesterton, 1906

Welsh hymn melody
Evans' *Hymnau a Thonau*, 1865

1. O God of earth and al - tar, Bow down and hear our cry;
2. From all that ter - ror teach - es, From lies of tongue and pen,
3. Tie in a liv - ing teth - er The priest and prince and thrall;

Our earth - ly rul - ers fal - ter; Our peo - ple drift and die;
From all the eas - y speech - es That com - fort cru - el men,
Bind all our lives to - geth - er; Smite us and save us all;

The walls of gold en - tomb us; The swords of scorn di - vide;
From sale and prof - a - na - tion Of hon - or and the sword,
In ire and ex - ul - ta - tion, A - flame with faith, and free,

Take not thy thun - der from us, But take a - way our pride.
From sleep and from dam - na - tion, De - liv - er us, good Lord!
Lift up a liv - ing na - tion, A sin - gle sword to thee. A - men.

498 O God of Every Nation

LLANGLOFFAN 7.6.7.6.D.

William W. Reid, Jr., 1958; alt., 1972

Welsh hymn melody
Evans' *Hymnau a Thonau*, 1865

1. O God of ev - ery na - tion, Of ev - ery race and land,
2. From search for wealth and pow - er And scorn of truth and right,
3. Lord, strength-en all who la - bor That men may find re - lease
4. Keep bright in us the vi - sion Of days when war shall cease,

Re - deem the whole cre - a - tion With your al - might - y hand;
From trust in bombs that show - er De - struc-tion through the night,
From fear of rat - tling sa - ber, From dread of war's in - crease;
When ha - tred and di - vi - sion Give way to love and peace,

Where hate and fear di - vide us And bit - ter threats are hurled,
From pride of race and sta - tion And blind-ness to your way,
When hope and cour - age fal - ter, Your still small voice be heard;
Till dawns the morn-ing glo - rious When broth - er - hood shall reign

In love and mer - cy guide us And heal our strife-torn world.
De - liv - er ev - ery na - tion, E - ter - nal God, we pray.
With faith that none can al - ter, Your serv - ants un - der - gird.
And Christ shall rule vic - to - rious O'er all the world's do - main. A - men.

O God of Light, Your Word, a Lamp Unfailing 499

CHARTERHOUSE 11.10.11.10.

Sarah E. Taylor, 1952; alt., 1972

David Evans, 1927

1. O God of light, your Word, a lamp un-fail-ing, Shines through the
2. From days of old, through swift-ly roll-ing ag-es, You have re-
3. Un-dimmed by time, the Word is still re-veal-ing To sin-ful
4. To all the world the mes-sage you are send-ing, To ev-ery

dark-ness of our earth-ly way, O'er fear and doubt, o'er black de-
vealed your will to mor-tal men, Speak-ing to saints, to proph-ets,
men your jus-tice and your grace; And quest-ing hearts that long for
land, to ev-ery race and clan; And myr-iad tongues, in one great

spair pre-vail-ing, Guid-ing our steps to your e-ter-nal day.
kings, and sag-es, Who wrote the mes-sage with im-mor-tal pen.
peace and heal-ing See your com-pas-sion in the Sav-ior's face.
an-them blend-ing, Ac-claim with joy your won-drous gift to man. A-men.

500
O God, Our Faithful God

O GOTT, DU FROMMER GOTT 6.7.6.7.6 6 6 6.

Johann Heermann, 1630
Trans. by Catherine Winkworth, 1858; alt., 1956, 1972

Attr. to Ahasuerus Fritsch, 1679
Harm. by J. S. Bach, 1726

1. O God, our faith-ful God, O foun-tain ev - er flow - ing,
2. And grant us, Lord, to do, With read - y heart and will - ing,
3. If dan - gers gath - er round, Still keep us calm and fear - less;

With - out whom noth - ing is, All per - fect gifts be - stow - ing,
What - ev - er you com - mand, Our call - ing here ful - fill - ing;
Help us to bear the cross When life is dark and cheer - less,

Grant us a faith - ful life, And give us, Lord, with - in, Com-
And do it when we ought, With zeal and joy - ful - ness; And
To o - ver - come our foes With words and ac - tions kind; O

mit - ment free from strife, A soul un - hurt by sin.
bless the work we've wrought, For you must give suc - cess.
God, your will dis - close, Your coun - sel let us find. A - men.

Words altered from *Hymnal for Colleges and Schools*, edited by E. Harold Geer; used by permission of Yale University Press.

O God, This Child from You Did Come

501

SHEPHERDS' PIPES C.M.D.

Frank A. Brooks, Jr., 1972

Annabeth McClelland Gay, 1952

1. O God, this child from you did come, To you it shall re-turn;
2. Real acts of love and words of truth We hope to teach this child,
3. Of flesh and blood this child is made, In im-age of your-self.

But to our trust and love you chose To send it for some years.
And con-stant may our guid-ance be In like-ness of your Son.
To men we come; on earth we live—Our pur-pose clear to serve.

Be-cause we thank you for this life That to our lives has come,

To-geth-er we do pledge our-selves To help this child serve you. A-men.

502 O God, Who by a Star Did Guide

ST. BERNARD C.M.

John Mason Neale, 1842; alt., 1972

Tochter Sion, Cologne, 1741
Arr. attr. to John Richardson, 1851

1. O God, who by a star did guide The
2. Al - though by stars you do not lead Your
3. As yet we know you but in part, But
4. O Sav - ior, give us then your grace, For

Wise Men on their way, Un - til it came and
serv - ants now be - low, Your Ho - ly Spir - it,
still we trust your word, That bless - ed are the
pure in heart we'd be, That we may see you,

stood be - side The place where Je - sus lay:
when they need, Will show them how to go.
pure in heart, For they shall see the Lord.
face to face, Through all e - ter - ni - ty. A - men.

O God, Whose Will Is Life and Peace

THIRD MODE MELODY C.M.D.

503

Rolland W. Schloerb, 1948; alt., 1972

Thomas Tallis, ca. 1567
Rhythm alt.

1. O God, whose will is life and peace For all the sons of men,
2. O God, whose ways shall lead to peace, En - light - en us, we pray;
3. O God, who calls all men to peace, We join with ev - ery - one

Let not our hu - man hates re - lease The sword's dread power a - gain.
Dis - pel our dark - ness and in - crease The light a - long our way.
Who does his part that wars may cease And jus - tice may be done.

For - give our nar - row-ness of mind; De - stroy false pride, we plead;
Il - lu - mine those who lead the lands, That they may make at length
En - a - ble us to take the way The Prince of Peace has trod;

De - liv - er us and all man-kind From self-ish-ness and greed.
The laws of right to guide the hands That wield the na-tions' strength.
Cre - ate the will to build each day The fam - i - ly of God. A - men.

504 O God, You Are the Father

GOSTERWOOD 7.6.7.6.D.

St. Columba (521-597)
Trans. by Duncan Macgregor, 1897; alt., 1972

Traditional English melody, collected and
harm. by Ralph Vaughan Williams, 1906

1. O God, you are the Fa - ther Of all that have be - lieved,
2. High in the heav-enly Zi - on You reign, our God a - dored,
3. You to the meek and low - ly Your se - crets do un - fold;

From whom all hosts of peo - ple Have life and power re - ceived.
And in the com - ing glo - ry You shall be sov - ereign Lord;
O God, who can do all things, All things good, new and old.

O God, you are the Mak - er Of all cre - at - ed things,
Be - yond our knowl-edge shin - ing, The ev - er - last - ing light:
We walk se - cure and bless - ed In ev - ery clime or coast,

The righ-teous Judge of judg - es, Th'al-might-y King of kings.
In - ef - fa - ble in lov - ing, Un-think-a - ble in might.
In name of God the Fa - ther, And Son, and Ho - ly Ghost. A-men.

O Holy City, Seen of John

505

MORNING SONG 8.6.8.6.8.6.

Walter Russell Bowie, 1909; alt., 1972

Kentucky Harmony, ca.1815
Harm. by C. Winfred Douglas, 1940

May be sung in unison

1. O ho - ly cit - y, seen of John, Where Christ, the Lamb, does reign, With - in whose four - square walls shall come No night, nor need, nor pain, And where the tears are wiped from eyes That shall not weep a - gain!

2. O shame to us who rest con - tent While lust and greed for gain In street and shop and ten - e - ment Wring gold from hu - man pain, And bit - ter lips in blind de - spair Cry, "Christ has died in vain"!

3. Give us, O God, the strength to build The cit - y that has stood Too long a dream, whose laws are love, Whose ways are broth - er - hood, And where the sun that shines be - comes God's grace for hu - man good.

4. Al - read - y in the mind of God That city ris - es fair: Lo, how its splen - dor chal - leng - es The souls that great - ly dare, And bids us seize the whole of life And build its glo - ry there. A - men.

506

O How Shall We Receive You

ST. THEODULPH 7.6.7.6.D.

Paul Gerhardt, 1653
Trans. by Arthur Tozer Russell, 1851, and others
As in *Hymnal for Colleges and Schools*, 1956; alt., 1972

Melchior Teschner, 1615

1. O how shall we re - ceive you, How meet you on your way,
2. Your Zi - on palms is spread-ing, And branch-es fresh and fair;
3. Love caused your in - car - na - tion; Love blessed hu - man - i - ty.
4. You came, O Lord, with glad - ness, In mer - cy and good - will,

Blest hope of ev - ery na - tion, Our soul's de - light and stay?
Our souls, to praise a - wak - ing, An an - them shall pre - pare.
Your thirst for our sal - va - tion Pro - cured our lib - er - ty.
To bring an end to sad - ness And bid our fears be still.

O Je - sus, Je - sus, give us Now by your own pure light
Un - end - ing thanks and prais - es From our glad hearts shall spring;
O love be - yond all tell - ing, That led you to em - brace.
We wel - come you, our Sav - ior; Come, gath - er us to you,

To know what-e'er is pleas - ing And wel-come in your sight.
And to your name the serv - ice Of all our powers we bring.
In love all loves ex - cel - ling, Our lost and trou-bled race.
That in your light e - ter - nal Our joy - ous home we'll view. A - men.

Words altered from *Hymnal for Colleges and Schools*, edited by E. Harold Geer; used by permission of Yale University Press.

O I Know the Lord

Negro spiritual

Negro spiritual

O   I know the Lord,   I know the Lord,   I know the Lord's laid his

hands on me. O   I know the Lord,   I know the Lord,

Fine

I   know   the   Lord's   laid   his   hands   on   me.

1. Did ev - er you   see the like be - fore—
2. O   was - n't that a hap - py   day
3.   Some seek the Lord and don't seek him right,   I know the Lord's laid his
4. My   Lord's done just what he   said,

See following page.

King   Je - sus preach - ing   to   the   poor?
When   Je - sus washed my   sins   a -   way?
hands on me.   They   fool all   day   and   pray   at   night.
He's healed the sick and raised the dead.

D.C.

I   know   the   Lord's   laid   his   hands   on   me.

O Jesus Christ, to You May Hymns Be Rising 509

CITY OF GOD 11.10.11.10.

Bradford G. Webster, 1954, 1969

Daniel Moe, 1957

1. O Je - sus Christ, to you may hymns be ris - ing,
2. Show us your Spir - it, brood - ing o'er each cit - y,
3. Grant us new cour - age, sac - ri - fi - cial, hum - ble,

In ev - ery cit - y for your love and care;
As you once wept a - bove Je - ru - sa - lem,
Strong in your strength to ven - ture and to dare;

In - spire our wor - ship, grant the glad sur - pris - ing
Seek - ing to gath - er all in love and pit - y,
To lift the fall - en, guide the feet that stum - ble,

That your blest Spir - it brings men ev - ery - where.
And heal - ing those who touch your gar - ment's hem.
Seek out the lone - ly and God's mer - cy share. A - men.

510 O Jesus, Joy of Loving Hearts

FEDERAL STREET L.M.

Latin, 12th century
Trans. by Ray Palmer, 1858; alt., 1972

Henry K. Oliver, 1832

1. O Je - sus, joy of lov - ing hearts, O fount of
2. Your truth un - changed has ev - er stood; You save those
3. We taste you, Lord, our liv - ing Bread, And long to
4. For you our rest - less spir - its yearn, Wher - e'er our
5. O Je - sus, ev - er with us stay, Make all our

life, O light of men, From the best bliss that earth im -
who up - on you call; To those who seek you, you are
feast up - on you still; We drink of you, the foun - tain -
change - ful lot is cast, Glad when to you our gaze we
mo - ments calm and bright; Chase the dark night of sin a -

parts We turn un - filled to you a - gain.
good, To them who find you all in all.
head, And thirst our souls from you to fill.
turn, Blest when our faith can hold you fast.
way, Shed o'er the world your ho - ly light. A - men.

O Little Town of Bethlehem

ST. LOUIS 8.6.8.6.7.6.8.6.

Phillips Brooks, 1868   Lewis H. Redner, 1868

1. O lit - tle town of Beth - le - hem, How still we see thee lie;
2. For Christ is born of Mar - y; And gath - ered all a - bove,
3. How si - lent - ly, how si - lent - ly The won - drous gift is given!
4. O ho - ly Child of Beth - le - hem, De - scend to us, we pray;

A - bove thy deep and dream-less sleep The si - lent stars go by.
While mor - tals sleep, the an - gels keep Their watch of won-dering love.
So God im-parts to hu - man hearts The bless - ings of his heaven.
Cast out our sin, and en - ter in, Be born in us to - day.

Yet in thy dark streets shin - eth The ev - er - last - ing Light;
O morn - ing stars, to - geth - er Pro-claim the ho - ly birth;
No ear may hear his com - ing, But in this world of sin,
We hear the Christ-mas an - gels The great glad ti - dings tell;

The hopes and fears of all the years Are met in thee to - night.
And prais - es sing to God the King, And peace to men on earth.
Where meek souls will re - ceive him, still The dear Christ en - ters in.
O come to us, a - bide with us, Our Lord Em-man - u - el. A-men.

Alternative Tune: FOREST GREEN

512   O Lord of Every Shining Constellation

LOMBARD STREET 11.10.11.10.

Albert F. Bayly, 1950; alt., 1968

Frederick George Russell, 1925

1. O Lord of ev - ery shin - ing con - stel - la - tion
2. You, Lord, have made the at - om's hid - den forc - es,
3. You, Lord, have stamped your im - age on your crea - tures,
4. Great Lord of na - ture, shap - ing and re - new - ing,

That wheels in splen - dor through the mid - night sky;
Your laws its might - y en - er - gies ful - fill;
And, though they mar that im - age, love them still;
You made us more than na - ture's sons to be;

Grant us your Spir - it's true il - lu - mi - na - tion
Teach us, to whom you give such rich re - sourc - es,
Lift up our eyes to Christ, that in his fea - tures
You help us tread, with grace our souls en - du - ing,

To read the se - crets of your work on high.
In all we use, to serve your ho - ly will.
We may dis - cern the beau - ty of your will.
The road to life and im - mor - tal - i - ty. A - men.

Words used by permission of Albert F. Bayly. Music used by permission of Industrial Christian Fellowship, London.

O Lord of Life, Where'er They Be

GELOBT SEI GOTT 8.8.8. with Alleluias

Frederick Lucian Hosmer, 1888; alt., 1972

Attr. to Melchior Vulpius, 1609
As in *Pilgrim Hymnal*, 1958

513

1. O Lord of life, wher-e'er they be, Safe in your own e-
2. All souls you call, both here and there Do rest with-in your
3. Your word is true, your ways are just; A-bove the chant-ed
4. Hap-py are they in God who rest, No more by fear and

ter-ni-ty, Now live your chil-dren glo-rious-ly:
shel-tering care; One prov-i-dence a-like they share:
"Dust to dust" Shall rise our song of grate-ful trust:
doubt op-pressed, Liv-ing or dy-ing, they are blest:

Al-le-lu-ia! Al-le-lu-ia! Al-le-lu-ia! A-men.

514   O Lord, Our God, Most Earnestly

STRACATHRO C.M.

From Psalm 63:1-8
The Psalter, 1912; alt., 1972

Charles Hutcheson, 1832
Harm. by Geoffrey Shaw, 1925

1. O Lord, our God, most ear - nest - ly Our
2. A - part from you we long and thirst, And
3. The lov - ing - kind - ness of our God Is
4. In you our souls are sat - is - fied, Our
5. O Sav - ior, 'neath your shel - tering wings Our

hearts would seek your face, With - in your ho - ly
none can sat - is - fy; We wan - der in a
life's se - cur - i - ty; So we will bless you
dark - ness turns to light, And joy - ful med - i -
souls de - light to dwell; Still clos - er to your

house once more To see your glo - rious grace.
des - ert land Where all the streams run dry.
while we live And pray un - ceas - ing - ly.
ta - tions fill The watch - es of the night.
side we press, For near you all is well. A - men.

O Lord, Our Lord, in All the Earth

DUNFERMLINE C.M.

From Psalm 8
The Psalter, 1912; alt., 1972

Scottish Psalter, 1615

515

1. O Lord, our Lord, in all the earth How ex - cel - lent your name! Your glo - ry you have spread a - far In all the star - ry frame.

2. When I re - gard the won - drous heavens, Your hand - i - work on high, The moon and stars you have or - dained, Oh, what is man! I cry.

3. Oh, what is man, in your re - gard To hold so large a place! And what the Son of man, that you Do vis - it him in grace!

4. On man your wis - dom has be - stowed A power none else has known; With hon - or you have crowned his head With glo - ry like your own.

5. Your might - y works and won - drous grace Your glo - ry, Lord, pro - claim. O Lord, our Lord, in all the earth How ex - cel - lent your name! A - men.

516 O Lord, Whose Gracious Presence Shone

PUER NOBIS (Praetorius) L.M.

Sts. 1, 2, 4, Marion Franklin Ham, 1912; alt., 1972
St. 3, Dalton E. McDonald, 1972

Trier MS., 15th century
Adapted by Michael Praetorius, 1609
Harm. by George R. Woodward, 1902

1. O Lord, whose gra - cious pres - ence shone A light to
2. Your grace and truth, your life that shed Un - dy - ing
3. We taste the wine, and so re - call Your sac - ri -
4. And lo, a - gain we seem to hear Your bless - ing

bless your fel - low - men, To you we fond - ly turn a -
ra - diance through all time, Your ten - der love, your faith sub -
fice up - on the cross— A life di - vine be - come as
on the loaf and cup—The pres - ence that was lift - ed

gain, As to a friend that we have known.
lime— Re - mem - ber - ing these, we break the bread.
loss, That love should live a - gain in all.
up A - gain to lov - ing hearts brought near. A - men.

O Lord, You Are Our God and King

DUKE STREET L.M.

517

From Psalm 145:1-7
The Psalter, 1912; alt., 1972

John Hatton, 1793

1. O Lord, you are our God and King, And we will
2. The Lord is great - ly to be praised; His great-ness
3. Up - on your glo - rious maj - es - ty And won-drous
4. Your match-less good - ness and your grace Your peo - ple

ev - er bless your name; We will ex - tol you
is be - yond our thought; From age to age the
works our minds shall dwell; Your deeds shall fill the
shall com - mem - o - rate, And all your truth and

ev - ery day, And ev - er - more your praise pro - claim.
sons of men Shall tell the won - ders God has wrought.
world with awe, And of your great - ness we will tell.
righ - teous-ness Our joy - ful songs shall cel - e - brate. A-men.

518 O Love, How Deep, How Broad, How High!

DEO GRACIAS L.M.

Latin, 15th century
Trans. by Benjamin Webb, 1851; alt.

"The Agincourt Song," England, ca. 1415
Arr. for *The Hymnal*, 1933

Unison

1. O love, how deep, how broad, how high!
2. For us bap - tized, for us he bore
3. For us to wick - ed men be - trayed,
4. For us he rose from death a - gain,

Be - yond man's gift to proph - e - sy,
His ho - ly fast, and hun - gered sore;
Scourged, mocked, in pur - ple robe ar - rayed,
For us he went on high to reign;

That God, the Son of God, should take
For us temp - ta - tions sharp he knew;
He bore the shame - ful cross and death,
For us he sent his Spir - it here

Our mor - tal form for mor - tals' sake!
For us the tempt - er o - ver - threw.
For us gave up his dy - ing breath.
To guide, to strength - en, and to cheer. A - men.

O Love That Wilt Not Let Me Go

ST. MARGARET 8.8.8.8.6.

519

George Matheson, 1882

Albert L. Peace, 1884

1. O Love that wilt not let me go,
   I rest my weary soul in thee;
   I give thee back the life I owe,
   That in thine o-cean depths its flow May rich-er, full-er be.

2. O Light that fol-lowest all my way,
   I yield my flick-ering torch to thee;
   My heart re-stores its bor-rowed ray,
   That in thy sun-shine's blaze its day May bright-er, fair-er be.

3. O Joy that seek-est me through pain,
   I can-not close my heart to thee;
   I trace the rain-bow through the rain,
   And feel the prom-ise is not vain That morn shall tear-less be.

4. O Cross that lift-est up my head,
   I dare not ask to fly from thee;
   I lay in dust life's glo-ry dead,
   And from the ground there blos-soms red Life that shall end-less be. A-men.

520 O Master, Let Me Walk with Thee

MARYTON L.M.

Washington Gladden, 1879

Henry Percy Smith, 1874

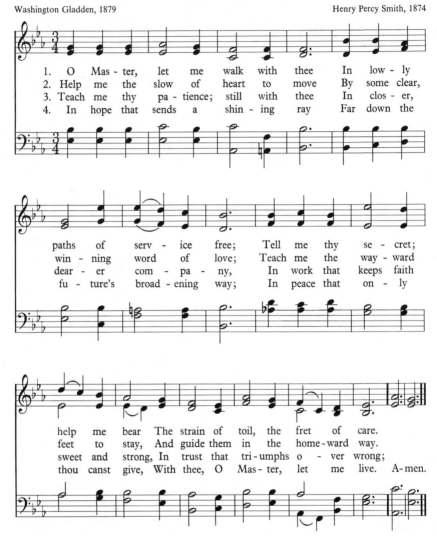

1. O Mas- ter, let me walk with thee In low- ly paths of serv- ice free; Tell me thy se- cret; help me bear The strain of toil, the fret of care.

2. Help me the slow of heart to move By some clear, win- ning word of love; Teach me the way- ward feet to stay, And guide them in the home- ward way.

3. Teach me thy pa- tience; still with thee In clos- er, dear- er com- pa- ny, In work that keeps faith sweet and strong, In trust that tri- umphs o- ver wrong;

4. In hope that sends a shin- ing ray Far down the fu- ture's broad- ening way; In peace that on- ly thou canst give, With thee, O Mas- ter, let me live. A- men.

O Morning Star, How Fair and Bright 521

FRANKFORT P.M.

Philipp Nicolai, 1599
Trans. by Catherine Winkworth, 1863; alt.

Attr. to Philipp Nicolai, 1599
Harm. by J. S. Bach, 1740

1. O Morn - ing Star, how fair and bright Your beams shine
*2. Come, heav - enly Bright - ness! Light di - vine! O deep with -
3. Re - joice, O heavens; and earth re - ply! With praise, you

forth in truth and light! O Sov-ereign meek and low - ly!
in our hearts now shine, And make you there an al - tar!
sin - ners, fill the sky, For this his in - car - na - tion.

O Root of Jes - se, Da - vid's Son, Our Lord and Mas - ter,
Fill us with joy and strength to be Your mem-bers joined with
In - car - nate God, put forth your power; Ride on, ride on, great

See following page.

you have won Our hearts to serve you sole - ly! You are   ho - ly,
u - ni - ty In love that can - not fal - ter! Toward you long - ing
Con - quer - or, Till all know your sal - va - tion.   A - men, A - men!

Fair and glo - rious, all - vic - to - rious, Rich in   bless - ing,
Does pos - sess us;   turn and bless us; Here in   sad - ness
Al - le - lu - ia! Al - le - lu - ia! Praise be   giv - en

Rule   and   might o'er   all   pos - sess - ing.
Eye   and   heart long   for   your   glad - ness!
Ev - er - more by   earth   and   heav - en.   A - men.

O My Soul, Bless God, the Father

STUTTGART 8.7.8.7.

From Psalm 103
Para. in *The Book of Psalms*, 1871; alt.

Psalmodia Sacra, 1715
Adapted in *Hymns Ancient & Modern*, 1861

523

1. O my soul, bless God, the Fa - ther; All with - in me bless his name; Bless the Fa - ther, and for - get not All his mer - cies to pro - claim;
2. He for - gives all your trans - gres - sions, Each dis - ease he gen - tly heals; He re - deems you from de - struc - tion, And with you so kind - ly deals.
3. Far as east from west is dis - tant, He has put a - way our sin; Like the pit - y of a fa - ther Has the Lord's com - pas - sion been.
4. As it was with - out be - gin - ning, So it lasts with - out an end; To their chil dren's chil - dren ev - er Shall his righ - teous - ness ex - tend:
5. Un - to such as keep his cov - enant And are stead - fast in his way; Un - to those who still re - mem - ber His com - mand - ments and o - bey.
6. Bless the Fa - ther, all his crea - tures, Ev - er un - der his con - trol, All through - out his vast do - min - ion; Bless the Fa - ther, O my soul. A - men.

524 O Sacred Head, Now Wounded

PASSION CHORALE 7.6.7.6.D.

Based on medieval Latin poem
Paul Gerhardt, 1656
Trans. by James W. Alexander, 1830

Hans Leo Hassler, 1601
Harm. by J. S. Bach, 1729

1. O sa-cred Head, now wound-ed, With grief and shame weighed down,
2. What thou, my Lord, hast suf-fered Was all for sin-ners' gain:
3. What lan-guage shall I bor-row To thank thee, dear-est Friend,

Now scorn-ful-ly sur-round-ed With thorns, thine on-ly crown;
Mine, mine was the trans-gres-sion, But thine the dead-ly pain.
For this thy dy-ing sor-row, Thy pit-y with-out end?

O sa-cred Head, what glo-ry, What bliss, till now was thine!
Lo, here I fall, my Sav-ior! 'Tis I de-serve thy place;
O make me thine for-ev-er; And should I faint-ing be,

Yet, though de-spised and gor-y, I joy to call thee mine.
Look on me with thy fa-vor, Vouch-safe to me thy grace.
Lord, let me nev-er, nev-er Out-live my love to thee. A-men.

O Sing a New Song to the Lord

SONG 67 C.M.

From Psalm 96
Para. in the Scottish Psalter, 1650; alt.

Prys's Welsh Psalter, 1621

525

1. O sing a new song to the Lord; Sing all the earth to God, To God sing, bless his name, show still His sav - ing health a - broad.

2. Great hon - or is be - fore his face, And maj - es - ty di - vine; Strength is with - in his ho - ly place, And there does beau - ty shine.

*3. O give un - to the liv - ing Lord, You men of ev - ery tribe, All glo - ry give un - to the Lord, And might - y power as - cribe.

4. O give the glo - ry to the Lord That to his name is due; Come all in - to his courts, and bring An of - fer - ing with you.

5. In beau - ty of his ho - li - ness, O all the earth through - out Fear him whom we im - plore. A - men.

O Sing a Song of Bethlehem

KINGSFOLD C.M.D.

Traditional English melody collected
by Lucy Broadwood (1858-1929)
Arr. and harm. by Ralph Vaughan Williams, 1906

Louis F. Benson, 1899

1. O sing a song of Beth - le - hem, Of shep-herds watch-ing there,
2. O sing a song of Naz - a - reth, Of sun - ny days of joy;
3. O sing a song of Gal - i - lee, Of lake and woods and hill,
4. O sing a song of Cal - va - ry, Its glo - ry and dis - may;

And of the news that came to them From an - gels in the air:
O sing of fra - grant flow - ers' breath, And of the sin - less boy:
Of him who walked up - on the sea And bade its waves be still:
Of him who hung up - on the tree, And took our sins a - way:

The light that shone on Beth - le - hem Fills all the world to - day;
For now the flowers of Naz - a - reth In ev - ery heart may grow;
For though, like waves on Gal - i - lee, Dark seas of trou - ble roll,
For he who died on Cal - va - ry Is ris - en from the grave,

Of Je - sus' birth and peace on earth The an - gels sing al - way.
Now spreads the fame of his dear name On all the winds that blow.
When faith has heard the Mas - ter's word, Falls peace up - on the soul.
And Christ, our Lord, by heaven a - dored, Is might - y now to save. A-men.

O Sons and Daughters, Let Us Sing!

O FILII ET FILIAE 8.8.8. with Alleluias

Jean Tisserand (d. 1494) and others
Trans. by John Mason Neale, 1851; alt.

Probably French, ca. 15th century
As in *Pilgrim Hymnal*, 1958

527

Alleluia! Alleluia! Alleluia!

1. O sons and daughters, let us sing! The King of heaven, the glorious King, O'er death today rose triumphing.
2. That Easter morn at break of day, The faithful women went their way To seek the tomb where Jesus lay.
3. An angel clad in white they see, Who sat, and spoke unto the three, "Your Lord has gone to Galilee." Alleluia!
4. How blest are they who have not seen, And yet whose faith has constant been; For they eternal life shall win.
5. On this most holy day of days, Our hearts and voices, Lord, we raise To you, in jubilee and praise.

A - men.

528 O Spirit of the Living God

WINCHESTER NEW L.M.

James Montgomery, 1823; alt., 1972

Musikalisches Handbuch, Hamburg, 1690
Arr. in *Old Church Psalmody*, 1864

1. O Spir - it of the liv - ing God, In
2. Give tongues of fire and hearts of love To
3. Be dark - ness, at your com - ing, light; Con -
4. O Spir - it of the Lord, pre - pare All
5. Bap - tize the na - tions; far and nigh The

1. all the full - ness of your grace, Wher - e'er the foot of
2. preach the rec - on - cil - ing word; Give power and bless - ing
3. fu - sion, or - der in your path; Souls with - out strength in -
4. the round earth her God to meet; And breathe a - broad like
5. tri - umphs of the cross re - cord; The name of Je - sus

1. man has trod, De - scend on our re - bel - lious race.
2. from a - bove, When - e'er the joy - ful sound is heard.
3. spire with might; Bid mer - cy tri - umph o - ver wrath.
4. morn - ing air, Till hearts of stone be - gin to beat.
5. glo - ri - fy, Till ev - ery kin - dred call him Lord. A - men.

O Splendor of God's Glory Bright

WAREHAM L.M.

Ambrose of Milan (ca. 340-397)
Translation composite
As in *The Methodist Hymnal*, 1935; alt., 1972

William Knapp, 1738

1. O splen - dor of God's glo - ry bright, From light e -
ter - nal bring - ing light; O Light of life, light's
liv - ing spring, True day, all days il - lu - min - ing.

2. Con - firm our will to do the right, And keep our
hearts from en - vy's blight; Let faith her ea - ger
fires re - new, And hate the false, and love the true.

3. O joy - ful be the pass - ing day With thoughts as
clear as morn - ing's ray, With faith like noon - tide
shin - ing bright, Our souls un - shad - owed by the night.

4. Dawn's glo - ry gilds the earth and skies; Let Him, our
per - fect morn, a - rise; The Fa - ther's help his
chil - dren claim, And sing the Fa - ther's glo - rious name. A - men.

Alternative Tune: PUER NOBIS

530 O Where Are Kings and Empires Now

ST. ANNE C.M.

Arthur Cleveland Coxe, 1839; alt.

Attr. to William Croft, 1708

1. O where are kings and em - pires now Of
2. We mark her good - ly bat - tle - ments And
3. For not like king - doms of the world Your
4. Un - shak - en as e - ter - nal hills, Im -

old that went and came? But, Lord, your church is
her foun - da - tions strong; We hear with - in the
ho - ly church, O God, Though earth - quake shocks are
mov - a - ble she stands, A moun - tain that shall

pray - ing yet, A thou - sand years the same.
sol - emn voice Of her un - end - ing song.
threat - ening her And tem - pests are a - broad,
fill the earth, A house not made by hands. A - men.

O Wondrous Type, O Vision Fair 531

DEO GRACIAS L.M.

Latin hymn, 15th century
Trans. by John Mason Neale, 1854; alt.

"The Agincourt Song," England, ca. 1415
Arr. for *The Hymnal*, 1933

1. O won - drous type, O vi - sion fair
2. With shin - ing face and bright ar - ray,
3. And faith - ful souls in vi - sion see
4. O Fa - ther, with th'e - ter - nal Son,

Of glo - ry that the church shall share,
Christ deigns to man - i - fest to - day
The heights of God's own mys - ter - y;
And Ho - ly Spir - it, ev - er One,

Which Christ up - on the moun - tain shows
What glo - ry shall be theirs a - bove
For which in joy - ful strains we raise
Be pleased to bring us by your grace

Where bright - er than the sun he glows.
Who joy in God with per - fect love.
The voice of prayer, the hymn of praise.
To see your glo - ry face to face. A - men.

532 O Word of God Incarnate

MUNICH 7.6.7.6.D.

William Walsham How, 1867; alt., 1972

Neuvermehrtes . . . Meiningisches Gesangbuch, 1693
Adapted by Felix Mendelssohn, 1847

1. O Word of God in - car - nate, O Wis - dom from on high,
2. The church from her dear Mas - ter Re - ceived the gift di - vine,
3. It floats e'er like a ban - ner Be - fore God's host un - furled;
4. O make your church, dear Sav - ior, A lamp of pur - est gold,

O Truth un-changed, un - chang-ing, O Light of our dark sky,
And still that light is lift - ed O'er all the earth to shine.
It shines out like a bea - con A - bove the dark -ening world.
To bear be - fore the na - tions Your true light, as of old.

We praise you for the ra - diance That from the hal - lowed page,
It is the chest so pre - cious Where gems of truth are stored;
It is the chart and com - pass That o'er life's surg - ing waves,
O teach your wan-dering pil - grims By this their path to trace,

A lan - tern to our foot-steps, Shines on from age to age.
It is the heaven-drawn pic - ture Of Christ, the liv - ing Word.
'Mid mists and rocks and quick-sands, Still guides to Christ who saves.
Till, clouds and dark - ness end - ed, They see you face to face. A-men.

O Worship the King All-glorious Above

LYONS 10.10.11.11.

Based on Psalm 104
Robert Grant, 1833; alt.

Attr. to J. Michael Haydn (1737-1806)
Gardiner's *Sacred Melodies*, 1815

1. O wor-ship the King all-glo-rious a-bove,
2. O tell of his might, O sing of his grace,
3. The earth with its store of won-ders un-told,
4. Your boun-ti-ful care, what tongue can re-cite?
5. We chil-dren of dust are fee-ble and frail;

O grate-ful-ly sing his power and his love;
Whose robe is the light, whose can-o-py space.
Al-might-y, your power has found-ed of old,
It breathes in the air, it shines in the light;
In you we do trust, nor find you to fail;

Our Shield and De-fend-er, the An-cient of Days,
His char-iots of wrath the deep thun-der-clouds form,
Es-tab-lished it fast by a change-less de-cree,
It streams from the hills; it de-scends to the plain,
Your mer-cies how ten-der, how firm to the end,

Pa-vil-ioned in splen-dor and gird-ed with praise.
And dark is his path on the wings of the storm.
And round it has cast, like a man-tle, the sea.
And sweet-ly dis-tills in the dew and the rain.
Our Mak-er, De-fend-er, Re-deem-er, and Friend! A-men.

For lower key, see "You Servants of God, Your Master Proclaim."

534

Of the Father's Love Begotten

DIVINUM MYSTERIUM 8.7.8.7.8.7.7.

Aurelius Clemens Prudentius (348-ca. 410)
Trans. by John Mason Neale, 1851,
and Henry W. Baker, 1859; alt., 1972

Plainsong, Mode V, 12th century (?)
Harm. by C. Winfred Douglas, 1940

Unison

1. Of the Fa-ther's love be-got-ten, Ere the worlds be-gan to be,
2. O you heights of heaven, a-dore him; An-gel hosts, his prais-es sing;
3. Christ, to you, with God the Fa-ther, And the Spir-it, one in three,

He is Al-pha and O-meg-a, He the Source, the End-ing he,
Powers, do-min-ions, bow be-fore him, And ex-tol our God and King;
Hymn and chant and high thanks-giv-ing And un-wea-ried prais-es be:

Of the things that are, that have been, And that
Let no tongue on earth be si - - - lent, Ev-ery
Hon-or, glo-ry, and do-min - - - ion, And e-

fu-ture years shall see, Ev-er-more and ev-er-more!
voice in con-cert ring, Ev-er-more and ev-er-more!
ter-nal vic-to-ry, Ev-er-more and ev-er-more! A - men.

Music used by permission of The Church Pension Fund.

Oh, Freedom!

Negro spiritual

Negro spiritual
Harm. by Joan M. Salmon, 1972

1. Oh, free - dom! oh, free-dom! oh, free - dom for me!
2. Dy - ing sin - ner! dy - ing sin-ner! dy - ing sin - ner all my days!
3. Trust-ing Je - sus! trust-ing Je - sus! trust-ing Je - sus all my days!

And be - fore I'd be a slave, I'd be bur - ied in my grave,

And go home to my Lord and be free. (and be free.)

536 On a Bethlehem Hill

Peter Scholtes, 1967

White spiritual
Harm. by Richard D. Wetzel, 1972

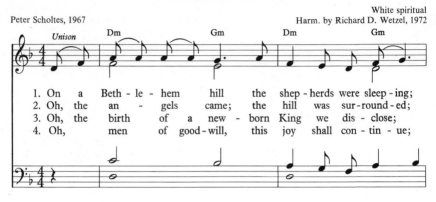

1. On a Beth - le - hem hill the shep - herds were sleep - ing;
2. Oh, the an - gels came; the hill was sur - round - ed;
3. Oh, the birth of a new - born King we dis - close;
4. Oh, men of good - will, this joy shall con - tin - ue;

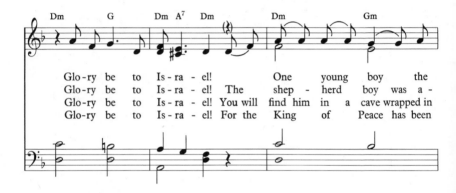

Glo-ry be to Is - ra - el! One young boy the
Glo-ry be to Is - ra - el! The shep - herd boy was a -
Glo-ry be to Is - ra - el! You will find him in a cave wrapped in
Glo-ry be to Is - ra - el! For the King of Peace has been

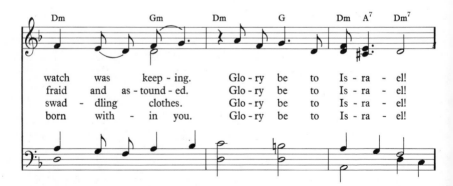

watch was keep - ing. Glo - ry be to Is - ra - el!
fraid and as - tound - ed. Glo - ry be to Is - ra - el!
swad - dling clothes. Glo - ry be to Is - ra - el!
born with - in you. Glo - ry be to Is - ra - el!

Glo-ry, glo-ry, glo-ry, glo-ry, Glo-ry be to Is-ra-el!

Glo-ry, glo-ry, glo-ry, glo-ry, Glo-ry be to Is-ra-el!

538 On This Day Earth Shall Ring

PERSONENT HODIE 6.6.6.6.6. with Refrain

Piae Cantiones, 1582
Trans. by Jane M. Joseph, 1924

Piae Cantiones, 1582
As in *Hymnal for Colleges and Schools*, 1956

1. On this day earth shall ring With the song chil-dren sing
2. His the doom, ours the mirth; When he came down to earth
3. God's bright star, o'er his head, Wise Men three to him led;
4. On this day an-gels sing; With their song earth shall ring,

To the Lord, Christ our King, Born on earth to save us!
Beth-le-hem saw his birth; Ox and ass be-side him
Kneel they low by his bed, Lay their gifts be-fore him,
Prais-ing Christ, heav-en's King, Born on earth to save us;

Id-e-o—o—o, Id-e-o—

Him the Fa-ther gave us. O, Id-e-o, Id-e-o, Id-e-
From the cold would hide him.
Praise him and a-dore him.
Peace and love he gave us. O, Id-e-o—o—o, Id-e-

O,—— Id-e-o—o—o,

o—o, Id-e-o glo-ri-a in ex-cel-sis De-o!*

o—o,

Id-e-o,

Unison

*"Therefore let us give glory to God in the highest."

Once in Royal David's City

IRBY 8.7.8.7.8.7.

Cecil Frances Alexander, 1848; alt.

Henry J. Gauntlett, 1849

1. Once in roy - al Da - vid's cit - y Stood a low - ly
2. He came down to earth from heav - en Who is God and
3. Je - sus is our child - hood's pat - tern, Day by day like
4. And our eyes at last shall see him, Through his own re -

cat - tle shed, Where a moth - er laid her ba - by
Lord of all, And his shel - ter was a sta - ble,
us he grew; He was lit - tle, weak, and help - less,
deem - ing love; For that child so dear and gen - tle

In a man - ger for his bed: Mar - y was that moth - er
And his cra - dle was a stall: With the poor, and mean, and
Tears and smiles like us he knew: And he com - forts us in
Is our Lord in heaven a - bove, And he leads his chil - dren

mild, Je - sus Christ, her lit - tle child.
low - ly, Lived on earth our Sav - ior ho - ly.
sad - ness, And he shares in all our glad - ness.
on To the place where he is gone. A - men.

540 Once to Every Man and Nation

EBENEZER (TON-Y-BOTEL) 8.7.8.7.D.

James Russell Lowell, 1845; alt.

Thomas John Williams, 1890

1. Once to ev-ery man and na-tion Comes the mo-ment to de-cide,
2. Then to side with truth is no-ble, When we share her wretch-ed crust,
3. By the light of burn-ing mar-tyrs, Christ, your bleed-ing feet we track,
4. Though the cause of e-vil pros-per, Yet 'tis truth a-lone is strong;

In the strife of truth with false-hood, For the good or e-vil side;
Ere her cause bring fame and prof-it, And 'tis pros-perous to be just;
Toil-ing up new Cal-varies ev-er With the cross that turns not back;
Though her por-tion be the scaf-fold, And up-on the throne be wrong,

Some great cause, God's new Mes-si-ah, Of-fering each the bloom or blight,
Then it is the brave man choos-es While the cow-ard stands a-side,
New oc-ca-sions teach new du-ties, Time makes an-cient good un-couth;
Yet that scaf-fold sways the fu-ture, And, be-hind the dim un-known,

And the choice goes by for-ev-er 'Twixt that dark-ness and that light.
Till the mul-ti-tude make vir-tue Of the faith they had de-nied.
They must up-ward still and on-ward, Who would keep a-breast of truth.
Stands our God with-in the shad-ow Keep-ing watch a-bove his own. A-men.

Music copyright by Gwenlyn Evans, Ltd.; used by permission.

One Table Spread

541

MANNITTO 10.4.10.4.12.10.

Dalton E. McDonald, 1972

Donald D. Kettring, 1972

1. One ta-ble spread through-out the whole wide earth—The King's own feast!
2. See bread and wine, the to-kens of God's grace—This is our meal.
3. Give thanks to God that peace may here be found With-in his plan;

From ev-ery na-tion men shall come to share, From west and east.
Here we re-call our Lord up-on the cross—His love is real!
Our part to hear and heed his new com-mand:"Love God and man!"

All now is read-y, and our Host in-vites us in:
Take it not light-ly; this is God's own sac-ri-fice
Now is re-vealed the glo-ry of the Fa-ther, Son,

"Both bad and good are guests. Let us be-gin."
For all our need,and his love will suf-fice.
And God the Ho-ly Spir-it, three in one. A-men.

542 Onward, Christian Soldiers

ST. GERTRUDE 6.5.6.5.D. with Refrain

Sabine Baring-Gould, 1864; alt.

Arthur S. Sullivan, 1871

1. On - ward, Chris - tian sol - diers, March - ing as to war,
2. Like a might - y ar - my Moves the church of God;
3. Crowns and thrones may per - ish, King-doms rise and wane,
4. On - ward, then, you peo - ple, Join our hap - py throng,

With the cross of Je - sus Go - ing on be - fore:
Broth - ers, we are tread - ing Where the saints have trod;
But the church of Je - sus Con - stant will re - main;
Blend with ours your voic - es In the tri - umph song;

Christ the roy - al mas - ter Leads a - gainst the foe;
We are not di - vid - ed, All one bod - y we,
Gates of hell can nev - er 'Gainst that church pre - vail;
Glo - ry, laud, and hon - or Un - to Christ the King;

For - ward in - to bat - tle, See, his ban - ners go.
One in hope and doc - trine, One in char - i - ty.
We have Christ's own prom - ise, And that can - not fail.
This through count-less ag - es Men and an - gels sing.

On - ward, Chris-tian sol - diers, March-ing as to war,

With the cross of Je - sus Go - ing on be - fore. A - men.

544 Open Now the Gates of Beauty

NEANDER (UNSER HERRSCHER) 8.7.8.7.7.7.

Benjamin Schmolck, 1732
Trans. by Catherine Winkworth, 1863; alt., 1972

Joachim Neander, 1680

1. O - pen now the gates of beau - ty, Zi - on, let us
2. Here, O God, we come be - fore you; To this com - pa -
3. Here our faith in - crease and quick - en, Let us keep your
4. Speak, O Lord, and we will hear you; Let your will be

en - ter there, Where we may in joy - ful du - ty
ny come down; Where we find you and a - dore you,
gift di - vine; And when - e'er temp - ta - tions thick - en
done in - deed. May we un - dis - turbed draw near you

Wait for him who an - swers prayer. O how bless - ed
There with joy our lives you crown; In our hearts to
May your word still o'er us shine, As our guid - ing
While your peo - ple you do feed; Here of life the

is this place, Filled with sol - ace, light, and grace!
you we bow, Let them be your tem - ple now.
star through life, As our com - fort in all strife.
foun - tain flows, Here is balm for all our woes. A - men.

Our Faith Is in the Christ Who Walks with Men 545

WAREHAM L.M.

Thomas Curtis Clark (1877-1953)

William Knapp, 1738

1. Our faith is in the Christ who walks With men today, in street and mart; The con - stant friend who thinks and
talks With those who seek him with the heart.

2. His gos - pel calls for liv - ing men, With sing - ing
blood and minds a - lert; Strong men, who fall to rise a -
gain, Who strive and bleed, with cour - age girt.

3. We serve no God whose work is done, Who rests with-
in his fir - ma - ment; Our God, his la - bors but be -
gun, Toils ev - er - more, with power un - spent.

4. God was and is and e'er shall be; Christ lived and
loved—and loves us still; And man goes for - ward, proud and
free, God's pres - ent pur - pose to ful - fill. A - men.

546
Our Father, by Whose Name
RHOSYMEDRE 6.6.6.6.8.8.8.

F. Bland Tucker, 1941, 1972

John D. Edwards, ca. 1840

1. Our Fa - ther, by whose name All fa - ther - hood is known,
*2. O Christ, your - self a child With - in an earth - ly home,
3. O Spir - it, who can bind Our hearts in u - ni - ty,

Who in your love pro - claim Each fam - i - ly your own,
With heart still un - de - filed, You did to man - hood come;
And teach us so to find The love from self set free,

Bless now all par - ents, guard - ing well, With con - stant love as
Our chil - dren bless, in ev - ery place, That they may all be -
In all our hearts such love in - crease, That ev - ery home, by

sen - ti - nel, The homes in which your peo - ple dwell.
hold your face, And, know - ing you, may grow in grace.
this re - lease, May be the dwell - ing place of peace. A - men.

Our Father, Which Art in Heaven 547

West Indian folk tune
Melody set down by Olive Pattison, 1945
Harm. by Richard D. Wetzel, 1972

Our Fa-ther, which art in heav-en, Hal-low-ed - a - be thy name.

Thy king-dom come, thy will be done, Hal-low-ed - a - be thy name.

On the earth as it is in heav-en. Give us this day our dai - ly bread;

And for-give us all our tres-pass-es, As we for-give those who

tres-pass a-gainst us; And leave us not to the dev-il to be tempt-ed,

*Repeat Refrain A or B as indicated after alternate lines.

See following page.

Our God, Our Help in Ages Past

ST. ANNE C.M.

Based on Psalm 90:1-5
Isaac Watts, 1719; alt.

Attr. to William Croft, 1708

1. Our God, our help in ag - es past, Our
2. Be - fore the hills in or - der stood, Or
3. A thou - sand ag - es in your sight Are
4. Time, like an ev - er - roll - ing stream, Bears
5. Our God, our help in ag - es past, Our

hope for years to come, Our shel - ter from the
earth re - ceived her frame, From ev - er - last - ing
like an eve - ning gone; Short as the watch that
all its sons a - way; They fly for - got - ten,
hope for years to come, O be our guard while

storm - y blast, And our e - ter - nal home:
you are God, To end - less years the same.
ends the night Be - fore the ris - ing sun.
as a dream Dies at the o - pening day.
life shall last, And our e - ter - nal home. A - men.

550 Pardoned Through Redeeming Grace

AUS DER TIEFE 7.7.7.7.

Edward Osler, 1836; alt., 1972

Attr. to Martin Herbst, 1676

1. Par - doned through re - deem - ing grace, In your
2. This our sac - ri - fice re - ceive, Hum - bly
3. By the hal - lowed out - ward sign, By the
4. Called to bear the Chris - tian name, May our

bless - ed Son re - vealed, Wor - ship - ing be -
of - fered through your Son; Quick - en us in
cleans - ing grace with - in, Seal us with your
vows and life ac - cord, And our ev - ery

fore your face, Lord, to you our - selves we yield.
him to live; Lord, in us your will be done.
own de - sign; Wash and keep us pure from sin.
deed pro - claim "Ho - li - ness un - to the Lord!" A - men.

Praise, My Soul, the King of Heaven

LAUDA ANIMA (PRAISE, MY SOUL) 8.7.8.7.8.7.

Based on Psalm 103
Henry Francis Lyte, 1834; alt.

John Goss, 1869

1. Praise, my soul, the King of heav - en; To his feet your
2. Praise him for his grace and fa - vor To our fa - thers
3. Fa - ther - like he tends and spares us; Well our fee - ble
4. Come, then, help us to a - dore him, Till we see him

trib - ute bring; Ran - somed, healed, re - stored, for - giv - en,
in dis - tress; Praise him still the same as ev - er,
frame he knows; In his hands he gen - tly bears us,
face to face; Glad - ly wor - ship we be - fore him,

Ev - er - more his prais - es sing: Al - le - lu - ia!
Slow to chide, and swift to bless: Al - le - lu - ia!
Res - cues us from all our foes. Al - le - lu - ia!
Dwell - ers now in time and space. Al - le - lu - ia!

Al - le - lu - ia! Praise the ev - er - last - ing King.
Al - le - lu - ia! Glo - rious in his faith - ful - ness.
Al - le - lu - ia! Wide - ly yet his mer - cy flows.
Al - le - lu - ia! Praise with us the God of grace. A - men.

552 Praise the Lord, His Glories Show

LLANFAIR 7.7.7.7. with Alleluias

Based on Psalm 150
Henry Francis Lyte, 1834; alt., 1972

Robert Williams, 1817
Harm. by David Evans, 1927

1. Praise the Lord, his glo - ries show,
2. Earth to heaven, and heaven to earth, Al - le - lu - ia!
3. Praise the Lord, his mer - cies trace,

Saints with - in his courts be - low,
Tell his won - ders, sing his worth, Al - le - lu - ia!
Praise his prov - i - dence and grace,

An - gels round his throne a - bove,
Age to age and shore to shore, Al - le - lu - ia!
All that he for man has done,

All that see and share his love.
Praise him, praise him ev - er - more! Al - le - lu - ia!
All he sends us through his Son.

A-men.

Praise the Lord, Who Reigns Above

AMSTERDAM 7.6.7.6.7.7.7.6.

553

Based on Psalm 150
Charles Wesley, 1743

Foundery Collection, 1742

1. Praise the Lord, who reigns a - bove And keeps his court be - low;
2. Cel - e - brate th'e - ter - nal God With harp and psal - ter - y;
3. Him, in whom they move and live, Let ev - ery crea - ture sing,

Praise the ho - ly God of love, And all his great - ness show;
Tim - brels soft and cym - bals loud In his high praise a - gree;
Glo - ry to their Mak - er give, And hom - age to their King.

Praise him for his no - ble deeds, Praise him for his match - less power;
Praise him, ev - ery tune - ful string; All the reach of heav - enly art,
Hal - lowed be his name be - neath, As in heaven on earth a - dored;

Him from whom all good pro - ceeds Let earth and heaven a - dore.
All the powers of mu - sic bring, The mu - sic of the heart.
Praise the Lord in ev - ery breath; Let all things praise the Lord. A - men.

Praise the Lord! You Heavens, Adore Him

AN DIE FREUDE 8.7.8.7.D.

Based on Psalm 148
Sts. 1, 2, anon., ca. 1801; alt., 1972
St. 3, Edward Osler, 1836; alt., 1972

Anon. setting of Schiller's
"Hymn to Joy," Berlin, 1799

1. Praise the Lord! you heavens, a - dore him; Praise him, an - gels in the
2. Praise the Lord! for he is glo - rious; Nev-er shall his prom-ise
3. Wor-ship, hon - or, glo - ry, bless-ing, Lord, we of - fer as our

height; Sun and moon, re - joice be - fore him, Praise him,
fail. God has made his saints vic - to - rious; Sin and
gift. Young and old, your praise ex - press - ing, Our glad

all you stars of light. Praise the Lord, for he has
death shall not pre - vail. Praise the God of our sal -
songs to you we lift. All the saints in heaven a -

Alternative Tune: AUSTRIAN HYMN

spo - ken; Worlds his might - y voice o - beyed; Laws which
va - tion! Hosts on high, his power pro - claim; Heaven and
dore you, We would join their glad ac - claim; As your

nev - er shall be bro - ken For their guid - ance he has made.
earth and all cre - a - tion, Laud and mag - ni - fy his name.
an - gels serve be - fore you, So on earth we praise your name. A-men.

556 Praise to God, Immortal Praise

ORIENTIS PARTIBUS 7.7.7.7.

Anna L. Barbauld, 1772; alt.

Medieval French melody
Harm. by Ralph Vaughan Williams, 1906

1. Praise to God, im - mor - tal praise, For the love that crowns our days; Boun - teous source of ev - ery joy, Let your praise our tongues em - ploy.

2. Flocks that whit - en all the plain, Yel - low sheaves of rip - ened grain, Clouds that drop their o'er the smil - ing land! All that lib - eral fat - tening dews, Suns that tem - perate warmth dif - fuse:

3. All that spring with boun - teous hand Scat - ters o'er the smil - ing land! All that lib - eral au - tumn pours From her rich o'er - flow - ing stores—

4. These to you, our God, we owe, Source whence all our bless - ings flow, And for these our souls shall raise Grate - ful vows and sol - emn praise. A - men.

Praise to the Lord, the Almighty

LOBE DEN HERREN P.M.

557

Joachim Neander, 1680
Trans. by Catherine Winkworth, 1863; alt.

Adapted from Stralsund Gesangbuch, 1665
As in *The Chorale Book for England*, 1863

1. Praise to the Lord, the Al-might-y, the King of cre - a - tion!
2. Praise to the Lord, who o'er all things is won-drous-ly reign - ing,
3. Praise to the Lord, who does pros-per your way and de - fend you;
4. Praise to the Lord! O let all that is in me a - dore him!

O my soul, praise him, for he is your health and sal - va - tion!
Shel-tering you un - der his wings and so gen-tly sus - tain - ing.
Sure - ly his good-ness and mer - cy shall ev - er at - tend you!
All that have life and breath, come now with prais-es be - fore him!

All you that hear, Now to his tem - ple draw near;
Have you not seen? All that is need - ful has been
Pon - der a - new What the Al - might - y can do,
Let the A - men Sound from his peo - ple a - gain:

Join - ing in glad ad - o - ra - tion.
Grant - ed in all his or - dain - ing.
Who with his love does be - friend you.
Glad - ly al - ways we a - dore him. A - men.

558 Praise We Our Maker While We've Breath

OLD 113TH 8.8.8.D.

From Psalm 146
Para. by Isaac Watts, 1719; alt., 1737, 1972

Attr. to Matthäus Greiter, 1525
Alt. and abr. in English use
Harm. by V. Earle Copes, 1964

1. Praise we our Mak - er while we've breath; And when our voice
   is lost in death, Praise shall em - ploy our no - bler powers.
   Our days of praise shall ne'er be past, While life, and thought,
   and be - ing last, Or im - mor - tal - i - ty en - dures.

2. The Lord gives vi - sion to the blind; The Lord sup - ports
   the faint - ing mind; He sends the la - boring con - science peace.
   He helps the stran - ger in dis - tress, The wid - ow and
   the fa - ther - less, And grants the pris - oner sweet re - lease.

3. Blest is the man whose hopes re - ly On Is - rael's God;
   he made the sky And earth and seas, with all their train.
   His truth for - ev - er stands se - cure; He saves th'op-pressed,
   he feeds the poor, And none shall find his prom - ise vain. A - men.

Put Forth, O God, Your Spirit's Might 559

DUNDEE (FRENCH) C.M.

Howard Chandler Robbins, 1937; alt., 1972

Scottish Psalter, 1615

1. Put forth, O God, your Spir - it's might And bid your church in - crease, In breadth and length, in depth and height, Her u - ni - ty and peace.

2. Let works of dark - ness dis - ap - pear Be - fore your con - quering light. Let ha - tred and tor - ment - ing fear Pass with the pass - ing night.

3. Let the a - pos - tles' con - stan - cy Be ours from age to age; Their stead - fast faith our u - ni - ty, Their peace our her - i - tage.

4. O Judge di - vine of hu - man strife! O Van - quish - er of pain! To know you is e - ter - nal life, To serve you is to reign. A - men.

Words altered from *The New Church Hymnal*; used by permission of Fleming H. Revell Company, publisher.

560

Rejoice and Be Merry
GALLERY CAROL 11.11.11.11.

Old church gallery book

Old church gallery book
Arr. by Martin Shaw, 1928

1. Re - joice and be mer - ry in songs and in mirth!
2. A heav - en - ly vi - sion ap - peared in the sky;
3. Like - wise a bright star in the sky did ap - pear,
4. And when they were come, they their trea - sures un - fold,

O praise our Re - deem - er, all mor - tals on earth!
Vast num - bers of an - gels the shep - herds did spy,
Which led the Wise Men from the east to draw near;
And un - to him of - fered myrrh, in - cense, and gold.

For this is the birth - day of Je - sus our King,
Pro - claim - ing the birth - day of Je - sus our King,
They found the Mes - si - ah, sweet Je - sus our King,
So bless - ed for - ev - er be Je - sus our King,

Who brought us sal - va - tion— his prais - es we'll sing!

Rejoice, O Pure in Heart

MARION S.M. with Refrain

Edward H. Plumptre, 1865; alt.
Refrain added, 1883

Arthur H. Messiter, 1883

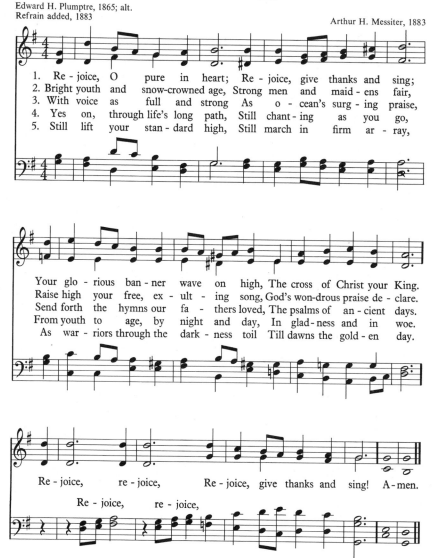

1. Re - joice, O pure in heart; Re - joice, give thanks and sing;
2. Bright youth and snow-crowned age, Strong men and maid - ens fair,
3. With voice as full and strong As o - cean's surg - ing praise,
4. Yes on, through life's long path, Still chant - ing as you go,
5. Still lift your stan - dard high, Still march in firm ar - ray,

Your glo - rious ban - ner wave on high, The cross of Christ your King.
Raise high your free, ex - ult - ing song, God's won-drous praise de - clare.
Send forth the hymns our fa - thers loved, The psalms of an - cient days.
From youth to age, by night and day, In glad-ness and in woe.
As war - riors through the dark - ness toil Till dawns the gold - en day.

Re - joice, re - joice, Re - joice, give thanks and sing! A - men.
Re - joice, re - joice,

562

Rejoice, the Lord Is King

DARWALL'S 148TH 6.6.6.6.8.8.

Charles Wesley, 1746; alt.

John Darwall, 1770; alt., ca. 1778

1. Re - joice, the Lord is King: Your Lord and King a - dore!
2. His King - dom can - not fail, He rules o'er earth and heaven;
3. He all his foes shall quell, Shall all our sins de - stroy,

Re - joice, give thanks, and sing, And tri - umph
The keys of death and hell Are to our
The church his work shall tell With ev - er -

ev - er - more: Je - sus given: Lift up your heart, lift up your voice!
last - ing joy:

Re - joice, a - gain I say, re - joice! A - men.

Ride On! Ride On in Majesty!

ST. DROSTANE L.M.

Henry H. Milman, 1827; alt., 1972

John B. Dykes, 1862

1. Ride on! Ride on in maj - es - ty! Hark! all the tribes ho -
2. Ride on! Ride on in maj - es - ty! In low - ly pomp ride
3. Ride on! Ride on in maj - es - ty! The wing - ed squad - rons
4. Ride on! Ride on in maj - es - ty! Your last and fierc - est
5. Ride on! Ride on in maj - es - ty! In low - ly pomp ride

san - na cry; Your hum - ble beast pur - sues his way
on to die: O Christ, your tri - umphs now be - gin
of the sky Look down with sad and won - dering eyes
strife is nigh; The Fa - ther on his sap - phire throne
on to die; Bow your meek head to mor - tal pain,

Where crowds the palms and gar - ments lay.
O'er cap - tive death and con - quered sin.
To see th' ap-proach - ing sac - ri - fice.
Ex - pects his own a - noint - ed Son.
Then take, O God, your power, and reign. A - men.

564 Rise Up, O Men of God!

FESTAL SONG S.M.

William Pierson Merrill, 1911; alt., 1972

William H. Walter, 1894

1. Rise up, O men of God! Have done with
2. Rise up, O men of God! His king-dom
3. Rise up, O men of God! How long the
4. Lift high the cross of Christ! Tread where his

less-er things; Give heart and soul and
tar-ries long; Bring in the day of
church must wait, Her strength un-e-qual
feet have trod; As broth-ers of the

mind and strength To serve the King of kings.
broth-er-hood And end the night of wrong.
to her task. Rise up, and make her great!
Son of Man, Rise up, O men of God. A-men.

Savior of the Nations, Come

565

NUN KOMM, DER HEIDEN HEILAND 7.7.7.7.

Attr. to Ambrose of Milan (ca. 340-397)
Para. by Martin Luther, 1524
Trans. by William M. Reynolds, 1850; alt.

Based on plainsong melody
Eyn Enchiridion . . ., Erfurt, 1524
As in *Songs of Syon*, 1910

1. Sav - ior of the na - tions, come, Vir - gin's Son, make
2. From the Fa - ther forth he came, And re - turns un -
3. You, the Fa - ther's on - ly Son, Have o'er sin the
4. Bright - ly does your man - ger shine; Glo - rious is its

here your home. Mar - vel now, O heaven and
to the same, Cap - tive lead - ing death and
vic - tory won. Bound - less shall your king - dom
light di - vine. Let not sin o'er - cloud this

earth, That the Lord chose such a birth.
hell. High the song of tri - umph swell!
be; When shall we its glo - ries see?
light; Ev - er be our faith thus bright. A - men.

566
Send Down Your Truth, O God

AYLESBURY S.M.

Chetham's *A Book of Psalmody*, 1718
Adapted in *A Book of Psalm Tunes*, 1724
Harm. and arr. by Martin Shaw, 1931

Edward Rowland Sill, 1867; alt., 1972

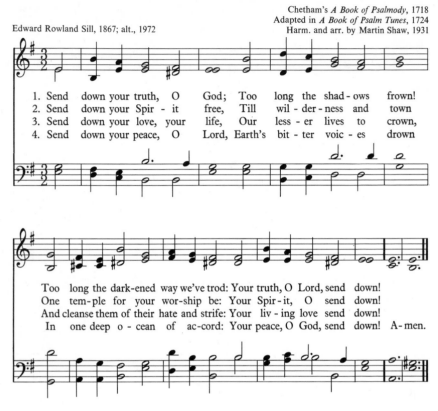

1. Send down your truth, O God; Too long the shad-ows frown!
2. Send down your Spir - it free, Till wil - der-ness and town
3. Send down your love, your life, Our less - er lives to crown,
4. Send down your peace, O Lord, Earth's bit - ter voic - es drown

Too long the dark-ened way we've trod: Your truth, O Lord, send down!
One tem-ple for your wor-ship be: Your Spir-it, O send down!
And cleanse them of their hate and strife: Your liv - ing love send down!
In one deep o - cean of ac-cord: Your peace, O God, send down! A-men.

Silent Night, Holy Night

STILLE NACHT Irregular

Joseph Mohr, 1818
Trans. by John Freeman Young, ca. 1863

Franz Grüber, 1818

1. Si - lent night, ho - ly night! All is calm, all is bright
2. Si - lent night, ho - ly night! Shep - herds quake at the sight;
3. Si - lent night, ho - ly night! Son of God, love's pure light

Round yon vir - gin moth - er and Child. Ho - ly In - fant so ten - der and mild,
Glo - ries stream from heav - en a - far, Heav - enly hosts sing al - le - lu - ia:
Ra - diant beams from thy ho - ly face, With the dawn of re - deem - ing grace,

Sleep in heav - en - ly peace, Sleep in heav - en - ly peace.
Christ, the Sav - ior, is born! Christ, the Sav - ior, is born!
Je - sus, Lord, at thy birth, Je - sus, Lord, at thy birth. A - men.

1. Stille Nacht, heilige Nacht!
   Alles schläft, einsam wacht
   Nur das traute, hochheilige Paar.
   Holder Knabe im lockigen Haar,
   Schlaf' in himmlischer Ruh',
   Schlaf' in himmlischer Ruh'!

2. Stille Nacht, heilige Nacht!
   Hirten erst kundgemacht
   Durch der Engel Alleluja,
   Tönt es laut von fern und nah:
   Christ der Retter ist da,
   Christ der Retter ist da!

3. Stille Nacht, heilige Nacht!
   Gottes Sohn, o wie lacht
   Lieb' aus deinem göttlichen Mund,
   Da uns schlägt die rettende Stund':
   Christ, in deiner Geburt,
   Christ, in deiner Geburt!

568 Sing Praise to God, Who Reigns Above

MIT FREUDEN ZART 8.7.8.7.8.8.7.

Johann J. Schütz, 1675
Trans. by Frances E. Cox, 1864; alt.

Bohemian Brethren Hymnal, 1566

1. Sing praise to God, who reigns a-bove, The God of all cre - a - tion,
2. What God's al-might-y power has made, In mer-cy he is keep-ing;
*3. Then all our glad-some way a - long, We sing a - loud in prais-ing,
4. All you who name Christ's ho - ly name, Give God all praise and glo - ry;

The God of power, the God of love, The God of our sal - va - tion;
By morn-ing glow or eve-ning shade His eye is nev - er sleep-ing;
That men may hear the grate-ful song Our voic - es all are rais-ing;
All you who own his power, pro-claim A - loud the won - drous sto - ry!

With heal-ing balm our souls he fills, And ev - ery faith - less
With - in the king - dom of his might, All things are just and
Be joy - ful in the Lord, O heart, Both soul and bod - y,
Cast each false i - dol from his throne, The Lord is God, and

mur - mur stills: To God all praise and glo - ry.
good and right: To God all praise and glo - ry.
bear your part: To God all praise and glo - ry.
he a - lone: To God all praise and glo - ry. A - men.

Sing to the Lord of Harvest

WIE LIEBLICH IST DER MAIEN 7.6.7.6.D.

569

Johann Steurlein, 1581
Arr. as hymn tune by Jan Bender, 1967

John S. B. Monsell, 1866; alt.

1. Sing to the Lord of har-vest, Sing songs of love and praise:
2. By him the clouds drop fat-ness, The des-erts bloom and spring,
3. Bring to his sa-cred al-tar The gifts his good-ness gave,

With joy-ful hearts and voic-es Your al-le-lu-ias raise.
The hills leap up in glad-ness, The val-leys laugh and sing.
The gold-en sheaves of har-vest, The souls he died to save.

By him the roll-ing sea-sons In fruit-ful or-der move;
He bless-es from his full-ness All things with large in-crease,
Your hearts lay down be-fore him When at his feet you fall,

Sing to the Lord of har-vest A joy-ous song of love.
He crowns the year with good-ness, With plen-ty and with peace.
And with your lives a-dore him, Who gave his life for all. A-men.

570   Sinner, Please Don't Let This Harvest Pass

Negro spiritual
Harm. by Robert E. Grooters, 1972

Negro spiritual

So Lowly Does the Savior Ride

EPWORTH CHURCH C.M.

571

Almer M. Pennewell, 1946; alt., 1972

V. Earle Copes, 1964

1. So low - ly does the Sav - ior ride A pal - try
bor - rowed beast, Nor pomp, nor show, nor loft - y pride,
Nor boast a - bove the least.

2. His scep - ter is his kind - li - ness, His gran - deur
is his grace, His roy - al - ty is ho - li - ness,
And love is in his face.

3. 'Tis thus the great Mes - si - ah came To break the
ty - rants' will, To heal the peo - ple of their shame,
And no - ble - ness in - still.

4. Ride on, O King, ride on your way, While men of
low de - gree Ex - alt and ush - er in the day
Of peace we long to see. A - men.

572 Somebody's Knocking at Your Door

Negro spiritual

Negro spiritual

Some-bod-y's knock-ing at your door, Some-bod-y's knock-ing at your

door. O sin-ner, why don't you an-swer? Some-bod-y's knock-ing at your door.

1. Knocks like Je - sus,
2. Can't you hear him? Some-bod-y's knock-ing at your door.
3. An - swer Je - sus.

Knocks like Je - sus,
Can't you hear him? Some-bod-y's knock-ing at your door.
An - swer Je - sus.

O sin - ner, why don't you an -swer? Some-bod-y's knock-ing at your door.

Son of God, Eternal Savior

573

IN BABILONE 8.7.8.7.D.

Somerset Corry Lowry, 1893; alt., 1972

Traditional Dutch melody
Harm. by Julius Röntgen, ca. 1906

1. Son of God, e - ter - nal Sav - ior, Source of life and truth and grace,
2. Lord, as you have lived for oth - ers, So may we for oth - ers live;
*3. Come, O Christ, and reign a - mong us, King of love and Prince of Peace;
4. See the Christ-like host ad - vanc-ing, High and low - ly, great and small,

Son of Man, whose birth in - car - nate Hal - lows all our hu - man race;
Free - ly have your gifts been grant-ed, Free - ly may your serv - ants give.
Hush the storm of strife and pas - sion, Bid its cru - el dis - cords cease.
Linked in bonds of com - mon serv - ice For the com - mon Lord of all.

You, our Head, who, throned in glo - ry, For your own do ev - er plead,
Yours the gold and yours the sil - ver, Yours the wealth of land and sea,
By your pa - tient years of toil - ing, By your si - lent hours of pain,
As you prayed and as you la - bored That your peo - ple should be one,

Fill us with your love and pit - y, Heal our wrongs, and help our need.
We, the stew-ards of your boun-ty, Faith - ful to our trust should be.
Quench our fe-vered thirst of plea-sure, Shame our self - ish greed of gain.
Grant, O grant our hope's fru - i - tion: Here on earth your will be done. A-men.

Words altered from *The English Hymnal*; used by permission of Oxford University Press. Music used by permission of F. E. Röntgen.

574 Spirit Divine, Attend Our Prayers

NUN DANKET ALL' (GRÄFENBERG) C.M.

Andrew Reed, 1829

Crüger's *Praxis Pietatis Melica*, 1653

1. Spir - it di - vine, at - tend our prayers, And make this
2. Come as the light: to us re - veal Our emp - ti -
3. Come as the fire: and purge our hearts Like sac - ri -
4. Come as the dove: and spread your wings, The wings of
5. Spir - it di - vine, at - tend our prayers; Make a lost

house your home; De - scend with all your
ness and woe; And lead us in those
fi - cial flame; Let our whole soul an
peace - ful love; And let the church on
world your home; De - scend with all your

gra - cious powers; O come, great Spir - it, come!
paths of life Where all the righ - teous go.
of - fering be To our re - deem - er's name.
earth be - come Blest as the church a - bove.
gra - cious powers; O come, great Spir - it, come! A - men.

Spirit of God, Descend Upon My Heart

MORECAMBE 10.10.10.10.

Attr. to George Croly, 1867

Frederick C. Atkinson, 1870

1. Spir - it of God, de - scend up - on my heart;
2. I ask no dream, no proph - et ec - sta - sies,
3. Hast thou not bid us love thee, God and King?
4. Teach me to feel that thou art al - ways nigh;
5. Teach me to love thee as thine an - gels love,

Wean it from earth; through all its puls - es move;
No sud - den rend - ing of the veil of clay,
All, all thine own, soul, heart, and strength, and mind;
Teach me the strug - gles of the soul to bear,
One ho - ly pas - sion fill - ing all my frame;

Stoop to my weak - ness, might - y as thou art,
No an - gel vis - i - tant, no o - pening skies;
I see thy cross— there teach my heart to cling:
To check the ris - ing doubt, the reb - el sigh;
The bap - tism of the heaven - de - scend - ed Dove,

And make me love thee as I ought to love.
But take the dim - ness of my soul a - way.
O let me seek thee, and O let me find!
Teach me the pa - tience of un - an - swered prayer.
My heart an al - tar, and thy love the flame. A - men.

576   Spirit of God, Man's Hope in All the Ages

L'OMNIPOTENT 11.10.11.10.

Frank von Christierson, 1967

Comp. or adapted by Louis Bourgeois, 1551
As in *Pilgrim Hymnal*, 1958

1. Spir - it of God, man's hope in all the ag - es,
2. Spir - it of love, grant us the ho - ly wis - dom
3. Spir - it of jus - tice, lead us in the bat - tle
4. Spir - it of Christ, the broth - er of the fall - en;

Bring - er of light in dark - ness, love in strife;
To love you first, and then our broth - er man;
For hu - man rights a - gainst all hu - man sin.
Friend of the friend - less, cham - pion of the poor,

Wis - dom of all the wise, and truth of sag - es,
To give our - selves in love to all who need us;
Help us be bold when man ex - ploits his broth - er
Lead forth your church in joy - ous con - se - cra - tion,

Show us the mean - ing and the goal of life.
To work with all ac - cord - ing to your plan.
To stand with Christ, and in his spir - it win.
Serv - ing the King - dom goals for - ev - er - more. A - men.

Spread, O Spread the Mighty Word

577

GOTT SEI DANK 7.7.7.7.

Jonathan Friedrich Bahnmaier, 1827
Trans. by Catherine Winkworth, 1858; alt.; and
Arthur W. Farlander and C. Winfred Douglas, 1938

Freylinghausen's *Geistreiches Gesangbuch*, 1704; alt.

1. Spread, O spread the might-y word, Spread the king - dom
2. Word of how the Fa - ther's will Made the world, and
3. Word of how the Sav - ior's love Earth's sore bur - den
4. Might - y word God's Spir - it gave, Man for heav - enly
5. Word of life, most pure and strong, Word for which the

of the Lord, That to earth's re - mot - est bound
keeps it, still; How his on - ly Son he gave,
does re - move; How for - ev - er, in its need,
life to save; Word through whose all - ho - ly might
na - tions long, Spread a - broad, un - til from night

Men may heed the joy - ful sound.
Man from sin and death to save.
Through his death the world is freed.
Man can will and do the right.
All the world a - wakes to light. A - men.

Words used by permission of The Church Pension Fund.

578 Strong Son of God, Immortal Love

ROCKINGHAM OLD L.M.

Alfred Tennyson, 1850

Psalmody in Miniature, 1783
Adapted by Edward Miller, 1790

1. Strong Son of God, im - mor - tal Love, Whom we, that
   have not seen thy face, By faith, and faith a - lone, em -
   brace, Be - liev - ing where we can - not prove,

2. Thou seem - est hu - man and di - vine, The high - est,
   ho - liest man - hood, thou. Our wills are ours, we know not
   how; Our wills are ours to make them thine.

3. Our lit - tle sys - tems have their day; They have their
   day and cease to be; They are but bro - ken lights of
   thee, And thou, O Lord, art more than they.

4. Let knowl - edge grow from more to more, But more of
   rev - erence in us dwell, That mind and soul, ac - cord - ing
   well, May make one mu - sic as be - fore. A - men.

Take Thou Our Minds, Dear Lord

579

HALL 10.10.10.10.

William H. Foulkes; sts. 1-3, 1918;
st. 4, ca. 1920

Calvin W. Laufer, 1918

1. Take thou our minds, dear Lord, we hum-bly pray;
2. Take thou our hearts, O Christ, they are thine own;
3. Take thou our wills, Most High! Hold thou full sway;
4. Take thou our-selves, O Lord, heart, mind, and will;

Give us the mind of Christ each pass-ing day;
Come thou with-in our souls and claim thy throne;
Have in our in-most souls thy per-fect way;
Through our sur-ren-dered souls thy plans ful-fill.

Teach us to know the truth that sets us free;
Help us to shed a-broad thy death-less love;
Guard thou each sa-cred hour from self-ish ease;
We yield our-selves to thee— time, tal-ents, all;

Grant us in all our thoughts to hon-or thee.
Use us to make the earth like heaven a-bove.
Guide thou our or-dered lives as thou dost please.
We hear, and hence-forth heed, thy sov-ereign call. A - men.

580 Thanks to God, Whose Word Was Spoken

LAUDA ANIMA (PRAISE, MY SOUL) 8.7.8.7.8.7.

R. T. Brooks, 1954

John Goss, 1869

1. Thanks to God, whose Word was spo - ken In the deed that
2. Thanks to God, whose Word in - car - nate Glo - ri - fied the
3. Thanks to God, whose Word is an - swered By the Spir - it's

made the earth. His the voice that called a na - tion,
flesh of man. Deeds and words and death and ris - ing
voice with - in. Here we drink of joy un - mea - sured,

His the fires that tried her worth. God has spo - ken;
Tell the grace in heav - en's plan. God has spo - ken;
Life re - deemed from death and sin. God is speak - ing;

God has spo - ken; Praise him for his o - pen Word.
God has spo - ken; Praise him for his o - pen Word.
God is speak - ing; Praise him for his o - pen Word. A - men.

That Easter Day with Joy Was Bright 581

PUER NOBIS (Praetorius) L.M.

Latin hymn, before 8th century
Trans. by John Mason Neale, 1851; alt.

Trier MS., 15th century
Adapted by Michael Praetorius, 1609
Harm. by George R. Woodward, 1902

1. That Eas-ter Day with joy was bright, The sun shone out with fair-er light, When, to their long-ing eyes re-stored, Th' a-pos-tles saw their ris-en Lord.

2. O Je-sus, King of gen-tle-ness, Do all our in-most hearts pos-sess, And we to you will ev-er raise The trib-ute of our grate-ful praise.

3. O Lord of all, with us a-bide In this our joy-ful Eas-ter-tide; From ev-ery weap-on death can wield, Your own re-deemed for-ev-er shield.

4. All praise, O ris-en Lord, we give To you, who, dead, a-gain do live; To God the Fa-ther e-qual praise, And God the Ho-ly Ghost, we raise. A-men.

Music altered from *The Cowley Carol Book*, No. 21; used by permission of A. R. Mowbray & Co. Limited.

582 The Church's One Foundation

AURELIA 7.6.7.6.D.

Samuel J. Stone, 1866, 1868; alt., 1972   Samuel S. Wesley, 1864

1. The church's one foun - da - tion Is Je - sus Christ her Lord;
2. E - lect from ev - ery na - tion, Yet one o'er all the earth,
3. Mid toil and trib - u - la - tion, And tu - mult of her war,
4. Yet she on earth has un - ion With God the Three in One,

She is his new cre - a - tion By wa - ter and the word:
Her char - ter of sal - va - tion One Lord, one faith, one birth;
She waits the con - sum - ma - tion Of peace for - ev - er - more;
And mys - tic sweet com - mu - nion With those whose rest is won:

From heaven he came and sought her To be his ho - ly bride;
One ho - ly name she bless - es, Par - takes one ho - ly food,
Till with the vi - sion glo - rious Her long - ing eyes are blest,
O hap - py ones and ho - ly! Lord, give us grace that we,

With his own blood he bought her, And for her life he died.
And to one hope she press - es, With ev - ery grace en - dued.
And the great church vic - to - rious Shall be the church at rest.
Like them, the meek and low - ly, May live e - ter - nal - ly. A - men.

The Day of Pentecost Arrived

583

LAND OF REST C.M.

Frank A. Brooks, Jr., 1972

Folk song, adapted as American folk hymn
Arr. by Annabel Morris Buchanan, 1938

1. The day of Pen - te - cost ar - rived, To one place man - y came. Tongues as of fire ap - peared to them. They spoke in dif - ferent ways.
2. Un - har - nessed joy was there re - leased. Strong pow - er they re - ceived. No ex - pla - na - tions were re - quired. They cel - e - brat - ed faith.
3. Not on - ly laws and an - cient creeds We some - times fail to grasp, But acts of love and broth - er - hood, O God, we would af - firm.
4. Our in - hi - bi - tions make us die, To you and to all men, Do make us free, O God our friend, And hear our new - found praise.
5. In nar - row ways of life and faith We all do sure - ly walk. But Pen - te - cost is nev - er far, And grace to all is free. A - men.

584

The Day of Resurrection!

LANCASHIRE 7.6.7.6.D.

John of Damascus (675?-749?)
Trans. by John Mason Neale, 1862; alt.

Henry Smart, 1836

1. The day of res - ur - rec - tion! Earth, tell it out a - broad!
2. Our hearts be pure from e - vil, That we may see a - right
3. Now let the heavens be joy - ful, Let earth her song be - gin;

The Pass - o - ver of glad - ness, The Pass - o - ver of God!
The Lord in rays e - ter - nal Of res - ur - rec - tion light,
Let the round world keep tri - umph, And all that is there - in;

From death to life e - ter - nal, From this world to the sky,
And, lis-tening to his ac - cents, May hear, so calm and plain,
Let all things seen and un - seen Their notes of glad - ness blend,

Our Christ has brought us o - ver With hymns of vic - to - ry.
His own "All hail!" and, hear-ing, May raise the vic - tor strain.
For Christ the Lord has ris - en, Our Joy that has no end. A - men.

The First Nowell the Angel Did Say

THE FIRST NOWELL Irregular

Traditional English carol

Traditional English carol
Harm. by John Stainer, 1871

1. The first Now-ell the an-gel did say Was to cer-tain poor
2. They look-ed up and saw a star Shin-ing in the
3. And by the light of that same star, Three Wise Men
4. This star drew nigh to the north-west, O'er Beth-le-
5. Then en-tered in those Wise Men three, Fell rev-erent-

shep-herds, in fields as they lay, In fields where they lay
east be-yond them far, And to the earth it
came from coun-try far; To seek for a king was
hem it took its rest, And there it did both
ly up-on their knee, And of-fered there in

keep-ing their sheep, On a cold win-ter's night that was so deep.
gave great light, And so it con-tin-ued both day and night.
their in-tent, And to fol-low the star wher-ev-er it went.
stop and stay, Right o-ver the place where Je-sus lay.
his pres-ence Their gold, and myrrh, and fran-kin-cense.

Now-ell, Now-ell, Now-ell, Now-ell, Born is the King of Is-ra-el! A-men.

586 The Friends of Christ Together

ES FLOG EIN KLEINS WALDVÖGELEIN 7.6.7.6.D.

David W. Romig, 1965

Memmingen MS., 17th century
Harm. by George R. Woodward, 1904

1. The friends of Christ to - geth - er, In pa - tience born of love
2. Our faith grows tired of wait - ing; The church is torn a - part,
3. The thun - der of the Spir - it Will burst on us a - new,

For God and for each oth - er, Sought wis - dom from a - bove.
Our self - ish - ness and hat - ing, A spear thrust to his heart!
If we, like them, can hear it And find God's work to do.

They heard the Mas - ter say - ing, His last words in that hour, "Stay
The hun - gry cry for feed - ing, In - jus - tice rules a - gain, And
Come, Ho - ly Spir - it, burn us, En - flame us with your power, And

in the cit - y pray - ing Till you are clothed with power."
Christ's hands are still bleed - ing Be - cause of cru - el men.
by your might re - turn us To Je - sus in this hour! A - men.

The God of Abraham Praise

LEONI (YIGDAL) 6.6.8.4.D.

Daniel ben Judah Dayyan, ca. 1400
Trans. by Newton Mann, 1885;
and William Channing Gannett, 1910; alt.

Traditional Hebrew melody
Transcribed by Meyer Lyon, ca. 1770

1. The God of A-braham praise, All prais - ed be his name,
2. His spir - it still flows free, High surg - ing where it will;
3. He has e - ter - nal life Im - plant - ed in the soul;

Who was, and is, and is to be, And still the same!
In proph - et's word he spoke of old And he speaks still.
His love shall be our strength and stay, While ag - es roll.

The one e - ter - nal God, Ere aught that now ap - pears;
Es - tab - lished is his law, And change - less it shall stand,
Praise to the liv - ing God! All prais - ed be his name

The first, the last: be - yond all thought His time - less years!
Deep writ up - on the hu - man heart, On sea, or land.
Who was, and is, and is to be, And still the same! A - men.

588 The Great Creator of the Worlds

TALLIS' ORDINAL C.M.

From Epistle to Diognetus, 2d or 3d century
Para. by F. Bland Tucker, 1939, 1972

Thomas Tallis, ca. 1567

1. The great Cre - a - tor of the worlds, The
2. He sent no an - gel of his host To
3. He sent him not in wrath and power, But
4. He sent him down as send - ing God; As

sov - ereign God of heaven, His ho - ly and im -
bear this might - y word, But him through whom the
grace and peace to bring, In kind - ness, as a
man he came to men; As one with us he

mor - tal truth To men on earth has given.
worlds were made, The ev - er - last - ing Lord.
king might send His son, him - self a king.
dwelt with us, And died and lives a - gain. A - men.

The Head That Once Was Crowned with Thorns 589

ST. MAGNUS C.M.

Thomas Kelly, 1820

Attr. to Jeremiah Clark, 1707

1. The head that once was crowned with thorns Is crowned with glo - ry now; A roy - al di - a - dem a - dorns The might - y vic - tor's brow.
2. The high - est place that heaven af - fords Is his, is his by right; The King of kings, and Lord of lords, And heaven's e - ter - nal light.
3. The joy of all who dwell a - bove, The joy of all be - low, To whom he man - i - fests his love And grants his name to know.
4. To them the cross, with all its shame, With all its grace, is given; Their name an ev - er - last - ing name, Their joy the joy of heaven. A - men.

590 The King of Love My Shepherd Is

ST. COLUMBA 8.7.8.7.

Psalm 23
Para. by Henry W. Baker, 1868; alt., 1972

Ancient Irish melody
Arr. by Robert Carwithen, 1972

1. The King of love my shep-herd is, Whose good-ness fails me nev-er; I noth-ing lack if I am his, And he is mine for-ev-er.
2. Where streams of liv-ing wa-ter flow My ran-somed soul he's lead-ing, And where the ver-dant pas-tures grow With food ce-les-tial feed-ing.
*3. Per-verse and fool-ish oft I strayed, But yet in love he sought me, And on his shoul-der gen-tly laid, And home, re-joic-ing, brought me.
*4. In death's dark vale I fear no ill With you, dear Lord, be-side me; Your rod and staff my com-fort still, Your cross be-fore to guide me.
5. You spread a ta-ble in my sight; Your grace so rich be-stow-ing; And O what trans-port of de-light From your pure cup is flow-ing!
6. And so through all the length of days Your good-ness fails me nev-er; Good Shep-herd, may I sing your praise With-in your house for-ev-er. A-men.

The Lone, Wild Bird

591

PROSPECT L.M.

Henry Richard McFadyen, 1925; alt., 1968

Southern folk hymn
Harm. by David N. Johnson, 1968

1. The lone, wild bird in loft - y flight Is
2. The ends of earth are in thy hand, The

still with thee, nor leaves thy sight.
sea's dark deep and far - off land.

And I am thine! I rest in thee.

Great Spir - it, come, and rest in me. A - men.

592

The Lord's My Shepherd

CRIMOND C.M.
(First Tune)

Psalm 23
Para. in the Scottish Psalter, 1650

Jessie Seymour Irvine, 1872
Harm. by T. C. L. Pritchard, 1929; alt., 1955

1. The Lord's my shep - herd, I'll not want; He makes me down to lie In pas - tures green; He lead - eth me The qui - et wa - ters by.
2. My soul he doth re - store a - gain; And me to walk doth make With - in the paths of righ - teous - ness, E'en for his own name's sake.
3. Yea, though I walk in death's dark vale, Yet will I fear none ill; For thou art with me; and thy rod And staff me com - fort still.
4. My ta - ble thou hast fur - nish - ed In pres - ence of my foes; My head thou dost with oil a - noint, And my cup o - ver - flows.
5. Good - ness and mer - cy all my life Shall sure - ly fol - low me; And in God's house for - ev - er - more My dwell - ing place shall be. A - men.

The Lord's My Shepherd

EVAN C.M.
(Second Tune)

Psalm 23
Para. in the Scottish Psalter, 1650

William H. Havergal, 1846

593

1. The Lord's my shep - herd, I'll not want; He
2. My soul he doth re - store a - gain; And
3. Yea, though I walk in death's dark vale, Yet
4. My ta - ble thou hast fur - nish - ed In
5. Good - ness and mer - cy all my life Shall

makes me down to lie In pas - tures green; He
me to walk doth make With - in the paths of
will I fear none ill; For thou art with me;
pres - ence of my foes; My head thou dost with
sure - ly fol - low me; And in God's house for -

lead - eth me The qui - et wa - ters by.
righ - teous - ness, E'en for his own name's sake.
and thy rod And staff me com - fort still.
oil a - noint, And my cup o - ver - flows.
ev - er - more My dwell - ing place shall be. A - men.

594   # The Man Who Once Has Found Abode
TALLIS' CANON L.M.

From Psalm 91
Para. in *The Book of Psalms*, 1871; alt., 1972

Thomas Tallis, ca. 1657

1. The man who once has found abode
With in the se - cret place of God Shall with al - might - y God a - bide And in his shad - ow safe - ly hide.

2. I of the Lord my God will say, "He is my ref - uge and my stay; To him for safe - ty I will flee; My God, in him my trust shall be."

3. His out - spread pin - ions shall you hide; Be - neath his wings shall you a - bide; His faith - ful - ness as - sured and true Shall be a shield pro - tect - ing you.

4. No night - ly ter - rors shall a - larm; No dead - ly shaft by day shall harm, Nor pes - ti - lence that walks by night, Nor plagues that waste in noon - day light.

5. Be - cause your trust is God a - lone, Your dwell - ing place the High - est One, No e - vil shall up - on you come, Nor plague ap - proach your guard - ed home. A - men.

*May be sung as a canon.

The Spacious Firmament on High

CREATION L.M.D.

Joseph Addison, 1712

Franz Joseph Haydn, 1798

1. The spa-cious fir-ma-ment on high, With all the
2. Soon as the eve-ning shades pre-vail, The moon takes
3. What though in sol-emn si-lence all Move round this

blue e-the-real sky, And span-gled heavens, a shin-ing frame,
up the won-drous tale, And night-ly to the lis-tening earth
dark ter-res-trial ball? What though no re-al voice nor sound

Their great O-rig-i-nal pro-claim: Th'un-wea-ried sun, from
Re-peats the sto-ry of her birth; While all the stars that
A-mid the ra-diant orbs be found? In rea-son's ear they

See following page.

day to day, Does his Cre-a - tor's power dis-play, And pub-lish-
round her burn, And all the plan - ets in their turn, Con-firm the
all re-joice And ut - ter forth a glo - rious voice; For - ev - er

es to ev - ery land The work of an al-might-y hand.
ti - dings as they roll, And spread the truth from pole to pole.
sing - ing, as they shine, "The hand that made us is di - vine." A-men.

The Strife Is O'er, the Battle Done

597

VICTORY (PALESTRINA) 8.8.8. with Alleluias

Symphonia Sirenum Selectarum, 1695
Trans. by Francis Pott, 1861; alt.

Giovanni P. da Palestrina, 1591
Adapted by William Henry Monk, 1861

Al - le - lu - ia! Al - le - lu - ia! Al - le - lu - ia!

org.

1. The strife is o'er, the bat - tle done;
2. The powers of death have done their worst,
3. The three sad days have quick - ly sped;
4. He closed the yawn - ing gates of hell;
5. Lord, by your wounds on Cal - va - ry

The vic - to - ry of life is won; The song of
But Christ their le - gions has dis - persed: Let shouts of
He ris - es glo - rious from the dead: All glo - ry
The bars from heaven's high por - tals fell: Let hymns of
From death's dread sting your serv - ants free, That we may

tri - umph has be - gun.
ho - ly joy out - burst.
to our ris - en Head! Al - le - lu - ia!
praise his tri - umphs tell.
live e - ter - nal - ly. A - men.

org.

598   The True Light That Enlightens Man

Based on John 1:9-17
John Ylvisaker, 1964

Spiritual (?)
Arr. by John Ylvisaker, 1964
Harm. by Paul Abels, 1966

1. The true light that en-light-ens man,
2. And to all who be-lieve in him, Al-le-lu - ia!
3. Word made flesh has dwelt with man,
4. For the law through Mo-ses came,

Came to earth from God's right hand,
Gave he free-dom from the bonds of sin, Al-le-lu - ia!
We shall live with him a - gain,
Grace and truth in Je-sus' name,

Glo - ry be to thee, O Lord, Al - le - lu - ia!

Praise to thee, O Son of God, Al - le - lu - ia!

Thee We Adore, O Hidden Savior, Thee
599

ADORO TE DEVOTE 10.10.10.10.

Attr. to Thomas Aquinas (ca. 1225-1274)
Trans. by James Russell Woodford, 1850; alt.

Plainsong, Solesmes form
Arr. by J. H. Arnold, 1933

1. Thee we a - dore, O hid - den Sav - ior, thee,
2. O blest me - mo - rial of our dy - ing Lord,
3. Foun - tain of good - ness, Je - sus, Lord and God,
4. O Christ, whom now be - neath a veil we see,

Who at this bless - ed feast art pleased to be;
Who liv - ing Bread to men doth here af - ford!
Cleanse us, un - clean, with thy most cleans - ing blood;
May what we thirst for soon our por - tion be,

Both flesh and spir - it in thy pres - ence fail,
O may our souls for - ev - er feed on thee,
In - crease our faith and love, that we may know
To gaze on thee un - veiled, and see thy face,

Yet here thy pres - ence we de - vout - ly hail.
And thou, O Christ, for - ev - er pre - cious be!
The hope and peace which from thy pres - ence flow.
The vi - sion of thy glo - ry and thy grace. A - men.

600

There Is a Balm in Gilead

Negro spiritual
Arr. by Harold Moyer, 1956

Negro spiritual

There is a balm in Gil-e-ad To make the wound-ed whole,

There is a balm in Gil-e-ad To heal the sin-sick soul.

Unison

1. Some-times I feel dis-cour-aged, And think my work's in
2. Don't ev-er feel dis-cour-aged, For Je-sus is your
3. If you can-not preach like Pe-ter, If you can-not pray like

D.C.

vain, But then the Ho-ly Spir-it Re-vives my soul a-gain.
friend, And if you lack for knowl-edge, He'll not re-fuse to lend.
Paul, You can tell the love of Je-sus And say, "He died for all."

Arrangement of music from *The Youth Hymnary*; used by permission of Faith and Life Press.

There's a Wideness in God's Mercy

IN BABILONE 8.7.8.7.D.

Frederick W. Faber, 1854

Traditional Dutch melody
Harm. by Julius Röntgen, ca. 1906

1. There's a wide-ness in God's mer-cy, Like the wide-ness of the sea;
2. For the love of God is broad-er Than the mea-sure of man's mind;

There's a kind-ness in his jus-tice, Which is more than lib-er-ty.
And the heart of the E-ter-nal Is most won-der-ful-ly kind.

There is no place where earth's sor-rows Are more felt than up in heaven;
If our love were but more sim-ple, We should take him at his word;

There is no place where earth's fail-ings Have such kind-ly judg-ment given.
And our lives would be all sun-shine In the sweet-ness of our Lord. A-men.

Music used by permission of F. E. Röntgen.

602 This Is My Father's World

TERRA BEATA S.M.D.

Maltbie D. Babcock, 1901

Traditional English melody
Adapted by Franklin L. Sheppard, 1915; alt.
Harm. for *The Hymnbook*, 1955

1. This is my Fa-ther's world, And to my lis-tening ears All
2. This is my Fa-ther's world: The birds their car - ols raise, The
3. This is my Fa-ther's world: Oh, let me ne'er for - get That

na - ture sings, and round me rings The mu - sic of the spheres.
morn-ing light, the lil - y white, De - clare their mak - er's praise.
though the wrong seems oft so strong, God is the rul - er yet.

This is my Fa-ther's world: I rest me in the thought Of
This is my Fa-ther's world: He shines in all that's fair; In the
This is my Fa-ther's world: The bat - tle is not done; Je -

rocks and trees, of skies and seas; His hand the won - ders wrought.
rus-tling grass I hear him pass, He speaks to me ev-ery-where.
sus who died shall be sat - is - fied, And earth and heaven be one. A-men.

Thou Whose Purpose Is to Kindle

603

LADUE CHAPEL 8.7.8.7.D.

Elton Trueblood, 1966

Ronald Arnatt, 1968

1. Thou whose pur - pose is to kin - dle Now ig - nite us with thy
2. Thou who, in thy ho - ly gos - pel, Wills that man should tru - ly
3. Lord, who still a sword de - liv - ers Rath - er than a plac - id

fire; While the earth a - waits thy burn - ing, With thy pas -
live, Make us sense our share of fail - ure, Our tran - quil -
peace, With thy sharp - ened word dis - turb us, From com - pla -

- sion us in - spire. O - ver - come our sin - ful calm - ness,
- li - ty for - give. Teach us cour - age as we strug - gle
- cen - cy re - lease! Save us now from sat - is - fac - tion,

Words from *The Incendiary Fellowship*, by Elton Trueblood; copyright ©
1967 by David Elton Trueblood; used by permission of Harper & Row,
Publishers. Music used by permission of Ronald Arnatt.

See following page.

AlternativeTune: AUSTRIAN HYMN

Rouse us with   re-demp-tive shame;   Bap - tize with   thy fier - y
In all lib -   er - a - ting strife;   Lift the small - ness of our
When we pri -   vate - ly are free,   Yet are un - dis-turbed in

spir - it,   Crown our lives   with tongues of   flame.
vi - sion   By thine own   a - bun - dant   life.
spir - it   By our broth - er's mis - er - y.   A - men.

Throned Upon the Awful Tree

605

ARFON 7.7.7.7.7.7.

John Ellerton, 1875; alt., 1972

Traditional melody, France and Wales
Adapted by Hugh Davies, ca. 1906

1. Throned up - on the aw - ful tree, Lamb of God, your grief we see. Dark - ness veils your an - guished face; None its lines of woe can trace. None can tell what pangs un - known Hold you si - lent and a - lone—

2. Si - lent through those three dread hours, Wres - tling with the e - vil powers, Left a - lone with hu - man sin, Gloom a - round you and with - in, Till th'ap - point - ed time is nigh, Till the Lamb of God may die.

3. Hark, that cry that peals a - loud Up - ward through the whelm - ing cloud! You, the Fa - ther's on - ly Son, You, his own a - noint - ed one, Till th'ap - point - ed You are ask - ing— can it be?— "Why have you for - sak - en me?"

4. Lord, should fear and an - guish roll Dark - ly o'er our sin - ful soul, You, who once were thus be - reft That your own might ne'er be left, Teach us by that bit - ter cry In the gloom to know you nigh. A - men.

606

'Tis the Gift to Be Simple
(Simple Gifts)

Shaker song
Harm. by Richard D. Wetzel, 1972

Shaker song

'Tis the gift to be sim - ple, 'tis the gift to be free, 'Tis the

gift to come down where we ought to be, And

when we find our - selves in the place just right, 'Twill

be in the val - ley of love and de - light.

When true sim - plic - i - ty is gained, To bow and to bend we shan't be a - shamed, To turn, turn will be our de - light Till by turn - ing, turn - ing we come round right.

608

To Abraham the Promise Came

THE BABE OF BETHLEHEM 8.7.8.7.D.

Traditional carol
Southern Harmony, 1835

American folk tune
Southern Harmony, 1835
Harm. by John Powell, 1934

1. To A - bra - ham the prom - ise came, And to his seed for -
2. His par - ents poor in earth - ly store, To en - ter - tain the
3. On that same night a glo - rious light To shep - herds there ap -
4. "The cit - y's name is Beth - le - hem, In which God hath ap -
5. When this was said, straight-way was made A glo - rious sound from

ev - er, A light to shine in I - saac's line, By
stran - ger They found no bed to lay his head, But
pear - ed, Bright an - gels came in shin - ing flame, They
point - ed, This glo - rious morn a Sav - ior's born, For
heav - en: Each flam - ing tongue an an - them sung, "To

Scrip - ture we dis - cov - er; Hail, prom - ised morn! the Sav - ior's
in the ox's man - ger: No roy - al things, as used by
saw and great - ly fear - ed. The an - gels said, "Be not a -
him hath God a - noint - ed; By this you'll know, if you will
men a Sav - ior's giv - en, In Je - sus' name, the glo - rious

Music from *Twelve Folk Hymns*, by John Powell; copyright 1934 by J. Fischer & Bro., renewed 1962; assigned to Belwin Mills Publishing Corp.; used by permission.

born, The glo-rious Me-di—a—tor—God's bless-ed Word made
kings, Were seen by those that found him, But in the hay the
fraid, Al-though we much a—larm you, We do ap-pear good
go To see this lit-tle stran-ger, His love-ly charms in
theme, We el-e-vate our voic-es, At Je-sus' birth be

flesh and blood, As—sumed the hu—man na—ture.
stran-ger lay, With swad-dling bands a—round him.
news to bear, As now we will in—form you.
Mar-y's arms, Both ly—ing in a man—ger."
peace on earth, Mean—while all heaven re—joic—es."

610
To Thee with Joy I Sing

Appalachian carol
Arr. by David N. Johnson, 1968

Appalachian carol
Adapted by David N. Johnson, 1968

1. To thee with joy I sing, Sweet Child that heaven did bring, Now
2. I greet thee, Prince of Peace: From sin give thy re - lease! Nor
3. Thy crib can scarce con - tain Thy love, our pre - cious gain; May
4. Now twi - light soft - ly comes: The Babe to sleep suc - cumbs; Play

Ju - dah's land shall ring With thy prais - es. Gen - tle
shall my tongue e'er cease From thy prais - es. Gen - tle
hymns new heights at - tain With thy prais - es. Gen - tle
soft - ly, flute and drums, To his prais - es. Gen - tle

Stran - ger, In that man - ger, In
Stran - ger, In that man - ger, In
Stran - ger, In that man - ger, In
Stran - ger, In that man - ger, In

Ju - dah's land we find thee, In - fant Sav - ior.
Ju - dah's land we find thee, In - fant Sav - ior.
Ju - dah's land we find thee, In - fant Sav - ior.
Ju - dah's land we find thee, Bless - ed Sav - ior. A - men.

Upon Your Great Church Universal

611

RENDEZ À DIEU 9.8.9.8.D

J. M. de Carbon-Ferrière, 1823
Trans. by Margaret House, 1949; alt., 1972

Comp. or adapted by Louis Bourgeois, 1543, 1551

1. Up - on your great church u - ni - ver - sal, The con - stant
2. O God, be mind - ful of your prom - ise Made to your
3. Spread the good news to all your peo - ple From ris - ing

ob - ject of your love, May your a - bun - dant grace pa - ter - nal
peo - ple through your Word; The Ho - ly Spir - it give us com - fort,
un - to set - ting sun; And let us hear the myr - iad voic - es

Be poured out free - ly from a - bove. Your chil - dren trust - ing in your
And teach us how to call you Lord. O - pen our eyes to see your
In theme and mu - sic raised as one! And on the far - thest dis - tant

See following page.

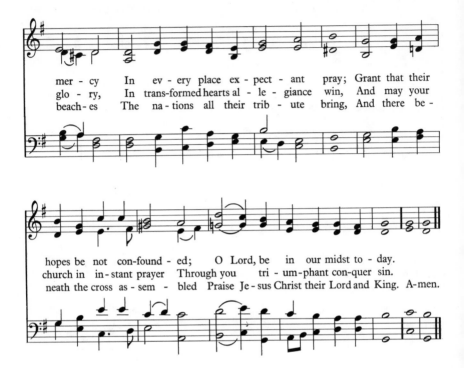

mer - cy   In   ev - ery place ex - pect - ant   pray; Grant that their
glo - ry,   In   trans-formed hearts al - le - giance   win,   And may your
beach - es   The   na - tions all their trib - ute   bring,   And there be -

hopes be not con-found - ed;   O Lord, be   in   our midst to - day.
church in in - stant prayer   Through you   tri - um-phant con-quer sin.
neath the cross as - sem - bled   Praise Je - sus Christ their Lord and King. A-men.

Veiled in Darkness Judah Lay

613

PITTSBURGH 7.7.7.7.7.7.

Douglas LeTell Rights, 1915; alt., 1972

Roland Leich, 1969

1. Veiled in dark-ness Ju-dah lay, Wait-ing for the prom-ised day,
2. Still the earth in dark-ness lies. Up from death's dark vale a-rise
3. Light of light, we hum-bly pray, Shine up-on your world to-day;

While a-cross the shad-owy night Streamed a flood of
Voic-es of a world in grief. Prayers of men who
Break the gloom of our dark night, Fill our souls with

glo-rious light, Heav-enly voic-es chant-ing then,
seek re-lief: Now our dark-ness pierce a-gain, "Peace on earth,
love and light, Send your bless-ed word a-gain,

peace on earth, good-will, good - will to men." A-men.

614 Wake, Awake, for Night Is Flying

WACHET AUF P.M.

Philipp Nicolai, 1599
Trans. by Catherine Winkworth, 1858, 1863; alt., 1972

Attr. to Philipp Nicolai, 1599
Harm. by J. S. Bach, 1731

1. Wake, a-wake, for night is fly - ing, The watch-men on the
2. Zi - on hears the watch-men sing - ing, And all her heart with

heights are cry - ing: A - wake, Je - ru - sa - lem, at last!
joy is spring - ing; She wakes, she ris - es from her gloom;

Mid-night hears the wel-come voic - es, And at the thrill-ing
For her Lord comes down all - glo - rious, The strong in grace, in

cry re-joic - es; Come forth, you vir-gins, night is past! The
truth vic-to - rious, Her Star is risen, her Light is come! Ah,

Bride-groom comes; a-wake, Your lamps with glad-ness take; Al - le - lu - ia! And
come now, bless-ed Lord, O Je - sus, Son of God! Al - le - lu - ia! We

for his mar-riage feast pre-pare, For you must go to meet him there.
fol - low till the halls we view Where you have bid us sup with you. A-men.

616 Walk Tall, Christian

WOOSTER 4.6.8.6.

Miriam Drury, 1969

Richard T. Gore, 1969

1. Walk tall, Chris - tian, Walk tall and have no fear; The Christ of God, whose child you are, He holds you in his care.
2. Walk true, Chris - tian, Keep faith come weal or woe; To up - right, pure, for - giv - ing souls, His boun - ties o - ver - flow.
3. Walk free, Chris - tian, Lay hold on deep, deep joy That age, nor loss, nor rude re - buff, Nor fail - ure, can de - stroy.
4. Walk proud, Chris - tian, As Christ's am - bas - sa - dor; His gos - pel and his church are judged By what his peo - ple are. A - men.

Watchman, Tell Us of the Night

617

ABERYSTWYTH 7.7.7.7.D.

John Bowring, 1825; alt., 1972

Joseph Parry, 1879

1. Watch-man, tell us of the night, What its signs of prom-ise are.
2. Watch-man, tell us of the night, High-er yet that star as-cends.
3. Watch-man, tell us of the night, For the morn-ing seems to dawn.

Trav - eler, o'er yon moun-tain's height, See that glo - ry - beam-ing star.
Trav - eler, bless-ed - ness and light, Peace and truth its course por-tends.
Trav - eler, dark-ness takes its flight, Doubt and ter - ror are with-drawn.

Watch-man, does its beau - teous ray Aught of joy or hope fore - tell?
Watch-man, will its beams a - lone Gild the spot that gave them birth?
Watch-man, let your wan-derings cease; Has-ten to your qui - et home.

Trav - eler, yes; it brings the day, Prom - ised day of Is - ra - el.
Trav - eler, ag - es are its own; See, it bursts o'er all the earth.
Trav - eler, lo, the Prince of Peace, Lo, the Son of God is come! A-men.

618 We Are Living, We Are Dwelling

BLAENHAFREN 8.7.8.7.D.

Arthur Cleveland Coxe, 1840; alt.

Traditional Welsh melody
as in *Hymns of the Kingdom of God*, 1923

1. We are liv-ing, we are dwell-ing In a grand and aw-ful time.
2. Will you play, then? will you dal-ly Far be-hind the bat-tle line?
3. Sworn to yield, to wa-ver, nev-er; Con-se-crat-ed, born a-gain;

In an age on ag-es tell-ing; To be liv-ing is sub-lime.
Up! it is Je-ho-vah's ral-ly; Your full strength with God's com-bine.
Sworn to be Christ's sol-diers ev-er, O for Christ at least be men!

Hark! the wak-ing up of na-tions, Hosts ad-vanc-ing to the fray;
Worlds are charg-ing, heaven be-hold-ing; You have but an hour to fight;
O let all the soul with-in you For the truth's sake go a-broad!

Hark! what sounds is all cre-a-tion's Groan-ing for the lat-ter day.
Now, the bla-zoned cross un-fold-ing, On, right on-ward for the right!
Strike! let ev-ery nerve and sin-ew Tell on ag-es, tell for God. A-men.

We Are One in the Spirit

619

(They'll Know We Are Christians by Our Love)

Peter Scholtes, 1966

Peter Scholtes, 1966
Harm. by Richard D. Wetzel, 1972

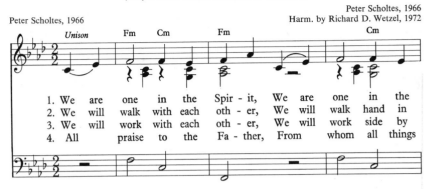

1. We are one in the Spir - it, We are one in the
2. We will walk with each oth - er, We will walk hand in
3. We will work with each oth - er, We will work side by
4. All praise to the Fa - ther, From whom all things

Lord, We are one in the Spir - it, We are one in the
hand, We will walk with each oth - er, We will walk hand in
side, We will work with each oth - er, We will work side by
come, And all praise to Christ Je - sus, His on - ly

Lord, And we pray that all un - i - ty may one day be re -
hand, And to - geth - er we'll spread the news that God is in our
side, And we'll guard each man's dig - ni - ty and save each man's
Son, And all praise to the Spir - it, who makes us

See following page.

We Bear the Strain of Earthly Care

AZMON C.M.

Ozora S. Davis, 1909

Carl G. Gläser, 1828
Arr. by Lowell Mason, 1839

621

1. We bear the strain of earth - ly care, But
2. Through din of mar - ket, whirl of wheels, And
3. The com - mon hopes that make us men Were
4. Our broth - er - hood still rests in him, The

bear it not a - lone; Be - side us walks our
thrust of driv - ing trade, We fol - low where the
his in Gal - i - lee; The tasks he gives are
broth - er of us all, And o'er the cen - turies

broth - er Christ And makes our task his own.
Mas - ter leads, Se - rene and un - a - fraid.
those he gave Be - side the rest - less sea.
still we hear The Mas - ter's win - some call. A - men.

622 We Believe in One True God

RATISBON 7.7.7.7.7.7.

Tobias Clausnitzer, 1668
Trans. by Catherine Winkworth, 1863; alt.

German melody, adapted in
J. G. Werner's *Choralbuch*, 1815

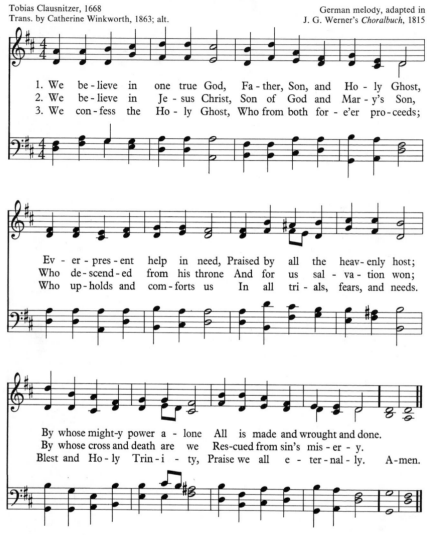

1. We be-lieve in one true God, Fa-ther, Son, and Ho-ly Ghost,
2. We be-lieve in Je-sus Christ, Son of God and Mar-y's Son,
3. We con-fess the Ho-ly Ghost, Who from both for-e'er pro-ceeds;

Ev-er-pres-ent help in need, Praised by all the heav-enly host;
Who de-scend-ed from his throne And for us sal-va-tion won;
Who up-holds and com-forts us In all tri-als, fears, and needs.

By whose might-y power a-lone All is made and wrought and done.
By whose cross and death are we Res-cued from sin's mis-er-y.
Blest and Ho-ly Trin-i-ty, Praise we all e-ter-nal-ly. A-men.

We Come Unto Our Fathers' God
NUN FREUT EUCH 8.7.8.7.8.8.7.

623

Thomas H. Gill, 1868; alt., 1972

Geistliche Lieder, Wittenberg, 1535

1. We come un-to our fa-thers'God; Their Rock is our sal-va-tion;
2. Their joy un-to their Lord we bring;Their song to us de-scend-ing;
3. You saints to come,take up the strain, The same sweet theme en-deav-or;

Th'e-ter-nal arms,their dear a-bode, We make our hab-i-ta-tion.
The Spir-it who in them did sing To us is mu-sic lend-ing:
Un-bro-ken be the gold-en chain! Keep on the song for-ev-er!

We bring you, Lord, the praise they brought, We seek you as your
His song in them, in us, is one; We raise it high, we
Safe in the same dear dwell-ing place, Rich with the same e-

saints have sought In ev-ery gen-er-a-tion.
send it on. The song is nev-er end-ing.
ter-nal grace, Bless the same bound-less Giv-er. A-men.

624 We Gather Together to Ask the Lord's Blessing

KREMSER 12.11.12.11.

Netherlands folk song
Trans. by Theodore Baker, 1919; alt., 1972

Netherlands folk song
Arr. by Eduard Kremser, 1877

1. We gath - er to - geth - er to ask the Lord's bless - ing;
2. Be - side us to guide us, our God with us join - ing,
3. We all do ex - tol you, O lead - er tri - um - phant,

He chas - tens and has - tens his will to make known;
Or - dain - ing, main - tain - ing his king - dom al - ways;
And pray that you still our de - fend - er will be.

The wick - ed op - press - ing now cease from dis - tress - ing.
So from the be - gin - ning the fight we were win - ning;
Let your con - gre - ga - tion es - cape trib - u - la - tion.

Sing prais - es to his name; he for - gets not his own.
You, Lord, were at our side, to you be all praise.
Your name be ev - er praised! O Lord, make us free! A - men.

We Greet You, Sure Redeemer from All Strife   625

TOULON 10.10.10.10.

Attr. to John Calvin, 1545
Trans. by Elizabeth L. Smith, 1868; alt.

Comp. or adapted by Louis Bourgeois, 1551
Abr. in English Psalters

1. We greet you, sure Re - deem - er from all strife,
2. You are the King of mer - cy and of grace,
3. You are the life, in which we do be - lieve,
*4. You have the true and per - fect gen - tle - ness,
5. Our hope is in no oth - er save in you;

Our on - ly Trust and Sav - ior of our life,
Reign - ing om - nip - o - tent in ev - ery place:
From you all sub - stance and our strength re - ceive;
You have no harsh - ness and no bit - ter - ness:
Our faith is built up - on your prom - ise true;

Who pain did un - der - go for our poor sake;
So come, O King, and our whole be - ing sway;
Sus - tain us by your faith and by your power,
O grant to us the grace in you we see
Lord, give us peace, and make us calm and sure,

We pray you from our hearts all cares to take.
Shine on us with the light of your pure day.
And give us strength in ev - ery try - ing hour.
That we may dwell in per - fect u - ni - ty.
That in your strength we ev - er - more en - dure. A - men.

626 We Love Your Kingdom, Lord

ST. THOMAS S.M.

Timothy Dwight, 1800; alt., 1972

Williams' *The Universal Psalmodist*, 1763
Abr. in *The New Universal Psalmodist*, 1770

1. We love your king - dom, Lord, The house of your a - bode, The church our blest Re - deem - er saved With his own pre - cious blood.
2. We love your church, O God, Her walls re - flect your plan, A sym - bol of love's cov - e - nant U - nit - ing God and · man.
3. For her our tears shall fall, For her our prayers as - cend; To her our cares and toils be given, Till toils and cares shall end.
4. Be - yond our high - est joy We prize her heav - enly ways, Her sweet com - mun - ion, sol - emn vows, Her hymns of love and praise. A - men.

We Praise You, O God, Our Redeemer, Creator 627

KREMSER 12.11.12.11.

Julia Cady Cory, 1902, 1956; alt., 1972

Netherlands folk song
Arr. by Eduard Kremser, 1877

1. We praise you, O God, our Re - deem - er, Cre - a - tor,
2. We wor - ship you, God of our fa - thers, we bless you;
3. With voic - es u - nit - ed our prais - es we of - fer,

In grate - ful de - vo - tion our trib - ute we bring.
Through life's storm and tem - pest our guide you have been.
And glad - ly our songs of true wor - ship we raise.

We lay it be - fore you, we kneel and a - dore you,
When per - ils o'er - take us, you will not for - sake us,
Our sins now con - fess - ing, we pray for your bless - ing;

We bless your ho - ly name, glad prais - es we sing.
And with your help, O Lord, life's bat - tles we win.
To you, our great Re - deem - er, for - ev - er be praise! A - men.

We Sing the Mighty Power of God

ELLACOMBE C.M.D.

Isaac Watts, 1715; alt.

Gesangbuch der herzogl. Wirtembergischen
Katholischen Hofkapelle, 1784

1. We sing the might-y power of God, That made the moun-tains rise;
2. We sing the good-ness of the Lord, That filled the earth with food;
3. There's not a plant or flower be-low But makes your glo-ries known;

That spread the flow-ing seas a-broad, And built the loft-y skies.
He formed the crea-tures with his word, And then pro-nounced them good.
And clouds a-rise, and tem-pests blow, By or-der from your throne;

We sing the Wis-dom that or-dained The sun to rule the day;
Lord, how your won-ders are dis-played, Wher-e'er we turn our eyes:
All crea-tures, man-y as they be, Are ev-er in your care,

The moon shines full at his com-mand, And all the stars o-bey.
If we sur-vey the ground we tread, Or gaze up-on the skies!
And ev-ery-where that man can be, We see your pres-ence there. A-men.

We Thank You, Lord, for Strength of Arm   629

O JESU 8.4.8.4.8.8.

Robert Davis, 1908; alt., 1972

Attr. to Johann Balthasar Reimann, 1747

1. We thank you, Lord, for strength of arm
2. We thank you, Lord, for shel - tered home
3. We thank you, Lord, for lav - ish love

To win our bread, And that, be-yond our need, is meat
In cold and storm, And that, be-yond our need, is room
On us be-stowed, E - nough to share with love - less folk

For friends un - fed: We thank you much for
For friends for - lorn: We thank you much for
To ease their load: Your love to us we

bread to live; We thank you more for bread to give.
place to rest, But more for shel - ter for our guest.
ill could spare, Yet dear - er is your love we share. A - men.

630

What Child Is This

GREENSLEEVES 8.7.8.7.6.8.6.7.

William Chatterton Dix, 1861

Traditional English melody

1. What child is this, who, laid to rest, On Mar-y's lap is sleep-ing?
2. Why lies he in such mean es-tate, Where ox and ass are feed-ing?
3. So bring him in-cense, gold, and myrrh; Come, peas-ant, king, to own him.

Whom an-gels greet with an-thems sweet, While shep-herds watch are keep-ing?
Good Chris-tian, fear, for sin-ners here The si-lent Word is plead-ing.
The King of kings sal-va-tion brings; Let lov-ing hearts en-throne him.

This, this is Christ the King, Whom shep-herds guard and an-gels sing!
Nails, spear, shall pierce him through, The cross be borne for me, for you.
Raise, raise the song on high! The vir-gin sings her lull-a-by.

Haste, haste to bring him laud, The Babe, the Son of Mar-y!
Hail, hail, the Word made flesh, The Babe, the Son of Mar-y!
Joy, joy, for Christ is born, The Babe, the Son of Mar-y!

What Makes a City Great and Strong?   631

LEICESTER 8.8.8.8.8.8.

Sts. 1-3, author unknown; alt., 1964
St. 4, Donald D. Kettring, 1972

John Bishop, ca. 1711
As in *Hymns for the Celebration of Life*, 1964

1. What makes a cit-y great and strong? Not ar-chi-tec-ture's
2. What makes a cit-y man can love? Not things that charm the
3. This is a cit-y that shall stand, A light up-on a
4. A cit-y warm with man's in-tent To serve the Christ who

grace-ful strength, Not fac-to-ries' ex-tend-ed length, But
out-ward sense, Not gross dis-play of op-u-lence, But
na-tion's hill, A voice that e-vil can-not still, A
came in love, As bea-cons light-ed from a-bove, With

men who see the civ-ic wrong, And give their lives to
right that wrong can-not re-move, And truth that fac-es
source of bless-ing to the land; Its strength not brick, nor
ra-diance of the One God sent; And quick-ened by the

make it right, And turn its dark-ness in-to light.
civ-ic shame To ban-ish it in hon-or's name.
stone, nor wood, But jus-tice, love, and broth-er-hood.
Spir-it's power We serve God in this place and hour. A-men.

632   What Star Is This, with Beams So Bright

PUER NOBIS (Praetorius) L.M.

Charles Coffin, 1736
Trans. by John Chandler, 1837; alt.

Trier MS., 15th century
Adapted by Michael Praetorius, 1609
Harm. by George R. Woodward, 1902

1. What star is this, with beams so bright, More love - ly than the noon - day light? 'Tis sent to an-nounce a new - born King, Glad ti - dings of our God to bring.

2. 'Tis now ful - filled what God de - creed, "From Ja - cob shall a star pro - ceed"; And lo! the East - ern sa - ges stand, To read in heaven the Lord's com - mand.

3. O Je - sus, while the star of grace Im - pels us on to seek your face, Let not our sloth - ful hearts re - fuse The guid - ance of your light to use.

4. To God the Fa - ther, heav - enly Light, To Christ, re - vealed in earth - ly night, To God the Ho - ly Ghost we raise An end - less song of thank - ful praise! A - men.

Music altered from *The Cowley Carol Book*, No. 21; used by permission of A. R. Mowbray & Co. Limited.

Whate'er Our God Ordains Is Right

WAS GOTT TUT 8.7.8.7.4.4.8.8.

Samuel Rodigast, ca. 1674
Trans. by Catherine Winkworth, 1858, 1863; alt., 1972

Attr. to Severus Gastorius, 1681
Harm. in *Common Service Book*, 1917

633

1. What-e'er our God or-dains is right, His ho-ly will a-bid-ing;
2. What-e'er our God or-dains is right; He nev-er will de-ceive us.
3. What-e'er our God or-dains is right; Here shall our stand be tak-en.

We will be still, what-e'er he does, And fol-low where he's guid-ing.
He leads us by the prop-er path; We know he will not leave us,
Though sor-row, need, or death be ours, Yet we are not for-sak-en.

He is our God; Though dark our road, He holds us that we
And take, con-tent, What he has sent; His hand can turn our
Our Fa-ther's care Is round us there; He holds us that we

shall not fall; Where-fore to him we leave it all.
griefs a-way, And pa-tient-ly we wait his day.
shall not fall, And so to him we leave it all. A-men.

Music slightly altered from *Common Service Book* of the United Lutheran Church; used by permission.

634 When Christ Comes to Die on Calvary

Henry L. Lettermann, 1966

Richard Hillert, 1966

1. When Christ comes to die on Cal - va - ry, Cre - at - ed things all
2. When Mar - y in doubt that Eas - ter dawn Be - lieves her Lord a -
3. When death with its ter - ror comes by night Dis - qui - et - ing my

hold their breath, They hide their face in the dark - ened sky, And
mong the dead, She weeps her shud - der - ing grief a - gainst The
sol - i - tude, My Christ who rose from the dead pro - claims The

noth - ing moves on that hill - side ex - cept A white lil - y blows,
stub - born stone in the gar - den and there A white lil - y blows,
emp - ty grave in the gar - den, and then A white lil - y blows,

blows, A white lil - y blows in the dark heart of spring!

When I Survey the Wondrous Cross

635

HAMBURG L.M.

Isaac Watts, 1707, 1709

Comp. or arr. by Lowell Mason, 1825

1. When I sur-vey the won-drous cross On which the
   Prince of glo-ry died, My rich-est gain I
   count but loss, And pour con-tempt on all my pride.

2. For-bid it, Lord, that I should boast, Save in the
   death of Christ my God. All the vain things that
   charm me most, I sac-ri-fice them to his blood.

3. See, from his head, his hands, his feet, Sor-row and
   love flow min-gled down. Did e'er such love and
   sor-row meet, Or thorns com-pose so rich a crown?

4. Were the whole realm of na-ture mine, That were a
   pres-ent far too small; Love so a-maz-ing,
   so di-vine, De-mands my soul, my life, my all. A-men.

Alternative Tune: ROCKINGHAM OLD

636

When Jesus Wept

St. 1, William Billings, 1770
Sts. 2-4, Frank A. Brooks, Jr., 1972

William Billings, 1770
Harm. by Richard D. Wetzel, 1972

1. When Jesus wept, the falling tear
2. When Jesus saw Jerusalem
3. When Jesus looks upon our towns;
4. Then let us haste to serve his cause

In mercy flowed beyond all bound;
Amid the palms and rowdy cheer,
Our churches rich; our brothers poor;
Forgetting race and station,

When Jesus groaned, a trembling fear
He stopped to look. His eyes grew dim.
"Hosannas" seem but empty sounds
Lest once again our chance is lost,

Seized all the guilty world around.
For misled men, he shed the tear.
To him who is our Savior sure.
And gone his visitation.

Stanzas 2-4 and music copyright 1972 by The Westminster Press.

*May be sung as a four-part canon unaccompanied.

When Morning Gilds the Skies

LAUDES DOMINI 6.6.6.D.

German hymn, 18th(?) century
Trans. by Edward Caswall, 1854, 1858; alt.

Joseph Barnby, 1868

1. When morn-ing gilds the skies, My heart a-wak-ing cries:
2. Does sad-ness fill my mind? A sol-ace here I find:
3. Let earth's wide cir-cle round In joy-ful notes re-sound:
4. Be this, while life is mine, My can-ti-cle di-vine:

May Je-sus Christ be praised! A-like at work and prayer
May Je-sus Christ be praised! Or fades my earth-ly bliss?
May Je-sus Christ be praised! Let air and sea and sky,
May Je-sus Christ be praised! Be this th'e-ter-nal song,

To Je-sus I re-pair: May Je-sus Christ be praised!
My com-fort still is this: May Je-sus Christ be praised!
From depth to height, re-ply: May Je-sus Christ be praised!
Through all the ag-es long: May Je-sus Christ be praised! A-men.

When Stephen, Full of Power and Grace

SALVATION C.M.D.

Based on Acts, chs. 6, 7
Jan Struther, 1931; alt., 1972

Kentucky Harmony, ca. 1815
Harm. by Kenneth Munson, 1964

Unison

1. When Ste-phen, full of power and grace, Went forth through-out the land, He bore no shield be - fore his face, No weap - on in his hand; But on - ly in his heart a flame
2. When Ste-phen preached a - gainst the laws And by those laws was tried, He had no friend to plead his cause, No spokes-man at his side; But on - ly in his heart a flame
3. When Ste-phen, young and doomed to die, . Fell crushed be - neath the stones, He had no curse nor venge - ful cry For those who broke his bones; But on - ly in his heart a flame
4. Let me, O Lord, your cause de - fend, A knight with - out a sword; No shield I ask, no faith - ful friend, No ven - geance, no re - ward; But on - ly in my heart a flame

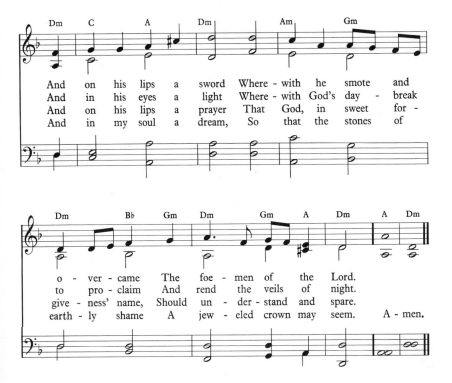

Lyrics under the first staff:

And   on   his   lips   a   sword   Where - with   he   smote   and
And   in   his   eyes   a   light   Where - with   God's   day - break
And   on   his   lips   a   prayer   That   God,   in   sweet   for -
And   in   my   soul   a   dream,   So   that   the   stones   of

Lyrics under the second staff:

o - ver - came   The   foe - men   of   the   Lord.
to   pro - claim   And   rend   the   veils   of   night.
give - ness' name,   Should   un - der - stand   and   spare.
earth - ly   shame   A   jew - eled   crown   may   seem.   A - men.

640   When We Are Tempted to Deny Your Son

PSALM 22 (abr.) 10.10.10.6.

David W. Romig, 1965

Comp. or adapted by Louis Bourgeois, 1542

1. When we are tempt - ed to de - ny your Son,
2. When we are tempt - ed to be - tray your Son,
3. When we for - get the cross that held your Son,
4. When doubt ob - scures the vic - tory of your Son,

Be - cause we fear the an - ger of the world,
Be - cause he leads us in a hard - er way,
And would a - void the bur - den of this life,
And faith is weak and all re - solve has fled,

And we are few who bear the in - sults hurled,
And makes de - mands we do not want to pay,
The cry for jus - tice and an end to strife,
Help us to know him ris - en from the dead,

Your will, O God, be done. A - men.

Words copyright 1972 by The Westminster Press.

Where Charity and Love Prevail

641

CHRISTIAN LOVE C.M.

Latin hymn, ca. 9th century
Para. by J. Clifford Evers, 1960

Paul Benoit (b. 1893)

1. Where char - i - ty and love pre - vail, There
2. With grate - ful joy and ho - ly fear His
3. For - give we now each oth - er's faults As
4. Let strife a - mong us be un - known, Let
5. Let us re - call that in our midst Dwells
6. No race nor creed can love ex - clude If

God is ev - er found; Brought here to - geth - er by Christ's
char - i - ty we learn; Let us with heart and mind and
we our faults con - fess; And let us love each oth - er
all con - ten - tion cease; Be his the glo - ry that we
God's be - got - ten Son; As mem - bers of his bod - y
hon - ored be God's name; Our broth - er - hood em - brac - es

love, By love are we thus bound.
soul Now love him in re - turn.
well In Chris - tian ho - li - ness.
seek, Be ours his ho - ly peace.
joined, We are in him made one.
all Whose Fa - ther is the same. A - men.

642   Where Cross the Crowded Ways of Life

GERMANY L.M.

Frank Mason North, 1903; alt., 1972

Attr. to Ludwig van Beethoven (1770-1827)
Gardiner's *Sacred Melodies*, 1815

1. Where cross the crowd - ed ways of life, Where sound the
2. In haunts of wretch - ed - ness and need, On shad - owed
*3. From ten - der child - hood's help - less - ness, From wom - an's
*4. The cup of wa - ter given for you Still holds the
5. O Mas - ter, from the moun - tain - side Make haste to
6. Till sons of men shall learn your love, And fol - low

cries of race and clan, A - bove the noise of self - ish
thresh - olds dark with fears, From paths where hide the lures of
grief, man's bur - dened toil, From fam - ished souls, from sor - row's
fresh - ness of your grace; Yet long these mul - ti - tudes to
where your feet have trod; Till glo - rious from your heaven a -

strife, We hear your voice, O Son of Man.
greed, We catch the vi - sion of your tears.
stress, Your heart has nev - er known re - coil.
view The sweet com - pas - sion of your face.
bide, O tread the cit - y's street a - gain;
bove Shall come the cit - y of our God. A - men.

While Shepherds Watched Their Flocks by Night 643

CHRISTMAS C.M.

Nahum Tate, 1702; alt., 1972

George Frederick Handel, 1728

1. While shep-herds watched their flocks by night, All seat-ed
2. "Fear not," said he — for might-y dread Had seized their
3. "To you, in Da-vid's town this day, Is born of
4. "The heav-enly Babe you there shall find To hu-man
5. Thus spoke the ser-aph, and forth-with Ap-peared a
6. "All glo-ry be to God on high, And to the

on the ground, The an-gel of the Lord came down,
trou-bled mind — "Glad ti-dings of great joy I bring
Da-vid's line, The Sav-ior, who is Christ, the Lord,
view dis-played, All mean-ly wrapped in swath-ing bands,
shin-ing throng Of an-gels prais-ing God, who thus
earth be peace: Good-will hence-forth, from heaven to men,

And glo-ry shone a-round, And glo-ry shone a-round.
To you and all man-kind, To you and all man-kind.
And this shall be the sign: And this shall be the sign:
And in a man-ger laid, And in a man-ger laid."
Ad-dressed their joy-ful song: Ad-dressed their joy-ful song:
Be-gin and nev-er cease! Be-gin and nev-er cease!" A-men.

644

You, Holy Father, We Adore

LASST UNS ERFREUEN L.M. with Alleluias

Calvin W. Laufer, 1931; alt., 1972

Geistliche Kirchengesäng, Cologne, 1623
Arr. and harm. by Ralph Vaughan Williams, 1906

1. You, ho - ly Fa - ther, we a - dore; We sing your prais-es o'er and o'er; Al-le-lu - ia, Al - le - lu - ia! With ser-aph throngs join heart and voice, Ac - claim your glo - ry and re - joice;
2. You fill the heaven and earth and sea With sov-ereign power and maj-es - ty; Al-le-lu - ia, Al - le - lu - ia! Yet where the poor in spir-it meet, There is your bless-ed mer - cy seat: Al-le-lu - ia,
3. Our souls on wings of rap-ture rise To swell the choirs of Par - a - dise: Al-le-lu - ia, Al - le - lu - ia! En - thralled and thrilled, we you a - dore, Our Lord and God for - ev - er-more.

Al-le-lu - ia, Al-le-lu - ia, Al-le-lu - ia, Al-le-lu - ia! A-men.

You Servants of God, Your Master Proclaim 645

LYONS 10.10.11.11.

Charles Wesley, 1744; alt.

Attr. to J. Michael Haydn (1737-1806)
Gardiner's *Sacred Melodies*, 1815

1. You serv - ants of God, your Mas - ter pro - claim,
2. Our God rules on high, al - might - y to save;
3. Sal - va - tion to God who sits on the throne!
4. Then let us a - dore, and give him his right,

And pub - lish a - broad his won - der - ful name;
And still he is nigh, his pres - ence we have.
Let all cry a - loud and hon - or the Son.
All glo - ry and power, and wis - dom and might,

The name, all - vic - to - rious, of Je - sus ex - tol;
The great con - gre - ga - tion his tri - umph shall sing,
The prais - es of Je - sus the an - gels pro - claim,
All hon - or and bless - ing, with an - gels a - bove,

His king - dom is glo - rious, and rules o - ver all.
As - crib - ing sal - va - tion to Je - sus, our King.
Fall down on their fac - es and wor - ship the Lamb.
And thanks nev - er ceas - ing, and in - fi - nite love. A - men.

646 Your Love, O God, Has All Mankind Created

L'OMNIPOTENT 11.10.11.10.

Albert F. Bayly, 1947; alt., 1972

Comp. or adapted by Louis Bourgeois, 1551
As in *Pilgrim Hymnal*, 1958

1. Your love, O God, has all man-kind cre - at - ed,
2. We bring you, Lord, in fer - vent in - ter - ces - sion
3. In pit - y look up - on your chil - dren's striv - ing
4. In - spire the church, mid earth's dis - cord-ant voic - es,
5. Un - til the ti - dings men have long a - wait - ed,

And led your peo - ple to this pres - ent hour.
The chil - dren of your world - wide fam - i - ly;
For life and free - dom, peace and broth - er - hood;
To preach the gos - pel of her Lord a - bove;
From north to south, from east to west shall ring;

In Christ we see love's glo - ry con - sum - mat - ed,
With con - trite hearts we of - fer our con - fes - sion,
Till, at the full - ness of your truth ar - riv - ing,
Un - til the day this war - ring world re - joic - es
And all man - kind, by Je - sus lib - er - at - ed,

Your spir - it man - i - fests his liv - ing power.
For we have sinned a - gainst your char - i - ty.
We find in Christ the crown of ev - ery good.
To hear the might - y har - mo - nies of love.
Pro - claims in ju - bi - la - tion Christ is King! A - men.

Words used by permission of Albert F. Bayly.

Indexes

Index of
Scripture and Scriptural Allusions

Scriptural quotations and allusions to be found in this book are listed below. Translations used in the services and prayers are the Revised Standard Version, the Phillips translation, the Jerusalem Bible, and the New English Bible. The page numbers printed in boldface type refer to hymns.

Guide for the Use of Prayers

The Guide for the Use of Prayers will help those who lead worship to locate particular prayers in this book. Prayers are indexed according to topics and the seasons of the Christian Year. References in the Guide indicate the page on which a prayer may be found, and the location of the prayer on the page. Thus, 154:5 refers to the fifth prayer printed on page 154; and 31:2 to the second prayer on page 31.

In addition to the prayers listed in the Guide, leaders of worship will discover that there are prayers within the litanies (see pp. 105–131). There are also petitions in the litanies that may be converted into brief and useful prayers with the addition of an address to God and a conclusion.

Love, for, 136:4; 140:2; 156:4; 158:1; 182:1; 183:5; 185:4; 186:1; 205:2

Management and labor, agreement between, 187:2
Marital difficulty, for those in, 186:1
Marriage service, prayers for, 67:1; 70:1
Married, newly, 67:1; 70:1; 184:4
Maundy Thursday, 41:3; 146:1; 146:2; 146:3
Men in the church, 201:4
Mental distress, for those in, 181:4
Middle years, for those in, 185:1
Military service, for those in, 187:3
Military service, for those who refuse, 187:4
Ministers of the word. *See* Church
Misfits, 182:3
Money, right use of, 199:1
Morning prayers, 56:1; 57:1; 57:2; 60:1; 205:3; 205:4

Nation, for the, 180:2
National crisis, in times of, 180:2
National significance, days of, 163:1; 163:2; 163:3
Natural resources, for right use of, 180:5
Neighbors, love of, 156:1; 156:5; 157:3; 179:2; 179:3; 182:3; 184:3; 205:2
New Year's Day, 138:4; 158:1; 158:2; 158:3
Night. *See* Evening prayers

Obedience, for, 28:1; 28:2; 47:2; 94:2; 97:1; 135:2; 140:3; 140:4; 141:1; 144:3; 149:2; 150:1; 152:1; 153:3; 154:1; 154:4; 156:1; 156:2; 161:3; 163:3
Oppression, victims of, 181:2
Ordination, prayers for, 93:1; 94:1; 94:2; 97:1
Orphans, 186:4
Overcome, that we may, 143:1; 149:1

Palm Sunday, 41:2; 144:1; 144:2; 144:3
Parents, 47:1; 183:4; 205:1
Patience, for, 140:5
Patriotism, for a right, 163:1

Peace:
between races, 179:3
inner, 72:1; 87:1; 141:3; 181:4
in the world, 32:1; 32:4; 136:2; 179:1; 179:2; 189:2
Pentecost, 41:7; 152:1; 152:2; 152:3; 153:1
Play, for a spirit of, 188:1
Power, a right use of, 180:3
Praise, that we may, 15:3; 15:5; 16:1; 135:3; 137:3; 138:2; 140:1; 150:1; 154:2; 155:1; 163:2
Prayer:
answer to, 33:4
for those we may forget in, 188:3
guidance in, 31:1; 188:3
Prayer after the Lord's Supper, 37:1; 55:1; 146:2; 160:2
Prayer for the Communion of Saints. *See* Communion of Saints
Prayer of confession. *See* Confession
Prayer of dedication. *See* Dedication
Prayer, eucharistic. *See* The Thanksgiving
Prayer for illumination. *See* Illumination
Prayer of intercession. *See* Intercession
Prayer of thanksgiving. *See* Thanksgiving
Prayer for use at home. *See* Home
Preach the good news, that we may, 140:5; 53:5; 188:2
Prejudice, 32:2; 179:3
Presbytery, meeting of. *See* Church
President, 32:3
Pride, 147:1; 155:3; 157:3
Prisoners, 182:2
Property, right use of, 199:1
Prophets, modern-day, 189:3
Prostitutes, 189:1

Racial peace. *See* Peace
Racketeers, 188:4
Reconciliation between men, 32:2; 200:4
Reformation Sunday, 161:1; 161:2; 161:3
Renewal, for, 136:3; 137:1; 147:1; 151:1; 160:1; 161:1; 161:3
Repentance, for, 26:2; 136:1; 142:2; 142:3; 143:4; 144:4; 147:3; 147:4; 161:1; 180:2

Guide for the Use of Hymns

The Guide for the Use of Hymns will enable the worship leader to find hymns appropriate to a part of the Service for the Lord's Day, a sacrament or act of the church, a season of the Christian or civil year, or one of several other observances.

The Guide includes thirty-five categories arranged under six major headings.

SERVICE FOR THE LORD'S DAY
Opening of Worship
After Confession and Pardon
After Old Testament Lesson
After Creed
After Offering
Conclusion of Worship

SACRAMENTS
Baptism
Lord's Supper

ACTS OF THE CHURCH
Confirmation
The Marriage Service
Witness to the Resurrection
—Funeral
Ordination
Installation

CHRISTIAN YEAR
Advent
Christmas

Epiphany
Lent
Palm Sunday
Good Friday
Easter Day
Ascension
Pentecost
Trinity Sunday

CIVIL YEAR
New Year
Memorial Day
Independence Day
Labor Day
Thanksgiving Day

OTHER OBSERVANCES
Christian Education
Ecumenism
Mission
Reformation Day
Stewardship
World Communion
World Peace

Service for the Lord's Day

OPENING OF WORSHIP

AFTER OFFERING

CONCLUSION OF WORSHIP

Sacraments

Acts of the Church

THE MARRIAGE SERVICE

WITNESS TO THE RESURRECTION—FUNERAL

ORDINATION

INSTALLATION

Christian Year

ADVENT

Other Observances

CHRISTIAN EDUCATION

WORLD COMMUNION

WORLD PEACE

Index of Familiar Hymns
with Unfamiliar First Lines

The hymns in this book are arranged in alphabetical order. However, the user of *The Worshipbook—Services and Hymns* is advised when searching to remember that the wording of many hymns has been modernized. In such cases *thee, thou,* and *ye* become *you; thy* becomes *your; hast* becomes *have.* "Cast thy burden" now reads, "Cast your burden." Similarly, "God hath spoken" now reads, "God has spoken." The user can generally locate such hymns without assistance.

The index below includes commonly used titles that differ from first lines. It includes familiar first lines that have been extensively altered for use in this book.

I sing the mighty power of God
see We sing the mighty power of God, 628

I thank thee, Lord, for strength of arm
see We thank you, Lord, for strength of arm, 629

I'll praise my Maker while I've breath
see Praise we our Maker while we've breath, 558

Jesus, thou joy of loving hearts
see O Jesus, joy of loving hearts, 510

Lord of the dance
see I danced in the morning, 426

Mary's Child
see Born in the night, Mary's Child, 312

O God, our help in ages past
see Our God, our help in ages past, 549

O God, thou faithful God
see O God, our faithful God, 500

O Lord, my God, most earnestly
see O Lord, our God, most earnestly, 514

O thou, who by a star didst guide
see O God, who by a star did guide, 502

O thou, whose gracious presence shone
see O Lord, whose gracious presence shone, 516

Rejoice, ye pure in heart
see Rejoice, O pure in heart, 561

Simple gifts
see 'Tis the gift to be simple, 606

The Babe of Bethlehem
see To Abraham the promise came, 608

Thee, holy Father, we adore
see You, holy Father, we adore, 644

They'll know we are Christians by our love
see We are one in the Spirit, 619

Thy love, O God, has all mankind created
see Your love, O God, has all mankind created, 646

Thy word is like a flaming sword
see God's word is like a flaming sword, 405

Unto the hills around do I lift up
see I to the hills will lift my eyes, 430

Ye servants of God, your Master proclaim
see You servants of God, your Master proclaim, 645

Index of Authors, Translators, and Sources

Index of Composers, Arrangers, and Sources

Alphabetical Index of Tunes

Metrical Index of Tunes